The South China Sea Arbitration

Toward an International Legal Order in the Oceans

Yoshifumi Tanaka

•HART•
OXFORD • LONDON • NEW YORK • NEW DELHI • SYDNEY

HART PUBLISHING

Bloomsbury Publishing Plc

Kemp House, Chawley Park, Cumnor Hill, Oxford, OX2 9PH, UK

HART PUBLISHING, the Hart/Stag logo, BLOOMSBURY and the Diana logo are trademarks of Bloomsbury Publishing Plc

First published in Great Britain 2019

A catalogue record for this book is available from the British Library.

Library of Congress Cataloging-in-Publication data

Names: Tanaka, Yoshifumi, author.

Title: The South China Sea arbitration : toward an international legal order in the oceans / Yoshifumi Tanaka.

Description: Oxford ; New York Hart, 2019. | Includes bibliographical references and index.

Identifiers: LCCN 2019029565 (print) | LCCN 2019029566 (ebook) | ISBN 9781509924813 (hardback) | ISBN 9781509924820 (Epub)

Subjects: LCSH: Philippines—Trials, litigation, etc. | China—Trials, litigation, etc. | South China Sea—International status. | Jurisdiction (International law) | Maritime boundaries.

Classification: LCC KZA1128.S58 T36 2019 (print) | LCC KZA1128.S58 (ebook) | DDC 341.4/480916472—dc23

LC record available at https://lccn.loc.gov/2019029565

LC ebook record available at https://lccn.loc.gov/2019029566

ISBN: HB: 978-1-50992-481-3
ePDF: 978-1-50992-483-7
ePub: 978-1-50992-482-0

Typeset by Compuscript Ltd, Shannon
Printed and bound in Great Britain by CPI Group (UK) Ltd, Croydon CR0 4YY

FSC www.fsc.org MIX Paper from responsible sources FSC® C013604

To find out more about our authors and books visit www.hartpublishing.co.uk. Here you will find extracts, author information, details of forthcoming events and the option to sign up for our newsletters.

Acknowledgements

I AM GRATEFUL to the University of Copenhagen, Faculty of Law and its Library for their support in the completion of this book. My thanks are also due to Sinead Moloney, Sasha Jawed and other Hart Publishing staff for their professional assistance. I thank Catherine Minahan for her thorough copy-editing.

Chapters 2, 3 and 4 of this book include some materials I have published previously, and I would like to thank the publishers and/or editors of the following periodicals for their permission to use my previous work:

- Y Tanaka, 'Reflections on the *Philippines/China* Arbitration: Award on Jurisdiction and Admissibility' (2016) 15 *The Law and Practice of International Courts and Tribunals* 305.
- Y Tanaka, 'Reflections on Historic Rights in the South China Sea Arbitration (Merits)' (2017) 32 *The International Journal of Marine and Coastal Law* 458.
- Y Tanaka, 'Reflections on the Interpretation and Application of Article 121(3) in the *South China Sea* Arbitration (Merits)' (2017) 48 *Ocean Development and International Law* 365.

When using the articles in this book, they were revised, modified and updated. The typescript of this book was completed in March 2019 at Copenhagen, Denmark. All websites were current as of that date.

Finally, I am grateful to my wife, Akiko, for all her support and prayer throughout my work.

Yoshifumi Tanaka
Copenhagen

Contents

List of Abbreviations

AFDI	*Annuaire français de droit international*
AJIL	*American Journal of International Law*
Art(s)	Article(s)
BYIL	*British Yearbook of International Law*
CBD	Convention on Biological Diversity
CJIL	*Chinese Journal of International Law*
CLCS	Commission on the Limits of the Continental Shelf
CSIL	Chinese Society of International Law
CMS	China Marine Surveillance
COLREGS	Convention on the International Regulations for Preventing Collisions at Sea
EEZ	exclusive economic zone
EFZ	exclusive fishery zone
EJIL	*European Journal of International Law*
GYIL	*German Yearbook of International Law*
ICJ	International Court of Justice
ICJ Rep	ICJ Reports
ICLQ	*International and Comparative Law Quarterly*
IJMCL	*International Journal of Marine and Coastal Law*
ILC	International Law Commission
ILM	*International Legal Materials*
IMO	International Maritime Organisation
ITLOS	International Tribunal for the Law of the Sea
ITLOS Rep	ITLOS Reports
LJIL	*Leiden Journal of International Law*

MPA	marine protected area
NILR	*Netherlands International Law Review*
NJIL	*Nordic Journal of International Law*
ODIL	*Ocean Development and International Law*
PCA	Permanent Court of Arbitration
PCIJ	Permanent Court of International Justice
RCADI	*Recueil des cours de l'Académie de droit international*
RECIEL	*Review of European Community and International Environmental Law*
RGDIP	*Revue générale de droit international public*
RIAA	*Reports of International Arbitral Awards*
UK	United Kingdom
UN	United Nations
UNCLOS	United Nations Convention on the Law of the Sea
UNDOALOS	United Nations Division for Ocean Affairs and the Law of the Sea
UNTS	*United Nations Treaty Series*
US	United States
WTO	World Trade Organization
YILC	*Yearbook of International Law Commission*
ZaöRV	*Zeitschrift für ausländisches öffentliches Recht und Völkerrecht*

Table of Cases

references are to page number

Table of Treaties and Other Instruments

references are to page number

NOTES VERBALE

NATIONAL MATERIAL

People's Republic of China

France

Indonesia

Japan

Mexico

Republic of the Philippines

Singapore

Timor-Leste

United Kingdom

United States of America

Viet Nam

Reports

1

Introduction

I. INTRODUCTION

INTERNATIONAL DISPUTES MAY often reflect the opposition of fundamental values or approaches underlying international law and community. As will be discussed in this book, the *South China Sea* arbitration between the Republic of the Philippines ('the Philippines') and the People's Republic of China ('China') vividly created vacillations such as: unilateralism versus multilateralism, states' interests versus community interests, and voluntary procedure versus the compulsory procedure of international dispute settlement. Given such fundamental oppositions, we would be faced with a choice that will affect the interpretation and application of rules of international law. Thus the *South China Sea* arbitration provides an interesting case-study when considering an aspect of the development of international law and community.

The *South China Sea* disputes are a complex mix, involving both territorial and maritime disputes. At present, multiple states claim territorial sovereignty over maritime features in the South China Sea.[1] In particular, the Spratly Islands are the site of longstanding territorial disputes between China, Taiwan and Viet Nam. The Philippines also claims territorial sovereignty over maritime features of the Spratly Islands that fall within the Kalayaan Island Group. Malaysia claims territorial sovereignty over several maritime features, and one reef lies within 200 nautical miles of Brunei Darussalam.[2] The Paracells are claimed by China, Taiwan and Viet Nam, and Scarborough Shoal is claimed by China, the Philippines and Taiwan.[3] The territorial disputes are linked to various maritime disputes in the same region, such as disputes regarding: entitlement to marine spaces, maritime delimitation, fisheries, the exploration and exploitation of mineral resources in the seabed and its subsoil, navigation and marine environmental protection.[4] Hence, the characterisation of the dispute is of critical importance in the *South China Sea* arbitration.

[1] TL McDorman, 'An International Law Perspective on Insular Features (Islands) and Low-tide Elevations in the South China Sea' (2017) 32 *IJMCL* 298, 299.

[2] R Beckman, 'The UN Convention on the Law of the Sea and the Maritime Disputes in the South China Sea' (2013) 107 *AJIL* 142, 144. Further, see DJ Dzurek, 'The Spratly Islands Dispute: Who's On First?' (1996) 2 *Maritime Briefing*, International Boundaries Research Unit.

[3] Beckman, n 2, 144–45.

[4] TL McDorman, 'The South China Sea *Tribunal Awards: A Dispute Resolution Perspective*' (2018) 3 *Asia-Pacific Journal of Ocean Law and Policy* 134, 134.

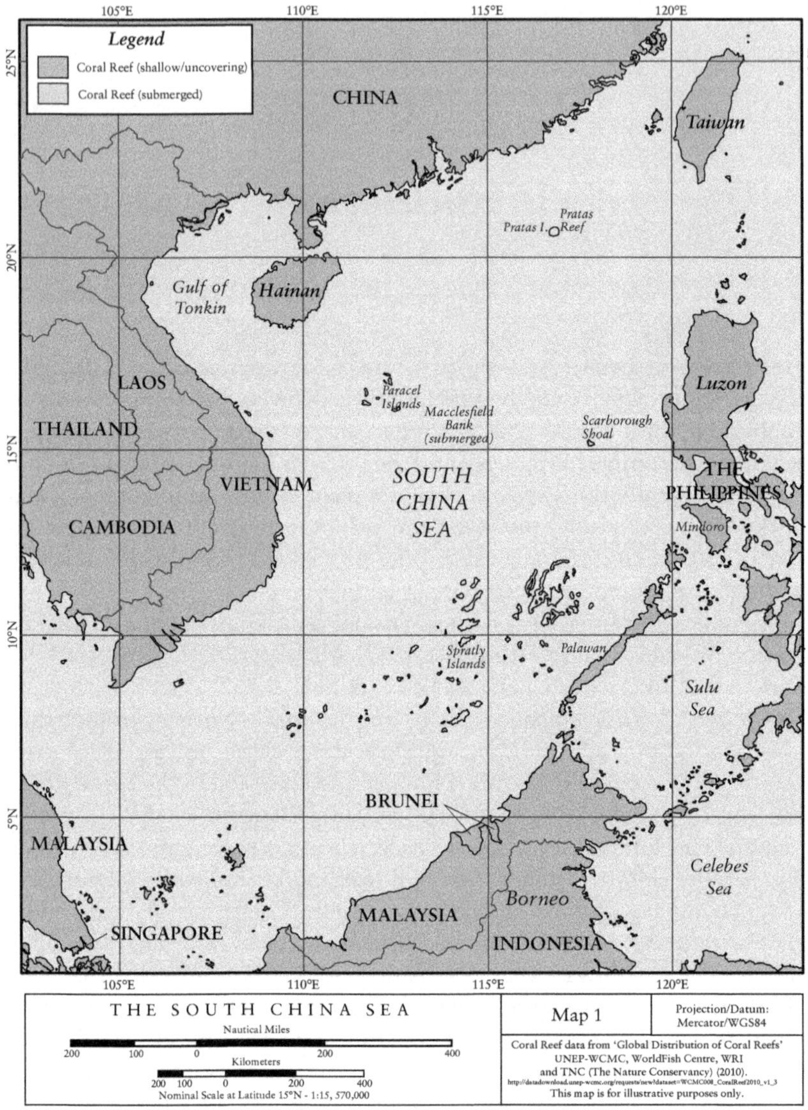

Figure 1.1 The South China Sea

Source: The *South China Sea* Arbitration Award (Merits), 9. Reproduced with permission of the Permanent Court of Arbitration (copyright holder).

The South China Sea, which covers around 3.5 million square kilometres, is a semi-enclosed sea in the western Pacific Ocean, surrounded by China, the Philippines, Viet Nam, Malaysia, Brunei, Singapore and Indonesia (see Figure 1.1).[5] It is a lifeline for oil and gas supplies from the Middle East, Africa, Australia and Southeast Asia to the large resource import-dependent countries of Northeast Asia.[6] Given that international energy markets depend on reliable transport routes, the freedom of navigation in the South China Sea is of critical importance.[7] Furthermore, the South China Sea is one of the world's important fishing grounds and is rich in biological diversity.[8] In particular, Scarborough Shoal and the Spratly Islands experience an extreme diversity of coastal fish and a high percentage of the living representatives of seagrasses, corals, giant clams, marine turtles and many other marine groups.[9] In addition, the energy reserves under the South China Sea are attracting growing attention.[10] If as much oil and gas exist in the South China Sea as is hoped, access to the potential oil and gas wealth will be crucial for the economic development of states in the region. In light of its economic, strategic and political importance, it would be no exaggeration to say that international disputes in the South China Sea may affect all countries that are linked to it.[11] In this sense, the peaceful settlement of the *South China Sea* disputes should be regarded as a crucial issue in international relations.[12]

[5] PCA Case No 2013–19. The *South China Sea* Arbitration Award (Merits) (hereinafter 'the *South China Sea* Arbitration Award (Merits)'), 12 July 2016, [3], available at https://pca-cpa.org/en/cases/7/. In this book, the relevant part of the Award will be indicated by paragraph numbers. For an overview of the South China Sea, see Keyuan Zou, 'The South China Sea' in D Rothwell, AG Oude Elferink, KN Scott and T Stephens (eds), *The Oxford Handbook of the Law of the Sea* (Oxford University Press, 2015) 626.

[6] Further, see C Rahman and M Tsamenyi, 'A Strategic Perspective on Security and Naval Issues in the South China Sea' (2010) 41 *ODIL* 315, 317–18; Hui Zhong and M White, 'South China Sea: Its Importance for Shipping, Trade, Energy and Fisheries' (2017) 2 *Asia-Pacific Journal of Ocean Law and Policy* 9, 12–18.

[7] Zhong and White, n 6, 17–18.

[8] ibid, 21–23; the *South China Sea* Arbitration Award (Merits), n 5, [823].

[9] Many of the species living in this region, such as the blue coral, the giant clam and the hawksbill turtle, are considered endangered according to the IUCN Red List of Threatened Species. KE Carpenter, *Eastern South China Sea Environmental Disturbances and Irresponsible Fishing Practices and their Effects on Coral Reefs and Fisheries* (22 March 2014), 5, reproduced in the Memorial of the Philippines, vol VII, Annex 240.

[10] Even though it is difficult to determine the amount of oil and natural gas in the South China Sea, the United States (US) Energy Information Agency estimates there to be approximately 11 billion barrels of oil reserves and 190 trillion cubic feet of natural gas reserves in this sea. According to the US Energy Information Administration, these numbers represent both proved and probable reserves, making them closer to a high-end estimate. US Energy Information Administration, 'South China Sea', 7 February 2013, available at https://www.eia.gov/beta/international/analysis_includes/regions_of_interest/South_China_Sea/south_china_sea.pdf. See also Zhong and White, n 6, 19–21. However, Owen and Schofield expressed their misgivings that optimism concerning the oil and gas potential of the South China Sea is often ill-founded: NA Owen and CH Shofield, 'Disputed South China Sea Hydrocarbons in Perspective' (2012) 36 *Marine Policy* 809. See also M Lim and N Lie, 'Condominium Arrangements as a Legal Mechanism for the Conservation of the South China Sea Large Marine Ecosystem' (2017) 2 *Asia-Pacific Journal of Ocean Law and Policy* 52, 75.

[11] Zhong and White, n 6, 23–24.

[12] Further, see G Till, 'The Global Significance of the South China Sea Disputes' in CJ Jenner and Tran Truong Thuy (eds), *The South China Sea: A Crucible of Regional Cooperation or Conflict-making Sovereignty Claims?* (Cambridge University Press, 2016) 13 et seq.

Apart from the Philippines, no states surrounding the South China Sea accepted the compulsory jurisdiction of the International Court of Justice (ICJ) pursuant to Article 36(2) of the Statute of the ICJ.[13] While all states surrounding the South China Sea ratified the UN Convention on the Law of the Sea (UNCLOS or 'the Convention'),[14] no states in the region chose the dispute settlement procedure pursuant to Article 287 of the Convention. Thus the states are to be deemed to have accepted arbitration in accordance with Annex VII to the Convention in accordance with Article 287(3). It follows that, unless otherwise agreed, arbitration under Annex VII to the UNCLOS is the only compulsory procedure of international dispute settlement when a dispute cannot be resolved through diplomatic means. The Philippines thus instituted arbitral proceedings against China in accordance with the UNCLOS. The *South China Sea* arbitration was bifurcated and the Annex VII Arbitral Tribunal issued its Award on Jurisdiction on 29 October 2015.[15] It then issued its Award on the Merits on 12 July 2016.[16] The Tribunal decided all issues unanimously.

Before examination of the *South China Sea* Arbitration Awards,[17] as a preliminary consideration, it is necessary to briefly review the course of the litigation in the *South China Sea* arbitration.

II. COURSE OF THE LITIGATION

According to the Philippines, under the authority of the Province of Hainan, China formally created a new administrative unit that included all of the maritime features and waters within the 'nine-dash line'[18] in June 2012. In November 2012, the provincial government of Hainan Province promulgated a law calling for the inspection, expulsion or detention of vessels 'illegally' entering the waters claimed by China within this area. This law went into effect on 1 January 2013.[19]

[13] Statute of the International Court of Justice (adopted 26 June 1945, entered into force 24 October 1945) 33 *UNTS* 993. The Philippines accepted the jurisdiction of the ICJ under Art 36(1) of the Statute of the ICJ on 18 January 1972. See at http://www.icj-cij.org/en/declarations/ph.

[14] Art 136 of the UN Convention on the Law of the Sea (adopted 10 December 1982, entered into force 16 November 1994) 1833 *UNTS* 3. The Philippines ratified the Convention on 8 May 1984, and China on 7 June 1996.

[15] PCA Case No 2013-19, the *South China Sea* arbitration (Jurisdiction and Admissibility) (hereinafter 'the *South China Sea* Arbitration Award (Jurisdiction and Admissibility)'), 29 October 2015, available at https://pca-cpa.org/en/cases/. Rules of procedure, written Submissions of the Philippines, transcripts and expert reports are available on the website.

[16] The *South China Sea* Arbitration Award (Merits), n 5.

[17] In this book, the phrase 'the *South China Sea* Arbitration Awards' includes both the 2015 Award on Jurisdiction and Admissibility and the 2016 Award on the Merits.

[18] While the vaguely-drawn demarcation line claimed by China in the South China Sea at various times has been referred to by different terminologies, this book uses the term 'nine-dash line' in accordance with the *South China Sea* Arbitration Award.

[19] Notification and Statement of Claim, [5], available at http://www.philippineembassy-usa.org/uploads/pdfs/embassy/2013/2013-0122-Notification%20and%20Statement%20of%20Claim%20on%20West%20Philippine%20Sea.pdf.

In response, by Notification and Statement of Claim dated 22 January 2013, the Philippines initiated arbitration proceedings against China in accordance with Articles 286 and 287 of the UNCLOS and Article 1 of Annex VII to the Convention. The Philippines, in its Notification and Statement of Claim, stressed that it

> does not seek in this arbitration a determination of which Party enjoys sovereignty over the islands claimed by both of them. Nor does it request a delimitation of any maritime boundaries. The Philippines is conscious of China's Declaration of 25 August 2006 under Article 298 of UNCLOS, and has avoided raising subjects or making claims that China has, by virtue of that Declaration, excluded from arbitral jurisdiction.[20]

China, in its Note Verbale to the Department of Foreign Affairs of the Philippines on 19 February 2013,[21] rejected the arbitration and returned the Notification and Statement of Claim to the Philippines.[22] In the Note Verbale of 19 February 2013, it claimed that 'At the core of the disputes between China and the Philippines in the South China Sea are the territorial disputes over some islands and reefs of the Nansha Islands.'[23] For China,

> [t]he territorial disputes between China and the Philippines are still pending and unresolved, but both sides have agreed to settle the disputes through bilateral negotiations. By initiating arbitration proceedings, the Philippines runs counter to the agreement between the two countries, and also contravenes the principles and spirit of the *Declaration on the Conduct of Parties in the South China Sea (DOC)*, and particularly 'to resolve their territorial and jurisdictional disputes by peaceful means, … through friendly consultations and negotiations by sovereign states directly concerned'.[24]

In the end, China chose not to appear before the Tribunal.[25]

In its Notification and Statement of Claim, the Philippines appointed Judge Rüdiger Wolfrum, a German national, as a member of the Tribunal in accordance with Article 3(b) of Annex VII to the UNCLOS. China did not appoint an arbitrator. Accordingly, on 23 March 2013, Judge Yanai, the President of the International Tribunal for the Law of the Sea (ITLOS), appointed Judge Stanislaw

[20] ibid, [7].

[21] Note Verbale from the Embassy of the People's Republic of China in Manila to the Department of Foreign Affairs of the Republic of the Philippines, No (13) PG-039, 19 February 2013. Reproduced in Memorial of the Philippines, vol. III, 30 March 2014, Annex 3.

[22] The *South China Sea* Arbitration Award (Jurisdiction and Admissibility), n 15, [27].

[23] Note Verbale, n 21.

[24] ibid.

[25] This is not the first time China had refused to appear before an international tribunal. In Denunciation of the Treaty of 2 November 1865 between China and Belgium, China did not take any steps in the proceedings. PCIJ Reports, Series A Nos 8, 14, 16, 18 and Series C No 16-1 (see in particular, Order, 1929, Series A No 18, 7). See also S Talmon, 'The South China Sea Arbitration: Is There a Case to Answer?' in S Talmon and Bing Bing Jia (eds), *The South China Sea Arbitration: A Chinese Perspective* (Hart Publishing, 2014) 18.

Pawlak, a national of Poland, as the second arbitrator pursuant to Article 3(c) and (e) of Annex VII to the Convention. On 24 April 2013, the President of ITLOS further appointed the remaining three arbitrators in accordance with Article 3(d) and (e) of Annex VII to the Convention. They were: Judge Jean-Pierre Cot, a national of France; Professor Alfred HA Soons, a national of the Netherlands; and Ambassador MCW Pinto, a national of Sri Lanka, as arbitrator and President of the Tribunal. Since Ambassador Pinto withdrew from the Tribunal on 21 June 2013, the President of ITLOS appointed Judge Thomas A Mensah, a national of Ghana, as arbitrator and President of the Tribunal, in accordance with Articles 3(e) and (f) of Annex VII to the Convention. Thus the Annex VII Arbitral Tribunal ('the Tribunal') was duly constituted on 21 June 2013.[26] Under Article 7(1) of the Rules of Procedure, '[a]ny arbitrator may be challenged if circumstances exist that give rise to justifiable doubts as to the arbitrator's impartiality or independence'. However, China did not legally challenge any arbitrator's impartiality or independence pursuant to Article 7(1).[27]

In the arbitral proceedings, the Philippines presented its 'strong interest in transparency and public access to information', and it proposed that the verbatim records of the hearing be published after review and correction. It also urged the Tribunal to consider opening the Hearing on Jurisdiction to the public.[28] While the Tribunal decided that the Registry would issue a press release at the time of the Hearing on Jurisdiction and would publish corrected transcripts shortly thereafter, it informed the Parties that the hearing would not be open to the public generally.[29] On 3 July 2015, however, the Tribunal informed the Parties that it had agreed to permit each of the Governments of Malaysia, Viet

[26] The Permanent Court of Arbitration (PCA) served as Registry for the Proceedings. The *South China Sea* Arbitration Award (Jurisdiction and Admissibility), n 15, [32]. In this connection, it must be stressed that the *South China Sea* Arbitration Award was rendered by the Annex VII Arbitral Tribunal, not the PCA. Further, see E Franckx, 'The Award of 12 July 2016 and Its Impact on the Clarification of Article 121(3) UNCLOS' in J Borton (ed), *Islands and Rocks in the South China Sea: Post-Hague Ruling* (Xlibris, 2017) 4–8. For the authority of the President of ITLOS to appoint arbitrators, see J Gao, 'Appointment of Arbitrators by the President of the ITLOS Pursuant to Article 3 of Annex VII to the LOS Convention: Some Tentative Observations' (2017) 16 *CJIL* 723.

[27] Hao Duy Phan and Lan Ngoc Nguyen, 'The South China Sea Arbitration: Bindingness, Finality, and Compliance with UNCLOS Dispute Settlement Decisions' (2018) 8 *Asian Journal of International Law* 36, 43. At the Press Conference, however, Vice Foreign Minister Liu Zhenmin said that 'the composition of the Arbitral Tribunal is actually the result of political manipulation'. *Vice Foreign Minister Liu Zhenmin at the Press Conference on the White Paper Titled China Adheres to the Position of Settling Through Negotiation the Relevant Disputes Between China and the Philippines in the South China Sea*, 13 July 2016, available at https://www.fmprc.gov.cn/nanhai/eng/wjbxw_1/t1381980.htm. The study of Chinese Society of International Law (CSIL) also criticised the composition of the Tribunal. CSIL, *The South China Sea Arbitration: A Critical Study* (Foreign Languages Press, 2018) 487–91, [902]–[911]. At the same time, it made clear that 'China, which maintains a non-acceptance and non-participation position, did not participate in the constitution of the Tribunal': ibid, 489, [906]. See also AC Robles, Jr, *The South China Sea Arbitration: Understanding the Awards and Debating with China* (Sussex Academic Press, 2019) 254 et seq.

[28] The *South China Sea* Arbitration Award (Jurisdiction and Admissibility), n 15, [71].

[29] ibid, [73].

Nam, Indonesia, Japan and Thailand to send small delegations of representatives to attend the hearing as observers. All observer delegations were reminded that their role would be to watch and listen, not to make statements.[30] However, Viet Nam actively expressed its view with regard to substantive issues in the *South China Sea* arbitration.[31] In addition, certain materials were made public by Taiwan.[32]

Pursuant to Article 31(1) of the Rules of Procedure, the expenses of the Tribunal, including the remuneration of its members, shall be borne by the Parties in equal shares. Under Article 33(1) of the Rules, the Registry may request each Party to deposit an equal amount as an advance for the expenses referred to in Article 31. Should either Party fail to make the requested deposit within 45 days after the receipt of the request, the Tribunal may so inform the Parties in order that one of them may make the payment by virtue of Article 33(3). While the Philippines paid its share of the deposit, China made no payments toward the deposit. Accordingly, the Philippines paid China's share.[33]

III. FRAMEWORK FOR ANALYSIS: TRIPLE VIEWPOINT

When analysing the *South China Sea* arbitration, three implications in particular merit being highlighted: the implications for the interpretation and application of rules of international law; the protection of community interests; and considerations relating to time.

A. Legal Implications of the *South China Sea* Arbitration Awards for the Interpretation and Application of International Law

The *South China Sea* arbitration is characterised by the diversity of issues at stake. Indeed the Philippines, in its application, presented some 15 Submissions to the Tribunal,[34] which, according to the Tribunal, could be divided into four categories.[35]

The first category concerns the source of maritime rights and entitlements in the South China Sea. Submissions No 1 and No 2 fall within the scope of this category. Specifically, the Philippines requested the Tribunal to declare that

[30] ibid, [84]. Although the US requested that the Tribunal should allow it to send a representative to observe the hearing, the Tribunal did not accede to the US request. The *South China Sea* Arbitration Award (Merits), n 5, [67].

[31] The *South China Sea* Arbitration Award (Jurisdiction and Admissibility), n 15, [183]–[184]. See also ch 2, section III of this book.

[32] The *South China Sea* Arbitration Award (Merits), n 5, [142].

[33] ibid, [110].

[34] The *South China Sea* Arbitration Award (Jurisdiction and Admissibility), n 15, [101].

[35] The *South China Sea* Arbitration Award (Merits), n 5, [7] et seq.

China's maritime entitlements in the South China Sea may not extend beyond those expressly permitted by the UNCLOS, and that China's claims to sovereign rights jurisdiction, and to 'historic rights', with respect to the maritime areas of the South China Sea encompassed by the so-called 'nine-dash line' are contrary to the Convention.

The second category relates to the legal status of maritime features in the South China Sea. In this regard, the Philippines sought a declaration that all of the features claimed by China in the Spratly Islands as well as Scarborough Shoal fall within the categories of submerged banks or low-tide elevations, and that none of these features generate an entitlement to an exclusive economic zone (EEZ) or to a continental shelf.[36]

The third category pertains to the lawfulness of China's actions in the South China Sea. Specifically, the Philippines claimed that China violated the UNCLOS by:

(a) interfering with the exercise of the Philippines' rights under the Convention, including with respect to fishing, oil exploration, navigation, and the construction of artificial islands and installations;
(b) failing to protect and preserve the marine environment by tolerating and actively supporting Chinese fishermen in the harvesting of endangered species and the use of harmful fishing methods that damage the fragile coral reef ecosystem in the South China Sea; and
(c) inflicting severe harm on the marine environment by constructing artificial islands and engaging in extensive land reclamation at seven reefs in the Spratly Islands.[37]

The fourth category concerns aggravation of the disputes between the Parties during the arbitral proceedings by China. In this regard, the Philippines claimed that since the commencement of this arbitration in January 2013, China had unlawfully aggravated and extended the dispute by restricting access to a detachment of Philippine marines stationed at Second Thomas Shoal, and by engaging in the large-scale construction of artificial islands and land reclamation at seven reefs in the Spratly Islands.[38] In addition, the Philippines sought a declaration that China must respect the rights and freedoms of the Philippines under the Convention and must comply with its duties under the Convention.[39]

In examining the Philippines' Submissions, the Tribunal clarified not a few murky issues concerning the interpretation or application of rules of the UNCLOS and international law. Examples include:

- The concepts of historic title and historic rights.
- The interpretation and application of Articles 13 and 121 of the UNCLOS.

[36] ibid, [8].
[37] ibid, [9].
[38] ibid, [10].
[39] ibid, [112].

- The obligation to protect the marine environment under Articles 192 and 194 of the Convention.
- The operation of law enforcement by vessels under the Convention on the International Regulations for Preventing Collisions at Sea (COLREGS) and Article 94 of the UNCLOS.
- The obligation regarding non-aggravation of disputes.

It is well known that judicial decisions may have implications for the development of international law, even though normally the principle of precedents does not apply in international adjudication. Concerning several issues of international law, the *South China Sea* Arbitration Awards may at the very least provide the basis for discussion in future jurisprudence. Thus the Awards must be examined from the perspective of the development of international law and the law of the sea.

B. Legal Implications of the *South China Sea* Arbitration Awards for the Protection of Community Interests

Particular attention must be given to the impact of the *South China Sea* arbitration on the protection of common interests of the international community or community interests.[40] As Bull observed, 'The maintenance of order in any society presupposes that among its members, or at least among those of its members who are politically active, there should be a sense of *common interests* in the elementary goals of social life.'[41] Thus the concept of common interests should be a crucial element in the maintenance of order in the international community. In fact, the emergence of the concept of community interests that encompass fundamental values shared by groups of states or the international community as a whole is one of the remarkable features that characterise contemporary international law.[42] In the words of Simma:

> [I]nternational law has undoubtedly entered a stage at which it does not exhaust itself in correlative rights and obligations running between states, but also incorporates common interests of the international community as a whole, including not only states but all human beings.[43]

[40] In this work, the terms 'common interests of the international community' and 'community interests' will be used interchangeably.

[41] H Bull, *The Anarchical Society: A Study of Order in World Politics*, 3rd edn (Palgrave, 2002) 151.

[42] Generally on this subject, see G Gaja, 'The Protection of General Interests in the International Community: General Course on Public International Law' (2012) 364 *RCADI* 9; E Benvenisti and G Nolte (eds), *Common Interests Across International Law* (Oxford University Press, 2018).

[43] B Simma, 'Universality of International Law from the Perspective of a Practitioner' (2009) 20 *EJIL* 265, 268.

This view was echoed by Judge Antônio Augusto Cançado Trindade, who stated that 'The growing consciousness of the need to bear in mind common values in pursuance of common interests has brought about a fundamental change in the outlook of International Law in the last decades.'[44]

As 'community interests' or 'common interests' are an elusive concept,[45] it is difficult to define it *a priori* in the abstract. As Simma noted, the existence of community interests does not derive from scientific abstraction but rather flows from the recognition of concrete problems.[46] In this connection, two points can be made.

First, community interests pertain to protection of a fundamental or crucial value shared by the international community as a whole or by contracting parties to a multilateral treaty. Hence community interests are collective by nature;[47] they generally refer to common interests of the international community as a whole but may also be interests common to parties to a particular multilateral treaty.[48] In any event, what is of particular importance is that community interests cannot be divided into the interests of each individual state.[49]

Second, strictly speaking, what international law protects concerns rights and interests reflected in specific norms of international law.[50] Norms of international law protecting community interests are sometimes called 'community interest norms'.[51] In essence, community interest norms can be regarded as obligations *erga omnes* or obligations *erga omnes partes*.[52] Some of such norms can also be considered as *jus cogens*. While norms of *jus cogens* considerably

[44] AA Cançando Trindade, 'International Law for Humankind: Towards a New *Jus Gentium*' (2005) 316 *RCADI* 9, 35.

[45] For an analysis of the concept of community interests, see I Feichtner, 'Community Interest' in R Wolfrum (ed), *Max Planck Encyclopedia of Public International Law* (Oxford University Press, 2011, online edn) [1] et seq; S Besson, 'Community Interests in International Law: Whose Interests Are They and How Should We Best Identify Them?' in Benvenisti and Nolte (eds), n 42, 36 et seq.

[46] Simma tentatively defines 'community interests' as 'a consensus according to which respect for certain fundamental values is not to be left to the free disposition of States individually or *inter se* but is recognized and sanctioned by international law as a matter of concern to all States': B Simma, 'From Bilateralism to Community Interest in International Law' (1994-IV) 250 *RCADI* 217, 233. According to Simma, examples of common interests include: international peace and security, solidarity between developed and developing countries, protection of the environment, the common heritage of mankind, and the protection of human rights: ibid, 235 et seq.

[47] Besson, n 45, 38.

[48] ibid, 39–40; Gaja, n 42, 22. As early as in 1951, the ICJ stated that in the Genocide Convention, 'the contracting States do not have any interests of their own; they merely have, one and all, a common interest'. *Reservations to the Convention on the Prevention and Punishment of the Crime of Genocide*, Advisory Opinion, [1951] ICJ Rep 15, 23.

[49] Besson, n 45, 39.

[50] See also Gaja, n 42, 21; Besson, n 45, 38.

[51] Feichtner, n 45, [2].

[52] See definition of obligations *erga omnes* by *Institut de droit international*, Resolution: Obligation *Erga Omnes* in International Law, Krakow Session 2005, available at http://www.idi-iil.org/app/uploads/2017/06/2005_kra_01_en.pdf. Crawford seems to assimilate 'communitarian norms' with obligations *erga omnes*. J Crawford, *Chance, Order, Change: The Course of International Law* (Brill/Nijhoff, 2014) 260.

overlap obligations *erga omnes*,[53] it is not suggested that all obligations *erga omnes* protecting community interests at the global level can be regarded as *jus cogens*.[54] As will be discussed in chapter 6, the concept of obligations *erga omnes (partes)* is key in the implementation of community interest norms.

At present, norms and concepts relating to community interests begin to be enshrined in positive international law,[55] and the law of the sea is no exception.[56] An illustrative example is provided by the principle of the common heritage of mankind. Under Article 136 of the UNCLOS, '[t]he Area and its resources are the common heritage of mankind', and activities in the Area shall be carried out for the benefit of mankind as a whole pursuant to Article 140(1) of the Convention.[57] The term 'mankind' is a trans-spatial concept, for it includes all the people on the planet. At the same time, it is trans-temporal, because 'mankind' includes both present and future generations.[58] It would seem to follow that 'the benefit of mankind' means the interest of all people in present and future generations.

[53] C Tams, *Enforcing Obligations* Erga Omnes *in International Law* (Cambridge University Press, 2005) 139–40.

[54] In this regard, some members of the International Law Commission (ILC) took the view that 'although all *jus cogens* norms were by definition *erga omnes*, not all *erga omnes* norms were necessarily imperative or of fundamental importance to the international community': (1998-II) *Yearbook of International Law Commission* 69, [279]. Judge Cançando Trindade also argued that 'By definition, all the norms of *jus cogens* generate necessarily obligations *erga omnes*. … In their turn, not all the obligations *erga omnes* necessarily refer to norms of *jus cogens*': Cançando Trindade, n 44, 354. In the discussion at the *Institut de Droit International*, Zemanek took a similar view: (2005) 71-I *Annuaire de l'Institut de Droit International* 166. For the relationship between *jus cogens* and obligations *erga omnes*, see also Tams, n 53, 157; S Villalpando, *L'émergence de la communauté internationale dans la responsabilité des Etats* (PUF, 2005) 106–08; J Verhoeven, 'Considérations sur ce qui est commun: Cours général de droit international public (2002)' (2008) 334 *RCADI* 9, 244; J-M Thouvenin, 'La saisine de la Cour internationale de Justice en cas de violation des règles fondamentales de l'ordre juridique international' in C Tomuschat and J-M Thouvenin (eds), *The Fundamental Rules of the International Legal Order* (Brill/Nijhoff, 2006) 311, 326–27; L Brilmayer and IY Tesfalidet, 'Third State Obligations and the Enforcement of International Law' (2011) 44 *New York University Journal of International Law and Politics* 1, 21–25; P Picone, 'The Distinction between Jus Cogens and Obligations Erga Omnes' in E Cannizzaro, *The Law of Treaties Beyond the Vienna Convention* (Oxford University Press, 2011) 411.

[55] Villalpando has persuasively demonstrated the emergence of community interests in positive international law by examining those concepts. S Villalpando, 'The Legal Dimension of the International Community: How Community Interests Are Protected in International Law' (2010) 21 *EJIL* 387. Wolfrum clearly stated that 'the existence of community interests is now accepted': R Wolfrum, 'Enforcing Community Interests Through International Dispute Settlement; Reality or Utopia?' in U Fastenrath et al (eds), *From Bilateralism to Community Interest, Essays in Honour of Judge Bruno Simma* (Oxford University Press, 2011) 1132, 1133.

[56] Generally on this subject, see Y Tanaka, 'Protection of Community Interests in International Law: The Case of the Law of the Sea' (2011) 15 *Max Planck Yearbook of United Nations Law* 329. See also JA Pastor Ridruejo, 'Le droit international à la veille du vingt et unième siècle: normes, faits et valeurs, Cours général de droit international public' (1998) 274 *RCADI* 9, 254.

[57] Under Art 1(1)(1) of the UNCLOS, 'the Area' refers to 'the sea-bed and ocean floor and subsoil thereof, beyond the limits of national jurisdiction'.

[58] R-J Dupuy, 'La notion de patrimoine commun de l'humanité appliquée aux fonds marins' in R-J Dupuy, *Dialectiques du droit international: souveraineté des Etats, communauté internationale et droits de l'humanité* (Pedone, 1999) 189 et seq; AC Kiss, 'La notion de patrimoine commun de l'humanité' (1982) 175 *RCADI* 99, 240.

As the scope of the international community is well beyond the community of states,[59] it may be reasonable to consider that the concept of the benefit of mankind is equivalent to the common interest of the international community as a whole. In light of the increasing importance of community interests at sea, it appears that a new paradigm that rests on common values or interests is emerging in the law of the sea. This new paradigm contrasts with the traditional paradigm in four respects.[60]

First, the traditional paradigm, which rests on the Westphalian conception of international law stressing the safeguarding of state sovereignty, aims to reconcile the individual interests of states in each jurisdictional zone. In contrast, the new paradigm aims to safeguard common interests of the international community or community interests at sea, by providing a legal framework for ensuring international cooperation in marine affairs.

Second, while the traditional paradigm is essentially governed by the principle of sovereignty and the principle of freedom, the new paradigm relies on the principle of cooperation.

Third, under the traditional paradigm, the state can be regarded as the primary subject of international law, since the reconciliation of individual interests of states constitutes the primary aim of the paradigm. By contrast, under the new paradigm, in addition to states, the role of non-state actors, in particular international institutions, is of particular importance, since international cooperation to promote community interests necessitates these institutions.

Fourth, under the traditional paradigm, compliance with rules of the law relies on the principle of reciprocity. According to this principle, compliance with rules of the law results from the interest that a state perceives in the reciprocal action of another state or states.[61] As the principle of reciprocity essentially governs bilateral and contractual relations between atomistic states,[62] however, the principle of reciprocity alone is inadequate to protect community interests.[63] Hence the new paradigm requires a more institutional approach to secure compliance with relevant rules.

In summary, it can be argued that the traditional paradigm essentially reflects the international law of coexistence,[64] and that the new paradigm reflects the

[59] In this respect, Judge Antônio Augusto Cançado Trindade argues that 'the conception of international community encompasses today all subjects of international law – States, international organizations, individuals, and humankind': Cançado Trindade, n 44, 219. See also P-M Dupuy, 'L'unité de l'ordre juridique international: Cours général de droit international public (2000)' (2002) 297 *RCADI* 9, 255.

[60] See also Y Tanaka, *The International Law of the Sea*, 3rd edn (Cambridge University Press, 2019) 5–6.

[61] The principle of reciprocity seeks to secure the national interest of each state on the basis of the symmetry of rights and obligations. Bull, n 41, 134; M Virally, 'Le principe de réciprocité dans le droit international contemporain' (1967) 122 *RCADI* 1, 19.

[62] Simma, n 46, 232–33.

[63] A Paulus, 'Reciprocity Revisited' in U Fastenrach et al (eds), *From Bilateralism to Community Interest: Essays in Honour of Judge Bruno Simma* (Oxford University Press, 2011) 113, 123.

[64] G Abi-Saab, 'Cours général de droit international public' (1987) 207 *RCADI* 9, 320.

international law of cooperation.[65] It must be stressed that the two paradigms are not mutually exclusive but are complementary; and that one paradigm is not replaced by another paradigm. In light of the dynamic nature of international law, including the law of the sea, however, the balance between the two paradigms may change over time. Given the increasing importance of the protection of community interests at sea, such as sustainable use of marine resources, marine environmental protection and the maintenance of maritime security, it appears that the new paradigm is gaining in importance in the law of the sea, even though it still remains embryonic.[66] The *South China Sea* arbitration should be considered within the broad context of the changing paradigm of the law of the sea.[67]

When considering the new paradigm, an essential question is whether and to what extent effective mechanisms for the protection of community interests exist in contemporary international law.[68] As discussed elsewhere, four models for protecting community interests can be identified:

> Model I. Protection of community interests through global international organisations in a centralised manner;
>
> Model II. Protection of community interests through the individual application of the law of *dédoublement fonctionnel*;
>
> Model III. Protection of community interests through the institutional application of the law of *dédoublement fonctionnel*; and
>
> Model IV. Protection of community interests through international adjudication.[69]

The best example of the first model, concerning the protection of community interests through an international organisation in a centralised manner, is the International Seabed Authority governing the Area.

The second model concerns the protection of community interests by the individual application of the law of *dédoublement fonctionnel* advocated by Georges Scelle.[70] Under this model, community interests are to be protected by each state, which would assume the role of organ of the international community. An example is the port state jurisdiction with regard to the regulation of vessel-source marine pollution under Article 218(1) of the UNCLOS.

[65] In this regard, it is well known that Friedmann pointed to the expansion of international law from international law of coexistence to international law of cooperation. Regarding this formula, see W Friedmann, 'General Course in Public International Law' (1969-II) 127 *RCADI* 39, 91–109.

[66] Tanaka, n 60, 6.

[67] See also ch 7 of this book.

[68] Cf Wolfrum, n 55, 1133.

[69] Tanaka, n 60, 540.

[70] Concerning the theory of the law of *dédoublement fonctionnel*, see G Scelle, 'Le phénomène juridique du dédoublement fonctionnel' in *Rechtsfragen der internationalen Organisation, Festschrift für Hans Wehberg zu seinem Geburtstag* (Klostermann, 1956) 324; A Cassese, 'Remarks on Scelle's Theory of "Role Splitting" (*dédoublement fonctionnel*) in International Law' (1990) 1 *EJIL* 210; M Nishiumi, 'Dédoublement fonctionnel de l'Etat et droit international contemporain: d'après la pensée de Georges Scelle' (in Japanese) (2001) 20 *Yearbook of World Law* 77.

The third model relates to the protection of community interests through the institutional application of the law of *dédoublement fonctionnel*. The establishment of the high seas marine-protected areas (MPAs) under the OSPAR Convention is a case in point.[71] By creating MPAs in areas beyond national jurisdiction, contracting parties to the OSPAR Convention, along with the supervision through the OSPAR Commission, can be thought to assume the role of an advocate of the international community in the protection of biological diversity on the high seas. The third model seeks to protect community interests through international institutions and arrangements. In so doing, this model attempts to overcome the deficiencies of the second model, namely, the lack of incentive of states, the lack of coordination and arbitral use of the concept of community interests.[72]

The fourth model concerns protection of community interests by international courts and tribunals. In this connection, international courts and tribunals can perform a dual function. First, an international court or tribunal decides, if appropriate, whether a rule of international law would be regarded as a community interest norm. Given that the concept of community interests may be used as an ideology to justify a policy of a state or a particular group of states, the review of the contents of community interests by a judicial body is crucial. Second, as international law rests essentially on a decentralised legal system, there is no centralised machinery for determining the breach of obligations concerning the protection of community interests. When an international dispute involving community interests is submitted to an international court or tribunal, the court or tribunal decides the breach of obligations protecting community interests in each specific case. In so doing, it assumes the role of an advocate in the protection of community interests.[73] The possible role of international adjudication in the settlement of international disputes involving community interests deserves serious consideration.[74] In fact, the Tribunal, in the *South China Sea* arbitration, addressed some issues relating to community interests, such as the protection of the marine environment and biological diversity.

[71] Convention for the Protection of the Marine Environment of the North-East Atlantic (adopted 22 September 1992, entered into force 25 March 1998). Text is available at https://www.ospar.org/convention/text. Further, see Y Tanaka, 'The Institutional Application of the Law of *Dédoublement Fonctionnel* in Marine Environmental Protection: A Critical Assessment of Regional Regimes' (2014) 57 *GYIL* 143.

[72] ibid, 149. See also Tanaka, n 56, 354.

[73] Tanaka, n 60, 541–42.

[74] For a pioneering study on this subject, see V Gowlland-Debbas, 'Judicial Insights into Fundamental Values and Interests of the International Community' in AS Muller et al (eds), *The International Court of Justice: Its Future Role after Fifty Years* (Nijhoff, 1997) 327. See also by the same writer, 'An Emerging International Public Policy?' in U Fastenrath et al (eds), *From Bilateralism to Community Interest: Essays in Honour of Judge Bruno Simma* (Oxford University Press, 2011) 241; M Benzing, 'Community Interests in the Procedure of International Courts and Tribunals' (2006) 5 *The Law and Practice of International Courts and Tribunals* 369.

Hence, the *South China Sea* arbitration provides an interesting insight into the protection of community interests through international adjudication.[75]

C. Legal Implications of the *South China Sea* Arbitration Awards for Considerations Relating to Time in International Law

Time was and continues to be a subject in various disciplines, including philosophy.[76] Given that the interpretation or application of rules of international law may be, more or less, influenced by time, elements relating to time should also constitute an issue that deserves serious consideration in the law.[77] In broad terms, it seems that the impact of time in international law can be divided into two categories.

The first is the impact of time on the interpretation or application of rules of international law. A typical example in this matter is evolutionary treaty interpretation. As discussed elsewhere, evolutionary interpretation may be at issue particularly in the interpretation of treaties concerning the protection of human rights, environmental treaties, the WTO law and constitutive instruments of international organisations.[78] The temporal issue also arises where a time element is incorporated in the interpretation of a concept or a rule itself. The concept of historic rights is an example.[79] Furthermore, time elements

[75] See ch 6, section IV of this book.

[76] In this connection, the distinction of three 'times' made by St Augustine merits particular attention. St Augustine, in *The Confessions*, stated 'Thus it is not properly said that there are three times, past, present, and future. Perhaps it might be said rightly that there are three times: a time present of things past; a time present of things present; and a time present of things future … The time present of things past is memory; the time present of things present is direct experience; the time present of things future is expectation.' *The Confessions of St Augustine*, ed and tr AC Outler (Dover Publications, 2002) 229. The distinction seems to be relevant to the interpretation or application of rules of international law. Indeed, treaty interpretation is governed by the memory of the past, ie the original will of the parties. In appropriate cases, the application of a rule of international law relies on historic evidence, which records the memory of the past. Some treaty provisions, such as environmental norms, are expected to change over time (ie evolutionary interpretation). It is beyond serious argument that rules of international law apply at the present time. Certain rules of international law must be interpreted or applied taking account of signs of the future. Under the precautionary approach, for instance, preventive measures must be taken in order to respond to probable or potential risks that cannot be objectively identified through present-day science but which might create environmental damage in the future. Generally on this issue, see Y Tanaka, 'Reflections on Time Elements in the International Law of the Environment' (2013) 73 *ZaöRV /Heidelberg Journal of International Law* 139.

[77] Concerning time elements in international law, the following studies are of particular interest: E McWhinney, 'The Time Dimension in International Law, Historical Relativism and Intertemporal Law' in J Makarczyk (ed), *Essays in International Law in Honour of Judge Manfred Lachs* (Nijhoff, 1984) 179; R Higgins, 'Time and the Law: International Perspectives on an Old Problem' (1997) 46 *ICLQ* 501; Société française pour le droit international, *Le droit international et le temps, Colloque de Paris* (Pedone, 2001).

[78] Tanaka, n 76, 143–44.

[79] See ch 3 of this book.

influence procedural rules of an international court or tribunal. The requirement of urgency in the prescription of provisional measures is a case in point.[80]

The second is the impact of time on space. As space and time are closely interlinked, an international spatial order cannot be immune from the influence of time. In international law, time elements may affect an international spatial order in at least three respects:[81]

(a) the acquisition of sovereignty over territory;
(b) the establishment of boundaries; and
(c) the entitlement to marine spaces.

As will be discussed in this book, considerations of time elements have significantly affected entitlements to marine spaces. Given that maritime entitlement directly influences an international spatial order in the oceans, the *South China Sea* Arbitration Award (Merits) provides an interesting insight into the interaction between space and time in international law.

IV. CONCLUSIONS

The *South China Sea* Arbitration Awards seem to highlight three key elements of an international spatial order:[82] *space*, *time*, and *community interests*. The three elements become particularly important when considering a legal order in the oceans. As Judge Paik, President of ITLOS, pointedly observed, the *South China Sea* Arbitration Awards can be thought to have implications that go far beyond the immediate dispute before the Tribunal.[83] Thus, noting the three legal implications previously mentioned, this book seeks to examine the *South China Sea* Arbitration Awards from the perspective of the development of public international law, including the law of the sea. To achieve the aim, general questions of international law are set out in the introduction to each chapter. An attempt is then made to find answers to the questions by analysing the *South China Sea* Arbitration Awards. Thus the focus of this book is to consider whether and to what extent the Awards furnish answers to the questions. This book focuses on legal issues only and does not aim to critically assess a policy of a particular state or states.

[80] On this issue, see Y Tanaka, 'The Requirement of Urgency in the Jurisprudence of ITLOS concerning Provisional Measures' in A Del Vecchio and R Virzo (eds), *Interpretations of the United Nations Convention on the Law of the Sea by International Courts and Tribunals* (Springer, 2019) 107.

[81] See ch 6, section V of this book.

[82] In this book, the term 'an international spatial order' means 'a spatial order in international law'.

[83] J-H Paik, 'South China Sea Arbitral Awards: Main Findings and Assessment' (2016) 20 *Max Planck Yearbook of United Nations Law* 367, 407.

FURTHER READING

Bautista, L and Arugay, AA (eds), 'Philippines v China, the South China Sea Arbitral Award: Implications for Policy and Practice' (2017) 9 *Asian Politics and Policy* 122.

Beckman, R, 'The UN Convention on the Law of the Sea and the Maritime Disputes in the South China Sea' (2013) 107 *AJIL* 142.

Beckman, R, Page, MR and Bernard, L (eds), *UNCLOS and the South China Sea* (Edward Elgar, 2014).

Benvenisti, E and Nolte, G (eds), *Common Interests Across International Law* (Oxford University Press, 2018).

Bull, H, *The Anarchical Society: A Study of Order in World Politics*, 3rd edn (Palgrave, 2002).

Buszynski, L and Roberts, CB (eds), *The South China Sea Maritime Dispute: Political, Legal and Regional Perspectives* (Routledge, 2015).

Cançando Trindade, AA, 'International Law for Humankind: Towards a New *Jus Gentium*' (2005) 316 *RCADI* 9.

Cassese, A, 'Remarks on Scelle's Theory of "Role Splitting" (*dédoublement fonctionnel*) in International Law' (1990) 1 *EJIL* 210.

Chinese Society of International Law (CSIL), 'The South China Sea Arbitration: A Critical Study' (2018) 17 *CJIL* 207.

——, *The South China Sea Arbitration: A Critical Study* (Foreign Languages Press, 2018).

Churchill, R, 'Dispute Settlement in the Law of the Sea: Survey for 2015, Part II and 2016' (2017) 32 *IJMCL* 379 (in particular, 393–403).

Cogliati-Banz, VP, 'The South China Sea Arbitration (The Republic of the Philippines v. The People's Republic of China)' (2016) 31 *IJMCL* 759.

Dzurek, DJ, 'The Spratly Islands Dispute: Who's On First?' (1996) 2 *Maritime Briefing*, International Boundaries Research Unit.

Feichtner, I, 'Community Interest' in R Wolfrum (ed), *Max Planck Encyclopedia of Public International Law* (Oxford University Press, 2011 online).

Fu-Kuo Liu and Spangler, J (eds), *South China Sea Lawfare: Legal Perspectives and International Responses to the Philippines v China Arbitration Case* (South China Sea Think Tank, 2016).

Gaja, G, 'The Protection of General Interests in the International Community: General Course on Public International Law' (2012) 364 *RCADI* 9.

Hao Duy Phan and Lan Ngoc Nguyen, 'The South China Sea Arbitration: Bindingness, Finality, and Compliance with UNCLOS Dispute Settlement Decisions' (2018) 8 *Asian Journal of International Law* 36.

Hiebert, M, Poling, GB and Cronin, C (eds), *In the Wake of Arbitration: Papers from the Sixth Annual CSIS South China Sea Conference* (Rowman & Littlefield Publishers, 2017).

Hsiung, JC, *South China Sea Disputes and US-China Contest* (World Scientific Publishing Co, 2018).

Hui Zhong and White, M, 'South China Sea: Its Importance for Shipping, Trade, Energy and Fisheries' (2017) 2 *Asia-Pacific Journal of Ocean Law and Policy* 9.

Jayakumar, S, Koh, T and Beckman, RC (eds), *South China Sea Disputes and Law of the Sea* (Edward Elgar, 2014).

Jayakumar, S, Koh, T, Beckman, R, Davenport, T and Hao Duy Phan (eds), *The South China Sea Arbitration: The Legal Dimension* (Edward Elgar, 2018).

Jenner, CJ and Tran Truong Thuy (eds), *The South China Sea: A Crucible of Regional Cooperation or Conflict-making Sovereignty Claims?* (Cambridge University Press, 2016).

Jing Huang and Biullo, A (eds), *Territorial Disputes in the South China Sea: Navigating Rough Waters* (Palgrave Macmillan, 2015).

Kassim, YR, *The South China Sea Disputes Flashpoints, Turning Points and Trajectories* (World Scientific Publishing Co, 2017).

Keyuan Zou, 'The South China Sea' in D Rothwell, AG Oude Elferink, KN Scott and T Stephens (eds), *The Oxford Handbook of the Law of the Sea* (Oxford University Press, 2015) 626–46.

Lim, M and Lie, N, 'Condominium Arrangements as a Legal Mechanism for the Conservation of the South China Sea Large Marine Ecosystem' (2017) 2 *Asia-Pacific Journal of Ocean Law and Policy* 52.

Lingqun Li, *China's Policy Towards the South China Sea: When Geopolitics Meets the Law of the Sea* (Routledge, 2018).

McDorman, TL, 'The South China Sea after 2009: Clarity of Claims and Enhanced Prospects for Regional Cooperation?' (2010) 24 *Ocean Yearbook* 507.

——, 'The South China Sea Arbitration' (2016) 20 *American Society of International Law Insights*, available at https://www.asil.org/insights/volume/20/issue/17/south-china-sea-arbitration.

——, 'The South China Sea Arbitration: Selected Legal Notes' (2017) 21 *Asian Yearbook of International Law* 1.

——, 'The South China Sea *Tribunal Awards*: *A Dispute Resolution Perspective*' (2018) 3 *Asia-Pacific Journal of Ocean Law and Policy* 134.

McGee, J, Gogarty, B and Smith, D, 'Associational Balance of Power and the Possibilities for International Law in South China Sea' (2017) 2 *Asia-Pacific Journal of Ocean Law and Policy* 88.

Nishimoto, K, 'The Significance of the South China Sea Arbitral Award from the Perspective of International Law' (in Japanese) (2017) 4 *Tohoku Law Review* 15.

Nong Hong, *UNCLOS and Ocean Dispute Settlement: Law and Politics in the South China Sea* (Routledge, 2012).

——, 'Exploring Maritime Dispute Management in the South China Sea' in B Courmont, F Lasserre and E Motte (eds), *Assessing Maritime Disputes in East Asia: Political and Legal Perspective* (Routledge, 2017) 141–67.

Owen, NA and Shofield, CH, 'Disputed South China Sea Hydrocarbons in Perspective' (2012) 36 *Marine Policy* 809.

Oxman, BH, 'The South China Sea Arbitration Award' (2017) 24 *University of Miami International and Comparative Law Review* 235.

Paik, J-H, 'South China Sea Arbitral Awards: Main Findings and Assessment' (2016) 20 *Max Planck Yearbook of United Nations Law* 367.

Rahman, C and Tsamenyi, M, 'A Strategic Perspective on Security and Naval Issues in the South China Sea' (2010) 41 *ODIL* 315.

Robles, AC Jr, *The South China Sea Arbitration: Understanding the Awards and Debating with China* (Sussex Academic Press, 2019).

Roy, N, *The South China Sea Disputes: Past, Present, and Future* (Lexington Books, 2016).

Scelle, G, 'Le phénomène juridique du dédoublement fonctionnel' in *Rechtsfragen der internationalen Organisation, Festschrift für Hans Wehberg zu seinem Geburtstag* (Klostermann, 1956) 324–42.

Simma, B, 'From Bilateralism to Community Interest in International Law' (1994-IV) 250 *RCADI* 217.

——, 'Universality of International Law from the Perspective of a Practitioner' (2009) 20 *EJIL* 265.

Storey, I and Cheng-Yi Lin (eds), *The South China Sea Dispute: Navigating Diplomatic and Strategic Tensions* (ISEAS Publishing, 2016).

Symposium on the South China Sea Arbitration, (2016) 110 *American Journal of International Law Unbound* 263.

Tams, C, *Enforcing Obligations* Erga Omnes *in International Law* (Cambridge University Press, 2005).

Tanaka, Y, 'Protection of Community Interests in International Law: The Case of the Law of the Sea' (2011) 15 *Max Planck Yearbook of United Nations Law* 329.

——, 'Reflections on Time Elements in the International Law of the Environment' (2013) 73 *ZaöRV /Heidelberg Journal of International Law* 139.

——, 'The Institutional Application of the Law of *Dédoublement Fonctionnel* in Marine Environmental Protection: A Critical Assessment of Regional Regimes' (2014) 57 *GYIL* 143.

Tran Truong Thuy and Le Thuy Trang, *Power, Law, and Maritime Order in the South China Sea* (Lexington Books, 2015).

Tran Truong Thuy, Welfield, JB and Le Thuy Trang (eds), *Building a Normative Order in the South China Sea: Evolving Disputes, Expanding Options* (Edward Elgar, 2019).

Tseng Hui-Yi, K, *Rethinking South China Sea Disputes: The Untold Dimensions and Great Expectations* (Routledge, 2017).

Villalpando, S, 'The Legal Dimension of the International Community: How Community Interests Are Protected in International Law' (2010) 21 *EJIL* 387.

Weisburd, AM, *Failings of the International Court of Justice* (Oxford University Press, 2016).

Wolfrum, R, 'Enforcing Community Interests Through International Dispute Settlement; Reality or Utopia?' in U Fastenrath, R Geiger, D-E Khan, A Paulus, S von Schorlemer and C Vedder (eds), *From Bilateralism to Community Interest, Essays in Honour of Judge Bruno Simma* (Oxford University Press, 2011) 1132–45.

Wu, S, Valencia, M and Nong Hong (eds), *UN Convention on the Law of the Sea and the South China Sea* (Ashgate, 2015).

Wu Shicun and Nong Hong (eds), *Recent Developments in the South China Sea Dispute: The Prospects of a Joint Development Regime* (Routledge, 2014).

Wu Shicun and Keyan Zou (eds), *Arbitration Concerning the South China Sea: Philippines versus China* (Routledge, 2016).

Yang Razali Kassim (ed), *The South China Sea Disputes: Flashpoints, Turning Points and Trajectories* (World Scientific Pub Co Inc, 2017).

Yann-Huei Song and Keyuan Zou, *Major Law and Policy Issues in the South China Sea: European and American Perspectives* (Ashgate, 2014).

Yen Hoang Tran, 'The South China Sea Arbitral Award: Legal Implications for Fisheries Management and Cooperation in the South China Sea' (2017) 6 *Cambridge International Law Journal* 87.

2

*Jurisdiction and Admissibility**

I. INTRODUCTION

THE JURISDICTION OF the Annex VII Arbitral Tribunal and the admissibility of the Philippines Submissions constituted a matter of extensive debate in the *South China Sea* arbitration. In this regard, the Chinese Government argued that 'the Arbitral Tribunal manifestly has no jurisdiction over the present arbitration'.[1] As the Annex VII Arbitral Tribunal stated in the *Arctic Sunrise* Arbitration Award, however:

> The fact that a party may contest the jurisdiction of the tribunal is not a basis on which a party can frustrate the effective discharge by that tribunal of its responsibility to adjudicate a dispute brought before it, including determining its own jurisdiction.[2]

Furthermore, under Article 288(4) of the UNCLOS, '[i]n the event of a dispute as to whether a court or tribunal has jurisdiction, the matter shall be settled by decision of that court or tribunal'. The power of an international court or tribunal to decide on the existence and extent of its own jurisdiction concerning any dispute before it – called the principle of *la compétence de la compétence* – is generally recognised in international law.[3] Accordingly, the question of whether the Arbitral Tribunal has jurisdiction is to be settled by decision of that tribunal itself.

In its Arbitration Award of 29 October 2015, the Tribunal found that it had jurisdiction to consider the Philippines' Submissions Nos 3, 4, 6, 7, 10, 11 and 13.[4]

* This chapter is derived in part from an article by the author: Y Tanaka, 'Reflections on the *Philippines/China* Arbitration: Award on Jurisdiction and Admissibility' (2016) 15 *The Law and Practice of International Courts and Tribunals* 305. Doi 10.1163/15718034-12341324.

[1] Position Paper of the Government of the People's Republic of China on the Matter of Jurisdiction in the South China Sea Arbitration Initiated by the Republic of the Philippines, 7 December 2014, [3]. See also ibid, [29] and [85]–[86], available at http://www.fmprc.gov.cn/mfa_eng/zxxx_662805/t1217147.shtml. Reproduced in Chinese Society of International Law (CSIL), *The South China Sea Arbitration: A Critical Study* (Foreign Languages Press, 2018) 525.

[2] The *Arctic Sunrise* Arbitration (Merits) (Kingdom of the Netherlands v Russian Federation), 14 August 2015, [368] available at https://pca-cpa.org/en/cases/21/.

[3] H Thirlway, *The International Court of Justice* (Oxford University Press, 2016) 38.

[4] PCA Case No 2013–19, the *South China Sea* Arbitration (Jurisdiction and Admissibility) (hereinafter 'the *South China Sea* Arbitration Award (Jurisdiction and Admissibility)'), 29 October 2015, [413]G.

These Submissions concern: the legal status of various maritime features as low-tide elevations, islands or rocks; traditional fishing activities of Philippines nationals at Scarborough Shoal; marine environmental protection at Scarborough Shoal and Second Thomas Shoal; and China's law enforcement activities in the vicinity of Scarborough Shoal. With regard to Submissions Nos 1, 2, 5, 8, 9, 12 and 14, however, the Tribunal reserved its consideration of its jurisdiction to the merits phase.[5] Thus the Tribunal did not dismiss any submission in the jurisdiction and admissibility phase.

The 2015 Arbitration Award on Jurisdiction and Admissibility raised, in particular, four issues that deserve serious consideration:

(a) How should irregular communications from a non-appearing state be treated in arbitral proceedings?
(b) How should communications by a third state be treated in the arbitral proceedings?
(c) Is it possible for a court or tribunal under Part XV of the UNCLOS to deal with a mixed dispute involving territorial and maritime issues at the same time?
(d) What are the legal implications of the interpretation of Article 281 of the UNCLOS for the development of dispute settlement in international law?

This chapter aims to examine the four issues by analysing the Arbitration Award of 2015. Following this introductory section, section II discusses the legal issues concerning the non-appearing state. Section III then addresses the treatment of communications by a third state. The chapter moves on to examine the issues of jurisdiction over the mixed dispute involving territorial sovereignty and maritime delimitation (section IV). Finally, this chapter analyses the Tribunal's interpretation of Article 281 of the UNCLOS (section V), before offering conclusions (section VI).

II. TREATMENT OF THE NON-APPEARING STATE

A. Irregular Communication Made by China

The treatment of the non-appearing state constitutes a crucial issue since it affects the arbitral proceedings as a whole. As pointed out earlier, China did not participate in the arbitral proceedings. However, it is not suggested that China completely ignored them. Rather, China sent various communications to the Tribunal with a view to advocating its claims as to the Sino-Philippines dispute. On 19 February 2013, China presented a Note Verbale to the Department of Foreign Affairs of the Philippines, rejecting the arbitration.[6] By a Note Verbale

[5] ibid, [413]H and I.
[6] The *South China Sea* Arbitration Award (Jurisdiction and Admissibility), n 4, [27].

dated 29 July 2013, China reiterated its position that it did not accept the arbitration initiated by the Philippines.[7] Furthermore, the Chinese Ambassador to the United Kingdom (UK) requested a meeting with the President of the Arbitral Tribunal. In response, on 14 November 2013, the Tribunal sent a letter to remind the Parties to refrain from *ex parte* communication with members of the Tribunal.[8]

Among various communications made by China, what is of particular importance is a 'Position Paper of the Government of the People's Republic of China on the Matter of Jurisdiction in the South China Sea Arbitration Initiated by the Republic of Philippines'.[9] This instrument was published on 7 December 2014, and the following day the Chinese Embassy requested that the PCA forward China's Position Paper and its English translation to the members of the Tribunal.[10] In the Position Paper, China stated that its rejection of and non-participation in the present arbitration were solidly grounded in international law.[11] According to the Paper, the Chinese Government had decided not to accept nor participate in the present arbitration in light of the manifest lack of jurisdiction on the part of the Arbitral Tribunal.[12] Moreover, the Chinese Ambassador to the Kingdom of the Netherlands wrote to the members of the Tribunal individually, setting out the Chinese Government's position on issues relating to the South China Sea arbitration, on 6 February 2015 (the Chinese Ambassador's First Letter) and 1 July 2015 (the Chinese Ambassador's Second Letter) respectively.[13] On 24 August 2015, China further published 'Foreign Ministry Spokesperson Hua Chunying's Remarks on the Release of the Transcript of the Oral Hearing on Jurisdiction by the South China Sea Arbitral Tribunal Established at the Request of the Philippines'.[14]

B. Treatment of Communication by China

As the Annex VII Arbitral Tribunal stated in the *Arctic Sunrise* Arbitration Award, the UNCLOS 'may not oblige a party to appear before a tribunal having jurisdiction under the Convention'.[15] Under Annex VII, Article 9 to the

[7] ibid, [37].
[8] ibid, [40].
[9] See n 1. Subsequently, China's arguments on the issue of jurisdiction and admissibility were amplified by CSIL, n 1, 33 et seq. As for China's arguments, this chapter will focus on the China's Position Paper, because this instrument was treated by the Tribunal as a plea concerning jurisdiction.
[10] The *South China Sea* Arbitration Award (Jurisdiction and Admissibility), n 4, [55]–[56].
[11] China's Position Paper, n 1, Pt V.
[12] ibid, [85].
[13] The *South China Sea* Arbitration Award (Jurisdiction and Admissibility), n 4, [64], [83].
[14] ibid, [96].
[15] *The Arctic Sunrise Arbitration*, n 2, [367].

UNCLOS and Article 25(1) of the Rules of Procedure,[16] however, it is clear that the non-appearance of one of the parties in dispute does not constitute a bar to the judicial proceedings. It must be stressed that as the International Tribunal for the Law of the Sea (ITLOS) highlighted in the *Arctic Sunrise* case, 'the non-appearing State is nevertheless a party to the proceedings'.[17] Thus, the eventual judgment is binding upon the non-appearing parties in accordance with Article 296(1) and Article 11 of Annex VII to the Convention.[18] This point was affirmed by the Arbitral Tribunal, stating that 'Despite its non-appearance, China remains a Party to these proceedings, with the ensuring rights and obligations, including that it will be bound by any decision of the Tribunal.'[19]

An issue that needs further consideration in the default case concerns the treatment of informal communications of a defaulting party. Experience suggests that more often than not, the non-appearing state indirectly defends its case and 'responds' to the allegations made against it, but it does so by means of a variety of unorthodox 'backstairs' or side-wind methods that avoid its entering a formal 'appearance' in the case.[20] On the one hand, to refuse to consider communications of this kind would create the risk of an international court or tribunal's giving judgment in ignorance of some highly important fact or allegation of law. On the other hand, to treat such communications as, in effect, pleadings would confer an unfair advantage on the absent state.[21] Thus a dilemma arises.

In the jurisprudence of the ICJ, the Court has taken account of informal communications. In the *Aegean Continental Shelf* case, for instance, Turkey submitted the 'Observations of the Turkish Government on the request of the Government of Greece for provisional measures dated 10 August 1976',[22] even though it refused to appear before the Court. In this regard, the Court explicitly

[16] The *South China Sea* Arbitration Award (Jurisdiction and Admissibility), n 4, [113]. See also *The 'Arctic Sunrise' case (Kingdom of the Netherlands v Russian Federation)*, Provisional Measures, ITLOS Case No 22, Order of 22 November 2013, [2013] ITLOS Rep 242, [48].

[17] *The 'Arctic Sunrise' case*, n 16, [51].

[18] Under Art 296(1) of the UNCLOS, '[a]ny decision rendered by a court or tribunal having jurisdiction under this section shall be final and shall be complied with by all the parties to the dispute'. Art 11 of Annex VII stipulates that 'The award shall be final and without appeal, unless the parties to the dispute have agreed in advance to an appellate procedure. It shall be complied with by the parties to the dispute.' See also G Fitzmaurice, 'The Problem of the "Non-Appearing" Defendant Government' (1980) 51 *BYIL* 89, 98; H Thirlway, *The Law and Procedure of the International Court of Justice: Fifty Years of Jurisprudence*, vol II (Oxford University Press, 2013) 1824.

[19] The *South China Sea* Arbitration Award (Jurisdiction and Admissibility), n 4, [114]. See also the *Arctic Sunrise* Arbitration (Merits), n 2, [367].

[20] *Military and Paramilitary Activities in and against Nicaragua (Nicaragua v United States of America)*, Merits, Judgment, [1986] ICJ Rep 14, 25, [31]. See also Thirlway, n 18, vol I, 1003; L Caflisch, 'Cent ans des règlement pacifique des différends interétatiques' (2001) 288 *RCADI* 245, 353.

[21] Thirlway, n 18, vol I, 1003.

[22] *Aegean Sea Continental Shelf (Greece v Turkey)*, Request for the Indication of Interim Measures of Protection, Order, [1976] ICJ Rep 3, 5, [7].

stated that '*having regard to the position taken by the Turkish Government in its observations communicated to the Court on 26 August 1976*, ..., it is necessary to resolve first of all the question of the Court's jurisdiction with respect to the case'.[23] In the *Nicaragua* case, the ICJ considered that 'it is valuable for the Court to know the views of both parties in whatever form those views may have been expressed'.[24] Furthermore, the ICJ in the *Nuclear Tests* case based its decision on a public statement by the French Government, which had not been submitted before it by any formal means.[25] In the words of Judge ad hoc Barwick, '[t]hose contents and that of the French *White Paper* on Nuclear Tests, published but not communicated to the Court during the hearing of the case, have in fact been fully considered'.[26] However, the ICJ's approach has been challenged by some writers since the non-appearing state is placed in a more advantageous position than that of an appearing party, at least in some respects.[27] For instance, Sir Gerald Fitzmaurice argued that since the non-appearing state was not technically entering any formal objection to the assuming of jurisdiction, the Court could have cut the jurisdictional phase of the case and proceeded straight to the merits.[28]

The Arbitral Tribunal in the *South China Sea* arbitration decided to treat the communications by China as effectively constituting a plea concerning the Tribunal's jurisdiction for the purposes of Article 20 of the Rules of Procedure.[29] As a consequence, arguably it may be said that China's statements and communications were treated as equivalent to preliminary objections. The Tribunal's approach seems to be in line with the jurisprudence of the ICJ.[30]

Article 9 of UNCLOS Annex VII seeks to balance the risk of prejudice that could be suffered by either party.[31] The Tribunal thus attempted to safeguard the procedural rights of the appearing and non-appearing states.[32]

[23] ibid, 13, [45] (emphasis added).

[24] The *Nicaragua* case [1986] ICJ Rep 25, [31].

[25] Thirlway, n 18, vol I, 1005.

[26] Dissenting Opinion of Judge Sir Garfield Barwick, *Nuclear Tests (Australia v France)*, Judgment, [1974] ICJ Rep 391, 401.

[27] Hans von Mangoldt and Andreas Zimmermann, 'Article 53' in A Zimmermann et al (eds), *The Statute of the International Court of Justice: A Commentary*, 2nd edn (Oxford University Press, 2012) 1347–48; T Davenport, 'Procedural Issues Arising from China's Non-participation in the South China Sea Arbitration' in S Jayakumar et al (eds), *The South China Sea Arbitration: The Legal Dimension* (Edward Elgar, 2018) 65, 75. For instance, communications of the non-appearing party are *de facto* exempt from the terms and conditions of the Rules of Court. See the *Aegean Sea Continental Shelf* case, Oral Arguments on Jurisdiction, 19 December 1978, CR 1978, Argument by Mr O'Connell, 319–20.

[28] Fitzmaurice, n 18, 107.

[29] The *South China Sea* Arbitration Award (Jurisdiction and Admissibility), n 4, [122]. See also Procedural Order No 4, [1.1], cited ibid, [68].

[30] See also Davenport, n 27, 84–85.

[31] The *South China Sea* Arbitration Award (Jurisdiction and Admissibility), n 4, [115].

[32] ibid, [117].

First, for the Philippines, the Arbitral Tribunal issued a request for Further Written Argument containing 26 questions, by implementing Article 25(2) of the Rules of Procedure.[33] Since China's communications, including its Position Paper, did not specify objections to the Tribunal's jurisdiction in a comprehensive manner, it was necessary for the Tribunal to raise 'possible' objections itself. Related to this, the Tribunal invited the Philippines to address these objections. For instance, since China did not invoke the 1976 Treaty of Amity as a basis for precluding the Tribunal's jurisdiction, the Tribunal invited the Philippines to address the effect of the Treaty with reference to Article 281 of the UNCLOS.[34] Likewise, China's Position Paper did not address any of the Philippines' allegations with regard to the breach of the Convention on Biological Diversity (CBD).[35] Accordingly, the Tribunal invited the Philippines to elaborate on the relationship between alleged violations of the CBD and the UNCLOS.[36] In so doing, the Tribunal might have seemed to furnish the Philippines with guidance on elaborating relevant issues. Arguably, this can be justified in light of Article 25(2) of the Rules of Procedure, as well as the absence of the respondent state.

Second, under Annex VII, Article 9, the rights of non-participating parties must be protected by ensuring that a tribunal will not simply accept the claim of the participating party. The Tribunal thus paid due regard to China's communications.[37] Yet it cannot pass unnoticed that China's communications presented after the deadline for the submission of the Counter-Memorial were equally considered by the Tribunal as if they were regular documents.[38] As a consequence, some communications made by China were *de facto* exempted from deadlines otherwise imposed upon the Parties by Article 20(2) of the Rules of Procedure. Here some doubts might be expressed regarding the procedural fairness of the treatment of communications made by the Parties in dispute. Despite this point, overall it would be fair to say that the Tribunal attempted to strike a sensitive balance between the procedural rights of the Philippines and China.[39]

[33] ibid, [121].

[34] ibid, [256]–[257].

[35] Convention on Biological Diversity (adopted 22 May 1992, entered into force 29 December 1993) 1760 *UNTS* 79.

[36] The *South China Sea* Arbitration Award (Jurisdiction and Admissibility), n 4, [275]–[276].

[37] ibid, [117].

[38] ibid, [122]. On 2 June 2014, the Tribunal issued the Procedural Order No 2 of 2 June 2014 and set 15 December 2014 as the date by which China should submit a Counter-Memorial: ibid, [52]. Yet the Chinese Ambassador's Second Letter was sent on 1 July 2015. In addition, the Presiding Arbitrator invited China to comment by 17 August 2015 on any matter raised during or after the Hearing on Jurisdiction: ibid, [92]. Yet 'Foreign Ministry Spokesperson Hua Chunying's Remarks' were published on 24 August 2015: ibid, [96].

[39] Davenport, n 27, 98.

III. TREATMENT OF THIRD PARTIES

A. Intervention by Third Parties in Arbitration

As multiple states were involved the *South China Sea* disputes, a question arises as to whether the *South China Sea* arbitration might affect the rights and interests of third parties. Here intervention by third parties in the arbitration is at issue. Intervention is a legal institution to safeguard rights and interests of third parties in judicial proceedings. Where a treaty contains a provision with regard to intervention by third states in arbitral proceedings,[40] no procedural problem arises. Unlike Annex VI (the Statute of ITLOS),[41] however, there is no provision concerning intervention under Annex VII. Nor do the Rules of Procedure contain any provision on this matter. An issue thus arises whether or not an intervention by a third party is permissible in arbitral proceedings under Annex VII to the UNCLOS.[42]

If the original parties to an arbitration consent to a request for intervention by a third state, such intervention may be allowed.[43] However, the issue is more controversial where one of the original parties objects to such an intervention in arbitral proceedings. In the *South China Sea* arbitration, China opposed intervention by other states,[44] while the Philippines considered that the Tribunal's broad discretion on procedural matters encompassed the power to permit intervention and to take any steps it might consider appropriate to request information from Viet Nam.[45]

Generally, there is no sufficient evidence to support intervention by third parties in arbitral proceedings. In this regard, the *Projet de règlement pour la procédure arbitrale internationale* adopted by the *Institut de droit international* stated in Article 16 that:

> Ni les parties, ni les arbitres ne peuvent d'office mettre en cause d'autres Etats ou des tierces personnes quelconques, sauf autorisation spéciale exprimée dans le compromis et consentement préalable du tiers.
>
> L'intervention spontanée d'un tiers n'est admissible qu'avec le consentement des parties qui ont conclu le compromis.[46]

[40] See, for instance, the 1899 Convention for the Pacific Settlement of International Disputes (Art 56), the 1907 Convention for the Pacific Settlement of International Disputes (Art 84), the 1928 General Act on the Pacific Settlement of International Disputes (Art 37), and the 1986 Vienna Convention on the Law of Treaties between States and International Organization or between International Organizations (Annex, II(4)).

[41] Arts 31 and 32.

[42] Generally on this issue, see S Yee, 'Intervention in an Arbitral proceeding under Annex VII to the UNCLOS?' (2015) 14 *CJIL* 79.

[43] ibid, 90.

[44] The *South China Sea* Arbitration Award (Jurisdiction and Admissibility), n 4, [64].

[45] ibid, [62], [185].

[46] Institut de droit international, *Projet de règlement pour la procédure arbitrale internationale*, Session de La Haye, 1875, available at http://www.justitiaetpace.org/idiF/resolutionsF/1875_haye_01_fr.pdf.

This view was echoed by a commentary on Article 62 of the ICJ Statute, stating that 'Generally, provisions for arbitral procedures provide for intervention only with the parties' consent.'[47] Furthermore, Brownlie has argued that 'Arbitration is litigation in conditions of privacy; no third-party intervention is possible.'[48]

In summary, where there is no provision permitting intervention by a third party in the Rule of Procedure and no consent of the original parties exists in this matter, a question arises whether a request for intervention in the arbitral proceedings may be accepted under Annex VII to the UNCLOS.[49] As we shall discuss, the Arbitral Tribunal in the *South China Sea* arbitration took a flexible approach to this matter.

B. Treatment of Communications by Viet Nam and Taiwan

Viet Nam did not apply to intervene in the proceedings of the *South China Sea* arbitration. In April 2014, however, it sent a Note Verbale to the Tribunal and stated that Viet Nam's legal interests and rights might be affected by the arbitration.[50] Having sought the views of the Parties, on 24 April 2014, the Tribunal agreed to grant Viet Nam access to the Memorial of the Philippines and its annexed documents, and noted that the Tribunal would consider in due course Viet Nam's request for access to any other relevant documents.[51] Furthermore, on 5 December 2014, the Vietnamese Embassy sent a Note Verbale to the Tribunal, accompanied by a 'Statement of the Ministry of Foreign Affairs of Viet Nam for the Attention of the Tribunal in the Proceedings between the Republic of the Philippines and the People's Republic of China' as well as annexed documents. In the Statement, Viet Nam clearly stated that undoubtedly the Tribunal had jurisdiction in these proceedings.[52] Related to this, the Tribunal said that it had taken note of Viet Nam's Statement of 5 December 2014.[53] On 7 December 2014, Viet Nam further delivered a 'Statement of the Ministry of Foreign Affairs of Viet Nam' to the Tribunal.[54]

On 22 December 2014, by sending a Note Verbale to the Tribunal, Viet Nam requested that it be furnished with a copy of Procedural Order No 3 and further communications between the Tribunal and the Parties. In this regard,

[47] C Chinkin, 'Article 62' in A Zimmermann, C Tomuschat, K Oellers-Frahm and CJ Tams (eds), *The Statute of the International Court of Justice: A Commentary*, 2nd edn (Oxford University Press, 2012) 1529, 1568.

[48] I Brownlie, 'The Peaceful Settlement of International Disputes' (2009) 8 CJIL 267, 277.

[49] Yee, n 42, 89.

[50] The *South China Sea* Arbitration Award (Jurisdiction and Admissibility), n 4, [47], [185].

[51] ibid, [49], [183].

[52] ibid, [54].

[53] ibid, [70].

[54] ibid, [183].

the Philippines stated that it would be appropriate to allow Viet Nam access to the requested documents and that the Philippines considered that the Tribunal's broad discretion on procedural matters encompassed the power to take any steps it might consider appropriate to request information from Viet Nam.[55] The Tribunal thus authorised the Registry to provide Viet Nam with a copy of Procedural Order No 3 on 17 February 2015.[56] A copy of the Philippines' Supplemental Written Submission and accompanying annexes was also made available to Viet Nam.[57] The Tribunal further agreed to permit each of the Governments of Viet Nam, Indonesia, Japan, Thailand and Malaysia to send small delegations of representatives to attend the hearing as observers.[58]

Notably, Viet Nam actively expressed its view with regard to substantive issues in the *South China Sea* arbitration. In the Statement of the Ministry of Foreign Affairs, Viet Nam reiterated its view that the Tribunal had jurisdiction in the arbitral proceedings, and expressed its expectation that the Tribunal's decision could contribute towards clarifying the legal positions of the parties in this case and interested third parties. Viet Nam also stated that matters of territorial sovereignty and maritime delimitation had deliberately been excluded from the Philippines' claim. Furthermore, it denied the legality of the Chinese nine-dash line. Concerning the maritime features mentioned in the Philippines' Memorial, Viet Nam claimed that none of these features was entitled to its own exclusive economic zone (EEZ) and continental shelf, since they were all low-tide elevations or rocks under Article 121(3) of the UNCLOS. It further alleged that Tribunal should apply Articles 60, 80, 94, 194, 206 and 300 of the UNCLOS.[59] In so doing, Viet Nam strongly supported the claims of the Philippines.

The Tribunal took the position that it would address the permissibility of Viet Nam's intervention in the proceedings only when Viet Nam made a formal application for such intervention.[60] In reality, however, it relied on Viet Nam's claim when considering whether any third parties were indispensable to the proceedings. In fact, 'in light of Viet Nam's own stance with respect to the proceedings', the Tribunal found that Viet Nam was not an indispensable third party and that its absence as a party did not preclude the Tribunal from proceeding with the arbitration.[61] Furthermore, the Tribunal ruled that its conclusion with regard to the difference between the present case and the precedents concerning the absence of an indispensable third party was supported

[55] ibid, [61]–[62], [185]. While China did not directly comment on Viet Nam's Statement, the Chinese Ambassador's First Letter expressed opposition to a procedure of intervention by other states, as being inconsistent with the general practices of international arbitration: ibid.

[56] ibid, [65].

[57] ibid, [67].

[58] ibid, [84].

[59] ibid, [183]–[184].

[60] ibid, [186].

[61] ibid, [187]. See also *Monetary Gold Removed from Rome in 1943 (Italy v France, United Kingdom of Great Britain and Northern Ireland and United States of America)*, Preliminary question, Judgment, [1954] ICJ Rep 19, 32.

by 'the position Viet Nam itself has taken in the present arbitration'.[62] Thus the *Monetary Gold* rule was not applied to this case.[63] Given that Viet Nam explicitly supported the jurisdiction of the Tribunal in this case, this seemed to be a reasonable conclusion.[64] Overall it can be observed that the Tribunal paid due regard to Viet Nam's interests by granting Viet Nam access to materials submitted by the Philippines and the Procedural Order, and that, to some extent at least, Viet Nam's claim did affect the Arbitration Award on Jurisdiction and Admissibility.

In addition, the Tribunal invited the Parties to comment on the new documents made public by Taiwan, such a document published by the 'Chinese (Taiwan) Society of International Law' and some remarks of Mr Ma Ying-jeou, then President of the Taiwan Authority of China, at an international press conference 'regarding Taiping [Itu Aba] Island in Nansha Islands'.[65] In this regard, the Philippines responded that it had chosen 'not to object to the Tribunal's consideration of Taiwan's most recent materials should the Tribunal itself find it appropriate to do so', in light of the exceptional difficulties China's non-appearance had created for the Tribunal.[66] The Tribunal thus fully considered 'certain materials made public by the Taiwan Authority of China'.[67]

The Tribunal's approach is not unprecedented. In the *Eritrea/Yemen* arbitration (Second Phase), the Kingdom of Saudi Arabia had written to the Registrar of the Tribunal on 31 August 1997 pointing out that its boundaries with Yemen were disputed, without attempting to intervene in the arbitral proceedings. It also suggested that the Tribunal should restrict its decision to areas 'that do not extend north of the latitude of the most northern point on Jabal al-Tayr Island'.[68] The Saudi Arabian claim was taken into account by the Tribunal, which stated that 'Reference has been made above to the need not to extend the boundary to areas that might involve third parties.'[69]

The *South China Sea* arbitration provides a precedent that a third party's claim can be taken into account by the Arbitral Tribunal, even if that party did not officially intervene in the proceedings; and that sending communication to the Arbitral Tribunal can provide a pragmatic solution for a third State

[62] The *South China Sea* Arbitration Award (Jurisdiction and Admissibility), n 4, [181]–[182].

[63] For this rule, see *Monetary Gold Removed from Rome in 1943*, n 61, 32.

[64] S Kaye, 'Jurisdiction in the *South China Sea Arbitration*: Application of the *Monetary Gold* Principle' in S Jayakumar et al (eds), *The South China Sea Arbitration: The Legal Dimension* (Edward Elgar, 2018) 45, 60.

[65] PCA Case No 2013-19, The *South China Sea* Arbitration Award (Merits) (hereinafter 'the *South China Sea* Arbitration Award (Merits)'), 12 July 2016, [89].

[66] Responses of the Philippines to the Tribunal's 1 April 2016 Request for Comments on Additional Materials regarding the Status of Itu Aba, 25 April 2016, [7]–[8].

[67] The *South China Sea* Arbitration Award (Merits), n 65, [142].

[68] *Second stage of the proceedings between Eritrea and Yemen (Maritime Delimitation)*, 17 December 1999, (2001) 22 *RIAA* 335, 344, [44].

[69] ibid, [164]. See also Yee, n 42, 98, fn 45.

to safeguard its interest in arbitral proceedings.[70] According to the Tribunal's approach, however, the distinction between formal intervention and *de facto* intervention by a third party will be thin.

IV. JURISDICTION OVER THE MIXED DISPUTE INVOLVING TERRITORIAL SOVEREIGNTY AND MARITIME DELIMITATION

A. The *South China Sea* Arbitration

The jurisdiction of the Annex VII Arbitral Tribunal is at the heart of the 2015 Award on Jurisdiction and Admissibility. In approaching this issue, the characterisation of the Parties' dispute is of particular importance. Yet the opinions of the Parties were sharply divided on this matter.

The Chinese view can be summarised in two points.[71] First, according to China, the essence of the subject-matter of the arbitration was territorial sovereignty over several maritime features in the South China Sea. Thus the Arbitral Tribunal would inevitably have to determine who had territorial sovereignty over the maritime features in the South China Sea in order to decide upon any of the Philippines' claims, including Submissions concerning China's historic rights. Nonetheless, a territorial dispute falls outside scope of the UNCLOS. Second, even if the Parties' dispute were to be concerned with the UNCLOS, the dispute would constitute an integral part of the maritime delimitation between the two countries. However, a maritime delimitation dispute is precluded from the compulsory procedures by virtue of the Declaration filed by China in 2006.[72]

In contrast, the Philippines claimed that none of its Submissions required the Tribunal to express any view at all as to the extent of China's sovereignty over land territory, or that of any other state.[73] According to the Philippines, its Submissions concerning the relationship between China's claimed historic

[70] ibid, 98.

[71] The *South China Sea* Arbitration Award (Jurisdiction and Admissibility), n 4, [133]–[139]; China's Position Paper, n 1, Pts II and IV.

[72] On 25 August 2006, China declared that 'The Government of the People's Republic of China does not accept any of the procedures provided for in Section 2 of Part XV of the Convention with respect to all the categories of disputes referred to in paragraph 1 (a) (b) and (c) of Art 298 of the Convention.' See at http://www.un.org/Depts/los/convention_agreements/convention_declarations.htm#China.

[73] Presentation by Sands, Hearing on Jurisdiction and Admissibility, Day 1, 7 July 2015, 61 et seq. In this regard, Sands argued that 'The determination of whether a particular feature is an island, or a rock, or a low-tide elevation, does not require any prior determination of which state has sovereignty over the feature. The fact that state A or state B or state C or state Z has sovereignty over a particular feature is entirely irrelevant to the question of its characterisation. The fact that two or more states may dispute the matter of sovereignty over a feature – assuming that there can be sovereignty at all – is entirely irrelevant to its characterisation': ibid, 65.

rights and the UNCLOS did not require any prior determination of sovereignty. Although the Philippines agreed with China that the land dominates the sea, it pointed to the corollary that without land, there can be no maritime entitlements on the basis of historic rights or otherwise.[74] Furthermore, the Philippines criticised China's contention on the ground that it conflated entitlement to maritime zones and delimitation of areas where those zones overlap.[75] In the words of the Philippines, '[t]he fact that resolution of delimitation issues may require the prior resolution of entitlement issues does not mean that entitlement issues are an integral part of the delimitation process itself'.[76] It follows that determination of the character of a particular maritime feature does not require any prior determination of which state has sovereignty over the feature.[77]

The Arbitral Tribunal took the position that it was entirely possible to approach the Philippines' Submissions from the premise that China was correct in its assertion of sovereignty over Scarborough Shoal and the Spratlys. In fact, the Philippines had expressly and repeatedly requested that the Tribunal refrain from ruling on sovereignty. Accordingly, the Tribunal did not consider that 'territorial dispute' was the appropriate characterisation of the Philippine claims in the proceedings.[78] Related to this, the Arbitral Tribunal stressed the difference of characterisation between the *South China Sea* case and the *Mauritius v United Kingdom* case concerning the *Chagos Marine Protected Area* (the *Chagos Marine Protected Area* arbitration).[79] In the words of the Tribunal:

> The Tribunal understands the majority's decision in that case [the *Chagos Marine Protected Area* arbitration] to have been based on the view both that a decision on Mauritius' first and second submissions would have required an implicit decision on sovereignty and that sovereignty was the true object of Mauritius' claims.[80]

However, the Tribunal did not consider that 'any of the Philippines' Submissions require an implicit determination of sovereignty'.[81] The tone of the *South China Sea* Arbitration Award seems to imply that if the Philippines' Submissions did require an implicit decision on sovereignty, the Tribunal could not determine the Submissions.

[74] ibid, 64; The *South China Sea* Arbitration Award (Jurisdiction and Admissibility), n 4, [143].

[75] Presentation by Oxman, Hearing on Jurisdiction and Admissibility, Day 2, 8 July 2015, 40.

[76] ibid, 46.

[77] Presentation by Sands, Hearing on Jurisdiction and Admissibility, Day 1, 7 July 2015, 64–65. See also Presentation by Sands, Hearing on Jurisdiction and Admissibility, Day 2, 8 July 2015, 3.

[78] The *South China Sea* Arbitration Award (Jurisdiction and Admissibility), n 4, [152]–[153].

[79] *Chagos Marine Protected Area (Mauritius v United Kingdom)*, Award of 18 March 2015 ('the *Chagos Marine Protected Area* Arbitration Award'), available at https://pca-cpa.org/en/cases/11/.

[80] The *South China Sea* Arbitration Award (Jurisdiction and Admissibility), n 4, [153].

[81] ibid.

Similarly, the Tribunal did not accept that the Parties' dispute was properly characterised as a maritime delimitation dispute.[82] In this regard, the Tribunal made an important statement:

> [A] dispute concerning the existence of an entitlement to maritime zones is distinct from a dispute concerning the delimitation of those zones in an area where the entitlements of parties overlap. While fixing the extent of parties' entitlements and the area in which they overlap will commonly be one of the first matters to be addressed in the delimitation of a maritime boundary, it is nevertheless a distinct issue. A maritime boundary may be delimited only between States with opposite or adjacent coasts and overlapping entitlements. In contrast, a dispute over claimed entitlements may exist even without overlap, where – for instance – a State claims maritime zones in an area understood by other States to form part of the high seas or the Area for the purposes of the Convention.[83]

The Tribunal did not provide any examples where a state claims maritime zones in part of the high seas or the Area.[84] In this regard, it is relevant to note that the Philippines, in the oral hearing, referred to Oki-no-Tori-Shima as 'a textbook example' in this matter. According to the Philippines, since China's coast is very far from Oki-no-Tori-Shima, no question of delimitation with China was implicated. Even so, China expressed the view that the application of Article 121(3) of the UNCLOS relates to the overall interests of the international community, and is an important legal issue of a general nature. The Philippines thus claimed that 'China recognises the fundamental distinction between an entitlement on the one hand, and delimitation on the other.'[85] The dispute concerning the legal status of Oki-no-Tori-Shima seemed to demonstrate that an entitlement dispute can exist independently of a maritime delimitation dispute.[86] In conclusion, the Tribunal found that disputes concerning the interpretation and application of the UNCLOS existed in all of the Philippines' Submissions.[87]

By stressing the difference between the *South China Sea* and the *Chagos Marine Protected Area* cases, the Arbitral Tribunal refrained from determining the jurisdictional issue with regard to a mixed dispute. As will be discussed next, however, the *Chagos Marine Protected Area* Arbitration Award covered this subject in more detail.

[82] ibid, [155].

[83] ibid, [156].

[84] In oral hearing, Judge Pawlak posed the question of whether there was 'any relevant jurisprudence or practice of states when entitlements to maritime features were decided separately from sovereignty over them'. Jurisdiction Hearing, Day 3, 13 July 2015, 62.

[85] Presentation by Oxman, Hearing on Jurisdiction and Admissibility, Day 2, 8 July 2015, 42.

[86] See also D Tamada, 'In the Matter of an Arbitration before an Arbitral Tribunal Constituted under Annex VII to the 1982 United Nations Convention on the Law of the Sea between the Republic of Philippines and the People's Republic of China, Award on Jurisdiction and Admissibility (29 October 2015)' (in Japanese) (2016) 66 *Kobe Law Journal* 125, 153.

[87] The *South China Sea* Arbitration Award (Jurisdiction and Admissibility), n 4, [178].

B. The *Chagos Marine Protected Area* Arbitration

In the *Chagos Marine Protected Area* arbitration,[88] Mauritius requested the Annex VII Arbitral Tribunal to declare, inter alia, that:

> (1) the United Kingdom is not entitled to declare an 'MPA' or other maritime zones because it is not the 'coastal State' within the meaning of inter alia Articles 2, 55, 56 and 76 of the Convention.[89]

In this regard, two questions arise: (i) What was the nature of the dispute encompassed in Mauritius' First Submission? (ii) To the extent that the Tribunal found the Parties' dispute to be, at its core, a matter of territorial sovereignty, to what extent does UNCLOS Article 288(1) permit a tribunal to determine issues of disputed land sovereignty as a necessary precondition to a determination of rights and duties in the adjacent sea?[90]

In the Arbitral Tribunal's view, it was clear that a dispute between the Parties existed with respect to sovereignty over the Chagos Archipelago. At the same time, a dispute existed between the Parties with regard to the MPA established by the UK. The views of the Parties also differed regarding the identity of the 'coastal State'. Thus the Tribunal was required to evaluate where the relative weight of the dispute lay.[91] According to the Tribunal, there was an extensive record documenting the Parties' dispute over sovereignty, although there was scant evidence that Mauritius was specifically concerned with the UK's implementation of the Convention on behalf of the British Indian Ocean Territory. Hence the Arbitral Tribunal found that Mauritius' First Submission was properly characterised as relating to land sovereignty over the Chagos Archipelago, and that the Parties' differing views on the 'coastal State' for the purposes of the Convention were simply one aspect of this larger dispute.[92]

The question of interest here is whether or not disputes regarding territorial sovereignty would fall within the scope of a dispute concerning the interpretation or application of the UNCLOS. The negotiating records of the Convention provide no explicit answer regarding jurisdiction over territorial sovereignty. In the Tribunal's view, this meant that none of the Conference participants expected that a long-standing dispute over territorial sovereignty would ever be

[88] The *Chagos Marine Protected Area* Arbitration Award, n 79. The members of the Arbitral Tribunal were: Professor Ivan Shearer, President, Judge Sir Christopher Greenwood, Judge Albert Hoffman, Judge James Kateka and Judge Rüdiger Wolfrum. For an analysis of the jurisdictional issues of the *Chagos Marine Protected Area* arbitration, see Lan Ngoc Nguyen, 'The Chagos Marine Protected Area Arbitration: Has the Scope of LOSC Compulsory Jurisdiction Being Clarified?' (2016) 31 *IJMCL* 120.

[89] The *Chagos Marine Protected Area* Arbitration Award, n 79, [163].

[90] ibid, [206].

[91] ibid, [209]–[211].

[92] ibid, [211]–[212].

considered to be a dispute 'concerning the interpretation or application of the Convention'.[93] The Tribunal thus concluded as follows.

Where a dispute concerns the interpretation or application of the UNCLOS, the jurisdiction of a court or tribunal pursuant to Article 288(1) extends to making such findings of fact or ancillary determinations of law as are necessary to resolve the dispute presented to it. However, where the 'real issue in the case' and the 'object of the claim' do not relate to the interpretation or application of the Convention, an incidental connection between the dispute and some matter regulated by the Convention is insufficient to bring the dispute as a whole within the ambit of Article 288(1). On the basis of the above considerations, the Tribunal in the *Chagos Marine Protected Area* arbitration found itself without jurisdiction to address Mauritius' First Submission.[94] Likewise, the Tribunal found that it could not deal with Mauritius' Second Submission since it was properly characterised as relating to the same dispute in respect of land sovereignty over the Chagos Archipelago as Mauritius' First Submission.[95]

Yet the majority opinion was challenged by Judges Kateka and Wolfrum. According to the two judges, in its Submission No 1, Mauritius only questioned the competence of the UK to be the coastal state in respect of establishing the MPA. Further, it initiated the arbitral proceedings against the UK only after the establishment of the MPA, and did not advance any argument concerning territorial sovereignty over the islands. Accordingly, the learned judges concluded that the Parties' dispute could not be qualified as a dispute about the sovereignty of the Chagos Archipelago.[96]

What is of particular interest concerns the two judges' view with regard to the jurisdiction of international courts under the UNCLOS. In their view, '[t]hat the drafters did not foresee the possibility does not in itself justify reading a limitation into the jurisdiction of the international courts and tribunals acting under Part XV of the Convention'.[97] The two learned judges considered that apart from the limitations and exceptions provided for in Articles 288(1), 297 and 298 of the UNCLOS, there is no justification to create another jurisdictional limitation beyond those of the Convention.[98] Thus they took the view that it is permissible to decide 'incidentally about sovereignty issues'.[99] However, the difference between the majority opinion and the two judges' dissenting opinion seems to be rather slim. In fact, Judges Kateka and Wolfrum accepted that under Article 288(1), 'a nexus between the case in question and the Convention

[93] ibid, [215].
[94] ibid, [221].
[95] ibid, [230].
[96] Dissenting and Concurring Opinion of Judge James Kateka and Judge Rüdiger Wolfrum, 3–5, paras 9–17, available at http://www.pcacases.com/web/sendAttach/1570.
[97] ibid, 7, [27].
[98] ibid, 11, [44].
[99] ibid, 12, [45].

has to exist'.[100] They also agreed that where the 'real issue in the case' and the 'object of the claim' do not relate to the interpretation or application of the Convention, an incidental connection between the dispute is insufficient to bring the dispute within the ambit of Article 288(1).[101]

In summary, according to the dictum of the Tribunal, if the 'real issue in the case' and the 'object of the claim' concern the interpretation or application of the Convention, the jurisdiction of an international court or tribunal under Article 288(1) may extend to issues ancillary to the real issue. In this regard, the Arbitral Tribunal made an important statement:

> The Tribunal does not categorically exclude that in some instances a minor issue of territorial sovereignty could be ancillary to a dispute concerning the interpretation or application of the Convention.[102]

The dictum of the Tribunal does seem to imply that the Arbitral Tribunal can adjudicate a 'minor issue of territorial sovereignty' ancillary to the real issue regarding the interpretation or application of the Convention that could fall within the ambit of Article 288(1). The dictum can be called the ancillary test.

C. The Ancillary Test

The ancillary test expressed in the *Chagos Marine Protected Area* Arbitration Award was not referred to in the 2015 *South China Sea* Arbitration Award. Although whether the test can be generalised needs further consideration, two issues in particular merit highlighting.

First, in applying the ancillary test, there is a need to identify the real issue of a particular dispute. In this regard, characterisation of a particular dispute is at issue.[103] The decision on the characterisation of the legal disputes must be made by the Tribunal on objective grounds, 'giving particular attention to the formulation of the dispute chosen by the Applicant'.[104] As shown in the *Chagos Marine Protected Area* arbitration, however, objective characterisation of a dispute is not free from controversy. Related to this, by referring to the

[100] ibid, 11, [45].

[101] ibid, 11–12, [45].

[102] The *Chagos Marine Protected Area* Arbitration Award, n 79, [221].

[103] S Talmon, 'The Chagos Marine Protected Area Arbitration: Expansion of the Jurisdiction of UNCLOS Part XV Courts and Tribunals' (2016) 65 *ICLQ* 927, 932–34.

[104] *Fisheries Jurisdiction (Spain v Canada)*, Jurisdiction of the Court, Judgment, [1998] ICJ Rep 432, 448, [30]; The *Chagos Marine Protected Area* Arbitration Award, n 79, 87, [208].

Teheran Hostage case,[105] the Arbitral Tribunal, in its Award of 2015, ruled that there are no grounds to 'decline to take cognizance of one aspect of a dispute merely because that dispute has other aspects, however important'.[106] Since international disputes are normally multifaceted, however, it may be less easy to determine which aspect of a dispute is the real issue concerning the interpretation or application of the UNCLOS.

The second and more contentious issue pertains to the question whether a territorial issue would fall within the ambit of Article 288(1) if it is ancillary to an issue concerning the interpretation or application of the UNCLOS.[107] Some argue that a mixed dispute would fall within the ambit of the jurisdiction of an international court or tribunal acting under the Convention. For example, Boyle argued:

> In some cases the delimitation of a maritime boundary may necessarily require a decision concerning disputed sovereignty over land, for example where an island is used as a basepoint for an EEZ or continental shelf claim. While parties to the Convention [UNCLOS] do have the option of excluding such disputes from compulsory jurisdiction under Article 298(1), the implication must be that, where this option is not exercised, a tribunal, including the ITLOS, may if necessary deal with both the land and the maritime dispute.[108]

Likewise Eiriksson, a former Judge of ITLOS, expressed the view that 'questions of maritime delimitation would often depend on questions of sovereignty over land territory and the Tribunal could not be expected to refrain from pronouncing on such questions in reaching a decision on the matter before it'.[109] This view seems to be echoed by Treves, a former Judge of ITLOS, stating that 'the argument *a contrario sensu* here considered seems sufficient to discard the view that whenever a case presents a land aspect, compulsory jurisdiction of the courts and tribunals competent under the Convention should automatically be excluded'.[110] Likewise, Judge Chandrasekhara Rao took the view that 'where no exclusionary declaration is applicable with respect to delimitation disputes under article 298, a court or tribunal would be competent to deal with a mixed

[105] *United States Diplomatic and Consular Staff in Tehran (United States v Iran)*, Questions of Jurisdiction and/or Admissibility, Judgment, [1980] ICJ Rep 3, 19–20, [36].

[106] The *South China Sea* Arbitration Award (Jurisdiction and Admissibility), n 4, [152].

[107] Generally on this issue, I Buga, 'Territorial Sovereignty Issues in Maritime Disputes: A Jurisdictional Dilemma for Law of the Sea Tribunals' (2012) 27 *IJMCL* 59.

[108] A Boyle, 'Dispute Settlement and the Law of the Sea Convention: Problems of Fragmentation and Jurisdiction' (1997) 46 *ICLQ* 37, 49.

[109] G Eiriksson, *The International Tribunal for the Law of the Sea* (Nijhoff, 2000) 113.

[110] T Treves, 'What have the United Nations Convention and the International Tribunal for the Law of the Sea to Offer as Regards Maritime Delimitation Disputes?' in R Lagoni and D Vignes (eds), *Maritime Delimitation* (Brill/Nijhoff, 2006) 63, 77.

dispute'.[111] Moreover, Judge Wolfrum, a former President of ITLOS, clearly stated:

> Issues of sovereignty or other rights over continental or insular land territory, which are closely linked or ancillary to maritime delimitation, concern the interpretation or application of the Convention and therefore fall within its scope.[112]

It is noteworthy that former and current members of ITLOS are supportive of the jurisdiction of international courts and tribunals acting under the UNCLOS with regard to a mixed dispute.

Where there is an agreement between the parties to settle territorial and marine disputes that are closely intertwined in the same proceedings, it may be possible to argue that an international court or tribunal acting under the UNCLOS should not decline the request by the parties.[113] Where such an agreement does not exist, however, the issue becomes more controversial. In this regard, it can be said that if a minor territorial issue could automatically preclude the jurisdiction of an international court or tribunal to deal with maritime delimitation, the dispute settlement system set out in the UNCLOS would be unduly restricted.[114] Accordingly, as the Arbitral Tribunal stated in the *Chagos Marine Protected Area* Arbitration Award, it may not be unreasonable to argue that a tribunal can adjudicate 'a minor issue of territorial sovereignty' in proceedings of the Annex VII Arbitral Tribunal.[115]

Even so, the further issue arises with regard to the scope of a minor issue of territorial sovereignty.[116] Unfortunately the Arbitral Tribunal in the *Chagos Marine Protected Area* arbitration did not provide any precision in this matter. A possible criterion in this regard may be the physical nature of the marine features concerned. Low-tide elevations are a case in point. In this regard, it is relevant to recall that the ICJ in *Qatar v Bahrain* (Merits) determined the sovereignty over a low-tide elevation, Fasht ad Dibal, on the basis of a maritime delimitation line.[117] In so doing, the Court treated such elevations as

[111] P Chandrasekhara Rao, 'Delimitation Disputes under the United Nations Convention on the Law of the Sea: Settlement Procedures' in TM Ndiaye and R Wolfrum (eds), *Law of the Sea, Environmental Law and Settlement of Disputes, Liber Amicorum Judge Thomas A Mensah* (Brill/Nijhoff, 2007) 877, 890.

[112] Statement by Judge Rüdiger Wolfrum, President of the International Tribunal for the Law of the Sea to the Informal Meeting of Legal Advisers of Ministries of Foreign Affairs, New York, 23 October 2006, p 6. See also R Wolfrum, 'The Settlement of Disputes Before the International Tribunal for the Law of the Sea: A Progressive Development of International Law or Relying on Traditional Mechanisms?' (2008) 51 *Japanese Yearbook of International Law* 140, 161.

[113] Boyle, n 108, 49; Buga, n 107, 67.

[114] See also Wolfrum, 'The Settlement of Disputes', n 112, 161; Buga, n 107, 67.

[115] *Chagos Marine Protected Area* Arbitration Award, n 79, [221].

[116] Talmon, n 103, 934–36.

[117] *Maritime Delimitation and Territorial Questions between Qatar and Bahrain (Qatar v Bahrain)*, Merits, Judgment, [2001] ICJ Rep 40, 109, [220].

part of the seabed, not as terrestrial territory.[118] Indeed, the Court in the 2012 *Nicaragua v Colombia* judgment clearly stated that 'low-tide elevations cannot be appropriated'.[119] Thus there appears to be some scope for arguing that a dispute regarding the territorial sovereignty over low-tide elevations can be regarded as a minor issue that is ancillary to the interpretation or application of the UNCLOS.

V. INTERPRETATION OF ARTICLE 281 OF THE UNCLOS

A. General Considerations

The interpretation of Article 281 of the UNCLOS is a debatable issue. Thus, finally, some consideration must be given to it. Article 281 sets out three requirements to activate the compulsory procedures under the Convention:

(a) no settlement has been reached by recourse to the agreed means;
(b) that agreement does not exclude resort to the procedures provided in the UNCLOS; and
(c) any agreed time limits have expired.[120]

If one of the requirements has not been met, the procedures under Part XV of the UNCLOS do not apply. In this regard, as will be seen next, the Tribunal's view in the *South China Sea* arbitration contrasts sharply with the view of the Annex VII Arbitral Tribunal in the *Southern Bluefin Tuna* arbitration.

B. The *Southern Bluefin Tuna Cases*

Although the *Southern Bluefin Tuna* dispute is well-known, some key points concerning interpretation of Article 281 must be briefly reviewed. The central issue in the 1999 *Southern Bluefin Tuna* cases before ITLOS was whether or not Article 16 of the 1993 Convention for the Conservation of Southern Bluefin Tuna ('the 1993 Convention')[121] precluded the application of compulsory procedures in the UNCLOS. Japan contended that recourse to the Arbitral Tribunal was excluded because the 1993 Convention provided for a dispute settlement procedure. However, Australia and New Zealand denied Japan's claim, since the 1993 Convention did not provide for a compulsory dispute settlement procedure

[118] Y Tanaka, 'Low-tide Elevations in International Law of the Sea: Selected Issues' (2006) 20 *Ocean Yearbook* 189, 203–07. See also ch 4, section II of this book.

[119] *Territorial and Maritime Dispute (Nicaragua v Colombia)*, Judgment, [2012] ICJ Rep 624, 641, [26].

[120] The *South China Sea* Arbitration Award (Jurisdiction and Admissibility), n 4, [195].

[121] Convention for the Conservation of Southern Bluefin Tuna (adopted 10 May 1993, entered into force 20 May 1994) 1819 *UNTS* 360.

entailing a binding decision, as required under Article 282 of the UNCLOS.[122] ITLOS was not persuaded by Japan's argument. According to the Tribunal, the fact that the 1993 Convention applied between the Parties 'does not preclude recourse to the procedures in Part XV, section 2, of the Convention on the Law of the Sea'.[123] It thus held that the requirements for invoking those procedures had been fulfilled and that the Arbitral Tribunal would prima facie have jurisdiction over the disputes.[124]

Nonetheless, the view of ITLOS was not echoed by the Annex VII Arbitral Tribunal at the merits stage. Article 16 of the 1993 Convention did not expressly exclude the applicability of any procedure, including the compulsory procedures of section 2 of Part XV of the UNCLOS. In the view of the Arbitral Tribunal, however, 'the absence of an express exclusion of any procedure in Article 16 is not decisive', since the dispute was not referable to adjudication by the ICJ or ITLOS, or to arbitration 'at the request of any party to the dispute' under Article 16 of the 1993 Convention.[125] The Arbitral Tribunal also pointed out that the wording of Article 16(1) and (2) had its essential origins in the terms of Article XI of the Antarctic Treaty.[126] According to the Arbitral Tribunal, 'it is obvious that these provisions are meant to exclude compulsory jurisdiction'.[127] It thus concluded that Article 16 of the 1993 Convention excluded any further procedure within the contemplation of Article 281(1) of the UNCLOS;[128] and that the Annex VII Tribunal lacked jurisdiction to entertain the merits of the dispute.[129]

However, the broad interpretation of Article 281 by the Arbitral Tribunal has been challenged by one of its members, Judge Keith, and literature.[130] Judge Keith, in his Separate Opinion, argued that clear wording is needed in order to

[122] *Southern Bluefin Tuna cases (New Zealand v Japan; Australia v Japan)*, Provisional Measures, ITLOS Case Nos 3 and 4, Order of 27 August 1999, [1999] ITLOS Rep 280, 294, [53]–[54].

[123] ibid, [55].

[124] ibid, 295, [61]–[62].

[125] The *Southern Bluefin Tuna* Arbitration Award, 4 August 2000, (2004) 23 *RIAA* 1, 43, [57].

[126] The Antarctic Treaty (signed 1 December 1959, entered into force 23 June 1961), 402 *UNTS* 71.

[127] The *Southern Bluefin Tuna* Arbitration Award, n 125, 44, [58].

[128] ibid, [59].

[129] ibid, 46, [65].

[130] For a critical assessment of the arbitral award, see, for instance, C Romano, 'The Southern Bluefin Tuna Dispute: Hints of a World to Come … Like it or Not' (2001) 32 *ODIL* 313; DA Colson and P Hoyle, 'Satisfying the Procedural Prerequisites to the Compulsory Dispute Settlement Mechanisms of the 1982 Law of the Sea Convention: Did the Southern Bluefin Tuna Tribunal Get It Right?' (2003) 34 *ODIL* 59; A Boyle, 'The Southern Bluefin Tuna Arbitration' (2001) 50 *ICLQ* 447; BH Oxman, 'Complementary Agreements and Compulsory Jurisdiction' (2001) 95 *AJIL* 277; P Chandrasekhara Rao and P Gautier, *The International Tribunal for the Law of the Sea: Law, Practice and Procedure* (Edward Elgar, 2018) 117. See also A Serdy, 'Article 281' in A Prölss (ed), *The United Nations Convention on the Law of the Sea: A Commentary* (Hart Publishing, 2017) 1820, 1822–23; A Caligiuri, 'Les conditions pour l'exercice de la function juridictionnelle par les cours et les tribunaux prevus dans la CNUDM' (2017) 121 *RGDIP* 945, 951.

exclude the compulsory procedures provided for in the UNCLOS.[131] Likewise Judge Wolfrum, in his Separate Opinion in the *MOX Plant* case, stated that 'An intention to entrust the settlement of disputes concerning the interpretation and application of the Convention to other institutions must be expressed explicitly in respective agreements.'[132] This view was supported by Gautier, a Registrar of ITLOS, stating that, 'In a matter of such great importance as the settlement of disputes, it seems logical to require that the decision to exclude the application of Part XV should be based on a clear and express manifestation of consent.'[133] Furthermore, Boyle clearly stated that '[o]f course, the decision of the *Bluefin Tuna* arbitrators may simply be wrong'.[134]

C. The *South China Sea* Arbitration

The opposition with regard to the interpretation of Article 281 re-emerged in the *South China Sea* arbitration. A pivotal issue that arises in this context is whether an express exclusion is required to preclude application of the Part XV dispute settlement procedures. Whereas the Philippines argued that the intent to exclude further procedures under the UNCLOS must be evident from the terms of the agreement itself, China considered an express exclusion unnecessary, and it subscribed to the majority view of the Annex VII Tribunal in *Southern Bluefin Tuna cases.*[135]

In approaching this issue, notably, the Annex VII Arbitral Tribunal departed from the broad interpretation taken in the *Southern Bluefin Tuna* arbitration, stating that 'the better view is that Article 281 requires some clear statement of exclusion of further procedures'.[136] The Tribunal's view relies on two legal

[131] Separate Opinion of Justice Sir Kenneth Keith in *Southern Bluefin Tuna* Arbitration Award, n 125, 53–55, [18]–[22]. In this connection, one may note with interest that the Virginia Commentary states that 'The last phrase of article 281, paragraph 1, envisages the possibility that the parties ... may also specify that this procedure shall be *an exclusive one* and that no other procedures (including those under Part XV) may be resorted to even if the chosen procedure should not lead to a settlement' (emphasis added). MH Nordquist, S Rosenne and LB Sohn (eds), *United Nations Convention on the Law of the Sea 1982: A Commentary*, vol V (Dordrecht, Nijhoff, 1989) 23–24. This view was referred to by Judge Keith, in *Southern Bluefin Tuna* Arbitration Award, n 125, 53–54, [18].

[132] Separate Opinion of Judge Wolfrum in the *MOX Plant case (Ireland v United Kingdom)*, Request for provisional measures, ITLOS Case No 10, Order of 3 December 2001, [2000] ITLOS Rep 95, 132.

[133] P Gautier, 'The Settlement of Disputes' in DJ Attard, M Fitzmaurice and NA Martínez Gutiérrez (eds), *The IMLI Manual on International Maritime Law*, vol I: *The Law of the Sea* (Oxford University Press, 2014) 533, 539.

[134] Boyle, n 130, 451. See also presentation by Boyle, Hearing on Jurisdiction and Admissibility, Day 2, 8 July 2015, 115–16.

[135] The *South China Sea* Arbitration Award (Jurisdiction and Admissibility), n 4, [222]–[223]. See also Memorial of the Philippines, vol I, 237–40, [7.64]–[7.73]; China's Position Paper, n 1, [82].

[136] The *South China Sea* Arbitration Award (Jurisdiction and Admissibility), n 4, [223].

grounds: the text of Article 281; and the integrity of the UNCLOS and its dispute settlement procedures.

First, the text of Article 281 provides for an 'opting out' of procedures under Part XV, in the sense that the compulsory procedures under the UNCLOS will apply where the parties' agreement 'does not exclude any further procedure'.[137] It does not contain an 'opting in' requirement whereby the parties must positively agree to Part XV procedures. Such an 'opting in' is only required where the parties have chosen an alternative compulsory and binding procedure, as set out in Article 282. Accordingly, the Part XV procedures are excluded by the alternative compulsory binding procedure, and 'the only way to make them available is for the parties to opt back in to them by "agreeing otherwise"'.[138] According to the Arbitral Tribunal, that distinction between Articles 281 and 282 is consistent with the overall design of the Convention as a system.[139]

Second, requiring express exclusion for Article 281 is consistent with the overall object and purpose of the Convention as a comprehensive agreement.[140] Considering that the dispute settlement system forms an integral part of the Convention, it is difficult to accept that the parties may remove a pivotal part of the Convention without clearly expressing an intention to do so.[141] The Tribunal thus explicitly supported the views of ITLOS in its provisional measures orders in the 1999 *Southern Bluefin Tuna cases*, as well as the Separate Opinion of Judge Keith in the 2000 *Southern Bluefin Tuna* Arbitral Award.[142] This would entail a decision not to accord precedential effect to the *Southern Bluefin Tuna* Arbitral Award.[143]

The interpretation of Article 281 is of critical importance since it significantly affects the effectiveness of the compulsory procedures of dispute settlement set out by the UNCLOS. It appears that the two different interpretations of Article 281 presented in the *Southern Bluefin Tuna* and *South China Sea* cases reflect two contrasting approaches to the dispute settlement system set out in the UNCLOS.[144]

The first is what might be called a voluntarist approach influenced by a Westphalian conception of international law stressing the safeguarding of state sovereignty. According to this approach, 'peaceful means of their own choice' prevails over the dispute settlement system set out in the UNCLOS, and primary

[137] ibid, [224].
[138] ibid.
[139] ibid.
[140] ibid, [225].
[141] ibid.
[142] ibid, [223].
[143] See also Tamada, n 86, 157.
[144] In his article of 2001, Oxman contrasted a substantive model (regime-building model) with a procedural model (the Westphalian model). Oxman, n 130, 279. Basically, the voluntarist approach corresponds to the procedural model and the objectivist model corresponds to the substantive model presented by Oxman.

emphasis is to be given to the restriction of the compulsory procedures under the Convention.[145] Under the voluntarist approach, the dispute settlement system of the UNCLOS is merely ancillary to political decisions of states. This approach is in line with the majority opinion in the *Southern Bluefin Tuna* arbitration.

The second is what might be called an objectivist approach. This approach stresses the international legal order beyond individual states. Under this approach, primary emphasis is given to the global system of dispute settlement set out in the UNCLOS since that system is integral to the international legal order presented by the Convention. The Tribunal in the *South China Sea* arbitration echoed this approach.

The two contrasting approaches seem to reflect the reality that an international legal system is currently in transition. Arguably, this period can be characterised by increasing legal and practical constrains on unilateral action as a principal means of law enforcement.[146] If, as Oxman pointedly observes, unilateralism was 'evil sought to be remedied' by the UNCLOS, the dispute settlement system under the UNCLOS must be viewed from a viewpoint of combating unilateralism at sea.[147] Importantly, the UNCLOS is intended to be comprehensive and universal in character with a view to establishing a new legal order in the oceans. The compulsory procedures set forth in Part XV of the Convention function as the cement to hold the whole structure together and to secure the integrity of the text.[148] Therefore, the international dispute settlement system, including the compulsory procedures, is a prerequisite to maintaining and developing the new international legal order in the oceans established by the UNCLOS.[149] However, the broad interpretation taken by the majority opinion in the *Southern Bluefin Tuna* arbitration runs the serious risk of undermining the compulsory procedures, since a regional agreement that simply contains no provision for compulsory procedures for dispute settlement could exclude resort to the compulsory procedures.[150] Hence one can say that the objectivist approach would provide a better way to consolidate the legal order established by the Convention.

After the *South China Sea* arbitration, the objectivist approach was further strengthened by the *Timor-Leste/Australia* Conciliation Commission.[151] On 11 April 2016, Timor-Leste invoked the compulsory conciliation procedures

[145] The *Southern Bluefin Tuna* Arbitration Award, n 125, 45–46, [63].
[146] Oxman, n 130, 312.
[147] ibid, 303.
[148] Boyle, n 108, 38.
[149] Oxman, n 130, 303.
[150] Colson and Hoyle, n 130, 67.
[151] The members of the Conciliation Commission were: Peter Taksøe-Jensen (Chairman), Rosalie Balkin, Abdul G Koroma, Donald McRae and Rüdiger Wolfrum. For a commentary on this conciliation, see Jianjun Gao, 'The Timor Sea Conciliation (Timor-Leste v Australia): A Note on the Commission's Decision on Competence' (2018) 49 *Ocean Development and International Law* 208; Y Tanaka, 'Maritime Boundary Delimitation by Conciliation' (2018) 36 *Australian Year Book of International Law* (forthcoming).

with a view to settling the dispute concerning 'the interpretation and application of Articles 74 and 83 of UNCLOS for the delimitation of the exclusive economic zone (EEZ) and the continental shelf between Timor-Leste and Australia including the establishment of the permanent maritime boundaries between the two States'.[152] However, Australia claimed that the Commission's competence was precluded by Article 281 in light of two instruments: the 2003 Exchange of Letters between the Prime Ministers of Timor-Leste and Australia; and the 2006 Treaty between Australia and the Democratic Republic of Timor-Leste on Certain Maritime Arrangements in the Timor Sea (CMATS). In this connection, Australia maintained that even though the Exchange of Letters did not constitute a binding agreement, a binding agreement is not required for the purposes of Article 281.[153] Referring to the *South China Sea* Arbitration Award (Jurisdiction and Admissibility), however, the Conciliation Commission considered that Article 281 does require a legally binding agreement.[154] A more debatable issue is whether CMATS alone would constitute an agreement within the meaning of Article 281 that precludes the compulsory procedures of the Convention. Under Article 4 of CMATS:

> [N]either Party shall commence or pursue any proceedings against the other Party before any court, tribunal or other dispute settlement mechanism that would raise or result in, either directly or indirectly, issues or findings of relevance to maritime boundaries or delimitation in the Timor Sea.

In interpreting this provision, the Conciliation Commission stated that Article 4 of CMATS does not seek settlement of the dispute by peaceful means of the parties' own choice,[155] while Article 281 requires the existence of an agreement 'to seek settlement of the dispute by a peaceful means of their own choice'. Nor does CMATS contain any procedure intended to provide for the settlement of maritime boundaries.[156] The Commission accordingly concluded that 'CMATS is not an agreement pursuant to Article 281 that would preclude recourse to compulsory conciliation pursuant to Article 298 and Annex V.'[157]

[152] Notification Instituting Conciliation under Section 2 of Annex V of UNCLOS, [5]. Even though Timor-Leste initiated two arbitration proceedings against Australia in 2013 and 2015, respectively, the two arbitrations were terminated according to the recommendation by the Conciliation Commission. *Report and Recommendations on the Compulsory Conciliation Commission between Timor-Leste and Australia on the Timor Sea*, 9 May 2018, [106], available at https://pca-cpa.org/en/cases/132/. Australia and Timor-Leste ratified the UNCLOS in 1994 and 2013, respectively. Pursuant to Art 298(1)(a)(i) of the UNCLOS, however, Australia precluded maritime delimitation disputes. See at http://www.un.org/Depts/los/settlement_of_disputes/choice_procedure.htm.

[153] A Conciliation Commission Constituted under Annex V to the 1982 United Nations Convention on the Law of the Sea between the Democratic Republic of Timor-Leste and the Commonwealth of Australia, Decision on Australia's Objections to Competence, 19 September 2016, [24].

[154] ibid, [55]–[58].

[155] ibid, [62].

[156] ibid, [63].

[157] ibid, [64].

The Commission's interpretation seems to have important implications: even if a treaty prohibits the recourse to any international court or tribunal with regard to disputes arising from the treaty, the compulsory procedures under the UNCLOS are to apply, unless that treaty provides alternative means of the parties' own choice. It appears that the Commission's interpretation of Article 281, along with the dictum in the *South China Sea* Arbitration Award (Jurisdiction and Admissibility), contributes to securing the application of the compulsory procedures under the UNCLOS.[158]

VI. CONCLUSIONS

This chapter examined four issues in particular: (i) the treatment of irregular communications from a non-appearing state; (ii) the treatment of the communications made by third parties; (iii) the Tribunal's jurisdiction with regard to a mixed dispute involving territorial and maritime issues; and (iv) the interpretation of Article 281 of the UNCLOS. The consideration in this chapter can be summarised as follows.

First, the non-appearance of one of the parties in dispute may create a particular sensitivity associated with the treatment of irregular communications from a non-appearing state. The Arbitral Tribunal, in its Award of 2015, treated China's informal communications as *de facto* constituting preliminary objections. It is argued that the Tribunal's approach corresponds to the practice of the ICJ. The judicial practice suggests that irregular communications from a non-appearing state are not *a priori* precluded from consideration by an international court or tribunal. Given that communications from a non-appearing state may include some important fact or allegation of law, it would be unwise for the Tribunal to refuse to take account of such communications. Yet it cannot pass unnoticed that the irregular communications made by China were *de facto* exempted from the Rules of Procedure of the Tribunal, while the Philippines complied with the Rules. Here a tension arises between the need for information and the fairness of the treatment of materials submitted by the parties in dispute.

Second, even though Viet Nam did not formally apply to intervene in the arbitral proceedings, it was allowed to access to relevant documents and materials, and its view was taken into account by the Tribunal. Accordingly, there appears to be some scope to consider that the position of Viet Nam was similar to that of a *de facto* non-party intervener. If this is the case, the distinction between formal intervention and *de facto* intervention by a third party will become slim.

[158] Tanaka, n 151.

Third, the dictum in the *Chagos Marine Protected Area* arbitration does seem to imply that in appropriate cases, the Arbitral Tribunal can adjudicate a 'minor' issue of territorial sovereignty ancillary to the interpretation or application of the UNCLOS. The ancillary test can furnish a criterion to determine the question whether an international court or tribunal has jurisdiction to adjudicate a mixed dispute under the UNCLOS. Yet the interpretation of a 'real' or 'ancillary' issue may differ among the judges, as well as between the parties in dispute. Furthermore, the scope of the 'minor' territorial issue needs further clarification.

Fourth, the difference of interpretation of Article 281 of the UNCLOS that emerged in the *Southern Bluefin Tuna* arbitration and *South China Sea* arbitration reflects two contrasting approaches to the international dispute settlement system under the UNCLOS. According to a voluntarist approach, a treaty that contains no explicit provision for the compulsory procedures of dispute settlement set out under the UNCLOS can preclude resort to the procedures. In contrast, according to an objectivist approach, the decision to exclude the application of the compulsory procedures under the UNCLOS requires a clear manifestation of consent. It is argued that the two contrasting approaches show vacillation between the safeguarding of state sovereignty and the establishment of the international legal order presented by the UNCLOS. The Tribunal, in its Award of 2015, clearly supported the objectivist approach. This approach will have implications for securing the effectiveness of the dispute settlement system as an integral part of the Convention.

FURTHER READING

Beckman, R, 'The UN Convention on the Law of the Sea and the Maritime Disputes in the South China Sea' (2013) 107 *AJIL* 142.

——, 'Jurisdictional Issues in the South China Sea Arbitration' in S Jayakumar et al (eds), *The South China Sea Arbitration: The Legal Dimension* (Edward Elgar, 2018) 19–44.

Boyle, A, 'Dispute Settlement and the Law of the Sea Convention: Problems of Fragmentation and Jurisdiction' (1997) 46 *ICLQ* 37.

——, A, 'The Southern Bluefin Tuna Arbitration' (2001) 50 *ICLQ* 447.

Brownlie, I, 'The Peaceful Settlement of International Disputes' (2009) 8 *CJIL* 267.

Buga, I, 'Territorial Sovereignty Issues in Maritime Disputes: A Jurisdictional Dilemma for Law of the Sea Tribunals' (2012) 27 *IJMCL* 59.

Caflisch, L, 'Cent ans de règlement pacifique des différends interétatiques' (2001) 288 *RCADI* 245.

Caligiuri, A, 'Les conditions pour l'exercice de la function juridictionnelle par les cours et les tribunaux prevus dans la CNUDM' (2017) 121 *RGDIP* 945.

Chinkin, C, 'Article 62' in A Zimmermann et al (eds), *The Statute of the International Court of Justice: A Commentary*, 2nd edn (Oxford University Press, 2012) 1529–72.

Colson, DA and Hoyle, P, 'Satisfying the Procedural Prerequisites to the Compulsory Dispute Settlement Mechanisms of the 1982 Law of the Sea Convention: Did the Southern Bluefin Tuna Tribunal Get It Right?' (2003) 34 *ODIL* 59.

Davenport, T, 'Procedural Issues Arising from China's Non-participation in the South China Sea Arbitration' in S Jayakumar et al (eds), *The South China Sea Arbitration: The Legal Dimension* (Edward Elgar, 2018) 65–99.

Eiriksson, G, *The International Tribunal for the Law of the Sea* (Nijhoff, 2000).

Fitzmaurice, G, 'The Problem of the "Non-Appearing" Defendant Government' (1980) 51 *BYIL* 89.

——, *The Law and Procedure of the International Court of Justice*, vol I (Cambridge University Press, 1993).

Gau, MS, 'The Shino-Philippine Arbitration of the South China Sea Nine-Dash Line Dispute: Applying the Rule on Default of Appearance' (2014) 28 *Ocean Yearbook* 81.

——, 'The Jurisdictional Rulings of the South China Sea Arbitration: Possible Errors in Fact and in Law' (2017) 31 *Ocean Yearbook* 197.

Gautier, P, 'The Settlement of Disputes' in DJ Attard, M Fitzmaurice and NA Martínez Gutiérrez (eds), *The IMLI Manual on International Maritime Law*, vol I: *The Law of the Sea* (Oxford University Press, 2014) 533–76.

Jia, BB, 'The Curious Case of Article 281: A "Super" Provision within UNCLOS?' (2015) 46 *ODIL* 266.

Kaye, S, 'Jurisdiction in the *South China Sea Arbitration*: Application of the *Monetary Gold* Principle' in S Jayakumar et al (eds), *The South China Sea Arbitration: The Legal Dimension* (Edward Elgar, 2018) 45–64.

Keyuan Zou and Qiang Ye, 'Interpretation and Application of Article 298 of the Law of the Sea Convention in Recent Annex VII Arbitrations: An Appraisal' (2017) 48 *ODIL* 331.

Klein, N, 'Expansions and Restrictions in the UNCLOS Dispute Settlement Regime: Lessons from Recent Decisions' (2016) 15(2) *CJIL* 403.

——, 'The Vicissitudes of Dispute Settlement under the Law of the Sea Convention' (2017) 32 *IJMCL* 332.

Kolb, R, *The International Court of Justice* (Oxford, Hart Publishing, 2013).

Lan Ngoc Nguyen, 'The Chagos Marine Protected Area Arbitration: Has the Scope of LOSC Compulsory Jurisdiction Being Clarified?' (2016) 31 *IJMCL* 120.

Nordquist, MH, Rosenne, S and Sohn, LB (eds), *United Nations Convention on the Law of the Sea 1982: A Commentary*, vol V (Nijhoff, 1989).

Oxman, BH, 'Complementary Agreements and Compulsory Jurisdiction' (2001) 95 *AJIL* 277.

Parlett, K, 'Jurisdiction of the Arbitral Tribunal in Philippines v China under UNCLOS and in the Absence of China' (2016) 110 *AJIL Unbound* 266.

Rao, PC, 'Delimitation Disputes under the United Nations Convention on the Law of the Sea: Settlement Procedures' in TM Ndiaye and R. Wolfrum (eds), *Law of the Sea, Environmental Law and Settlement of Disputes, Liber Amicorum Judge Thomas A Mensah* (Brill/Nijhoff, 2007) 877–97.

Rao, PS, 'The South China Sea Arbitration (The Philippines v China): Assessment of the Award on Jurisdiction and Admissibility' (2016) 15 *CJIL* 265.

Romano, C, 'The Southern Bluefin Tuna Dispute: Hints of a World to Come ... Like it or Not' (2001) 32 *ODIL* 313.

Serdy, A, 'Article 281' in A Prölss (ed), *The United Nations Convention on the Law of the Sea: A Commentary* (Hart Publishing, 2017) 1820–24.

Sofaer, AD, 'The Philippine Law of the Sea Action against China: Relearning the Limits of International Adjudication' (2016) 15 *CJIL* 393.

Talmon, S, 'The South China Sea Arbitration: Observations on the Award on Jurisdiction and Admissibility' (2016) 15 *CJIL* 309.

——, 'The Chagos Marine Protected Area Arbitration: Expansion of the Jurisdiction of UNCLOS Part XV Courts and Tribunals' (2016) 65 *ICLQ* 927.

——, 'The South China Sea Arbitration and the Finality of "Final" Awards' (2017) 8 *Journal of International Dispute Settlement* 388.

Talmon, S and Bing Bing Jia (eds), *The South China Sea Arbitration: A Chinese Perspective* (Hart Publishing, 2014).

Tamada, D, 'In the Matter of an Arbitration before an Arbitral Tribunal Constituted under Annex VII to the 1982 United Nations Convention on the Law of the Sea between the Republic of Philippines and the People's Republic of China, Award on Jurisdiction and Admissibility (29 October 2015)' (in Japanese) (2016) 66 *Kobe Law Journal* 125.

Tanaka, Y, 'Low-Tide Elevations in International Law of the Sea: Selected Issues' (2006) 20 *Ocean Yearbook* 189.

——, 'Reflections on the *Philippines/China* Arbitration: Award on Jurisdiction and Admissibility' (2016) 15 *The Law and Practice of International Courts and Tribunals* 305.

Thirlway, H, *The Law and Procedure of the International Court of Justice: Fifty Years of Jurisprudence*, 2 vols (Oxford University Press, 2013).

Treves, T, 'What have the United Nations Convention and the International Tribunal for the Law of the Sea to Offer as Regards Maritime Delimitation Disputes?' in R Lagoni and D Vignes (eds), *Maritime Delimitation* (Brill/Nijhoff, 2006) 63–78.

von Mangoldt, H and Andreas Zimmermann, 'Article 53' in A Zimmermann et al (eds), *The Statute of the International Court of Justice: A Commentary*, 2nd edn (Oxford University Press, 2012) 1324–54.

Wensheng Qu, 'The Issue of Jurisdiction Over Mixed Disputes in the Chagos Marine Protection Area Arbitration and Beyond' (2016) 47 *ODIL* 40.

Whomersley, C, 'The South China Sea: The Award of the Tribunal in the Case Brought by Philippines against China – A Critique' (2016) 15 *CJIL* 239.

Wolfrum, R, 'The Settlement of Disputes Before the International Tribunal for the Law of the Sea: A Progressive Development of International Law or Relying on Traditional Mechanisms?' (2008) 51 *Japanese Yearbook of International Law* 140.

Yee, S, 'The South China Sea Arbitration (The Philippines v China): Potential Jurisdictional Obstacles or Objections' (2014) 13 *CJIL* 663.

——, 'The South China Sea Arbitration: the Clinical Isolation and/or One-sided Tendencies in the Philippines' Oral Arguments' (2015) 14 *CJIL* 423.

——, 'Intervention in an Arbitral Proceeding under Annex VII to the UNCLOS?' (2015) 14 *CJIL* 79.

——, 'The South China Sea Arbitration Decisions on Jurisdiction and Rule of Law Concerns' (2016) 15 *CJIL* 219.

Yu Mincai, 'China's responses to the Compulsory Arbitration on the South China Sea Dispute: Legal Effects and Policy Options' (2014) 45 *ODIL* 1.

Xinjun Zhang, 'Nonappearance and Procedural delicacy: Some Observations on the Tribunal's Handling of Jurisdiction in the South China Sea Arbitration' (2018) 117(2) *The Journal of International Law and Diplomacy* 50.

3

The 'Nine-dash Line' and China's Claim to Historic Rights in the South China Sea[*]

I. INTRODUCTION

CHINA'S CLAIMED HISTORIC rights to marine spaces encompassed by the so-called 'nine-dash line' constituted one of the most debatable issues in the *South China Sea* arbitration. In this regard, the Philippines, in its Submissions Nos 1 and 2, claimed:

> (1) China's maritime entitlements in the South China Sea, like those of the Philippines, may not extend beyond those expressly permitted by the United Nations Convention on the Law of the Sea …;
>
> (2) China's claims to sovereign rights jurisdiction, and to 'historic rights' with respect to the maritime areas of the South China Sea encompassed by the so called 'nine dash line' are contrary to the Convention and without lawful effect to the extent that they exceed the geographic and substantive limits of China's maritime entitlements expressly permitted by UNCLOS.[1]

In the Tribunal's view, the dispute reflected in the Philippines' Submissions Nos 1 and 2 is evident from the diplomatic exchange between the Parties.[2] In fact, in response to China's Note Verbales of 7 May 2009, which enclosed a map depicting the 'nine-dash line' in the South China Sea,[3] the Philippines, in the Note Verbales of 5 April 2011,[4] countered that China's claim would have

[*] This chapter is derived in part from an article by the author: Y Tanaka, 'Reflections on Historic Rights in the South China Sea Arbitration (Merits), (2017) 32 *The International Journal of Marine and Coastal Law* 458. Doi 10.1163/15718085-12322037.

[1] PCA Case No 2013–19. The *South China Sea* Arbitration Award (Merits) (hereinafter 'the *South China Sea* Arbitration Award (Merits)'), 12 July 2016, [169].

[2] PCA Case No 2013-19, the *South China Sea* arbitration (Jurisdiction and Admissibility) (hereinafter 'the *South China Sea* Arbitration Award (Jurisdiction and Admissibility)'), 29 October 2015, [169].

[3] Note Verbale from the Permanent Mission of the People's Republic of China to the United Nations to the Secretary-General of the United Nations, No CML/17/2009 (7 May 2009); Note Verbale from the Permanent Mission of the People's Republic of China to the United Nations to the Secretary-General of the United Nations, No CML/18/2009 (7 May 2009).

[4] Note Verbale from the Permanent Mission of the Republic of the Philippines to the United Nations to the Secretary-General of the United Nations, No 000228 (5 April 2011), cited in the *South China Sea* Arbitration Award (Jurisdiction and Admissibility), n 2, [165].

no basis under international law, specifically the UNCLOS. However, China's Note of 14 April 2011 clearly stated that the contents of the Philippines' Note Verbale were 'totally unacceptable to the Chinese Government'.[5] The Tribunal thus considered that 'a dispute is readily apparent in the text and context of this exchange.'[6] However, the Tribunal's jurisdiction to consider the Philippines' Submissions Nos 1 and 2 would be dependent on whether historic rights are covered by the exclusion from jurisdiction over 'historic bays or titles' in Article 298. Accordingly, the Tribunal, in the 2015 Award on Jurisdiction and Admissibility, reserved a decision on its jurisdiction with respect to the Philippines' Submissions Nos 1 and 2.[7]

As will be discussed in this chapter, the Tribunal, in its Award on the Merits, considered that the exception to jurisdiction in Article 298(1)(a)(i) was limited to disputes involving historic titles, not historic rights. The Tribunal thus held that it had jurisdiction to consider the Philippines' Submissions Nos 1 and 2.[8] It eventually concluded that

> as between the Philippines and China, China's claims to historic rights, or other sovereign rights or jurisdiction, with respect to the maritime areas of the South China Sea encompassed by the relevant part of the 'nine-dash line' are contrary to the Convention and without lawful effect to the extent that they exceed the geographic and substantive limits of China's maritime entitlements under the Convention.[9]

To support this conclusion, the Tribunal provided detailed review with regard to the concept of 'historic rights' and the relationship between China's claimed historic rights and the UNCLOS. Given that the topic of historic rights has long been an unsatisfactory subject due to absence of detailed analysis,[10] the *South China Sea* Arbitration Award (Merits) provides an important insight into this subject.[11] Against that background, this chapter examines the following issues:

(a) What is the difference between historic title and historic rights in international law?
(b) What is the relationship between the historic rights and the UNCLOS?
(c) What are the requirements to establish historic rights?
(d) What is the role of the time element in the identification of historic rights?

This chapter proceeds in four sections. Following this Introduction, the chapter addresses the concept of historic rights (section II). It then examines

[5] Note Verbale from the Permanent Mission of the People's Republic of China to the Secretary-General of the United Nations, No CML/8/2011 (14 April 2011).

[6] The *South China Sea* Arbitration Award (Jurisdiction and Admissibility), n 2, [167].

[7] ibid, [398]–[399]. See also [393].

[8] The *South China Sea* Arbitration Award (Merits), n 1, [229].

[9] ibid, [1203]B(2). See also [277]–[278].

[10] A notable exception is CR Symmons, *Historic Waters in the Law of the Sea: A Modern Re-appraisal* (Brill/Nijhoff, 2008). This is the only monograph on this subject in recent years.

[11] For an analysis of the issues of historic rights in the *South China Sea* Arbitral Award on Merits, see, in particular, CR Symmons, 'Historic Rights in the Light of the Award in the South China Sea Arbitration: What Remains of the Doctrine Now?' in S Jayakumar et al (eds), *The South China Sea Arbitration: The Legal Dimension* (Edward Elgar, 2018) 101.

the Tribunal's view on the legality of China's claimed historic rights to the South China Sea at the three phases: (i) China's historic rights prior to the entry into force of the Convention in 1996, (ii) China's historic rights when the Convention entered into force in relation to China in 1996, and (iii) China's historic rights after the entry into force of the Convention in 1996 (section III). Finally, conclusions are presented in section IV.

II. THE CONCEPT OF HISTORIC RIGHTS

A. The 'Nine-dash Line'

Above all, it is necessary to review the background of the 'nine-dash line' claimed by China. What has become known as the 'nine-dash line', which is also called 'U-shaped line' or 'nine-dotted line', first appeared on an official Chinese map in 1948.[12] While originally the 1948 map featured 11 dashes, the two dashes in the Gulf of Tonkin were removed in 1953.[13] As the Tribunal observed, the extent of the rights asserted within the 'nine-dash line' only became clear with China's Notes Verbales of 7 May 2009 (see Figure 3.1).[14] In the Notes Verbales, the Chinese Government claimed that:

> China has indisputable sovereignty over the islands in the South China Sea and the adjacent waters, and enjoys sovereign rights and jurisdiction over the relevant waters as well as the seabed and subsoil thereof (see attached map). The above position is consistently held by the Chinese Government, and is widely known by the international community.[15]

A map of the South China Sea with the 'nine-dash line' was attached as part of the notes. This was the first time that the China officially used the 'nine-dash line' to defend its claims to the South China Sea.[16] In this regard, on 12 May 2016,

[12] The *South China Sea* Arbitration Award (Merits), n 1, [181]. In addition, the Tribunal indicated that '[a] similar line had also appeared in privately produced cartography as early as 1933': ibid. According to Li Jimning and Li Dexia, the origin of the 'nine-dash line' dates back to 1947. Li Junming and Li Dexia, 'The Dotted Line on the Chinese Map of the South China Sea: A Note' (2003) 34 *ODIL* 287. See also US Department of State, *Limits in the Seas No 143 China: Maritime Claims in the South China Sea*, 5 December 2014, 3. But Sheng-Ti Gau argued that a map with the 'eleven-dash line', ie 'Map of Location of the South China Sea Island', was published in December 1946: M Sheng-Ti Gau, 'The U-Shaped Line and a Categorization of the Ocean Disputes in the South China Sea' (2012) 43 *ODIL*, 58. Franckx and Benatar also took the same view: E Franckx and M Benatar, 'Dots and Lines in the South China Sea: Insights from the Law of Map Evidence' (2012) 2 *Asian Journal of International Law* 89, 90–91.

[13] The *South China Sea Arbitration Award (Merits)*, n 1, para. 181. See also Zhuguo Gao and Bing Bing Jia, 'The Nine-Dash Line in the South China Sea: History, Status, and Implications' (2013) 107 *AJIL* 98, 103.

[14] The *South China Sea* Arbitration Award (Merits), n 1, [275].

[15] CML/17/2009 and CML/18/2009, Memorial of the Philippines, vol VI, Annexes 191 and 192. CML/17/2009 is also available at http://www.un.org/Depts/los/clcs_new/submissions_files/mysvnm33_09/chn_2009re_mys_vnm_e.pdf.

[16] Keyuan Zou, 'China's U-Shaped Line in the South China Sea Revisited' (2012) 43 *ODIL* 18, 23; see also CR Symmons, 'Rights and Jurisdiction over Resources and Obligations of Coastal States' in

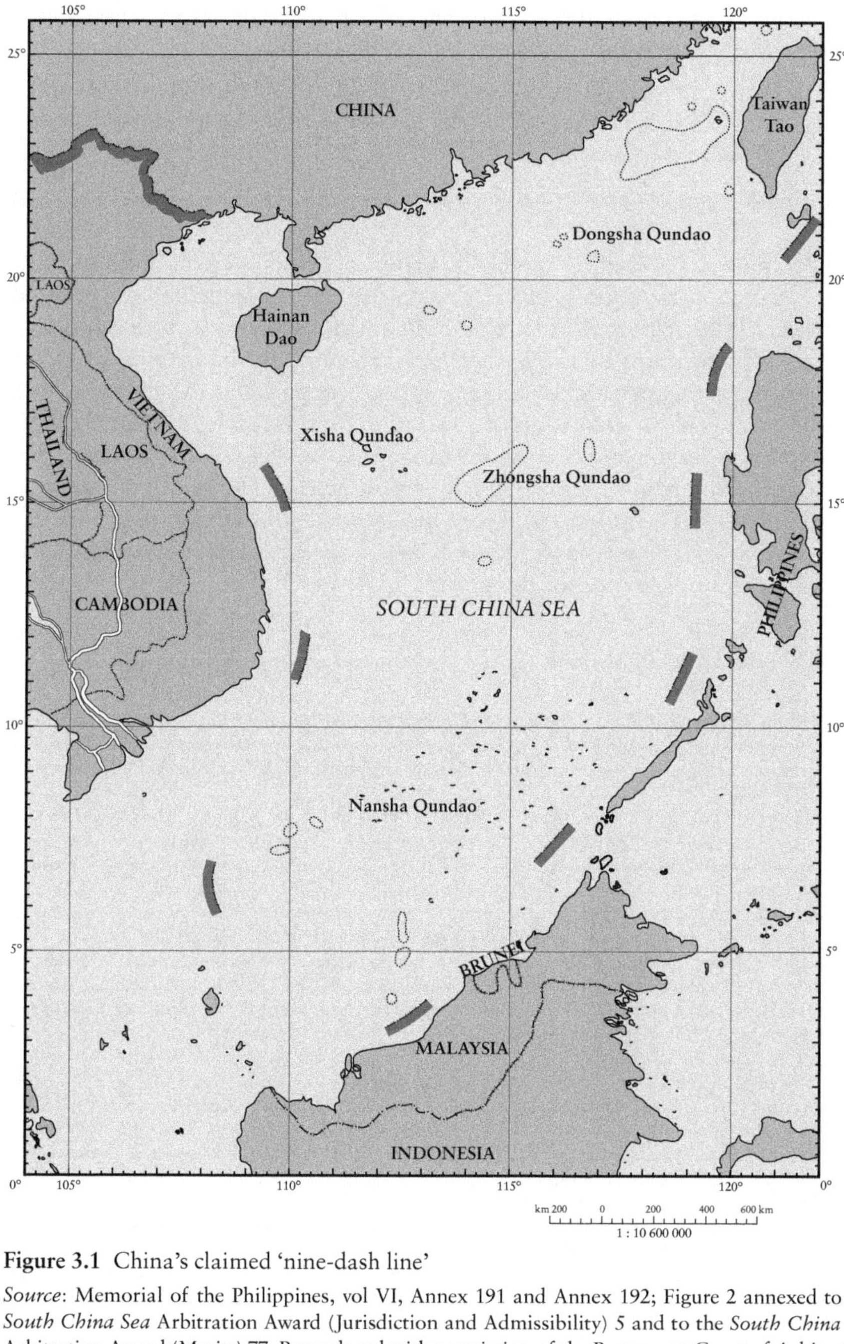

Figure 3.1 China's claimed 'nine-dash line'

Source: Memorial of the Philippines, vol VI, Annex 191 and Annex 192; Figure 2 annexed to the *South China Sea* Arbitration Award (Jurisdiction and Admissibility) 5 and to the *South China Sea* Arbitration Award (Merits) 77. Reproduced with permission of the Permanent Court of Arbitration (copyright holder).

the Director-General of the Department of Treaty and Law at the Chinese Ministry of Foreign Affairs made the following statement:

> Early in 1948, the dotted line was mapped on China's official map. It was a confirmation of China's rights in the South China Sea formed throughout the history, instead of creation of new claims.[17]

Yet China has not clarified its understanding of the meaning of the 'nine-dash line'.[18]

The 'nine-dash line' is merely a series of nine broken lines; it lacks precise geographical coordinates.[19] The dashes are not uniformly distributed. A geographic description of the 'nine-dash line' is further complicated because the sizes and locations of the dashes vary according to the maps consulted.[20] In addition, the map with the 'nine-dash line' attached to the Note Verbales of 2009 contained no indication of the datum, that is a reference employed in geodesy for measurement.[21] A new vertical map with the 'ten-dash line' was published by Sinomaps in 2013 and later reproduced by Hunan Map Publishing House in 2014.[22] The new vertical map includes a tenth dash located to the east of Taiwan. Like the previous 'nine-dash line', however, the 'ten-dash line' lacks coordinates to indicate the location of the 10 dashes.[23]

Tran Truong Thuy and Le Thuy Trang (eds), *Power, Law, and Maritime Order in the South China Sea* (Lexington Books, 2015) 145, 153. That line encompasses approximately 2,000,000 square kilometres of marine space, which is equal to around 22% of China's land area. US Department of State, n 12, 4.

[17] Ministry of Foreign Affairs, People's Republic of China, *Briefing by Xu Hong, Director-General of the Department of Treaty and Law on the South China Sea Arbitration Initiated by the Philippines*, 12 May 2016, available at http://www.fmprc.gov.cn/mfa_eng/wjbxw/t1364804.shtml.

[18] The *South China Sea* Arbitration Award (Merits), n 1, [180]. In this regard, US Department of State indicated three different interpretations: (i) dashed line as a claim to island, (ii) dashed line as a national boundary, and (iii) dashed line as a historic claim: US Department of State, n 12, 11 et seq. See also Jinming and Dexia, n 12, 291; Keyuan Zou and Liu Xinchang, 'The U-Shaped Line and Historic Rights in the Philippines v China Arbitration Case' in Shicun Wu and Keyuan Zou (eds), *Arbitration Concerning the South China Sea: Philippines Versus China* (Routledge, 2016) 127, 132; T Ikeshima, 'China's Dashed Line in the South China Sea: Legal Limits and Future Prospects' (2013) 10 *Waseda Global Forum* 17, 19.

[19] M Miyoshi, 'China's "U-Shaped Line" Claim in the South China Sea: Any Validity Under International Law?' (2012) 43 *ODIL*, 1; F Dupuy and P-M Dupuy, 'A Legal Analysis of China's Historic Rights Claim in the South China Sea' (2013) 107 *AJIL* 124, 132; CR Symmons, 'Historic Waters and Historic Rights in the South China Sea: A Critical Appraisal' in S Wu, M Valencia and Nong Hong (eds), *UN Convention on the Law of the Sea and the South China Sea* (Ashgate, 2015) 191, 221.

[20] US Department of State, n 12, 4–5; Symmons, n 19, 221. See also Ikeshima, n 18, 31–32.

[21] Franckx and Benatar, n 12, 111.

[22] ibid, 3. The map from Hunan Map Publishing House is available at http://en.people.cn/n/2014/0624/c90882-8745925.html. Yet it is unclear how the new map of 2014 is endorsed by the Chinese Government. It seems that commentators' views are divided on this matter. In this regard, see Symmons, n 19, 215, fn 129.

[23] Symmons, n 19, 219. As the Tribunal in the *South China Sea* arbitration consistently refers to the 'nine-dash line', not the 'ten-dash line', this chapter will also refer to the 'nine-dash line'.

It remains less clear whether maps are to be understood as evidence supporting China's claim to the South China Sea.[24] In any event, as the International Court of Justice (ICJ) stated in the *Frontier Dispute* case, 'maps merely constitute information which varies in accuracy from case to case; of themselves, and by virtue solely of their existence, they cannot constitute a territorial title'.[25]

According to the Court, only if maps are annexed to an official text of which they form an integral part may they acquire legal force.[26] Given that China's Note Verbales of 7 May 2009 lack geographical coordinates, some doubts can be expressed regarding whether the 2009 Note Verbales can be regarded as the official text to provide the basis of China's claim to the South China Sea. In any case it is debatable whether maps indicating the 'nine-dash line' can serve as the basis of China's claim to the South China Sea due to the lack of precision, clarity and consistency.[27] In this regard, the view of Max Huber, sole arbitrator in the *Island of Palmas* case, bears quoting: 'The first condition required of maps that are to serve as evidence on points of law is their geographical accuracy.'[28] Curiously China's Note Verbale of 14 April 2011 made no reference to the 'nine-dash line', while claiming sovereignty and related rights and jurisdiction in the South China Sea supported by 'abundant historical and legal evidence'.[29]

B. Distinction between Historic Title and Historic Rights

China, in its various statements, claimed its historic rights to the South China Sea.[30] According to the Tribunal, however, China has never expressly clarified

[24] Dupuy and Dupuy, n 19, 131.

[25] *Frontier Disputes (Burkina Faso/Republic of Mali)*, Judgment, [1986] ICJ Rep 554, 582, [54].

[26] ibid. Furthermore, Judge Oda, in his Separate Opinion in the *Kasikili/Sedudu* case, stated that '[a] map on its own, with no other supporting evidence, cannot justify a political claim'. Separate Opinion of Judge Oda in *Kasikili/Sedudu Island (Botswana/Namibia)*, Judgment of 13 December 1999, [1999] ICJ Rep1045, 1134, [40]. See also Dupuy and Dupuy, n 19, 133–34; Miyoshi, n 19, 4–5; L Caflisch, 'Les frontières, limites et délimitations internationales – Quelle importance aujourd'hui?' (2013) 368 *RCADI* 9, 36–38; H Thirlway, 'Territorial Disputes and Their Resolution in the Recent Jurisprudence of the International Court of Justice' (2018) 31 *Leiden Journal of International Law* 117, 134–35; K Del Mar, 'Evidence in Territorial Disputes' in MG Kohen and M Hébité (eds), *Research Handbook on Territorial Disputes in International Law* (Edward Elgar Publishing, 2018) 417, 424–28.

[27] United States Department of State, n 12, 18; Dupuy and Dupuy, n 19,132.

[28] *Island of Palmas (Netherlands v USA)*, Award of 4 April 1928, (1949) 2 *RIAA* 829, 853.

[29] Permanent Mission of the People's Republic of China to the United Nations (translation), CML/8.2011, 14 April 2011, available at http://www.un.org/Depts/los/clcs_new/submissions_files/mysvnm33_09/chn_2011_re_phl_e.pdf. See also Franckx and Benatar, n 12, 93. In this regard, Dupuy and Dupuy argued that the omission of the 'nine-dash line' in 2011 Note Verbale could be seen as an indication that the map is unrelated to the historic rights argument: Dupuy and Dupuy, n 19, 133.

[30] The *South China Sea* Arbitration Award (Merits), n 1, [200]. In fact, China repeatedly referred to rights formed 'throughout the long course of the history'. See, eg, *Briefing by Xu Hong*, n 17; Ministry of Foreign Affairs of the People's Republic of China, *Foreign Ministry Spokesperson Jiang Yu's Regular Press Conference on September 15, 2011*, 2. Memorial of the Philippines, vol V,

the nature or scope of its claimed historic rights.[31] The concept of historic rights constitutes a key element when examining the legality of China's claimed rights to the South China Sea.

The UNCLOS contains no provision concerning 'historic rights'. Nor does it provide any provision with regard to historic waters.[32] Although the term 'historic title' is referred to in Articles 15 and 298(1)(a)(i) of the UNCLOS,[33] the Convention provides no further precision with regard to the concept. And even though the term 'historic bay' is referred to in Articles 10(6) and 298(1)(a), no attempt is made to elucidate the concept of 'historic bay' in the Convention.[34] Accordingly, the issues of the temporal concepts, that is historic title, historic rights, historic waters and historic bay, are governed by customary international law.[35]

What is of particular importance in this regard is the distinction between 'historic rights' and 'historic title'. China precluded all of the optional exceptions referred to Article 298(1)(a), (b) and (c) from the compulsory procedures set out in the Convention.[36] As a consequence, 'disputes concerning the interpretation or application of articles 15, 74 and 83 relating to sea boundary delimitations, or those involving historic bays or titles' were precluded from the jurisdiction of the Annex VII Arbitral Tribunal by virtue of Article 298(1)(a). Hence the question of whether the concept of historic title covers that of historic rights is a crucial issue when establishing the jurisdiction of the Tribunal.

Notably, the Tribunal, in its Award on the Merits, made a clear distinction between the concept of historic rights and that of historic title. The Tribunal's view deserves to be quoted in full:

> The term 'historic rights' is general in nature and can describe any rights that a State may possess that would not normally arise under the general rules of international law, absent particular historical circumstances. Historic rights may include

30 March 2014, Annex 113. China also directly referred to its 'historic rights'. See, eg, Memorandum from the Embassy of the Republic of the Philippines in Beijing to the Secretary of Foreign Affairs of the Republic of the Philippines, No ZPE-064-2011-S, 21 June 2011, 6, para 8. Memorial of the Philippines, vol IV, 30 March 2014, Annex 72.

[31] The *South China Sea* Arbitration Award (Merits), n 1, [180].

[32] Bouchez defined 'historic waters' as 'waters over which the coastal State, contrary to the generally applicable rules of international law, clearly, effectively, continuously, and over a substantial period of time, exercises sovereign rights with the acquiescence of the community of States': LJ Bouchez, *The Regime of Bays in International Law* (Sijthoff, 1964) 281.

[33] In addition, Art 10(6) of the Convention refers to 'historic bay'.

[34] Symmons, n 19, 191.

[35] Symmons, n 10, 8; Zou Keyuan, 'Historic Rights in the South China Sea' in Wu et al, n 19, 242. The Preamble to the Convention affirms that 'matters not regulated by this Convention continue to be governed by the rules and principles of general international law'. See also *Continental Shelf (Tunisia/Libyan Arab Jamahiriya)*, Judgment, [1982] ICJ Rep 3, 74, [100].

[36] On 25 August 2006, China declared that 'The Government of the People's Republic of China does not accept any of the procedures provided for in Section 2 of Part XV of the Convention with respect to all the categories of disputes referred to in paragraph 1(a) (b) and (c) of Art 298 of the Convention.' See at http://www.un.org/depts/los/convention_agreements/convention_declarations.htm#China after ratification.

> sovereignty, but may equally include more limited rights, such as fishing rights or rights of access, that fall well short of a claim of sovereignty. 'Historic title', in contrast, is used specifically to refer to historic sovereignty to land or maritime areas. 'Historic waters' is simply a term for historic title over maritime areas, typically exercised either as a claim to internal waters or as a claim to the territorial sea, although 'general international law ... does not provide for a single "regime" for "historic waters" or "historic bays", but only for a particular régime for each of the concrete, recognised cases of "historic waters" or "historic bays".' Finally, a 'historic bay' is simply a bay in which a State claims historic waters.[37]

The Tribunal's view seems to be in line with the precedents on this subject. In this regard, the ICJ, in the *Norwegian Fisheries* case, took the view that 'By "historic waters" are usually meant waters which are treated as *internal waters* but which would not have that character were it not for the existence of an *historic title*.'[38] Given that internal waters are under the territorial sovereignty of the coastal state, the dictum of the Court can be interpreted to signify that historic title is to be linked to territorial sovereignty.[39] Furthermore, the 1962 Study prepared by the UN Secretariat stated that 'In principle, the scope of the historic title emerging from the continued exercise of sovereignty should not be wider in scope than the scope of the sovereignty actually exercised.'[40] According to the UN Secretariat Study, historic waters 'would be internal waters or territorial sea according to whether the sovereignty exercised over them in the course of the development of the historic title was sovereignty as over internal waters or sovereignty as over the territorial sea'.[41] In so stating, the 1962 UN Secretariat Study linked the historic title to sovereignty. As the Tribunal observed, the Study seemed to consider the term 'historic waters' as equivalent to historic title.[42]

In the *Qatar v Bahrain* case, the ICJ ruled that historic pearl fishing 'seems in any event never to have led to the recognition of an exclusive quasi-territorial right to the fishing grounds themselves or to the superjacent waters'.[43] While the concept of an 'exclusive quasi-territorial right' is not wholly unambiguous, the dictum of the Court seems to be interpreted to imply that historic pearl fishing is not equivalent to territorial sovereignty. More clearly, the Arbitral Tribunal,

[37] The *South China Sea* Arbitration Award (Merits), n 1, [225].

[38] *Fisheries (United Kingdom v Norway)*, Judgment of 18 December 1951, [1951] ICJ Rep 116, 130.

[39] By referring to Art 12 of the Geneva Convention on the Territorial Sea and Contiguous Zone, the Tribunal, in its Award on the Merits, took the view that 'As used in Article 12 of the 1958 Convention, "historic title" was clearly intended to have the same meaning as its usage in *Anglo-Norwegian Fisheries*, namely as an area of sea claimed exceptionally as internal waters (or, possibly, as territorial sea).' The *South China Sea* Arbitration Award (Merits), n 1, [221].

[40] *Juridical Regime of Historic Waters including Historic Bays: Study Prepared by the Secretariat*, A/CN.4/143, (1962) 2 *Yearbook of the International Law Commission* 1, 23, [164].

[41] ibid, [167].

[42] The *South China Sea* Arbitration Award (Merits), n 1, [222].

[43] *Maritime Delimitation and Territorial Questions between Qatar and Bahrain (Qatar v Bahrain)*, Merits, Judgment, [2001] ICJ Rep 40, 112–13, [236].

in the *Eritrea/Yemen* arbitration (First Stage), stated that historic rights are rights that fall short of territorial sovereignty.[44] The Arbitral Tribunal's view is echoed by some commentators. For example, Keyuan Zou argued that 'The term "historic rights" also covers certain special rights without involving a claim of full sovereignty.'[45] Symmons also stated that 'historic rights differ from "historic waters" in as much as they do not … amount to zonal claims to jurisdiction or *sovereignty*'.[46] Given that the lack of precision of the various 'historic' concepts may entail the risk of encouraging states to make historic claims of increasing scope to marine spaces,[47] the clarification of the concept of historic rights and that of historic title by the Tribunal can be thought to be a welcome development.[48]

C. The Legal Nature of China's Claimed Rights

On the basis of the distinction between historic rights and historic title, it is necessary to examine the nature of China's claimed rights in the South China Sea. In this regard, the Tribunal highlighted three instances that can be considered as examples of China's historic rights arising independently from the Convention:

- a notice of open blocks for petroleum exploration adjunct to the western edge of the nine-dash line by the China National Offshore Oil Cooperation;[49]
- China's objection to the Philippines' award of petroleum blocks within the nine-dash line; and
- China's declaration of a 'Summer Ban on Marine Fishing in the South China Sea Maritime Space'.[50]

[44] *Territorial Sovereignty and Scope of the Dispute (Eritrea and Yemen)*, Arbitral Award of 9 October 1998, (2001) 22 *RIAA* 209, 244, [126]. This interpretation is supported by Zhuguo Gao and Bing Bing Jia, n 13, 122.

[45] Keyuan Zou, n 16, 241.

[46] Emphasis added. Symmons, n 10, 5. See also Symmons, n 11, 108–13.

[47] Symmons, n 19, 192.

[48] Symmons argued that 'the Arbitral Tribunal incidentally clarified the meaning of various formerly interchangeably used terms relating to historic maritime claims, … such as "historic rights" … This clarity is a welcome development in a formerly arcane and obscure area of international law': Symmons, n 11, 125. With reservation, McDorman also stated that 'the analysis of the Tribunal's differences between historic title, historic rights and historic waters is a welcome clarification': TL McDorman, 'The South China Sea *Tribunal Awards: A Dispute Resolution Perspective*' (2018) 3 *Asia-Pacific Journal of Ocean Law and Policy* 134, 138.

[49] One of the blocks (Block BS16) lies beyond 200 nautical miles from any feature in the South China Sea claimed by China and beyond any possible extended continental shelf: ibid, [208]. See also US Department of State, n 12, 17.

[50] The *South China Sea* Arbitration Award (Merits), n 1, [208]–[211].

In this connection, it is crucial to note that China has unequivocally accepted the freedom of navigation and overflight in the South China Sea. In fact, China's Vice Foreign Minister explicitly stated:

> The Chinese side respects and safeguards the freedom of navigation and over-flight in the South China Sea to which all countries are entitled under international law … There has been and will be no obstruction to navigation and over-flight freedom in the South China Sea.[51]

China's Position Paper also emphasised that 'China always respects the freedom of navigation and overflight enjoyed by all States in the South China Sea in accordance with international law'.[52] The freedom of navigation in the South China Sea was also confirmed by the Chinese Foreign Ministry Spokesman on 24 January 2017.[53]

In international law, apart from the right of innocent passage,[54] states do not enjoy the freedom of navigation in the territorial sea. Nor do they enjoy the freedom of overflight above the territorial sea. Accordingly, it was the Tribunal's view that China's commitment to respect both freedom of navigation and overflight signified that China did *not* consider the sea areas within the 'nine-dash line' to be equivalent to its territorial sea or internal waters.[55] It must also be noted that China declared baselines for the territorial sea surrounding Hainan and the Paracel Islands.[56] As the Tribunal observed, it would be unnecessary for China to declare baselines if the waters both within and beyond 12 nautical miles of those islands already formed part of China's territorial sea or internal waters by virtue of a claim to historic rights through the 'nine-dash line'.[57]

Overall it can be concluded that China did not consider waters encompassed by the 'nine-dash line' to form part of its territorial sea or internal waters.[58] This is compatible with the fact that China invoked its historic rights in the South China Sea, not historic title that is linked to sovereignty.[59] In the word of the Tribunal, 'the dispositive proof that China's claim is not one to historic title lies

[51] The *South China Sea* Arbitration Award (Merits), n 1, [212]. See also the Philippines' Supplemental Documents, vol I, Annex 645.

[52] Position Paper of the Government of the People's Republic of China on the Matter of Jurisdiction in the South China Sea Arbitration Initiated by the Republic of the Philippines, 7 December 2014, [28]. The Position Paper is available at http://www.fmprc.gov.cn/mfa_eng/zxxx_662805/t1217147.shtml.

[53] The statement of Foreign Ministry Spokesperson Hua Chunying's Regular Press Conference on 24 January 2017, which stated that 'What we have been stressing is, China upholds the freedom of navigation enjoyed by countries under international law in the South China Sea, but we oppose intruding navigation that undermines sovereignty and security of coastal countries.' See at http://www.fmprc.gov.cn/mfa_eng/xwfw_665399/s2510_665401/t1433525.shtml.

[54] UNCLOS, Art 17.

[55] The *South China Sea* Arbitration Award (Merits), n 1, [213].

[56] ibid, [176].

[57] ibid, [213].

[58] ibid, [214].

[59] ibid, [227].

in China's conduct … which is incompatible with a claim that the waters of the South China Sea constitute China's territorial sea or internal waters'.[60]

This point was confirmed by Zhiguo Gao and Bing Bing Jia, stating that '[t]he nine-dash line, in the light of that body of national law, is not intended to assert a *historic* title of sovereignty over the sea areas, as enclosed by the lines, beyond what is allowed under international law';[61] and that 'the nine-dash line can be best defined, in view of China's long-standing practice, as a line to preserve both its title to territory and its historic rights.'[62] They also add that 'China has never impeded that freedom [of navigation and overflight] in the past, with or without the nine- or eleven-dash lines'.[63]

In the view of the Tribunal, 'the reference to "historic titles" in Article 298(1)(a)(i) of the Convention is accordingly a reference to claims of sovereignty over maritime areas derived from historical circumstances', and this provision is not intended to exclude jurisdiction over a broad and unspecified category of possible claims to historic rights falling short of sovereignty.[64] As the exception to jurisdiction in Article 298(1)(a)(i) is limited to disputes involving historic titles and China did not claim historic title to the waters of South China Sea, the dispute concerning China's historic rights was not precluded by this provision. Therefore, the Tribunal concluded that it had jurisdiction to consider the Philippines' Submissions Nos1 and 2.[65]

III. THREE PHASES OF ANALYSIS

A. General Considerations

The Tribunal then moved on to examine the legality of China's claimed historic rights. In this regard, it specified three questions:

(a) First, does the Convention, and in particular its rules for the exclusive economic zone and continental shelf, allow for the preservation of rights to living and

[60] ibid, [228].

[61] Zhuguo Gao and Bing Bing Jia, n 13, 108 (original emphasis). They also argued that '[t]here has also been no evidence that China has enforced its domestic law in those waters as if they were part of internal waters': ibid, 109.

[62] ibid, 123.

[63] ibid,119.

[64] The *South China Sea* Arbitration Award (Merits), n 1, [226].

[65] ibid, [229]. Beckman and Bernard already argued that 'Although Article 15 mentions historic title, it does not mention historic rights, and there are no provisions in UNCLOS on historic rights. Therefore, if China were to argue that it has the right under international law to exercise historic rights in the waters inside the nine dashed lines, a dispute could arise over whether such rights are consistent with UNCLOS, and such dispute would not be excluded by the declaration' (footnote omitted). R Beckman and L Bernard, 'Disputed Areas in the South China Sea: Prospects for Arbitration or Advisory Opinion', *Paper at the Third International Workshop, South China Sea: Cooperation for Regional Security and Development*, Hanoi, 2011, 15–16, available at http://cil.nus.edu.sg/wp/wp-content/uploads/2009/09/Beckman-Bernard-Paper-DAV-Conf-3-5-Nov-2011.pdf.

non-living resources that are at variance with the provisions of the Convention and which may have been established prior to the Convention's entry into force by agreement or unilateral act?

(b) Second, prior to the entry into force of the Convention, did China have historic rights and jurisdiction over living and non-living resources in the waters of the South China Sea beyond the limits of the territorial sea?

(c) Third, and independently of the first two considerations, has China in the years since the conclusion of the Convention established rights and jurisdiction over living and non-living resources in the waters of the South China Sea that are at variance with the provisions of the Convention? If so, would such establishment of rights and jurisdiction be compatible with the Convention?[66]

China ratified the UNCLOS in 1996. Thus the above questions can be rearranged in chronological order:

- *Phase I* – China's historic rights prior to the entry into force of the Convention for China in 1996.
- *Phase II* – China's historic rights when the Convention entered into force in relation to China in 1996.
- *Phase III* – China's historic rights after the entry into force of the Convention for China in 1996.

While the Tribunal addressed questions (a)–(c), the subsections following examine the three issues in chronological order.

B. Phase I: China's Historic Rights Prior to the Entry into Force of the Convention

The first issue is whether China established its historic rights prior to the entry into force of the UNCLOS. In its public statements, China repeatedly asserted its rights in the South China Sea on the basis of historic evidence. For instance, the Director-General of the Department of Treaty and Law at the Chinese Ministry of Foreign Affairs stated:

> I want to stress that China's sovereignty and relevant rights in the South China Sea were formed *throughout the long course of history* and have been maintained by the Chinese Government consistently.[67]

Furthermore, China's Position Paper stated:

> China has indisputable sovereignty over the South China Sea Islands (the Dongsha Islands, the Xisha Islands, the Zhongsha Islands and the Nansha Islands) and the

[66] The *South China Sea* Arbitration Award (Merits), n 1, [234].

[67] Ministry of Foreign Affairs, People's Republic of China, *Briefing by Xu Hong, Director-General of the Department of Treaty and Law on the South China Sea Arbitration Initiated by the Philippines* (12 May 2016) (emphasis added), available at http://www.fmprc.gov.cn/mfa_eng/wjbxw/t1364804.shtml.

> adjacent waters. Chinese activities in the South China Sea date back to over 2,000 years ago. China was the first country to discover, name, explore and exploit the resources of the South China Sea Islands and the first to continuously exercise sovereign powers over them.[68]

According to the Ministry of Foreign Affairs of China:

> Over the history, Chinese fishermen have resided on Taiping Dao for years, working and living there, carrying out fishing activities, digging wells for fresh water, cultivating land and farming, building huts and temples, and raising livestock. The above activities are all manifestly recorded in Geng Lu Bu (Manual of Sea Routes) which was passed down from generation to generation among Chinese fishermen, as well as in many western navigation logs before the 1930s.[69]

However, the Philippines challenged the existence of Chinese historic rights to the maritime areas of the South China Sea. The Philippines stressed in particular the absence of any documents evidencing any official Chinese activities in regard to any South China Sea feature prior to the beginning of the twentieth century.[70] Related to this, it indicated an interesting fact that for periods of the fourteenth century and for much of the fifteenth and sixteenth centuries, the Imperial Chinese Government actively prohibited maritime trade by Chinese subjects.[71] Overall the Philippines claimed that until 2009, any Chinese historical claims to the features of the South China Sea did not include a claim to the waters beyond their territorial sea.[72] While the views of the parties in dispute were sharply divided, both Parties commonly relied on historical evidence. Nonetheless, the Tribunal did not give much weight to historical evidence when examining the question of whether China has historically had rights to living and non-living resources beyond the limits of the territorial sea in the South China Sea.[73] Instead, the Tribunal addressed two issues that are intimately intertwined.

The first issue is whether China's historical activities in the South China Sea can be regarded as part of the freedom of the high seas. According to the Tribunal, China recognised that the South China Sea formed part of the high seas prior to the adoption of the Convention. To support this view, the Tribunal

[68] Position Paper, n 52, [4]. Furthermore, China's practice in the South China Sea prior to the 20th century is described by CSIL in some detail. See CSIL, *The South China Sea Arbitration: A Critical Study* (Foreign Languages Press, 2018) 279 et seq.

[69] Foreign Ministry Spokesperson Hua Chunying's Remarks on Relevant Issue about Taiping Dao, 3 June 2016, available at http://www.fmprc.gov.cn/mfa_eng/xwfw_665399/s2510_665401/2535_665405/t1369188.shtml.

[70] The *South China Sea* Arbitration Award (Merits), n 1, [197]; presentation by Mr Loewenstein, Merits Hearing Tr (Day 1), 89.

[71] Presentation by Mr Loewenstein, Merits Hearing Tr (Day 1), n 70, 81; the *South China Sea* Arbitration Award (Merits), n 1, [195].

[72] The *South China Sea* Arbitration Award (Merits), n 1, [199]; presentation by Mr Loewenstein, Merits Hearing Tr (Day 2), 2.

[73] The *South China Sea* Arbitration Award (Merits), n 1, [264].

referred to China's Declaration of the Government of the People's Republic of China on China's Territorial Sea of 4 September 1958, which expressly stated that it applies to 'the Dongsha Islands, the Xisha Islands, the Zhongsha Islands, the Nansha Islands and all other islands belonging to China *which are separated from the mainland and its coastal islands by the high seas*'.[74] The reference to the 'high seas' can be seen as an indication that China did not consider the South China Sea as comprising marine spaces under its exclusive jurisdiction on the basis of historic rights.[75] Indeed, it was 1998 when China declared its EEZ.[76] It seems to follow that China's navigation and trade in the South China Sea, as well as fishing beyond the territorial sea, represented the exercise of high seas freedoms.[77] As the Tribunal stated, the exercise of freedoms permitted under international law cannot give rise to a historic right, since it involves nothing that would call for the acquiescence of other states.[78] As China merely engaged in activities that were permitted to all states by international law, historical navigation and fishing beyond the territorial sea cannot form the basis for the emergence of a historic right.[79]

The second issue is whether China had engaged in activities that deviated from what was permitted under the freedom of the high seas and other states acquiesced in such activities. In the view of the Tribunal, 'historic rights are, in most instances, exceptional rights'.[80] To establish the exclusive historic right to living and non-living resources within the 'nine-dash line', it would be necessary to show that China had historically sought to prohibit or restrict the exploitation of such resources by the nationals of other states and that those states had acquiesced in such restrictions. Nonetheless, there was no evidence that would suggest that China historically regulated or controlled fishing in the South China Sea, beyond the limits of the territorial sea.[81] Furthermore, it would be theoretically impossible for China to regulate the non-living resources of the seabed since offshore oil extraction became possible in deep water areas only recently. In fact, with respect to the seabed, the Tribunal did not see any historical

[74] ibid, [269] (emphasis added by the Tribunal). The Declaration is available at http://www.chinausfocus.com/upload/file/2014/Annex1-4.pdf. See also Keyuan Zou and Liu Xinchang, n 18, 133.
[75] US Department of State, n 12, 19.
[76] Law on the Exclusive Economic Zone and the Continental Shelf, 26 June 1998, available at http://www.npc.gov.cn/englishnpc/Law/2007-12/11/content_1383573.htm. Art 14 of the Law stipulates that '[t]he provisions in this Law shall not affect the rights that the People's Republic of China has been enjoying ever since the days of the past'. According to the translation maintained by the UN Department of Ocean Affairs and the Law of the Sea, Art 14 provides that '[t]he provisions of this Act shall not affect the historical rights of the People's Republic of China'. The text of translation is available at http://www.un.org/Depts/los/LEGISLATIONANDTREATIES/PDFFILES/chn_1998_eez_act.pdf. In any case the Law provides no explanation about the meaning of China's claimed rights.
[77] The *South China Sea* Arbitration Award (Merits), n 1, [269].
[78] ibid, [268].
[79] ibid, [269]–[270].
[80] ibid, [268].
[81] ibid, [270].

activity that could have been restricted or controlled in the South China Sea.[82] Accordingly, the Tribunal held that China's ratification of the Convention in June 1996 did not extinguish historic rights in the waters of the South China Sea, but China relinquished the freedoms of the high seas there.[83]

What is of particular interest in this regard concerns the Tribunal's approach to historic rights. When examining the establishment of historic rights, it appears that an orthodox approach is to examine elements for formulating the rights. Elements of title to historic waters are summarised in the Study prepared by the UN Secretariat. They are:

- the exercise of authority over the area by the state claiming the historic right;
- the continuity of this exercise of authority; and
- the attitude of foreign states.[84]

According to the UN Secretariat Study, 'there seems to be fairly general agreement' on the three requirements.[85] In this regard, the Tribunal considered that the process is the same for claims to rights short of sovereignty, since historic waters are merely one form of historic right.[86] The Tribunal seemed to regard the three elements as requirements for formulating historic rights in customary international law.[87] If the three elements can be regarded as conditions for creating historic rights in customary international law, the practical application of the three elements is not free from difficulty since these elements are not wholly unambiguous.[88] This is particularly true of the temporal element. As O'Connell stated, '[t]he whole theory behind the doctrine of historic rights is that special situations crystallize as the result of historical evolution'.[89] Hence the temporal element, that is the passage of time, is at the heart of *historic* rights.[90]

[82] ibid.

[83] ibid, [271].

[84] UN Secretariat, n 40, 13, [80].

[85] ibid. In this regard, Churchill and Lowe considered that the three requirements were implicitly accepted by the ICJ in *Land, Island and Maritime Frontier Dispute (El Salvador v Honduras: Nicaragua intervening)*. Even though they did not specify a relevant paragraph, see [1992] ICJ Rep 593–594, [394]: R Churchill and AV Lowe, *The Law of the Sea*, 3rd edn (Manchester University Press, 1999) 44. According to Symmons, the UN document on historic waters has had an authoritative standing with the US courts. The commentators on historic bays and waters are also much in agreement on the requisite criteria. Symmons, n 10, 111–13. It appears that the US Department of State also supports the three elements as requirements for establishing the existence of a historic bay or historic title: US Department of State, n 12, 10. See also TL McDorman, 'Rights and Jurisdiction over Resources in the South China Sea: UNCLOS and the "Nine-dash Line"' in S Jayakumar, T Koh and RC Beckman (eds), *South China Sea Disputes and Law of the Sea* (Edward Elgar, 2014) 144, 153.

[86] The *South China Sea* Arbitration Award (Merits), n 1, [265]. See also CSIL, n 68, 269, [495].

[87] In fact, the Tribunal stated that 'the process for the formation of historic rights in international law is well summarised in the UN Secretariat's 1962 *Memorandum on the Juridical Regime of Historic Waters, Including Historic Bays*': The *South China Sea* Arbitration Award (Merits), n 1, [265].

[88] Symmons, n 19, 214. See also Symmons, n 10, 113–16.

[89] DP O'Connell, *The International Law of the Sea*, vol I, ed IA Shearer (Clarendon Press, 1982) 425.

[90] Concerning a historic title, the UN Secretariat took the view that the passage of time is essential. The UN Secretariat, n 40, 15, [103]. The same will hold true of historic rights.

In this connection, two issues arise. The first is how long the exercise of authority must continue and the second is at what time the opposition must occur in order to prevent the creation of historic rights.

The first issue concerns the establishment of historic rights. In this regard, it is generally considered that the state must exercise the authority for a considerable time for it to have developed into a usage.[91] In this regard, the ICJ in the *Tunisia/Libya* case ruled that '[h]istoric titles must enjoy respect and be preserved as they have always been by *long usage*'.[92] As the UN Secretariat admitted, however, 'no precise length of time can be indicated as necessary to build the usage on which the historic title must be based'.[93] The same consideration can apply with respect to historic rights. As a consequence, the length of time necessary for a historic right to emerge is a matter of subjective judgment.[94]

The second issue pertains to the prevention of such rights. It can be reasonably considered that opposition can be made only after the exercise of authority has begun. In practice, however, it may not be easy to determine exactly when a state commenced to exercise its jurisdiction over a certain marine space.[95] Furthermore, there is no precise time limit for the lapse of time necessary to allow the emergence of the historic rights.[96] Therefore, it may have to be admitted that rules concerning the key element of historic rights, that is the temporal element, remain obscure in customary international law.

As noted, the Tribunal, in its Arbitration Award on the Merits, did not take an approach that involved examining each and every element of historic rights.[97] Instead, the Tribunal focused on the freedom of the high seas and the exceptional nature of historic rights. As historical human activities beyond the territorial seas, such as navigation and fishing, are only part of the freedom of

[91] The UN Secretariat, n 40, 15, [103].

[92] *Continental Shelf (Tunisia/Libyan Arab Jamahiriya)* [1982] ICJ Rep 73, [100].

[93] The UN Secretariat, n 40, 15, [104]. According to the UN Secretariat, the adjective 'immemorial' is of little assistance, since taken literally 'immemorial' would be a wholly impractical notion: ibid.

[94] The UN Secretariat, n 40, 18, [123]; Miyoshi, n 19, 6. Symmons argued that as a working rule, 'the alleged historic claim should *usually* have existed for at least a century': Symmons, n 19, 157 (original emphasis).

[95] The 1962 UN Secretariat Study took the view that the time cannot begin to run until the exercise of sovereignty is to be effective and public: the UN Secretariat, n 40, 18, para. 124. See also Symmons, n 10, 139 et seq.

[96] The UN Secretariat, n 40, 19, [131].

[97] However, some commentators examined the question of whether China's historic claim to the South China Sea fulfilled the three conditions. For instance, Jinming and Dexia argued that 'Since the 1947 announcement of the dotted line in the South China Sea, the government of China has seldom practiced this kind of exclusive rights [*sic*] over the waters within the line. The occasional exercise of exclusivity is only focused on the islands within the line, but not the waters': Jinming and Dexia, n 12, 292. After examination of various sub-rules governing historic rights, Symmons concluded that the Chinese claim fails to make the mark on most of these rules: Symmons, n 19, 214–33. Furthermore, the US Department of State took the view that China's historic waters claim in the South China Sea would not pass any element of the three requirements: US Department of State, n 12, 21–22. Franckx and Benatar also reached a negative conclusion in this matter: Franckx and Benatar, n 12, 96.

the high seas, they do not create any rights. In this sense, historic evidence on navigation and/or fishing in the high seas does not provide a basis of historic rights, even if a state had engaged in navigation and/or fishing for a considerable time. Furthermore, as historic rights are exceptional rights, a state that claims such rights must prove that it had engaged in activities that are contrary to the freedom of the high seas. In light of the openness of the high seas, however, it is highly difficult if not impossible to successfully prove that a state had exclusively controlled living resources in the high seas and that other states had tolerated such restrictions. According to the Tribunal's approach, the role of the historical element is to be reduced almost to vanishing point.

C. Phase II: China's Historic Rights When the Convention Entered into Force in Relation to China in 1996

Even if China's claimed historic rights were established anterior to the entry into force of the UNCLOS for China, an issue arises whether the Convention allows the preservation of rights that are at variance with the Convention. In considering this issue, four propositions can be identified:

(a) The situation where the Convention expressly permits or preserves other international agreements: such agreements shall remain unaffected by virtue of Article 311(5) of the Convention.
(b) The situation where the Convention does not expressly permit or preserve a prior agreement, rule of customary international law or historic right: if their operation does not conflict with any provision of the Convention or to the extent that interpretation indicates that the Convention intended the prior agreements, rules or rights to continue in operation, such prior norms will not be incompatible with the Convention.
(c) The situation where rights and obligations arising independently of the Convention are not incompatible with its provisions: in this case, operation of the rights and obligations will remain unaltered in accordance with Article 311(2).
(d) The situation where independent rights and obligations have arisen prior to the entry into force of the UNCLOS but they are incompatible with its provisions: in this case, the Convention will prevail over the earlier, incompatible rights or obligations in accordance with Article 30(3) of the Vienna Convention on the Law of Treaties and Article 293 of the UNCLOS.[98]

Propositions (a), (b), and (c) will not create serious legal issues. However, proposition (d) needs careful consideration.

[98] The *South China Sea* Arbitration Award (Merits), n 1, [238].

No article of the Convention expressly provides for or permits the continued existence of historic rights to the living or non-living resources of the EEZ. A question of interest here is whether the Convention nevertheless intended the continued operation of historic rights that are at variance with it.[99] It is apparent that the coastal state alone has the sovereign rights to the living and non-living resources of the EEZ under the Convention.[100] As provided in Article 58, high seas rights and freedoms apply in the EEZ only to the extent they are not incompatible with the provisions of Part V of the Convention.[101] The costal state's sovereign rights in the EEZ are exclusive in the sense that other states cannot engage upon activities in the EEZ without the consent of the coastal State. Accordingly, as the Tribunal rightly stated, 'the notion of *sovereign* rights over living and non-living resources is generally incompatible with another State having historic rights to the same resources, if such historic rights are considered exclusive'.[102] Furthermore, under Article 62(3), 'the need to minimize economic dislocation in States whose nationals have habitually fished in the zone' constitutes merely one of the relevant *factors*, not rights, to be taken into account by the coastal state in giving access to any *surplus in the allowable catch*.[103] In the view of the Tribunal, 'the inclusion of this provision – which would be entirely unnecessary if traditional fishing rights were preserved in the exclusive economic zone – confirms that the drafters of the Convention did not intend to preserve such rights'.[104] In light of Article 62(3), any pre-existing claimed historic *rights* in another state's EEZ are to be phased out. Symmons thus stated that 'this provision [Article 62(3)] is the death knell of any continuing exercise of any meaningful claimed historic rights in a post-UNCLOS setting in an EEZ by a third State'.[105]

It must also be noted that the sovereign rights over the continental shelf set out in Article 77 of the Convention are also exclusive in the sense that even if the coastal state does not explore the continental shelf or exploit its natural resources, no one may undertake these activities without the express consent of

[99] ibid, [239].

[100] UNCLOS, Art 56(1); the *South China Sea* Arbitration Award (Merits), n 1, [243].

[101] ibid, [241].

[102] ibid, [243].

[103] In this regard, it must be noted that the coastal state has a broad discretion to determine the allowable catch. WT Burke, *The New International Law of Fisheries: UNCLOS 1982 and Beyond* (Oxford University Press, 1994) 47–48. According to Oda, as a matter of theory, the coastal state may always have the capacity to harvest the entire allowable catch, by introducing foreign capital and technology. S Oda, 'Fisheries Under the United Nations Convention on the Law of the Sea' (1983) 77 *AJIL* 739, 744.

[104] The *South China Sea* Arbitration Award (Merits), n 1, [804]. In this regard, Symmons argued that 'a plain reading of the Article 62 provision equally applies to supersede both "exclusive" and "non-exclusive" historic rights claimed in another state's EEZ or (by analogy) on its continental shelf': Symmons, n 11, 122.

[105] Symmons, n 11, 122.

the coastal state.[106] In this regard, it is important to note that the rights of the coastal state over the continental shelf are inherent rights.[107] It follows that the notion of sovereign rights over the continental shelf is incompatible with another state's historic rights over the same shelf.[108] In this connection, O'Connell's view deserves to be quoted:

> The establishment of the continental shelf doctrine as an autonomous legal institution, independent of other methods of territorial acquisition, implied the automatic attribution of the continental shelf to the coastal State. One of the aims behind the propagation of the doctrine was to annul any priority of claim in time or nature over the rights of the coastal State, so that, for example, the doctrines of historic rights or acquisitive prescription would not be available.[109]

In conclusion, the Tribunal made a clear statement:

> The Convention does not include any express provisions preserving or protecting historic rights that are at variance with the Convention. On the contrary, the Convention supersedes earlier rights and agreements to the extent of any incompatibility. The Convention is comprehensive in setting out the nature of the exclusive economic zone and continental shelf and the rights of other States within those zones. China's claim to historic rights is not compatible with these provisions.[110]

According to the Tribunal, the text and context of the Convention are clear in superseding any historic rights that a state may once have had in the areas that now form part of the EEZ and continental shelf of another state. In the words of the Tribunal, '[t]here is no ambiguity here'.[111] Related to this, it is of particular interest to note that China opposed any accommodation of historic fishing in the text of the Convention. During the negotiation of the UNCLOS, the Chinese Government stated:

> The super-Powers had for years wantonly plundered the offshore resources of developing coastal States, thereby seriously damaging their interests. Declaration of permanent sovereignty over such resources was a legitimate right, which should be respected by other countries. The super-Powers, however, while giving verbal recognition to the economic zone, were advocating the placing of restrictions on the sovereignty of coastal States over their resources. For example, one of them had proposed that the coastal State should allow foreign fishermen the right to fish within that zone in cases where the State did not harvest 100 per cent of the allowable catch. Such logic made no sense. The suggestion in fact harked back to that super-Power's

[106] UNCLOS, Art 77(2); Geneva Convention on the Continental Shelf, Art 2(2). The ICJ echoed this view in *North Sea Continental Shelf (Federal Republic of Germany/Denmark) (Federal Republic of Germany/Netherlands)*, Judgment of 20 February 1969, [1969] ICJ Rep 3, 22, [19]. See also Y Tanaka, *The International Law of the Sea*, 3rd edn (Cambridge University Press, 2019) 173.

[107] *North Sea Continental Shelf*, n 106, 22, [19].

[108] The *South China Sea* Arbitration Award (Merits), n 1, [244]. See also McDorman, n 85, 160.

[109] O'Connell, n 89, 482.

[110] The *South China Sea* Arbitration Award (Merits), n 1, [246].

[111] ibid, [247].

> well-known proposal that coastal States should be allowed only 'preferential rights' when fishing their own off-shore areas. Yet, the establishment of exclusive economic zones over the resources of which coastal States would exercise permanent sovereignty simply meant that the developing countries were regaining their long-lost rights and in no way implied a sacrifice on the part of the super-Powers.[112]

For the Tribunal,

> China's position, as asserted during the negotiation of the Convention, is incompatible with a claim that China would be entitled to historic rights to living and non-living resources in the South China Sea that would take precedence over the exclusive economic zone rights of the other littoral States. China never advanced such a claim during the course of the negotiations, notwithstanding that the South China Sea and the question of sovereignty over the Spratly Islands was raised on several occasions in exchanges between China and the Philippines during the work of the Seabed Committee and between China and Viet Nam during the Third UN Conference.[113]

It must also be noted that reservations are clearly prohibited in Article 309 of the UNCLOS. The prohibition is crucial to maintaining the integrity of the Convention. According to the Tribunal, it is simply inconceivable that the drafters of the UNCLOS anticipated that the resulting Convention would be subordinate to broad claims of historic rights.[114]

Under the Tribunal's approach, historical evidence cannot provide a basis for exercising rights that are contrary to the Convention.[115] This point was echoed by the ICJ in the *Gulf of Maine* case. There, the US claimed that the delimitation line should take account of longstanding use by US fishermen in Georges Bank. However, the claim was rejected by the Chamber of the ICJ. In the words of the Chamber:

> Until very recently, as the Chamber has recalled, these expanses were part of the high seas and as such freely open to the fishermen not only of the United States and Canada but also of other countries, and they were indeed fished by very many nationals of the latter. … But after the coastal States had set up exclusive 200-mile fishery zones, the situation radically altered. Third States and their nationals found themselves deprived of any right of access to the sea areas within those zones and of any position of advantage they might have been able to achieve within them.[116]

[112] Statement of Mr Ling Ching, 'Summary Records of Meetings of the Second Committee, 24th Meeting', UN Doc A/CONF.62/C.2/SR.24, 1 August 1974, *Official Records of the Third United Nations Conference on the Law of the Sea, Volume II*, 187, [2], available at http://legal.un.org/diplomaticconferences/1973_los/vol2.shtml.

[113] The *South China Sea* Arbitration Award (Merits), n 1, [252] (footnotes omitted).

[114] ibid, [254].

[115] See also the US Department of State, n 12, 23.

[116] *Delimitation of the Maritime Boundary in the Gulf of Maine Area (Canada/United States of America)*, Judgment, [1984] ICJ Rep, 246, 341–42, [235].

Following the dictum of the Chamber,[117] China could no longer rely on historic rights in the South China Sea to the extent that it became part of the EEZ of another state, even if it had such rights.

At first sight, a contrary indication might be ascribed to the 1974 *Fisheries Jurisdiction* cases. In these cases, the ICJ accepted the preferential rights of the coastal state in adjacent waters.[118] However, it ruled that

> [t]he concept of preferential rights is not compatible with the exclusion of all fishing activities of other States. A coastal State entitled to preferential rights is not free, unilaterally and according to its own uncontrolled discretion, to determine the extent of those rights.[119]

At the time of the judgment, however, the EEZ was not established in customary international law. Nor was it enshrined in the Convention. It must be considered that the dictum on the preferential rights became obsolete after the adoption of the Convention. Thus, as the Tribunal observed, the *South China Sea* arbitration differs fundamentally from the *Fisheries Jurisdiction* cases.[120]

On the other hand, the Arbitral Tribunal, in the *Eritrea/Yemen* arbitration (Second Stage: Maritime Delimitation), ruled that '[t]he traditional fishing regime is not limited to the territorial waters of specified islands' and it 'operates throughout those waters beyond the territorial waters of each of the Parties', that is, into their EEZs.[121] In this case, however, the Arbitral Tribunal was allowed to take into account 'the opinion it will have formed on questions of territorial sovereignty, the United Nations Convention on the Law of the Sea, and any other pertinent factor'.[122] Consequently, the applicable law in the *Eritrea/Yemen* arbitration was not limited to the Convention, and the *South China Sea* arbitration is distinct from the *Eritrea/Yemen* arbitration.[123] In this regard, the Tribunal made clear that

> the Tribunal disagrees with the conclusions of the tribunal in *Eritrea v Yemen* (which held that the traditional fishing regime in the Red Sea extended throughout the maritime zones of those States) and considers that that tribunal was able to reach the conclusions it did only because it was permitted to apply factors other than the Convention itself under the applicable law provisions of the parties' arbitration agreement.[124]

[117] See also United States Department of State, n 12, 20.

[118] *Fisheries Jurisdiction (United Kingdom of Great Britain and Northern Ireland v Iceland)*, Judgment, [1974] ICJ Rep 3, 23, [56]; *Fisheries Jurisdiction (Federal Republic of Germany v Iceland)*, Judgment, [1974] ICJ Rep 175, 192, [44].

[119] *Fisheries Jurisdiction (Federal Republic of Germany v Iceland)* [1974] ICJ Rep 196, [54]; 196, [54]; *Fisheries Jurisdiction (United Kingdom of Great Britain and Northern Ireland v Iceland)* [1974] ICJ Rep 27, [62].

[120] The *South China Sea* Arbitration Award (Merits), n 1, [258].

[121] The *Eritrea/Yemen* arbitration, Award of 17 December 1999, (2001) 22 *RIAA* 335, 361, [109]. See also Memorial of the Philippines, vol I, 30 March 2014, [4.68].

[122] Art 2(3) of the Arbitral Agreement, The *Eritrea/Yemen* arbitration, n 121, Annex I – The Arbitral Agreement, 375.

[123] The *South China Sea* Arbitration Award (Merits), n 1, [259].

[124] ibid, [803].

In any case it is clear that China's claimed historic rights do not derive from the Convention.[125] Given that these rights are at variance with the rules of the Convention with regard to the EEZ and the continental shelf, and that China is bound by the Convention, there is no scope to argue that China can exercise the historic rights in the South China Sea under the Convention. The Tribunal thus concluded that

> upon China's accession to the Convention and its entry into force, any historic rights that China may have had to the living and non-living resources within the 'nine-dash line' were superseded, as a matter of law and as between the Philippines and China, by the limits of the maritime zones provided for by the Convention.[126]

According to the Tribunal's approach, states cannot validate historic rights that are at variance with the UNCLOS on the basis of a time element, that is historical evidence. Thus a time element has no role to play in this context.

D. Phase III: China's Exceptional Rights Since the Convention Entered into Force in 1996

The last issue to be addressed is whether China acquired rights or jurisdiction at variance with the Convention in the years since the Convention entered into force in 1996.[127] According to the Tribunal, '[i]nternational law is not static'.[128] The Tribunal thus refers to subsequent practice that may bear on the interpretation of treaty pursuant to Article 31 of the Vienna Convention on the Law of Treaties, or a formation of a new rule of customary international law that may emerge to modify the provisions of a treaty.[129]

In this regard, the Tribunal took the view that a claim of modification of the Convention by state practice would be required to fulfil the same requirements with regard to historic rights:

- the assertion by a state of a right at variance with the Convention;
- acquiescence therein by the other states parties; and

[125] This point was affirmed by some Chinese commentators. For instance, Keyuan Zou clearly stated that 'Since there are no express legal provisions in the LOS Convention that can be used as a legal basis to support China's U-shaped line, China is unable to use the LOS Convention to defend its unilateral line in the South China Sea': Keyuan Zou, n 16, 28–29. See also Jia Zhuguo Gao and Bing Bing Jia, n 13, 121.

[126] The *South China Sea* Arbitration Award (Merits), n 1, [262]. According to McDorman, 'the Tribunal clearly and correctly rejected the idea … that a State a party to the LOS Convention can have historic rights to fish or to the resources of the seafloor within the 200 nm zone of another State': TL McDorman, 'The South China Sea Arbitration: Selected Legal Notes' (2017) 21 *Asian Yearbook of International Law* 1, 15.

[127] The *South China Sea* Arbitration Award (Merits), n 1, [273].

[128] *Ibid*, [274].

[129] *Ibid*.

- the passage of sufficient time to establish beyond doubt the existence of both the right and a general acquiescence.[130]

The above requirements were not met, however. China's Law on the Exclusive Economic Zone and Continental Shelf refers to historic rights, but without anything that would enable another state to know the nature or extent of the rights claimed.[131] According to the Tribunal, the extent of the rights asserted within the 'nine-dash line' only became clear with China's Notes Verbales of May 2009. Since that date, China's claims have been clearly objected to by other states.[132] For instance, Viet Nam claimed:

> China's claim over the islands and adjacent waters in the Eastern Sea (South China Sea) as manifested in the map attached with Notes Verbale CLM/17/2009 and CLM/18/2009 has no legal, historical or factual basis, therefore is null and void.[133]

The Philippines also sent a diplomatic note to the United Nations and stated that China's claim to relevant waters as well as the seabed and subsoil thereof, as reflected in the so-called 'nine-dash line' map, had no basis in international law, specifically the Convention.[134] Furthermore, Indonesia stated that 'the so called "nine-dotted-lines map" as contained in the above circular note Number: CML/17/2009 dated 7th May 2009, clearly lacks international legal basis and is tantamount to upset the UNCLOS 1982'.[135]

Thus it must be admitted that there has been no acquiescence.[136] Accordingly, it cannot be considered that China acquired historic rights since the Convention entered into force in 1996. All in all, the Tribunal's examination of China's claims to historic rights in the three phases led to the conclusion that the China's claims were contrary to the Convention; and that the Convention superseded any historic rights, or other sovereign rights or jurisdiction, in excess of the limits imposed therein.[137]

[130] *Ibid*, [275].

[131] In 1998, Viet Nam already protested that 'it shall not recognize any so-called "historical interests" which are not in consistence with international law and violate the sovereignty, the sovereign rights of Viet Nam and Viet Nam's legitimate interests in its maritime zones and continental shelf in the Eastern Sea as mentioned in article 14 of the above-mentioned law [Law on the Exclusive Economic Zone and the Continental Shelf] of the People's Republic of China': (1998) 38 *Law of the Sea Bulletin* 55.

[132] ibid. See also the US Department of State, n 12, 22. For reactions of states to China's nine-dash line, see Keyuan Zou, n 16, 26–28.

[133] Permanent Mission of the Socialist Republic of Viet Nam to the United Nations, No 86/HC-2009, 8 May 2009, available at http://www.un.org/Depts/los/clcs_new/submissions_files/mysvnm33_09/vnm_chn_2009re_mys_vnm_e.pdf.

[134] Philippine Mission to the United Nations, 11-00494 No 000228, 5 April 2011, available at http://www.un.org/Depts/los/clcs_new/submissions_files/mysvnm33_09/phl_re_chn_2011.pdf.

[135] Permanent Mission of the Republic of Indonesia, No 480/POL-703/VII/10, 8 July 2010, available at http://www.un.org/Depts/los/clcs_new/submissions_files/mysvnm33_09/idn_2010re_mys_vnm_e.pdf.

[136] The *South China Sea* Arbitration Award (Merits), n 1, [275].

[137] ibid, [1203]B(2).

IV. CONCLUSIONS

This chapter has examined the Tribunal's view of China's claimed 'historic rights' to marine spaces encompassed by the 'nine-dash line' in its Award on the Merits. The principal points of this chapter may be summarised as follows.

First, according to the Tribunal, the concept of 'historic title' refers to historic sovereignty to land or maritime areas. In contrast, the concept of 'historic rights' includes limited rights that fall well short of a claim of sovereignty. In this respect, the concept of historic rights is distinct from that of historic title. As the exception to jurisdiction in Article 298(1)(a)(i) is limited to disputes involving historic titles, a dispute concerning historic rights to marine spaces is not precluded by that provision. The Tribunal's interpretation of the concepts of 'historic rights' and 'historic title' may have general implications beyond the Parties in dispute.[138]

Second, the Convention contains no express provisions preserving or protecting historic rights that are at variance with the Convention. Therefore, it is argued that the UNCLOS supersedes earlier rights and agreements to the extent of any incompatibility. Accordingly, the exercise of exceptional rights that are at variance with the Convention cannot be defended on the basis of the long course of history. In this sense, historic rights play a less prominent role after the entering into force of the Convention.[139]

Third, according to the Study prepared by the UN Secretariat, three requirements must be fulfilled in order to establish historic title or historic rights. They are:

- the exercise of authority over the area by the state claiming the historic right;
- the continuity of this exercise of authority; and
- the attitude of foreign states.

However, there are no clear rules with regard to the questions as to how long the exercise of authority must continue and at what time the opposition must occur in order to prevent the creation of historic rights. Hence the practical application of the requirements encounters difficulties. In this regard, it is noteworthy that the Tribunal, in its Arbitration Award on the Merits, did not take an approach of examining each and every requirement to establish the historic rights, and that it decided the validity of China's claimed historic rights by focusing on the freedom of the high seas and the exceptional nature of historic rights.

Fourth, the Tribunal, in its Arbitration Award on the Merits, took an approach that minimises the role of the historical element when determining

[138] Symmons, n 11, 125.

[139] Symmons thus argued that any historic rights of a non-sovereign and exceptional nature are 'today of little practical legal value to claimants'. CR Symmons, 'First Reactions to the *Philippines v China* Arbitration Award Concerning the Supposed Historic Claims of China in the South China Sea' (2016) 1 *Asia-Pacific Journal of Ocean Law and Policy* 260, 267.

the legality of China's claimed historic rights in the South China Sea. Given that rules concerning the elements are not wholly unambiguous, the Tribunal's approach seems to be an option well worth considering to avoid any controversy with regard to historical evidence.

Finally, when considering the historic rights, particular attention must be paid to the relativity of historic evidence in international law. Historic evidence is relative in the sense that it is limited in space and time. Thus the value of historic evidence in international law needs to be considered in relation to the paradigm or principle governing a certain *space* at a certain period of *time*. Prior to the introduction of the UNCLOS system, in particular prior to the Second World War, nearly all of the South China Sea formed part of the high seas.[140] Accordingly, the South China Sea was governed by the cardinal principle at that time, that is, the freedom of the seas. As human activities on the high seas are only part of the freedom of the seas, as the Tribunal ruled, they do not create any rights. After the introduction of the UNCLOS system, the value of historic evidence relies on its compatibility with the Convention. Historic evidence is also relative in the sense that its values relies on the reaction of other states. States are not bound by the unilateral conduct of a particular state. Therefore, to establish historic rights, it is necessary to prove that a particular state has historically sought to preclude or restrict the activities of the nationals of other states, and that those other states have acquiesced in such restrictions. In the South China Sea, there was no adequate evidence that proved the existence of such restrictions by China and acquiescence by other states. In summary, it can be said that the mere accumulation of events or episodes cannot, by itself, create historic rights in international law.

FURTHER READING

Beckman, R and Bernard, L, 'Disputed Areas in the South China Sea: Prospects for Arbitration or Advisory Opinion', *Paper at the Third International Workshop, South China Sea: Cooperation for Regional Security and Development*, Hanoi, 2011, 1–19, available at http://cil.nus.edu.sg/wp/wp-content/uploads/2009/09/Beckman-Bernard-Paper-DAV-Conf-3-5-Nov-2011.pdf.

Bouchez, LJ, *The Regime of Bays in International Law* (Sijthoff, 1964).

Caflisch, L, 'Les frontières, limites et délimitations internationales – Quelle importance aujourd'hui?' (2013) 368 *RCADI* 9.

Del Mar, K, 'Evidence in Territorial Disputes' in MG Kohen and M Hébité (eds), *Research Handbook on Territorial Disputes in International Law* (Edward Elgar Publishing, 2018) 417–36.

Dupuy, F and Dupuy, P-M, 'A Legal Analysis of China's Historic Rights Claim in the South China Sea' (2013) 107 *AJIL* 124.

[140] The *South China Sea* Arbitration Award (Merits), n 1, [269].

Dutton, PA, 'An Analysis of China's Claim to Historic Rights in the South China Sea' in Yann Huei Song and Keyuan Zou, *Major Law and Policy Issues in the South China Sea: European and American Perspectives* (Ashgate, 2014) 57–73.

Franckx, E and Benatar, M, 'Dots and Lines in the South China Sea: Insights from the Law of Map Evidence' (2012) 2 *Asian Journal of International Law* 89.

Ikeshima, T, 'China's Dashed Line in the South China Sea: Legal Limits and Future Prospects' (2013) 10 *Waseda Global Forum* 17.

Li Junming and Li Dexia, 'The Dotted Line on the Chinese Map of the South China Sea: A Note' (2003) 34 *ODIL* 287.

Kanehara, A, 'Validity of International Law in the South China Sea Arbitral Award (Merits)' (in Japanese) (2017) 659 *Kokusai Mondai* 25.

——, 'Validity of International Law over Historic Rights: The Arbitral Award (Merits) on the South China Sea Dispute' (2017) 61 *Sophia Law Review* 27.

Keyuan Zou, 'China's U-Shaped Line in the South China Sea Revisited' (2012) 43 *ODIL* 18.

——, 'Historic Rights in the South China Sea' in S Wu, M Valencia and Nong Hong (eds), *UN Convention on the Law of the Sea and the South China Sea* (Ashgate, 2015) 239–50.

Kopela, S, 'Historic Titles and Historic Rights in the Law of the Sea in the Light of the South China Sea Arbitration' (2017) 48 *ODIL* 181.

Ma Xinmin, 'Merits Award Relating to Historic Rights in the South China Sea Arbitration: An Appraisal' (2018) 8 *Asian Journal of International Law* 12.

McDorman, TL, 'Rights and Jurisdiction over Resources in the South China Sea: UNCLOS and the "Nine-dash Line"' in S Jayakumar, T Koh and RC Beckman (eds), *South China Sea Disputes and Law of the Sea* (Edward Elgar, 2014) 144–63.

——, 'The Law of the Sea Convention and the U-Shaped Line: Some Comments' in Shicun Wu and Keyuan Zou (eds), *Arbitration Concerning the South China Sea: Philippines Versus China* (Routledge, 2016) 147–55.

Miyoshi, M, 'China's "U-Shaped Line" Claim in the South China Sea: Any Validity Under International Law?' (2012) 43 *ODIL* 1.

O'Connell, DP, *The International Law of the Sea*, vol I, ed IA Shearer (Clarendon Press, 1982).

Sakamoto, S, 'Legal Status of the Nine-Dash Line: Historic Waters or Historic Rights' (2017) 69 *Doshisya Law Review* 1.

Sheng-Ti Gau, M, 'The U-Shaped Line and a Categorization of the Ocean Disputes in the South China Sea' (2012) 43 *ODIL* 57.

Symmons, CR, *Historic Waters in the Law of the Sea: A Modern Re-appraisal* (Brill/Nijhoff, 2008).

——, 'Historic Waters and Historic Rights in the South China Sea: A Critical Appraisal' in S Wu, M Valencia and Nong Hong (eds), *UN Convention on the Law of the Sea and the South China Sea* (Ashgate, 2015) 191–238.

——, 'First Reactions to the *Philippines v China* Arbitration Award Concerning the Supposed Historic Claims of China in the South China Sea' (2016) 1 *Asia-Pacific Journal of Ocean Law and Policy* 260.

——, 'Historic Rights in the Light of the Award in the South China Sea Arbitration: What Remains of the Doctrine Now?' in S Jayakumar et al (eds), *The South China Sea Arbitration: The Legal Dimension* (Edward Elgar, 2018) 101–27.

Tanaka, Y, 'Reflections on Historic Rights in the South China Sea Arbitration (Merits)' (2017) 32 *The International Journal of Marine and Coastal Law* 458.

Thirlway, H, 'Territorial Disputes and Their Resolution in the Recent Jurisprudence of the International Court of Justice' (2018) 31 *Leiden Journal of International Law* 117.

UN Secretariat, *Juridical Regime of Historic Waters including Historic Bays: Study Prepared by the Secretariat*, A/CN.4/143, (1962) 2 *Yearbook of the International Law Commission* 1.

United States Department of State, *Limits in the Seas No 143 China: Maritime Claims in the South China Sea*, 5 December 2014, 1–24.

Zhuguo Gao and Bing Bing Jia, 'The Nine-Dash Line in the South China Sea: History, Status, and Implications' (2013) 107 *AJIL* 98.

Zou Keyuan and Liu Xinchang, 'The U-Shaped Line and Historic Rights in the Philippines v China Arbitration Case' in Shicun Wu and Keyuan Zou (eds), *Arbitration Concerning the South China Sea: Philippines Versus China* (Routledge, 2016) 127–46.

4

The Legal Status of Maritime Features in the South China Sea[*]

I. INTRODUCTION

THIS CHAPTER EXAMINES the Tribunal's approach to the legal status of maritime features in the South China Sea. Many maritime features exist there. If these features could be regarded as 'fully entitled islands' and these islands belonged to China, China would be able to claim a 200-nautical mile exclusive economic zone (EEZ) around the islands. Accordingly, the legal status of marine features in the South China Sea constituted an issue of considerable importance in the *South China Sea* Arbitration. In this regard, the Philippines raised multiple issues,[1] including two principal issues. The first was whether a maritime feature is above water at high tide (ie a high-tide feature) and the second question was whether a high-tide feature can be considered as a 'fully entitled island'. This chapter seeks to address these two issues. In so doing, it will attempt to examine three main questions, with specific focus on the temporal elements:

(a) How is it possible to determine the legal status of maritime features above/below high tide?
(b) What is the territoriality of low-tide elevations? And is it possible to appropriate low-tide elevations in international law?
(c) How should Article 121(3) of the UNCLOS be interpreted?

Following this introduction, this chapter addresses the legal status of maritime features as above/below water at high tide (section II). It then discusses the legal status of maritime features as rocks/islands (section III). The chapter moves on to examine the Tribunal's interpretation and application of Article 121(3) of the UNCLOS (section IV), before offering conclusions (section V).

[*] This chapter is derived in part from an article by the author: Y Tanaka, 'Reflections on the Interpretation and Application of Article 121(3) in the *South China Sea* Arbitration (Merits)' (2017) 48 *Ocean Development and International Law* 365. Doi: 10.1080/00908320.2017.1349529.

[1] See the Philippines' Submissions Nos 3, 4, 5, 6 and 7. PCA Case No 2013–19, The *South China Sea* Arbitration Award (Merits) (hereinafter 'the *South China Sea* Arbitration Award (Merits)'), Judgment of 12 July 2016, [112].

II. THE LEGAL STATUS OF MARITIME FEATURES AS ABOVE/BELOW WATER AT HIGH TIDE

A. General Considerations

In its Submissions Nos 4 and 6, the Philippines claimed:

> (4) Mischief Reef, Second Thomas Shoal and Subi Reef are low-tide elevations that do not generate entitlement to a territorial sea, exclusive economic zone or continental shelf, and are not features that are capable of appropriation by occupation or otherwise;
>
> ...
>
> (6) Gaven Reef and McKennan Reef (including Hughes Reef) are low-tide elevations that do not generate entitlement to a territorial sea, exclusive economic zone or continental shelf, but their low-water line may be used to determine the baseline from which the breadth of the territorial sea of Namyit and Sin Cowe, respectively, is measured.[2]

The Philippines maintained that each of the five maritime features mentioned in its Submissions Nos 4 and 6 was a low-tide elevation.[3] China did not set out its position concerning all of the maritime features at issue in the arbitral proceedings. However, the Tribunal reiterated the view of China in its Award on Jurisdiction that 'a dispute is not negated by the absence of granular exchanges with respect to each and every individual feature.'[4]

In light of China's public statements and diplomatic correspondence, the Tribunal understood that China considered Huangyan Dao (Scarborough Shoal) to be an island and that Mischief Reef and Fiery Cross Reef were high-tide features, entitled to have at least a territorial sea.[5] In this connection, the Tribunal also referred to China's comments on the entitlements of the maritime features of the Spratly Islands, which stated that 'China's Nansha Islands is [sic] fully entitled to Territorial Sea, Exclusive Economic Zone (EEZ) and Continental Shelf.'[6]

[2] The *South China Sea* Arbitration Award (Merits), n 1, [281]. The Philippines regarded Namyit and Sin Cowe as 'rocks' occupied by Viet Nam. Memorial of the Philippines, vol I, 265, [7.145]. For a detailed description of maritime features in the South China Sea, see JM Van Dyke and DL Bennett, 'Islands and the Delimitation of Ocean Space in the South China Sea' (1993) 10 *Ocean Yearbook* 54.

[3] The *South China Sea* Arbitration Award (Merits), n 1, [292].

[4] PCA Case No 2013–19. The *South China Sea* Arbitration (Jurisdiction and Admissibility) (hereinafter 'the *South China Sea* Arbitration Award on Jurisdiction'), 29 October 2015, [170].

[5] ibid, [299]–[300]. In this regard, the Tribunal referred to the following documents: Department of Foreign Affairs, Republic of the Philippines, *Record of Proceedings: 10th Philippines–China Foreign Ministry Consultations* (30 July 1998); Ministry of Foreign Affairs, People's Republic of China, *Chinese Foreign Ministry Statement Regarding Huangyandao* (22 May 1997); Note Verbale from the Embassy of the People's Republic of China in Manila to the Department of Foreign Affairs, Republic of the Philippines, No 15 (PG)-214 (28 June 2015).

[6] ibid, [301]. See also Note Verbale from the Permanent Mission of the People's Republic of China to the Secretary-General of the United Nations, No CML/8/2011 (14 April 2011). Reproduced in the Philippines' Memorial, vol VI, Annex 201.

In its Award on Jurisdiction, the Tribunal ruled that these Submissions did not reflect disputes concerning sovereignty over maritime features. It also held that these Submissions did not concern maritime boundary delimitation. It thus concluded that, subject to a caveat with respect to the possible effects of any overlapping entitlements, it had jurisdiction to address the matters raised in the Philippines' Submissions Nos 4 and 6.[7] Furthermore, as the Tribunal observed, the question of whether maritime features were above or below water at high tide was also implicated by the Philippines' Submissions Nos 3 and 7. The Tribunal thus decided to examine the status of all 10 features identified in the Philippines' Submissions.[8]

Before examining the maritime features, it is necessary to clarify the terminology. According to the Tribunal, the generic category of features that meet the definition of an island in Article 121(1) is 'high-tide features'. The term 'rocks' refers to high-tide features that 'cannot sustain human habitation or economic life of their own', and which are disqualified from generating an EEZ or continental shelf pursuant to Article 121(3). High-tide features that are not rocks and which enjoy the same entitlements as other land territory pursuant to Article 121(2) are called 'fully entitled islands'. It follows that 'rocks' and 'fully entitled islands' are both sub-sets of the broader category of 'high-tide features'. A feature that is exposed at low tide but covered with water at high tides is referred to as a 'low-tide elevation'. Maritime features that are fully submerged even at low tide are referred to as 'submerged features'.[9]

B. Interpretation of Article 13 of the UNCLOS

Under Article 13(1) of the UNCLOS, a low-tide elevation is 'a naturally formed area of land which is surrounded by and above water at low tide but submerged at high tide'.[10] Three issues arise with regard to Article 13.

The first issue concerns the condition regarding natural formation. This condition is included in the definition of both a low-tide elevation and an island in Articles 13 and 121(1), respectively. In the *South China Sea* arbitration this point is crucial, since many of the features in the South China Sea have been subject to substantial human modification as large islands.[11] In this regard,

[7] The *South China Sea* Arbitration Award (Jurisdiction and Admissibility), n 4, [401] and [403].

[8] The *South China Sea* Arbitration Award (Merits), n 1, [282].

[9] ibid, [280]. The terms 'high-tide features', 'fully entitled islands' and 'submerged features' are not used in the UNCLOS.

[10] The ICJ has held that Art 13 reflects customary international law. *Maritime Delimitation and Territorial Questions between Qatar and Bahrain (Qatar v Bahrain)*, Judgment, [2001] ICJ Rep 40, 100, [201]; *Territorial and Maritime Dispute (Nicaragua v Colombia)*, Judgment, [2012] ICJ Rep 624, 693, [182].

[11] The *South China Sea* Arbitration Award (Merits), n 1, [306]. See also ibid, [976].

importantly, the Tribunal stressed that '[a]s a matter of law, human modification cannot change the seabed into a low-tide elevation or a low-tide elevation into an island'.[12]

Second, the meaning of 'high tide' is open to question. Whereas the height datum selected by the Philippines was 'Mean High Water', Chinese charts referred to 'high tide' as comprising 'Mean High Water Springs' or 'Mean Higher High Waters'. In this regard, the Tribunal took a flexible approach, stating that 'either Mean Higher High Water or Mean High Water Springs would be an appropriate approximation of "high tide" if determined on the basis of Chinese nautical charts'.[13] In any event, the Tribunal considered that '[u]ltimately, however, the tidal range in the South China Sea is comparatively small and the selection of a vertical datum will, in most instances, make no difference regarding the status of a feature'.[14] The approach of the Tribunal contrasted with that taken by the ICJ in the *Nicaragua v Colombia* case. There, the Court applied the Highest Astronomical Tide (HAT) as the vertical datum when examining the status of Quitasueño. As noted, however, the Tribunal, in its Arbitration Award (Merits), did not follow this approach, stating that the International Hydrographic Organisation specifically recommends that Highest Astronomical Tide be used 'as the datum for vertical clearances (*ie*, bridges), but only for this purpose'.[15] In the view of the Tribunal, neither the UNCLOS nor customary international law specified any particular high-water datum.[16] Accordingly, the Tribunal held that 'States are free under the Convention to claim a high-tide feature or island on the basis of any high-water datum that reasonably corresponds to the ordinary meaning of the term "high tide" in Articles 13 and 121.'[17] As commenters indicate, the sea level used as a reference in charts has evolved over time.[18] The sea level might also alter due to changes in the environment, such as climate

[12] ibid, [305].

[13] ibid, [313]. However, the Mean Higher High Water and Mean High Water Spring are very different means. In this regard, see Y Lyons, Luu Quang Hung and P Tkalich, 'Determining High-tide Features (or Islands) in the South China Sea under Article 121(1): a Legal and Oceanography Perspective' in S Jayakumar et al (eds), *The South China Sea Arbitration: The Legal Dimension* (Edward Elgar, 2018) 128, 135.

[14] The *South China Sea* Arbitration Award (Merits), n 1, [313]. Yet some commentators cast doubt on whether the difference between Mean Higher Water Springs and Mean Higher High Water remains less significant in the context of low-lying atolls. Lyons, Luu Quang Hung and Tkalich, n 13, 136–37.

[15] The *South China Sea* Arbitration Award (Merits), n 1, [310].

[16] ibid, [311]. SD Murphy, 'International Law Relating to Islands' (2017) 386 *RCADI* 9, 44. In the United States v Alaska case of 1997, the Special Master's Report indicated that 'high tide' was understood as 'mean high water' according to well-established US practice. The US Supreme Court would seem to be supportive of this view. Report of the Special Master, J Keith Mann, March 1996, No 84, Original, the Supreme Court of the United States, 234–36; 521 United States Reports, Cases Adjudged in the Supreme Court at October Term 1996 (Washington DC, 2000) 30–32. However, this does not mean that it is an internationally accepted standard.

[17] The *South China Sea* Arbitration Award (Merits), n 1, [311].

[18] Lyons, Luu Quang Hung and Tkalich, n 13, 142.

change. Here one may find the impact of time elements on the identification of low-tide elevations.

The third issue relates to the territoriality of low-tide elevations.[19] In this regard, the Tribunal, in its Award on the Merits, took the view that low-tide elevations form part of the territorial sea or continental shelf of coastal states, stating that:

> With respect to the status of low-tide elevations, the Tribunal considers that notwithstanding the use of the term 'land' in the physical description of a low-tide elevation, such low-tide elevations do not form part of the land territory of a State in the legal sense. Rather they form part of the submerged landmass of the State and fall within the legal regimes for the territorial sea or continental shelf, as the case may be.[20]

The Tribunal thus confirmed the view of the ICJ in the *Nicaragua v Colombia* case that 'low-tide elevations cannot be appropriated'.[21]

The Tribunal's view must be examined from the perspective of the development of case law on this subject. The leading case on this matter is *Qatar v Bahrain* (Merits) (2001). There, sovereignty over a low-tide elevation, Fasht ad Dibal, was in issue. Whereas Qatar argued that Fasht ad Dibal as a low-tide elevation could not be appropriated, Bahrain contended that low-tide elevations by their very nature were territory, and thus could be appropriated in accordance with the criteria that pertain to the acquisition of territory.[22] However, the ICJ was not persuaded by Bahrain's argument. According to the Court, it was only in the context of the law of the sea that a number of permissive rules had been established with regard to low-tide elevations situated a relatively short distance from the coast.[23] A low-tide elevation situated beyond the limits of territorial sea cannot have a territorial sea of its own. This means that a low-tide elevation *per se* does not generate the same rights as an island or other territory. The Court accordingly considered that low-tide elevations cannot, from the viewpoint of the acquisition of sovereignty, be fully assimilated with islands or other land territory.[24]

To decide on sovereignty over a low-tide elevation, the ICJ provisionally drew two hypothetical equidistance lines. In either hypothesis, Fasht ad Dibal would largely or totally fall on the Qatari side of the adjusted equidistance line. In conclusion, the Court ruled that 'As Fasht ad Dibal is thus situated in the territorial sea of Qatar, it falls for that reason under the sovereignty of that

[19] For an analysis of this issue, see Y Tanaka, 'Low-Tide Elevations in International Law of the Sea: Selected Issues'(2006) 20 *Ocean Yearbook* 189, 198–207.

[20] The *South China Sea* Arbitration Award (Merits), n 1, [309]. See also Memorial of the Philippines, vol I, 139–40, [586].

[21] The *South China Sea* Arbitration Award (Merits), n 1, [309]; *Nicaragua v Colombia*, Judgment, n 10, [2012] ICJ Rep 624, 641, [26].

[22] *Qatar v Bahrain* (Merits), n 10, [2001] ICJ Rep 100, [200].

[23] ibid, 101–02, [205].

[24] ibid, 102, [206]–[207].

State.'[25] It follows that in the *Qatar v Bahrain* case (Merits), the ICJ considered a low-tide elevation to be part of the seabed, not terrestrial territory.

The dictum in the *Qatar v Bahrain* judgment was confirmed by the ICJ in the 2008 *Malaysia/Singapore* case.[26] There, the Court noted that a low-tide elevation called South Ledge fell within the apparently overlapping territorial waters generated by the mainland of Malaysia, Pedra Branca and Middle Rocks. The Court thus found that sovereignty over South Ledge belonged to the state in whose territorial waters it was located.[27] In so ruling, the Court did not assimilate low-tide elevations to land territory or islands.[28] As noted, this position was confirmed by the ICJ in the 2012 *Nicaragua v Colombia* case.[29] The ICJ's view was echoed by Sir Gerald Fitzmaurice, stating that:

> It is a well-established rule of international law that territory, in order to be capable of appropriation in sovereignty, must be situated permanently above high-water mark, and not consist e.g. of a drying-rock, only uncovered at low tide, unless it is already within the territorial waters of appropriable territory.[30]

As provided in Article 13(1) of the UNCLOS, low-tide elevations can be used as basepoints only if situated within the breadth of the territorial sea.[31] In other words, low-tide elevations generate territorial seas on the basis of the fact that they are already under the territorial sovereignty of coastal states. However, the fact that low-tide elevations may be used as basepoints does not necessarily

[25] ibid, 109, [220].

[26] *Case Concerning Sovereignty over Pedra Branca/Pulau Batu Puteh, Middle Rocks and South Ledge (Malaysia/Singapore)*, Judgment, [2008] ICJ Rep 12, 100–01, [296].

[27] ibid, 101, [297]–[299].

[28] Y Tanaka, 'Passing of Sovereignty: the *Malaysia/Singapore* Territorial Dispute before the ICJ' (2008) 3 *Hague Justice Journal* 5, 11.

[29] *Nicaragua v Colombia*, Judgment, n 10, [2012] ICJ Rep 624, 641, [26]. However, China, in its Position Paper, criticised the ICJ's view. According to the Position Paper, the ICJ 'did not point to any legal basis for this conclusory statement. Nor did it touch upon the legal status of low-tide elevations as components of an archipelago, or sovereignty or claims of sovereignty that may have long existed over such features in a particular maritime area'. Position Paper of the Government of the People's Republic of China on the Matter of Jurisdiction in the South China Sea Arbitration Initiated by the Republic of the Philippines, 7 December 2014, para 25, available at http://www.fmprc.gov.cn/mfa_eng/zxxx_662805/t1217147.shtml.

[30] G Fitzmaurice, *The Law and Procedure of the International Court of Justice*, vol I (Cambridge University Press, 1993) 286–87.

[31] It may be relevant to recall that Basis of Discussion No 14 at the 1930 Hague Conference for the Codification of International Law already stated that 'In order that an island may have its own territorial waters, it is necessary that it should be permanently above the level of high tide. In order that an island lying within the territorial waters of another island or of the mainland may be taken into account in determining the belt of such territorial waters, it is sufficient for the island to be above water at low tide.' Reproduced in S Rosenne (ed), *League of Nations: Conference for the Codification of International Law 1930*, vol II (Oceana, 1975) 272. See also C Symmons, 'Some Problems Relating to the Definition of "Insular Formations" in International Law: Islands and Low-Tide Elevations', *Maritime Briefing* 1 No 5 (International Boundaries Research Unit, 1995) 14–15; G Guillaume, 'Les haute-fonds découvrants en droit international' in *La mer et son droit, Mélanges offerts à Laurent Lucchini et Jean-Pierre Que'neudec* (Pedone, 2003) 287, 288.

suggest that they enjoy the same status as islands. Furthermore, under Article 7(4) of the UNCLOS:

> Straight baselines shall not be drawn to and from low-tide elevations, unless lighthouses or similar installations which are permanently above sea level have been built on them or except in instances where the drawing of baselines to and from such elevations has received general international recognition.[32]

This provision also shows that low-tide elevations should be distinguished from islands.[33] It appears that the legal distinction between low-tide elevations and land territory is currently well established in international law.

C. Evidence on the Status of Maritime Features as Above/Below Water at High Tide

A particular issue that arises in this context concerns evidence on the legal status of maritime features. According to the Tribunal, '[a]s a general matter, the most accurate determination of whether a particular feature is or is not above water at high tide would be based on a combination of methods, including potentially direct, in-person observation covering an extended period of time across a range of weather and tidal conditions.'[34] Yet this approach is impossible where, as in the South China Sea, human modifications have obscured the original status of a maritime feature, or where political considerations restrict in-person observation. In such circumstances, the legal status of maritime features must be determined on the basis of the 'best available evidence of the *previous* status of the feature'.[35]

As for evidence on the status of maritime features, the Philippines relied heavily on remote sensing through satellite imagery.[36] However, the Tribunal did not accept the degree of accuracy or certainty that the Philippines gave to

[32] By applying this provision, the Court of Arbitration in the *Eritrea/Yemen* dispute (Second Phase) ruled that Eritrea could not use Negileh Rock as a straight baseline of the territorial sea since the rock appeared not to be above water at any state of the tide. The *Eritrea/Yemen Arbitration* (Second Phase: Maritime Delimitation), Award of 17 December 1999, (2001) 22 *RIAA* 335, 367–368, [141]–[146].

[33] The 1958 Geneva Convention on the Territorial Sea and the Contiguous Zone contained a similar provision: 'Baselines shall not be drawn to and from low-tide elevations, unless lighthouses or similar installations which are permanently above sea level have been built on them' (Art 4(3)). Bowett indicates that, in relation to the drawing of baselines under the straight baselines method provided for in Art 4 of the 1958 Geneva Convention on the Territorial Sea, the assimilation of low-tide elevations to islands did not occur. DW Bowett, *The Legal Regime of Islands in International Law* (Oceana, 1979) 12.

[34] The *South China Sea* Arbitration Award (Merits), n 1, [321]. In this regard, the ICJ, in the *Nicaragua v Colombia* case ([2012] ICJ Rep 644, [36]), ruled that the Court 'has to make sure that it has before it evidence sufficient to satisfy that a maritime feature meets the test of being above water at high tide'.

[35] The *South China Sea* Arbitration Award (Merits), n 1, [306] (original emphasis).

[36] ibid, [322].

such imagery, since the resolution of the satellite imagery being used by the Philippines was insufficient to establish the presence or absence of high-tide features.[37] Instead, the Tribunal considered that 'more convincing evidence concerning the status of features in the South China Sea is to be found in nautical charts, records of surveys, and sailing directions.'[38] Specifically the Tribunal relied particularly on:

- a survey conducted by the British Royal Navy between 1862 and 1868;
- surveys conducted by the British Royal Navy and the Imperial Japanese Navy in the 1920s and 1930s; and
- sailing directions.[39]

On the basis of the above materials, the Tribunal ruled that the following features were regarded as high-tide features:

(a) Scarborough Shoal;
(b) Cuarteron Reef;
(c) Fiery Cross Reef;
(d) Johnson Reef;
(e) McKennan Reef; and
(f) Gaven Reef (North).

In contrast, the following features were regarded as low-tide elevations:

(a) Hughes Reef;
(b) Gaven Reef (South);
(c) Subi Reef;
(d) Mischief Reef; and
(e) Second Thomas Shoal.[40]

These low-tide elevations do not generate entitlements to a territorial sea, EEZ or continental shelf.[41]

It was noteworthy that the Tribunal independently obtained evidence to decide the legal status of maritime features. The Tribunal's own inquiry relied on Article 22(2) of the Rules of Procedure, which provided that the Tribunal may 'take all appropriate measures in order to establish the facts'. The active use of its power of inquiry seems to be in contrast with the practice of the ICJ, which has used its power to seek evidence in a more modest manner.[42] In the

[37] ibid; see also at [326].
[38] ibid, [327].
[39] ibid, [329]–[332].
[40] ibid, [382]–[383] and [1203]B(3), (4), (5).
[41] ibid.
[42] A Riddell and B Plant, *Evidence before the International Court of Justice* (British Institute of International and Comparative Law, 2009) 70; M Benzing, 'Evidentiary Issues' in

South China Sea arbitration, arguably the Tribunal's own inquiry was relevant because of the inadequacy of the evidence submitted by the Philippines and the lack of materials deriving from the non-appearance of the respondent state.[43] However, the application of the Tribunal's approach needs careful consideration in two respects.

First, the Tribunal placed much weight on historical records when deciding the legal status of maritime features as above/below high tide. In this regard, it must be remembered that the Tribunal took this approach in the particular situation where human modifications had already obscured the original status of a maritime feature. Where a maritime feature maintains its original form, the legal status of the maritime feature needs to be ascertained on the basis of the current form. In fact, when examining whether Quitasueño is above water at high tide, the ICJ stressed that 'what is relevant to the issue before it is the contemporary evidence'.[44] Accordingly, the relevance of historical records may vary according to particular situations.

Second, there is no guarantee that historical records are always clear and consistent. In some cases, the description of a maritime feature may differ according to the records used. With regard to Mischief Reef, for instance, the Tribunal referred to five different records:

- the surveys by HMS *Herald* in 1933 and 1938;
- Imperial Japanese Navy Chart No 525;
- China's Chart No 18500; and
- Chinese Navy Headquarters sailing directions (2011).

Yet the description contained in the records was inconsistent with regard to Mischief Reef. Despite the absence of any reference to a high-tide feature at Mischief Reef, HMS *Herald*'s description referred to a drying rock with a height of five feet above Mean Low Water Springs.[45] Imperial Japanese Navy Chart No 525 showed no feature above water at high tide.[46] In contrast, China's Chart No 18500 depicted a height of one metre above Mean Sea Level at the location of that rock. Chinese Navy Headquarters sailing directions described rocks exposed at half-tide.[47]

A Zimmermann et al (eds), *The Statute of the International Court of Justice: A Commentary*, 2nd edn (Oxford University Press, 2012) 1238; T Davenport, 'Procedural Issues Arising from China's Non-participation in the South China Sea Arbitration' in Jayakumar et al (eds), n 13, 65, 96.

[43] See also Y Lee-Iwamoto, 'Legal Implications of the Awards and Procedure in the South China Sea Arbitration' (in Japanese) (2018) 177 (2) *The Journal of International Law and Diplomacy* 30, 39–41.

[44] *Nicaragua v Colombia*, Judgment, n 10, 644, [36].

[45] The *South China Sea* Arbitration Award (Merits), n 1, [374].

[46] ibid, [375].

[47] ibid, [376]–[377].

The Tribunal took the view that the clear evidence from direct observations – to 'drying rocks' by HMS *Herald* and to rocks exposed 'during half-tide' in the Chinese sailing directions – was more convincing. In this regard, the Tribunal considered it inconceivable that a high-tide rock or feature could have been overlooked or gone unmentioned in light of the amount of time spent by HMS *Herald* in surveying Mischief Reef and the knowledge of tidal conditions apparent in the above description.[48] Yet this seems to be a matter of speculation. In any event, where the description of a maritime feature varies according to survey records, the relevance of the records is subject to the judgment of the Tribunal.

III. THE LEGAL STATUS OF MARITIME FEATURES AS ROCKS/ISLANDS

A. General Considerations

The second question concerns the legal status of maritime features as rocks or islands for the purposes of Article 121 of the UNCLOS. The question relates to the Philippines' Submissions Nos 3, 5 and 7, respectively. The Philippines submitted that:

> (3) Scarborough Shoal generates no entitlement to an exclusive economic zone or continental shelf;
>
> ...
>
> (5) Mischief Reef and Second Thomas Shoal are part of the exclusive economic zone and continental shelf of the Philippines;
>
> ...
>
> (7) Johnson Reef, Cuarteron Reef and Fiery Cross Reef generate no entitlement to an exclusive economic zone or continental shelf.[49]

Related to this, the Philippines claimed that all four of the high-tide features identified in its Submissions Nos 3 and 7 – Scarborough Shoal, Johnson Reef, Cuarteron Reef and Fiery Cross Reef – are rocks under Article 121(3) of the Convention.[50] According to the Philippines, none of the features in the Spratly Islands is capable, based on its own natural elements, of sustaining both human habitation and economic life of its own.[51] To support its claim, the Philippines submitted expert analyses of the natural conditions of Itu Aba.[52] According to the Philippines, maritime features in the South China Sea generate only the territorial sea (see Figure 4.1).

[48] ibid, [377].
[49] ibid, [385].
[50] ibid, [423].
[51] ibid, [426]. See also Memorial of the Philippines, vol I, [5.96]–[5.114].
[52] See, for instance, Dr RT Bailey, *Groundwater Resources Analysis of Itu Aba* (9 March 2016) (Annex 878); Dr RT Bailey, *Supplemental Report on Groundwater Resources Analysis of Itu Aba*

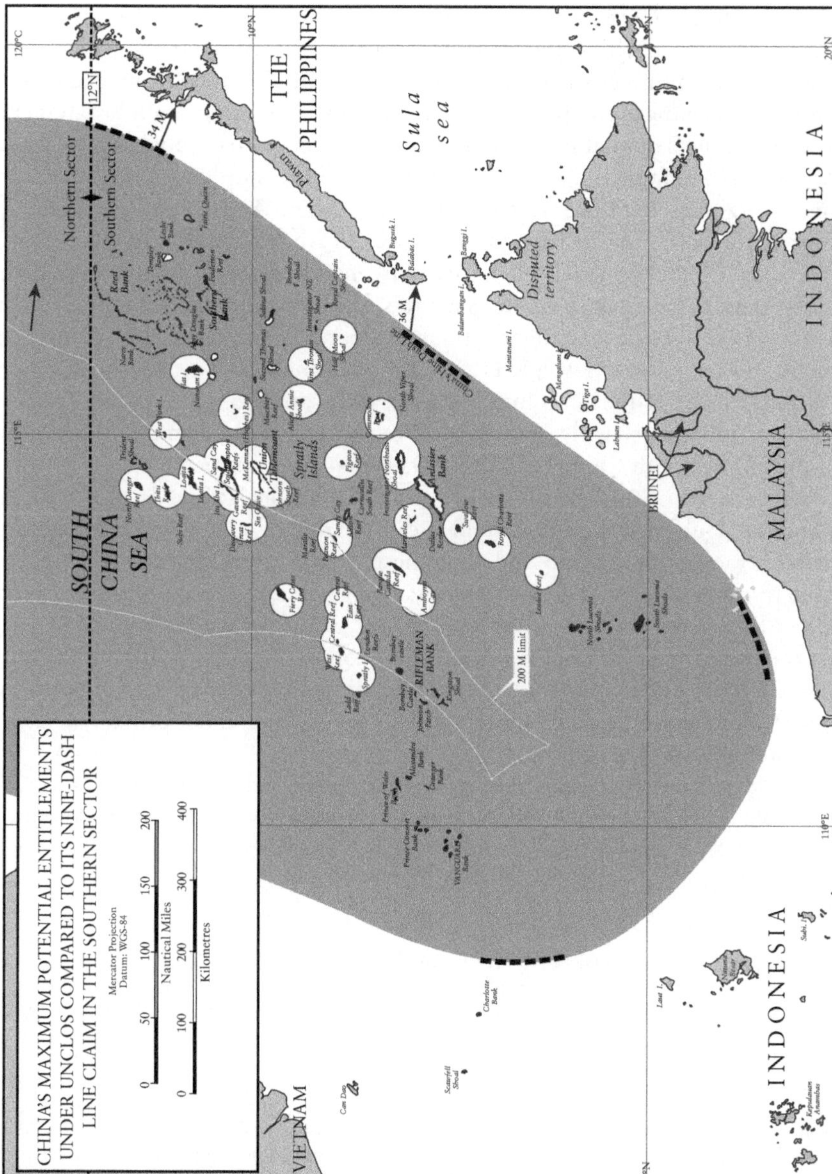

Figure 4.1 China's maximum potential of entitlements under the UNCLOS compared to its nine-dash line claim in the southern sectors

Source: Memorial of the Philippines, Figure 4.2; Award on Jurisdiction, 51. Reproduced with permission of the Permanent Court of Arbitration (copyright holder).

Even though China did not clarify its position on the application of Article 121(3) to each of the maritime features identified in the Philippines' Submissions, China's position on this subject can be discerned from its own law, diplomatic exchanges and public statements.[53] By examining China's statements and actions, the Tribunal found that China considers Scarborough Shoal, which is known as 'Huangyan Dao' in China, to be a fully entitled island.[54] Furthermore, in light of the statement of China's Foreign Ministry Spokesperson of 3 June 2016, China can be thought to regard Itu Aba as a fully entitled island.[55] In the view of the Tribunal, China had also made general statements that the Spratly Islands group as a whole generates full maritime entitlements, while it had not made specific statements about the status of Johnson Reef, Cuarteron Reef, Fiery Cross Reef, Gaven Reef (North) or McKennan Reef for the purposes of Article 121(3) of the Convention.[56] Overall it can be observed that the views of the parties were sharply divided with regard to the legal status of maritime features in the South China Sea and/or their maritime entitlements.

In its Award on Jurisdiction and Admissibility, the Tribunal ruled that the Philippines' Submissions Nos 3 and 7 did not relate to a dispute concerning sovereignty over the feature and that these Submissions did not concern sea boundary delimitation. The Tribunal thus concluded that it had jurisdiction to address the matters raised in the Philippines' Submissions Nos 3 and 7.[57] On the other hand, the Tribunal reserved a decision on its jurisdiction with respect to the Philippines' Submission No 5 for consideration in conjunction with the merits of the Philippines' claims, since this Submission did not possess an exclusively preliminary character.[58]

The legal status of maritime features is governed by Article 121 of the UNCLOS. Article 121 contains three provisions that set out a definition (paragraph 1), a general rule (paragraph 2) and an exception to that general rule (paragraph 3).[59] A contentious issue arises with regard to the interpretation

(20 April 2016) (Annex 911); Dr PP Motavalli, *Soil Resources and Potential Self-Sustaining Agricultural Production on Itu Aba* (9 March 2016) (Annex 879); Dr PP Motavalli, *Second Supplemental Expert Report on Soil Resources and Potential Self-Sustaining Agricultural Production on Itu Aba* (2 June 2016) (Annex 934). These reports are available at https://pca-cpa.org/en/cases/7/.

[53] The *South China Sea* Arbitration Award, n 1, [450].

[54] ibid, [465].

[55] ibid, [466]. Related to this, Taiwan also asserted that Itu Aba indisputably qualified as an 'island' under Art 121. Ministry of Foreign Affairs of the Republic of China (Taiwan), *Statement on the South China Sea*, 7 July 2015, Annex 656 and *ROC Government Reiterates Its Position on South China Sea Issues*, 31 October 2015, Annex 657 of Supplemental Documents of the Philippines, vol I, 19 November 2015, available on the PCA website, n 1. See also the *South China Sea* Arbitration Award, n 1, [449].

[56] The *South China Sea* Arbitration Award, n 1, [469]–[472].

[57] The *South China Sea* Arbitration Award (Jurisdiction and Admissibility), n 4, [400] and [404].

[58] ibid, [402].

[59] For a detailed examination of legislative history of Art 121, see R Kolb, 'L'interprétation de l'article 121, paragraph 3, de la Convention de Montego Bay sur le droit de la mer: les "roches qui ne se prêtent pas à l'habitation humaine ou à une vie économique propre …"' (1994) 40 *Annuaire Français de Droit International* 876; MH Nordquist, 'Textual Interpretation of Article 121 in

and application of Article 121(3), which reads 'Rocks which cannot sustain human habitation or economic life of their own shall have no exclusive economic zone or continental shelf.' The Convention contains no definition of 'rocks'. In the view of the Tribunal, the word 'rock' under Article 121(3) is not limited to maritime features composed of solid rock. Accordingly, the geological and geomorphological characteristics of a high-tide feature are not relevant to its classification pursuant to Article 121(3).[60] In this regard, the Tribunal made it clear that '[w]ithin Article 121, rocks are a category of island'.[61] The Tribunal's view is supported by commentators. For instance, Gjetnes has argued that 'a rock is a particular type of island' and 'the purely geological definition of rock must be rejected in the interpretation of Article 121(3)'.[62] This view was echoed by Kolb.[63] Furthermore, Lowe clearly stated that '[r]ocks *are* islands; they are a sub-category of "islands"'.[64] It follows that the definition provided in Article 121(1) also applies to 'rocks'.[65]

B. Interpretation of Article 121(3) of the UNCLOS

i. Qualitative Requirements

In interpreting Article 121(3) of the UNCLOS, the Tribunal focused on two types of requirements: qualitative and temporal requirements. Article 121(3) contains two qualitative requirements for maritime features to be fully entitled islands: the capacity to sustain 'human habitation' and 'economic life of their own'. The capacity of a feature must be objectively determined.[66] A pivotal question

the UN Convention on the Law of the Sea' in HP Hestermeyer et al (eds), *Coexistence, Cooperation and Solidarity: Liber Amicorum Rüdiger Wolfrum*, vol I (Leiden, Brill/Njihoff, 2012) 991; MH Nordquist, 'UNCLOS Article 121 and Itu Aba in the South China Sea Final Award: A Correct Interpretation?' in Jayakumar et al (eds), n 13, 176, 179–84; and United Nations, Office for Ocean Affairs and the Law of the Sea, *The Law of the Sea: Régime of Islands, Legislative History of Part VIII (Article 121) of the United Nations Convention on the Law of the Sea* (United Nations, 1988).

60 The *South China Sea* Arbitration Award (Merits), n 1, [540].

61 ibid, [481].

62 M Gjetnes, 'The Spratlys: Are They Rocks or Islands?' (2001) 32 *ODIL* 191, 193.

63 Kolb, n 59, 904. See also B Kwiatkowska and AHA Soons, 'Entitlement to Maritime Areas of Rocks Which Cannot Sustain Human Habitation or Economic Life of Their Own' (1990) 21 *The Netherlands Yearbook of International Law* 139, 151; and G Xue, 'How Much Can A Rock Get? A Reflection from the Okinotorishima Rocks' in MH Nordquist, et al (eds), *The Law of the Sea Convention: US Accession and Globalization* (Brill/Nijhoff, 2012) 341, 355.

64 Presentation by Professor Lowe in the *Maritime Delimitation in the Black Sea (Romania v Ukraine)*, Verbatim Record, CR 2008/20, 4 September 2008, 41, para 11 (original emphasis), available on the ICJ website at http://www.icj-cij.org/en.

65 Gjetnes, n 62, 194. In this connection, the ICJ, in Nicaragua v Colombia, stressed the integrity of the three provisions of Art 121. According to the Court, 'the legal régime of islands set out in UNCLOS Article 121 forms an indivisible régime, all of which (as Colombia and Nicaragua recognise) has the status of customary international law': [2012] ICJ Rep 624, 674, [139].

66 The *South China Sea* Arbitration Award (Merits), n 1, [545].

is whether, objectively, the feature is 'apt, able to, or lends itself to human habitation or economic life', not whether the feature actually does sustain human habitation or an economic life.[67] In considering this question, four issues merit discussion.

The first issue is whether the requirement of 'human habitation' and that of 'an economic life of their own' must be met for a feature to be entitled to an EEZ and continental shelf at the same time (cumulative interpretation), or whether one will suffice (disjunctive interpretation). The Philippines urged the Tribunal to adopt the cumulative interpretation, stating that 'As a matter of logic, the combination of a negative verb form with the disjunctive "or" creates a cumulative requirement. It is, in essence, a double negative.'[68] This is not an isolated view. For instance, Van Dyke, Morgan and Gurish regarded the phrase 'capable of sustaining human habitation or economic life of their own' as covering a single concept.[69] This view is also supported by Kolb[70] and Franckx.[71]

However, the Tribunal declined to adopt the cumulative interpretation, stating that 'the ability to sustain *either* human habitation *or* an economic life of its own would suffice to entitle a high-tide feature to an exclusive economic zone and continental shelf'.[72] The Tribunal's disjunctive interpretation relies on its analysis of the structure of the language of Article 121(3). The Tribunal focused on the parallel structure of a single sentence of this provision. It noted that the first clause of Article 121(3) is not the only negation of a disjunction within the provision and that the same construction is repeated in the second half of the paragraph, which provides that such rocks 'shall have no exclusive economic zone *or* continental shelf'.[73] According to the Tribunal, the logical construction is that 'a rock which fails to meet the criteria of the paragraph shall have no exclusive economic zone [and shall have] no continental shelf.'[74] In the view of the Tribunal, it is not plausible that the drafters of the Convention would have employed a strictly logical construction for one clause within the parallel structure of a single sentence and departed from such construction for the other. The Tribunal thus interpreted that a rock would be disentitled from an EEZ and continental shelf only if it were to lack both the capacity to sustain human habitation and the capacity to sustain an economic life of its own.

[67] ibid, [483].

[68] Presentation by Mr Martin, Merits Hearing (Day 2), 25 November 2015, 84; Memorial of the Philippines, vol I, 145, [5.103].

[69] JM Van Dyke, JR Morgan and J Gurish, 'The Exclusive Economic Zone of the Northwestern Hawaiian Islands: When Do Uninhabited islands Generate an EEZ?' (1988) 25 *San Diego Law Review* 425, 437.

[70] Kolb, n 59, 906.

[71] E Franckx, 'The Regime of Islands and Rocks' in DJ Attard, M Fitzmaurice and NA Martínex Gutiérrez (eds), *The IMLI Manual on International Maritime Law*, vol I: *The Law of the Sea* (Oxford University Press, 2014) 99, 117.

[72] The *South China Sea* Arbitration Award (Merits), n 1, [544]. See also ibid, [496].

[73] Emphasis added.

[74] ibid, [495].

In other words, 'an island that is able to sustain either human habitation or an economic life of its own is entitled to both an exclusive economic zone *and* a continental shelf.'[75] In reality, however, it appears difficult to imagine economic life totally detached from human life. Therefore the Tribunal went on to add that as a practical matter, a maritime feature will ordinarily possess an economic life of its own only if it is also inhabited by a stable human community,[76] and that the two requirements will 'in most instances go hand in hand'.[77] In so stating, it appears that the Tribunal attempted to reconcile the disjunctive interpretation with the cumulative interpretation at the practical level. In this sense, the Tribunal's interpretation is close to a compromise between the two interpretations in reality.

The second issue pertains to the requirement for an island to be 'naturally formed'. In this regard, the Philippines claimed that a feature's capacity to sustain human habitation and economic life must be determined by reference to its natural conditions. According to the Philippines, '[a] contrary rule would create perverse incentives for states to undertake such actions to extend their maritime zones to the detriment of other coastal states and/or the common heritage of mankind.'[78] The Philippines' view was supported by the Tribunal:

> Just as a low-tide elevation or area of seabed cannot be legally transformed into an island through human efforts, the Tribunal considers that a rock cannot be transformed into a fully entitled island through land reclamation. The status of a feature must be assessed on the basis of its natural condition.[79]

There is little doubt that the dictum applied to the land reclamation being promoted and undertaken by China in the South China Sea. In fact, the Tribunal ruled that China's reclamation activities at Mischief Reef, which was originally a low-tide elevation, had evolved into the creation of an artificial island.[80]

Furthermore, the Tribunal held:

> If States were allowed to convert any rock incapable of sustaining human habitation or an economic life into a fully entitled island simply by the introduction of technology and extraneous materials, then the purpose of Article 121(3) as a provision of limitation would be frustrated. It could no longer be used as a practical restraint to prevent States from claiming for themselves potentially immense maritime space.[81]

[75] ibid, [496].

[76] ibid, [544].

[77] ibid, [543]. In this regard, the Philippines argued that in this case, the result would be the same whether the criteria were disjunctive or conjunctive: ibid, [417]; presentation by Reichler, Merits Hearing (Day 4), 30 November 2015, 8–9; presentation by Schofield, ibid, 45.

[78] Presentation by Mr Martin, Merits Hearing, n 68, 72.

[79] The *South China Sea* Arbitration Award (Merits), n 1, [508]. See also Presentation by Mr Sands, Merits Hearing (Day 2), 25 November 2015, 18.

[80] The *South China Sea* Arbitration Award (Merits), n 1, [1037]. Since Mischief Reef lies within the Philippines' EEZ and continental shelf, only the Philippines could construct or operate such an artificial island. Thus China's activities were contrary to Art 60 of the Convention: ibid, [1035]–[1036] and [1043].

[81] ibid, [509].

In reality, many of the high-tide features had been significantly modified from their natural condition. Accordingly, when examining the natural conditions of high-tide features in the Spratly Islands, the Tribunal considered 'historical evidence of conditions on the features – prior to the advent of the exclusive economic zone as a concept or the beginning of significant human modification – to represent a more reliable guide to the capacity of the features to sustain human habitation or economic life.'[82] The Tribunal's interpretation is essentially static in the sense that the capacity of a maritime feature is fixed at a certain moment in the past.[83] The question of interest here is whether the capacity of a maritime feature to sustain human habitation or economic life of its own may change over time.

In this regard, it must be noted that historical evidence of human habitation or economic life of its own can only serve as evidence of capacity in the past, and that the past capacity must continue to exist for a maritime feature to be a fully entitled island.[84] If the past capacity has been lost, the feature can no longer be regarded as a fully entitled island.[85] The logic of this suggests the possibility that a maritime feature may subsequently obtain natural conditions to sustain human habitation or economic life of its own.[86] As the Tribunal accepted, 'Article 121(3) is concerned with the *capacity* of a maritime feature to sustain human habitation or an economic life of its own, not with whether the feature is presently, or has been, inhabited or home to economic life.'[87] As the capacity is a generic term, its content evolves over time.[88] Given that the environment is dynamic by nature, it seems reasonable to consider that natural conditions of a maritime feature may change through natural phenomena such as climate change.[89] Hence it appears difficult to completely preclude the possibility that the capacity of a maritime feature may change over time. Some commentators accept the variability of the legal status of maritime features with the passage of time. For instance, Charney stated that 'the application of Article 121(3) to

[82] ibid, [578].

[83] See also I Papanicolopulu, 'The Land Dominates the Sea (Dominates the Land Dominates the Sea)' (2018) 47 *Questions of International Law Zoom-in* 39, 47.

[84] Kwiatkowska and Soons, n 63, 162.

[85] JI Charney, 'Rocks That Cannot Sustain Human Habitation' (1999) 93 *AJIL* 863, 867. See also Choo-Ho Park, 'The Changeable Legal Status of Islands and "Non-Islands" in the Law of the Sea: Some Instances in the Asia-Pacific Region' in DD Caron and HN Scheiber (eds), *Bringing New Law to Ocean Waters* (Nijhoff, 2004) 483, 484 and 486–87.

[86] See also Kwiatkowska and Soons, n 63, 162.

[87] The *South China Sea* Arbitration Award (Merits), n 1, [545].

[88] According to Judge Higgins, a 'generic term' is 'a known legal term, whose content the Parties expected would change through time'. Declaration of Judge Higgins in *Kasikili/Sedudu Island (Botswana v Namibia)* [1999] ICJ Rep 1113, [2]. See also Report of the International Law Commission, Fifty-eighth session, General Assembly, Official Records Sixty-first session Supplement No 10 (A/61/10) (2006), 415–16, [23]. The evolutionary nature of a generic term has been affirmed by the international courts and tribunals. See Y Tanaka, 'Reflections on Time Elements in the International Law of the Environment' (2013) 73 *ZaöRV* 140, 150–54.

[89] Choo-Ho Park, n 85, 484.

a feature may vary over time'.[90] This view was echoed by Gjetnes, stating that 'The status of features may vary over time because the criteria in Article 121(3) will themselves be subject to change or new technologies and life conditions emerge.'[91] Furthermore, as a matter of practice, it would be difficult for humans to settle in a maritime feature or to sustain economic life without introducing some sorts of artificial addition. Even if a rock cannot be transformed into a fully entitled island through land reclamation,[92] there appears to be some scope to consider whether the introduction of an 'artificial addition' is completely prohibited under Article 121(3).

The third and related issue concerns the interpretation of the requirement of 'economic life of their own'. A contentious issue in this regard is whether external resources can be introduced to improve economic life in a maritime feature. The Tribunal's answer was no. For the Tribunal:

> Economic activity that is entirely dependent on external resources or devoted to using a feature as an object for extractive activities without the involvement of a local population would also fall inherently short with respect to this necessary link to the feature itself.[93]

In the view of the Tribunal:

> [T]he requirement in Article 121(3) that the feature itself sustain human habitation or economic life clearly excludes a dependence on external supply. A feature that is only capable of sustaining habitation through the continued delivery of supplies from outside does not meet the requirements of Article 121(3).[94]

Fourth, for the Tribunal, the phrase 'cannot sustain' means 'cannot, without artificial addition, sustain'.[95] Related to this, it further held that 'Where outside support is so significant that it constitutes a necessary condition for the inhabitation of a feature, however, it is no longer the feature itself that sustains human habitation.'[96] The phrase 'so significant' seems to imply that some minor outside support might be allowed to sustain human habitation,[97] while a feature

[90] Charney, n 85, 867–868.

[91] Gjetnes, n 62, 199. See also Murphy, n 16, 74–75 and 208–19.

[92] Transformation of a rock to a fully entitled island through land reclamation might be considered as an abuse of rights. See UNCLOS, Art 300. See also Kolb, n 59, 908.

[93] The *South China Sea* Arbitration Award (Merits), n 1, [543].

[94] ibid, [547]. In this regard, the Philippines, in its Memorial, stressed that '[t]o avoid classification as a "rock", the conditions supportive of economic life cannot be artificially created or injected from outside'. Memorial of the Philippines, vol I, 129, [5.50]. See also ibid, [5.48]. In his book published in 1979, Bowett had already argued that '[t]he phrase "of their own" means that a State cannot avoid a rock being denied both an EEZ and a shelf by injecting an artificial economic life, based on resources from its other land territory': Bowett, n 33, 34.

[95] The *South China Sea* Arbitration Award (Merits), n 1, [510].

[96] ibid, [550].

[97] Gjetnes, n 62, 199, argued that 'some sort of outside support should be allowed in realizing an island's economic opportunities, since in most cases this is necessary in order to realize an economic potential'. See also Kwiatkowska and Soons, n 63, 168–69; and Kolb, n 59, 908.

that is totally dependent for every human need does not meet the requirements of Article 121(3).[98] However, the Tribunal offered no further precision with regard to the degree of 'significant' dependence. Accordingly, one will be forced to decide the degree of significant dependence on a case-by-case basis. Since there is no objective standard to assess the degree of significant dependence, however, the decision will lack predictability, entailing the risk of subjectivity.

ii. Temporal Requirements

The temporal requirements are crucial in the interpretation of 'human habitation' in Article 121(3). Here the Tribunal made an important statement:

> [T]he human habitation with which the drafters of Article 121(3) were concerned was the habitation by a portion of the population for whose benefit the exclusive economic zone was being introduced. Taken together with notions of settlement and residence and the qualitative aspect inherent in the term habitation, it should be understood to refer to the habitation of a feature by a settled group or community for whom the feature is a home.[99]

Related to this, the Tribunal stressed the 'non-transient character' of the inhabitation.[100] In the words of the Tribunal:

> The term 'human habitation' should be understood to involve the inhabitation of the feature by a stable community of people for whom the feature constitutes a home and on which they can remain.[101]

The term 'a stable community of people' will be noted. Interestingly, in 1934, the existence of a stable community of people was presented by Gidel as a factor for a feature to be a fully entitled island.[102] This view was subsequently supported by other commentators.[103] The adjective 'stable' seems to signify that to fulfil the requirement of human habitation, a community of people must exist in a maritime feature for a certain period of time.[104] In fact, by referring to the

[98] According to Lowe, such a maritime feature 'is indistinguishable from a steel platform'. Presentation by Lowe in the *Maritime Delimitation in the Black Sea (Romania v Ukraine)*, Verbatim Record, CR 2008/31, 16 September 2008, 14, [21].

[99] The *South China Sea* Arbitration Award (Merits), n 1, [520].

[100] ibid, [542].

[101] ibid. In this connection, the Tribunal added that 'Such a community need not necessarily be large, and in remote atolls a few individuals or family groups could well suffice. Periodic or habitual residence on a feature by a nomadic people could also constitute habitation …': ibid, [542].

[102] G Gidel, *Le droit international public de la mer, Le temps de paix*, Tome III (reprint) (Duchemin, 1981) 684.

[103] See, for instance, Van Dyke and Brooks, who argued that '[t]he key factor must be whether the island can in fact support a stable population': JM Van Dyke and RA Brooks, 'Uninhabited Islands: Their Impact on the Ownership of the Oceans' Resources' (1983) 12 *ODIL* 265, 286. See also Kolb, n 59, 906; and Gjetnes, n 62, 196.

[104] Lowe argued that '[t]he reference to a "community" connotes a substantial degree of stability and permanence in the population continuing over a period of time': Lowe, Verbatim Record, n 64, 45, [31].

commentator's view, the Philippines stressed that 'a stable community of human beings [is a community] that is sustainable across time'.[105] The dictum of the Tribunal leads to an important consequence of precluding temporary military personnel, fishermen, lighthouse keepers, etc.[106]

For the survival of people, some essential needs must be met in a maritime feature. In this regard, the Tribunal considered that the following factors contribute to the natural capacity of a feature: the presence of water, food and shelter in sufficient quantities to enable a group of persons to live on the feature for an indeterminate period of time.[107] As shown by the phrase 'an indeterminate period of time', the Tribunal again stressed a temporal requirement concerning human habitation. Related to this, the Tribunal ruled that the ordinary meaning of 'sustain' in Article 121(3) contains a temporal concept. According to the Tribunal, this means that 'the support and provision must be over a period of time and not one-off or short-lived'.[108] Furthermore, the Tribunal took the view that 'in connection with sustaining human habitation, to "sustain" means to provide that which is necessary to keep humans alive and healthy over a continuous period of time, according to a proper standard.'[109] The requirement of 'a continuous period of time' can also be regarded as a temporal element.

As the Tribunal observed, the requirements to be fulfilled under Article 121(3) concern the capacity of a maritime feature to sustain human habitation or an economic life of its own. Whether the feature is presently inhabited or home to economic life is not the issue.[110] Nor is the size of a maritime feature a decisive factor. In this regard, the Tribunal held that 'size cannot be dispositive of a feature's status as a fully entitled island or rock and is not, on its own, a relevant factor,' even though size may correlate to the availability of water, food, living space and resources for an economic life.[111] Here the Tribunal referred to the

[105] Memorial of the Philippines, vol I, 126, [5.36].

[106] In this regard, Lowe argued that '[w]e also submit that the criterion of human habitation is not fulfilled where individuals are ordered to go, and to stay on, the rock by their employers. This is particularly, but not exclusively, the case where the employer is the State': Lowe, Verbatim Record, n 64, 45, [32]. This view is supported by Gjetnes, n 62, 197. The Philippines, in its Memorial, took the same view: Memorial of the Philippines, vol I, 146, [5.106].

[107] The *South China Sea* Arbitration Award (Merits), n 1, [546]. Gjetnes also considered that '[t]he availability of food, fresh water, and shelter may thus be chosen as the main characteristic of an island that is capable of sustainable human habitation': Gjetnes, n 62, 196. See also Xue, n 63, 356.

[108] The *South China Sea* Arbitration Award (Merits), n 1, [487].

[109] ibid. In the Tribunal's dictum, however, the level of a 'proper standard' remains less clear. While there is no objective standard on this matter, it would seem that a 'proper standard' requires a level more than mere survival of humans on a maritime feature. W Gullett, 'The South China Sea Arbitration's Contribution to the Concept of Juridical Islands' (2018) 47 *Questions of International Law Zoom-in* 5, 14.

[110] The *South China Sea* Arbitration Award (Merits), n 1, [545].

[111] ibid, [538]. In this regard, Hafetz argued that '[p]roposed guidelines based on size, however, were never adopted, and the text of Article 121(3) neither explicitly mentions size nor provides any guidelines to that effect': JL Hafetz, 'Fostering Protection of the Marine Environment and Economic Development: Article 121(3) of the Third Law of the Sea Convention' (2000) 15 *American University International Law Review* 583, 590–91. More generally, Nordquist and Phalen indicated that

view of the ICJ in *Nicaragua v Colombia*, where it ruled that 'international law does not prescribe any minimum size which a feature must possess in order to be considered an island'.[112] Yet it appears that focus of the Tribunal's dictum in the *South China Sea* Arbitration is not on the minimum size but on the *upper* size of a rock. The dictum of the Tribunal seems to imply that even if the size of a maritime feature is large enough, it may still fall within the scope of a rock for the purposes of Article 121(3) because it cannot sustain human habitation or economic life on its own.

If a feature is entirely barren of vegetation and lacks drinkable water and the foodstuffs necessary even for basic survival, it is clear that the feature lacks the capacity to sustain human habitation. In reality, however, evidence of physical conditions may be insufficient for features that fall close to the line. In this case, the Tribunal considered that 'the most reliable evidence of the capacity of a feature will usually be the historical use to which it has been put'.[113] For the Tribunal:

> If the historical record of a feature indicates that nothing resembling a stable community has ever developed there, the most reasonable conclusion would be that the natural conditions are simply too difficult for such a community to form and that the feature is not capable of sustaining such habitation.[114]

Furthermore, '[e]vidence of human habitation that predates the creation of exclusive economic zones may be more significant than contemporary evidence, if the latter is clouded by an apparent attempt to assert a maritime claim'.[115]

'objective criteria such as physical size, number of inhabitants, geographical location and other characteristics were proposed, deliberated upon and *rejected* for inclusion in the text of Article 121(3)': MH Nordquist and WG Phalen, 'Interpretation of UNCLOS Article 121 and Itu Aba (Taiping) in the South China Sea Arbitration Award' in MH Nordquist, JN Moore and R Long (eds), *International Marine Economy: Law and Policy* (Nijhoff, 2017) 30, 64–65 (original emphasis). Symmons' view is more nuanced. He argued that 'size as such has been abandoned as a feasible criterion of insular status, ... but, indirectly size may still be important because the geological phenomenon of a "rock" has been singled out for special treatment': C Symmons, *The Maritime Zones of Islands in International Law* (Nijhoff, 1979) 41. See also AG Oude Elferink, 'The Islands in the South China Sea: How Does Their Presence Limit the Extent of the High Seas and the Area and the Maritime Zones of the Mainland Coasts?' (2011) 32 *ODIL* 169, 173; and Kolb, n 59, 904. For a criticism on this point, see AG Oude Elferink, 'The South China Sea Arbitration's Interpretation of Article 121(3) of the UNCLOS: A Disquieting First', *The JCLOS Blog*, 7 September 2016, available at site.uit.no/jclos/files/2016/09/The-South-China-Sea-Arbitrations-Interpretation-of-Article-1213-of-the-UNCLOS-A-Disquieting-First.pdf.

[112] *Nicaragua v Colombia*, n 10, [2012] ICJ Rep 624, 645, [37]. See also *Qatar v Bahrain*, n 10, [2001] ICJ Rep 97, [185]. In a Judgment of 7 May 1996, the Norwegian Supreme Court held that Abel Island, which is 13.2 square kilometres in area, was too large to be a 'rock' within the meaning of Art 121(3) and that the island would be able to support a significant polar bear hunt, were such hunting not prohibited for conservation reasons. See R Churchill, 'Norway: Supreme Court Judgment on Law of the Sea Issues' (1996) 11 *IJMCL* 576, in particular, 579. While the judgment seemed to rely only on the size of the island, it also referred to a sort of economic activity, namely, the polar bear hunt.

[113] The *South China Sea* Arbitration Award (Merits), n 1, [549] (emphasis added).

[114] ibid, [549].

[115] ibid, [550].

It follows that in borderline circumstances, historical evidence prior to the advent of the EEZ as a concept or the beginning of significant human modification presents a more reliable guide to the capacity of the features to sustain human habitation or economic life.[116] Therefore, a temporal element, that is historical evidence, becomes a crucial factor in determining the legal status of maritime features that fall close to the line in terms of their capacity to sustain human habitation and an economic life of this own.

C. Application of Article 121(3)

On the basis of the above interpretation, the Tribunal determined the legal status of disputed maritime features in the South China Sea. Taking Scarborough Shoal as an example, according to the Tribunal, the protrusions above high tide at Scarborough Shoal were minuscule and they obviously could not sustain human habitation in their naturally formed state. Furthermore, they had no fresh water, vegetation or living space, and were remote from any feature possessing such features. Moreover, there was no evidence that Scarborough Shoal could independently sustain an economic life of its own.[117] Accordingly, the Tribunal concluded that Scarborough Shoal was a rock for the purposes of Article 121(3).[118] For similar reasons, the Tribunal ruled that Johnson Reef, Cuarteron Reef, Fiery Cross Reef, Gaven Reef (North) and McKennan Reef were 'rocks' for the purposes of Article 121(3).[119]

However, the legal status of Itu Aba was more debatable. Itu Aba, which is known as 'Taiping Dao' in China and 'Ligaw' in the Philippines, is the largest high-tide feature in the Spratly Islands, measuring approximately 1.4 kilometres in length and almost 400 metres at its widest point (0.43 square kilometres). Itu Aba is located at 200.6 nautical miles from the archipelagic baseline of the Philippine island of Palawan and 539.6 nautical miles from China's baseline point 39 (Dongzhou (2)) adjacent to the island of Hainan. There are multiple buildings, a lighthouse, a runway and port facilities on Itu Aba. Itu Aba is currently under the control of Taiwan.[120]

When examining the legal status of Itu Aba, the Tribunal examined the natural conditions, such as the presence of potable fresh water, vegetation and biology, soil and agricultural potential, the presence of fishermen, and commercial operations.[121] The Tribunal's examination relied on historical evidence of

[116] ibid, [578].
[117] ibid, [556].
[118] ibid, [554].
[119] ibid, [557]–[570].
[120] ibid, [401]. See also Memorial of the Philippines, vol I, 142–43, [5.96]–[5.97].
[121] The *South China Sea* Arbitration Award (Merits), n 1, [580]–[614].

conditions on the features prior to the advent of the EEZ as a concept or the beginning of significant human modification.[122] In this regard, the Tribunal considered that the principal high-tide features in the Spratly Islands, including Itu Aba, are capable of enabling the survival of small groups of people.[123] However, the Tribunal went on to add:

> [T]he features are not obviously habitable, and their capacity even to enable human survival appears to be distinctly limited. In these circumstances, and with features that fall close to the line in terms of their capacity to sustain human habitation, the Tribunal considers that the physical characteristics of the features do not definitively indicate the capacity of the features. Accordingly, the Tribunal is called upon to consider the historical evidence of human habitation and economic life on the Spratly Islands and the implications of such evidence for the natural capacity of the features.[124]

The Tribunal thus turned to examine the 'historical human habitation' and 'historical economic life of their own' of the features of the Spratly Islands.

The Tribunal first examined the historical human habitation of the features of the Spratly Islands. In this regard, a temporal requirement, that is the non-transient nature of the habitation, was of particular importance. According to the Tribunal, 'the criterion of human habitation is not met by the temporary inhabitation of the Spratly Islands by fishermen, even for extended periods', and '[t]his standard is not met by the historical presence of fishermen that appears in the record before the Tribunal.'[125] Applying this standard, the Tribunal considered that the fishermen were not the natural population of the Spratlys, including Itu Aba.[126] Furthermore, a crew of Formosan labourers, brought to the Spratly Islands to mine guano or capture sea turtles, did not suffice to establish a settled community within the meaning of 'human habitation' in Article 121(3), since their presence was inherently transient in nature.[127] Nor did the Tribunal consider that the military or other governmental personnel stationed on the features in the Spratly Islands by one or another of the littoral states sufficed to constitute 'human habitation' for the purposes of Article 121(3), since these groups were heavily dependent on outside supplies.[128] Overall the Tribunal observed that there was no indication that anything fairly resembling a stable human community had ever formed on the Spratly Islands. It thus concluded that Itu Aba, along with Thitu, West York, Spratly Island, South-West Cay and North-East Cay, was not capable of sustaining human habitation within the meaning of Article 121(3).[129]

[122] ibid, [578].
[123] ibid, [615].
[124] ibid, [616].
[125] ibid, [618].
[126] ibid.
[127] ibid, [619].
[128] ibid, [620].
[129] ibid, [622].

The Tribunal then moved on to examine the 'historical economic life of their own' of the features of the Spratly Islands. In this regard, the Tribunal specified two standards. The first standard concerned the feature-oriented nature of economic activity. In the words of the Tribunal, 'to constitute the economic life of the feature, economic activity must be oriented around the feature itself and not be focused solely on the surrounding territorial sea or entirely dependent on external resources'.[130] The second standard related to the linkage between a stable local community and economic activity. In this regard, the Tribunal considered that 'extractive economic activity, without the presence of a stable local community, necessarily falls short of constituting the economic life of the feature'.[131]

Applying the standards,[132] the Tribunal ruled that 'the history of extractive economic activity does not constitute, for the features of the Spratly Islands, evidence of an economic life of their own'; and that Itu Aba, Thitu, West York, Spratly Island, South-West Cay and North-East Cay were not capable of sustaining an economic life of their own within the meaning of Article 121(3).[133] In conclusion, the Tribunal held that none of the high-tide features in the Spratly Islands was capable of sustaining human habitation or an 'economic life of their own', and that the effect of Article 121(3) was that such features 'shall have no [EEZ] or continental shelf.'[134]

[130] ibid, [623]; see also [503].

[131] ibid, [623].

[132] Perhaps the standards might evoke the 'natural obligation to cultivate the land' ('obligation naturelle de cultiver la terre') claimed by Vattel. According to Vattel, the cultivation of the soil is an obligation imposed on man by nature. Vattel thus argued that other more industrious nations can come to take possession of a part of lands of those who choose to live by hunting and their flocks. For Vattel, the obligation to cultivate provided a basis for occupation. E de Vattel, *Le droit des gens, ou principes de la loit naturelle, Nouvelle édition par M.P. Pradier-Fodéré*, Tome I (Guillaumin et Cle, Libraires, 1863) 258–59, § 81. For an English translation of Emer de Vattel's *Le droit des gens*, see E de Vattel, *The Law of Nations; or Principles of the Law of Nature, Applied to the Conduct and Affairs of Nations and Sovereigns*, tr J Chitty (T and JW Johnson and Co, Law Booksellers, 1853) 34–36. The origin of Vattel's thought may seem to go back to Locke. Locke argued that '*As much land* as a man tills, plants, improves, cultivates, and can use the product of, so much is his *property*': J Locke, *Two Treaties of Government* (1764), 220, § 32 (original emphasis). (The book was originally published in 1689/90. The 1764 edition is available at https://oll.libertyfund.org/titles/locke-the-two-treatises-of-civil-government-hollis-ed.) To cultivate the soil, 'a stable community of people' would be needed. It would seem to follow that the standards mentioned in para 623 of the Award on the merits are linked to the interpretation of 'human habitation' at para 542 of the Award.

[133] The *South China Sea* Arbitration Award (Merits), n 1, [624]–[625].

[134] ibid, [626]. The Schofield Report submitted by the Philippines also concluded that 28 maritime features within the Spratly Islands elevated above the high-tide level were classified as 'rocks' consistent with Art 121(3) of UNCLOS. C Schofield, JRV Prescott and R van der Poll, *An Appraisal of the Geographical Characteristics and Status of Certain Insular Features in the South China Sea*, March 2015, 87, reproduced in Annex 513 to the Philippines' Supplemental Written Submission, vol IX. Notably, the Schofield Report relied on the disjunctive interpretation of Art 121(3) (see further section III.B.i of this chapter); presentation by Schofield, n 77, 45. As Gullett pointedly observed, if the Tribunal had classified Itu Aba as a fully entitled island, it would have needed to examine whether the next most substantial maritime features met the requirements set out in Art 121(3). Gullett thus argued that the decision of the Tribunal was 'elegant in the sense that it

In summary, the Tribunal applied the two-stage approach to the determination of the legal status of maritime features in the South China Sea. At the first stage, the Tribunal examined the natural conditions of a maritime feature. Where a maritime feature obviously lacked conditions to meet the essential survival needs of a human being, such as fresh water, vegetation or living space, that feature was to be regarded as a rock under Article 121(3) since it obviously could not sustain human habitation in its naturally formed state. Where the physical characteristics of the features did not definitively indicate the capacity of the features, at the second stage, the legal status of the features was to be determined on the basis of historical evidence, that is 'historical human habitation' and a 'historical economic life of their own'.

D. Mischief Reef and Second Thomas Shoal

Finally, the Tribunal examined the Philippines' Submission No 5 with regard to Mischief Reef and Second Thomas Shoal, both coral reefs located in the centre of the Spratly Islands.[135] As noted, the Tribunal ruled that there was no legal basis for any Chinese historic rights or sovereign rights and jurisdiction beyond those provided for in the UNCLOS, in the waters of the South China Sea encompassed by the 'nine-dash' line.[136] As Mischief Reef and Second Thomas Shoal are low-tide elevations, they generate no entitlement to maritime zones of their own. Furthermore, since high-tide features in the Spratly Islands are regarded as 'rocks' for the purposes of Article 121 of the Convention, they generate no EEZ or continental shelf. In addition, there is no high-tide feature that is located within 12 nautical miles of either Mischief Reef or Second Thomas Shoal.[137] Accordingly, the Tribunal held that 'there exists no legal basis for any entitlement by China to maritime zones in the area of Mischief Reef or Second Thomas Shoal' and that 'there is no situation of overlapping entitlement' that would call for maritime delimitation. Hence there was no possible basis for the application of the exception to jurisdiction provided in Article 298(1)(a)(i).[138]

A particular issue to be addressed in this context was whether Malaysia was indispensable to the arbitral proceedings. This issue relates to the application of the *Monetary Gold* principle.[139] In this regard, the Tribunal considered that 'the legal interests of Malaysia do not form "the very subject-matter of the

meant the Tribunal did not need to draw a line between the most substantial feature – Taiping Dao – and other features': Gullett, n 109, 36.

[135] The *South China Sea* Arbitration Award (Merits), n 1, [290].

[136] ibid, [631].

[137] ibid, [633].

[138] ibid, [634].

[139] *Monetary Gold Removed from Rome in 1943 (Italy v France, United Kingdom of Great Britain and Northern Ireland and United States of America)*, Judgment of 15 June 1954, Preliminary Question, [1954] ICJ Rep 19.

dispute" and are not implicated by the Tribunal's conclusions', and accordingly 'Malaysia's rights and interests do not engage the rule in *Monetary Gold*'.[140] It thus concluded that it had jurisdiction with regard to the Philippines' Submission No 5.

Both Mischief Reef and Second Thomas Shoal are located within 200 nautical miles of the Philippines' coast on the island of Palawan and there is no overlapping area of the entitlements there. The Tribunal thus held that as between the Philippines and China, Mischief Reef and Second Thomas Shoal form part of the EEZ and continental shelf of the Philippines.[141] It follows that Mischief Reef and Second Thomas Shoal belong to the Philippines. In consequence, the Sino-Philippines dispute with regard to the jurisdiction over Mischief Reef and Second Thomas Shoal was legally resolved by the Tribunal.

IV. ASSESSMENT OF THE TRIBUNAL'S INTERPRETATION AND APPLICATION OF ARTICLE 121(3)

On the basis of the above considerations, the Tribunal's interpretation and application of Article 121(3) must be examined in terms of their consistency with state practice and with the jurisprudence.

A. Consistency with State Practice

The first issue to be addressed is whether the Tribunal's interpretation is supported by state practice. As provisions of a treaty are interpreted and applied by the Contracting Parties to that treaty, the practice of the Parties may influence the interpretation of treaty provisions.[142] The Tribunal succinctly examined the relevance of state practice in the implementation of Article 121(3) by referring to Article 31(3) of the Vienna Convention on the Law of Treaties.[143] In accordance with this provision, 'any subsequent practice in the application of the treaty which establishes the agreement of the parties regarding its interpretation' shall be taken into account together with the context.[144] Referring to

[140] The *South China Sea* Arbitration Award (Merits), n 1, [640].

[141] ibid, [647].

[142] While, in some cases, the practice of international institutions in the interpretation and application of treaty provisions also needs to be examined, for the purposes of this chapter we shall focus on the practice of states.

[143] ibid, [552]. Vienna Convention on the Law of Treaties (adopted 22 May 1969, entered into force 27 January 1980) 1155 *UNTS* 331.

[144] The importance of subsequent practice was stressed by the International Law Commission (ILC). The Commission stated that '[t]he importance of such subsequent practice in the application of the treaty, as an element of interpretation, is obvious; for it constitutes objective evidence of the understanding of the parties as to the meaning of the treaty': (1966) 2 *Yearbook of the International Law Commission* 221, [15] (footnote omitted).

the jurisprudence of the ICJ[145] and the World Trade Organization (WTO),[146] the Tribunal considered that the threshold for accepting an agreement on interpretation by state practice is quite high.[147] It thus stated that 'as far as the case before it is concerned, there is no evidence for an agreement based upon State practice on the interpretation of Article 121(3) which differs from the interpretation of the Tribunal as outlined in the previous Sections'.[148] However, the Tribunal remained mute on the question of whether state practice supported its interpretation.[149]

Related to this, the Tribunal referred to the position of Viet Nam, Indonesia and the Philippines that the high-tide features in the Spratly Islands were 'rocks' for the purposes of Article 121(3) and should only be entitled to a 12-nautical mile territorial sea.[150] Malaysia also seemed to take a similar position.[151]

[145] In this connection, the Tribunal referred to the ICJ's *Advisory Opinion Concerning the Legality of the Use by a State of Nuclear Weapons in Armed Conflict* and the *Kasikili/Sedudu Island* case. After the examination of the practice of the World Health Organization (WHO), the Court stressed that the practice dealing with the legality of the use of nuclear weapons cannot be inferred from isolated passages of certain resolutions of the World Health Assembly: *Advisory Opinion Concerning the Legality of the Use by a State of Nuclear Weapons in Armed Conflict* [1996] ICJ Rep 66, 81–82, [27]. The ICJ, in the *Kasikili/Sedudu Island* case, held that events that occurred between 1947 and 1951 cannot constitute 'subsequent practice in the application of the treaty [of 1890] which establishes the agreement of the parties regarding its interpretation': *Kasikili/Sedudu Island (Botswana v Namibia)*, Judgment, [1999] ICJ Rep 1045, 1087, [63]. For an analysis of the jurisprudence concerning subsequent practice, see in particular G Nolte, 'Jurisprudence of the International Court of Justice and Arbitral Tribunals of Ad Hoc Jurisdiction Relating to Subsequent Agreements and Subsequent Practice: Introductory Report for the ILC Study Group on Treaties over Time' in G Nolte (ed), *Treaties and Subsequent Practice* (Oxford University Press, 2013) 170 et seq. See also G Distefano, 'La pratique subséquente des Etats parties à un traité' (1994) 40 *Annuaire Français de Droit International* 41.

[146] By way of example, in *Japan – Taxes on Alcoholic Beverages*, the Appellate Body stated that 'Generally, in international law, the essence of subsequent practice in interpreting a treaty has been recognized as a "concordant, common and consistent" sequence of acts or pronouncements which is sufficient to establish a discernible pattern implying the agreement of the parties regarding its interpretation': *Japan – Taxes on Alcoholic Beverages*, Report of the Appellate Body, AB-1996-2, WT/DS8/AB/R, 4 October 1996, WT/DS10/AB/R, WT/DS11/AB/R, 12–13.

[147] The *South China Sea* Arbitration Award (Merits), n 1, [552]. A commentary indicated that '[c]ase law reveals that subsequent practice is classified as an element for the interpretation of a treaty, but that it is out of the question to envisage an amendment or a termination of the treaty by lapse': J-M Sorel and VB Eveno, '1969 Vienna Convention Article 31' in O Corten and P Klein (eds), *The Vienna Conventions on the Law of Treaties: A Commentary*, vol I (Oxford University Press, 2011) 828.

[148] The *South China Sea* Arbitration Award (Merits), n 1, [553].

[149] N Klein, 'Islands and Rocks after the South China Sea Arbitration' (2016) 34 *Australian Year Book of International Law* 21, 27.

[150] The *South China Sea* Arbitration Award (Merits), n 1, [449]. In Viet Nam's 2009 Submissions to the Commission on the Limits of the Continental Shelf (CLCS), the 200-nautical mile limit delineated by Viet Nam is based on Viet Nam's straight baselines. Government of the Socialist Republic of Vietnam, 'partial Submission in Respect of Vietnam's Extended Continental Shelf: North Area (VNM-N, Part I: Executive Summary, April 2009, available at http://www.un.org/depts/los/clcs_new/submissions_files/vnm37_09/vnm2009n_executivesummary.pdf.

[151] The *South China Sea* Arbitration Award (Merits), n 1, [449]. In the Joint Submission of 2009 to the CLCS, the 200-nautical mile limit is based on straight baselines along the coasts of Viet Nam and Malaysia. Any insular features in the Spratly Islands were used in the construction of the 200-nautical

Furthermore, the Tribunal referred to the fact that China regards Okino-Tori-Shima (Okinotorishima) as a rock.[152] Yet there appears to be some scope to consider the question whether the practice of the limited number of states will be adequate to support the Tribunal's interpretation.

Opinions may often be divided with regard to the legal status of maritime features for the purposes of Article 121(3). For instance, France established an EEZ around the Kerguelen Islands,[153] even though, as Judge Vukas observed in the *Monte Confurco* case, the Kerguelen Islands are 'uninhabitable and uninhabited' islands.[154] Australia has proclaimed an EEZ around Heard Island and the MacDonald Islands,[155] even though Judge Vukas, in the *Volga* case, questioned whether Heard Island and the MacDonald Islands can generate the EEZ since there can be no permanent habitation.[156] Mexico has proclaimed an EEZ around Guadalupe, Isla Socorro, Isla Clarion, Isla San Benedicto and Isla Roca Partida in the Pacific. Apart from Guadalupe, however, some doubts can be expressed on whether the other four maritime features can sustain human habitation.[157]

mile limit. Joint Statement of the Republic of the Philippines and the People's Republic of China, Beijing, 21 October 2016, para 42, available at http://www.dfa.gov.ph/newsroom/dfa-releases/10748-joint-statement-of-the-republic-of-the-philippines-and-the-people-s-republic-of-china. See also TL McDorman, 'An International Law Perspective on Insular Features (Islands) and Low-tide Elevations in the South China Sea' (2017) 32 *IJMCL* 298, 304.

[152] The *South China Sea* Arbitration Award (Merits), n 1, [452]. China's view on Okinotorishima was referred to by the Philippines. See Memorial of the Philippines, vol I, 124–25, [5.29]–[5.31]. Recently the Chinese Government confirmed its position, stating that 'Okinotori reef does not meet the basic requirements to be recognised as [an] island': Foreign Ministry Spokesperson Lu Kang's Regular Press Conference on 2 January 2019. CSIL took the same view. CSIL, *The South China Sea Arbitration: A Critical Study* (Foreign Languages Press, 2018) 395, [719].

[153] France established an EEZ around the Kerguelen Islands in February 1978. Decree No 78–144 of 3 February 1978, creating an EEZ off the coasts of the French Southern and Antarctic Territories. See at http://www.un.org/depts/los/LEGISLATIONANDTREATIES/PDFFILES/FRA_1978_Decree144.pdf. See also W Gullett and C Schofield, 'Pushing the Limits of the Law of the Sea Convention: Australian and French Cooperative Surveillance and Enforcement in the Southern Ocean' (2007) 22 *IJMCL* 545, 548–49; C Schofield, 'The Trouble with Islands: The Definition and Role of Islands and Rocks in Maritime Boundary Delimitation' in Seoung-Yong Hong and JM Van Dyke (eds), *Maritime Boundary Disputes, Settlement Processes, and the Law of the Sea* (Nijhoff, 2009) 19, 30.

[154] Declaration of Judge Vukas in the *Monte Confurco Case (Seychelles v France)*, Application for Prompt Release, ITLOS Case No 6, [2000] ITLOS Rep 122. According to the French Government, the Kerguelen Islands are composed of a principal island, La Grande Terre, and more than 300 islands and islets covering a total area of 7,215 square kilometres. La Grande Terre covers 6,675 square kilometres. See at www.taaf.fr/L-archipel-de-Kerguelen.

[155] Gullett and Schofield, n 153, 547; Schofield, n 153, 30.

[156] Declaration of Vice-President Vukas in the *Volga case (Russian Federation v Australia)*, Application for Prompt Release, ITLOS Case No 11, [2002] ITLOS Rep 42 et seq. Heard Island is approximately 40 kilometres long and 20 kilometres wide. The island covers 368 square kilometres. See heardisland.antarctica.gov.au/about/location-geography. According to UNESCO, MacDonald Island covers only 100 hectares, which is equivalent to 1 square kilometre. See whc.unesco.org/en/list/577. Heard Island and the McDonald Islands were added to the UNESCO World Heritage list in December 1997. See heardisland.antarctica.gov.au/news/heard-island-and-mcdonald-islands-marine-reserve-expansion. See also Klein, n 149, 28–29.

[157] Van Overbeek argued that Mexico's claims to an EEZ around the four features appeared to be contrary to Art 121(3). W van Overbeek, 'Article 121(3) UNCLOS in Mexican State Practice in the

In some cases, the establishment of the EEZ around a maritime feature has resulted in protests. For instance, the Aves Island (Bird Island) is given full effect in Venezuela's maritime boundary agreements with the US (Puerto Rico),[158] France (Martinique and Guadeloupe)[159] and the Netherlands (Netherlands Antilles),[160] was the subject of protests by Antigua and Barbuda, St Kitts and Nevis, Saint Lucia, and the Saint Vincent and the Grenadines, respectively.[161] While the Japanese Government established a 200-mile EEZ around Okinotorishima in 1996,[162] China, Taiwan and the Republic of Korea have questioned the legal status of Okinotorishima as a fully entitled island.[163] The Japanese Government takes the view that it *is* a fully entitled island.[164] Here opinions are sharply divided with regard to Okinotorishima's legal status. However, with the notable exception of Rockall,[165] it is rare for coastal states to abandon an

Pacific' (1989) 4 *IJMCL* 252, 262–63. See also Kwiatkowska and Soons, n 63, 176; and Kolb, n 59, 896–97.

[158] Maritime Boundary Treaty between the United States and Venezuela in JI Charney and LM Alexander (eds), *International Maritime Boundaries*, vol I (Nijhoff, 1993) 701.

[159] Delimitation Treaty between Venezuela and the French Republic, ibid, 613.

[160] Delimitation Treaty between the Netherlands and Venezuela, ibid, 631. Aves Island is 375 metres in length and never more than 50 metres wide. JA Roach and RW Smith, *Excessive Maritime Claims*, 3rd edn (Nijhoff, 2012) 178. According to CW Dundas, 'Middle American and Caribbean Maritime Boundaries' in DA Colson and RW Smith (eds), *International Maritime Boundaries*, vol V (Nijhoff, 2005) 3411, Aves Island has an area of about 10 acres (40468.56 square metres). Dundas cited Kwiatkowska and Soons, who argued that Aves Island may qualify as a rock: Kwiatkowska and Soons, n 63, 180.

[161] See (1997) 35 *Law of the Sea Bulletin* 97.

[162] At high tide, only two natural features, ie Kitakojima and Higashikojima, remain above water. These features in their natural form were about the size of two king-size beds or four-and-a-half tatami mats. JM Van Dyke, 'The Romania-Ukraine Decision and Its Effect on East Asian Maritime Delimitation' in Seoung-Yong Hong and JM Van Dyke (eds), *Governing Ocean Resources: New Challenges and Emerging Regimes, A Tribute to Judge Choon-Ho Park* (Nijhoff, 2013) 41, 58.

[163] Yann-huei Song, 'Okinotorishima: A "Rock" or an "Island"? Recent Maritime Boundary Controversy between Japan and Taiwan/China' in Seoung-Yong Hong and Van Dyke (eds), n 153, 145, 146 and 151–54; Yann-huei Song, 'The Application of Article 121 of the Law of the Sea Convention to the Selected Geographical Features Situated in the Pacific Ocean' (2010) 9 *CJIL* 663, 668–74 and 691–94; JA Roach, 'Rocks versus Islands: Implications for Protection of the Marine Environment', in Jayakumar et al (eds), n 13, 247, 263–68; Republic of Korea, Note Verbale, 27 February 2009, and the People's Republic of China, Note Verbale, 6 February 2009, sent regarding Japan's submission of its outer limits of the continental shelf to Commission on the Limits of the Continental Shelf (CLCS), on the CLCS website at www.un.org/Depts/los/clcs. For an analysis of maritime features in East Asia, see Yann-huei Song, 'Article 121(3) of the Law of the Sea Convention and the Disputed Offshore Islands in East Asia: A Tribute to Judge Choon-Ho Park' in Seoung-Yong Hong and JM Van Dyke (eds), n 162, 61.

[164] See, for instance, Press Conference by Foreign Minister Fumio Kishida, 15 July 2016, available at https://www.mofa.go.jp/press/kaiken/kaiken4e_000290.html. At the Conference, the Foreign Minister stated that 'Oki-no-Tori Shima Island is an island that meets the criteria under UNCLOS'.

[165] Rockall is about 624 square metres in area. R Churchill, 'United Kingdom's Decision to Defer Accession to the UN Convention on the Law of the Sea: A Convincing Move?' (1997) 12 *IJMCL* 110, 114. At the beginning of 1977, the UK established an exclusive fishery zone around Rockall by the Fishery Limits Act 1976. However, it drew protests from Ireland, Denmark and Iceland. Accordingly, the UK gave up the 200-mile fishery zone when it acceded to the UNCLOS in 1997. See V Prescott and C Schofield, *The Maritime Political Boundaries of the World*, 2nd edn (Brill/Njihoff, 2005) 374–76; DH Anderson, 'British Accession to the UN Convention on the Law of the Sea' (1997) 46

established EEZ or continental shelf around marine formations because they constitute rocks under Article 121(3). It is also uncommon for coastal states to incorporate Article 121(3) into their national legislation. It would appear that the only example of such incorporation is the 1986 EEZ Federal Act of Mexico.[166] As noted, however, Mexico gave full effect to several minuscule islets in generating its EEZ.[167] Overall, it can be observed that the interpretation or application of Article 121(3) may differ significantly as between countries. It would be fair to say that no uniform interpretation or application of Article 121(3) can be identified in state practice.

B. Consistency with the Jurisprudence

The second issue is whether the Tribunal's interpretation is in line with the international jurisprudence. Even though legal effects given to maritime features have been discussed in the jurisprudence concerning maritime delimitations, it has been rare for an international court or tribunal to determine the legal status of maritime features.[168] Regarding the jurisprudence of the ICJ, six cases merit discussion.

The first is the 1993 *Jan Mayen* case.[169] Jan Mayen, which appertains to Norway, is 53 kilometres long and between 2.5 and 15 kilometres wide. Its total area is 377 square kilometres. There are neither trees nor bushes on Jan Mayen

ICLQ 761, 778–79; RR Churchill and AV Lowe, *The* Law of the Sea (Manchester University Press, 1999) 164. In this regard, Tony Lloyd, the Secretary of State for Foreign and Commonwealth Affairs, stated that 'Even before accession [to the UNCLOS], the UK's claim to 200-mile fishery limits based on Rockall was highly questionable. Rockall itself will remain part of Scotland with a 12-mile territorial sea, and will remain within British fishery limits, as will the Rockall Bank and the new deep water fisheries to the east of Rockall. Redrawing our fishery limits has no effect on our continental shelf to the west of Rockall': Foreign and Commonwealth Affairs, *Rockall*, 31 July 1997, col 482, available at https://publications.parliament.uk/pa/cm199798/cmhansrd/vo970731/text/70731w17.htm. As for the continental shelf, Churchill stated that 'at the time this claim was made the legal justification given for it was not only Rockall's entitlement as an island to its own continental shelf but also that the area of seabed concerned was a natural prolongation of the sea-bed of the west of Scotland': Churchill, 'United Kingdom's Decision to Defer Accession to the UN Convention on the Law of the Sea', 114–15. See also ED Brown, 'Rockall and the Limits of National Jurisdiction of the UK: Part 2' (1987) 2 *Marine Policy* 275, 292–94. Subsequently, Rockall was wholly ignored in delimiting the continental shelf boundary between the UK and Ireland in 1988. Report by DH Anderson in JI Charney and LM Alexander (eds), *International Maritime Boundaries*, vol II (Nijhoff, 1996) 1767, 1770; Prescott and Schofield, n 165, 375.

[166] EEZ Federal Act of Mexico (1986) 25 *ILM* 896, Art 51.

[167] W van Overbeek, n 157, 262; Kwiatkowska and Soons, n 63, 176; and Kolb, n 59, 896–97.

[168] ML Delabie, 'Le fragile équilibre entre prévisibilité juridique et opportunité judiciarei en matière de délimitation maritime: l'arrêt de la Court internationale de Justice du 19 novembre 2012 dans l'affaire du *Différend territorial et maritime (Nicaragua c Colombie)*' (2012) 58 *AFDI*, 223, 228.

[169] *Case concerning Maritime Delimitation in the Area between Greenland and Jan Mayen (Denmark v Norway)* [1993] ICJ Rep 38.

and there are relatively few plants.[170] It is inhabited by some 25 technical and other staff of the island's meteorological station, a LORAN (long-range radio navigation) station and the coastal radio station. There is a regular service by military aircraft, which permits personnel transfers and light cargo deliveries. The landing field can also be used for search-and-rescue operations and for emergency evacuation and medical assistance.[171] Bulk supplies are brought in by ship and uploaded in Hvalrossbukta (Walrus Bay) to support the human population.[172] Norway has established 12-mile territorial sea and 200-mile fishing zone around Jan Mayen.[173] Relying on the terminology of Article 121(3), Denmark maintained that Jan Mayen could not sustain and has not sustained human habitation or an economic life of its own.[174] Care should be taken, in that Denmark did not argue that Jan Mayen had no entitlement to a continental shelf or fishery zone; rather the argument was that the island of Jan Mayen could not be accorded full effect in the delimitation.[175]

Applying the Tribunal's interpretation in the *South China Sea* Arbitration, it is difficult to consider that Jan Mayen is a fully entitled island since there is no stable community or population and the life of people working on Jan Mayen is entirely dependent on external resources. Nonetheless, the ICJ, in the *Jan Mayen* case, did not question the legal status of Jan Mayen as a fully entitled island.[176] In fact, the Court defined the area of overlapping claims by a median line measured from Jan Mayen and Greenland and the 200-mile line from Greenland.[177] It drew the delimitation line that divides the continental shelf and fishery zones of Greenland and Jan Mayen.[178] As a consequence, Jan Mayen does have a continental shelf and a fishery zone. It can be said that the ICJ de facto treated Jan Mayen as an island, even though the Court did not directly examine the legal status of Jan Mayen for the purposes of Article 121(3). The status of Jan Mayen

[170] G Ulfstein, 'Jan Mayen' in R Wolfrum (ed), *Max Planck Encyclopedia of Public International Law* (Oxford University Press, 2009) [1]. Information on Jan Mayen may differ slightly according to sources. According to Norway, the length of the island is 53.6 kilometres; the breadth varies between 2.5 and 16 kilometres. The total area is 380 square kilometres (148 square miles). The *Jan Mayen* case, Counter-Memorial Submitted by Norway, 11 May 1990, 23, [78]. Norway regarded Jan Mayen as a fully entitled island: ibid, 133, [445]; T Pedersen, 'Denmark's Policies Toward the Svalbard Area' (2009) 40 *ODIL* 319, 324.

[171] Counter-Memorial Submitted by Norway, n 170, 23–28, [78]–[101]. According to Ulfstein, a private person had previously occupied the middle part of Jan Mayen. However, his heirs sold the property to the Norwegian Government in 1952: Ulfstein, n 170, [7].

[172] Counter-Memorial Submitted by Norway, n 170, 27, [96].

[173] Ulfstein, n 170, [4].

[174] The *Jan Mayen* case, n 174, [1993] ICJ Rep 65, [60]. See also See also Memorial of the Government of the Kingdom of Denmark, 31 July 1989, 97, [302] and the Reply of the Government of the Kingdom of Denmark, 31 January 1991, 32, [83]; 165, [452].

[175] The *Jan Mayen* case, n 174, [1993] ICJ Rep 73–74, [80].

[176] L Caflisch, 'Les espaces marins attachés à des îles ou roches' in M Forteau and J-M Thouvenin (eds), *Traité de droit international de la mer* (Pedone, 2017) 447, 485.

[177] The *Jan Mayen* case, n 174, [1993] ICJ Rep 78, [89].

[178] ibid, 79–81, [91]–[92].

as a fully entitled island was supported by the 1981 Conciliation Commission on the Continental Shelf Area between Iceland and Jan Mayen. The Conciliation Commission explicitly stated that 'Jan Mayen must be considered as an island' and that '[t]herefore, Jan Mayen is entitled to a territorial sea, an economic zone and a continental shelf'.[179] There seems to be an inconsistency between the Tribunal's interpretation of Article 121(3) in the *South China Sea* Arbitration on the one hand and the *Jan Mayen* case and the Conciliation between Iceland and Jan Mayen on the other hand.

The second case is *Qatar v Bahrain* (2001). There, the Court held that Qit'at Jaradah was an island that should be used for the determination of the equidistance line.[180] At the same time, the Court observed that Qit'at Jaradah 'is a very small island, uninhabited and without any vegetation'.[181] Thus, if its low-water line were to be used for determining a basepoint in the construction of the equidistance line, a disproportionate effect would be given to an insignificant maritime feature. The Court thus found that there was a circumstance warranting the choice of a delimitation line passing immediately to the east of Qit'at Jaradah.[182] As a consequence, Qit'at Jaradah was given only a narrow territorial sea on its eastern side. In any case the Court did not examine the question whether Qit'at Jaradah was a rock for the purposes of Article 121(3).

Third is the *Nicaragua v Honduras* case, where the Court had to consider whether Bobel Cay, Savanna Cay, Port Royal Cay and South Cay belonged to Honduras and fell within the definition of and regime applying to islands under Article 121, since the Parties did not dispute the fact that these marine features remain above water at high tide. At the same time, the Court noted that the Parties did not claim for these islands any maritime areas beyond the territorial sea.[183] Accordingly, in drawing the maritime delimitation line between Nicaragua and Honduras, the Court traced the 12-nautical mile arc of the territorial sea around the south of Bobel Cay until it reached the median line in the overlapping territorial seas of Bobel Cay, Port Royal Cay and South Cay (Honduras) and Edinburgh Cay (Nicaragua). Furthermore, the Court traced the arc of the outer limit of the 12-nautical mile territorial sea of South Cay round to the north until it connected with the bisector line.[184] The Court's solution produced the same effect as if the cays were rocks under Article 121(3), even though the Court did not make a finding regarding the legal status of these features.

[179] 'Report and Recommendations to the Governments of Iceland and Norway of the Conciliation Commission on the Continental Shelf Area Between Iceland and Jan Mayen' (1981) 20 *ILM* 797, 803–04. See also R Churchill, 'Maritime Delimitation in the Jan Mayen Area' (1985) 9 *Marine Policy* 16, 19–20; Roach, n 163, 262–63.

[180] *Qatar v Bahrain* (Merits), n 10, [2001] ICJ Rep 99, [195].

[181] ibid, 104, [219].

[182] ibid, 109, [219].

[183] *Territorial and Maritime Dispute between Nicaragua and Honduras in the Caribbean Sea (Nicaragua v Honduras)* [2007] ICJ Rep 659, 702, [137].

[184] ibid, 759, [320].

Fourth, in the *Black Sea* case, Romania claimed that Serpents' Island, which belongs to Ukraine, is a rock incapable of sustaining human habitation or economic life of its own and, consequently, has no EEZ or continental shelf as provided for in Article 121(3) of the Convention.[185] Serpents' Island is above water at high tide and has a surface area of approximately 0.17 square kilometres and a circumference of approximately 2,000 metres.[186] According to Romania, Serpents' Island is devoid of water sources other than rainfall and practically devoid of soil, vegetation and fauna,[187] and as a consequence it is incapable of sustaining human habitation.[188] Nor is it capable of sustaining any economic life of its own.[189] In contrast, Ukraine asserted that Serpents' Island is indisputably an island, and supports human habitation and economic and other activities.[190] While the ICJ did not examine the legal status of Serpents' Island for the purposes of Article 121(3), the Court did not select any base points on Serpents' Island for the construction of a provisional equidistance line between the Parties.[191] Instead, the Court attributed a 12-nautical mile territorial sea to Serpents' Island pursuant to an agreement between the Parties.[192] The Court's solution produces the same effect as treating Serpents' Island as a rock, even though the ICJ did not clearly express this opinion.

Fifth, in the 2012 *Nicaragua v Colombia* case, the legal status of Quitasueño was at issue.[193] Quitasueño is a large bank approximately 57 kilometres long and 20 kilometres wide. Among multiple marine features of Quitasueño, only one feature, named QS 32, is above water at high tide. It is a minuscule feature, barely 1 square metre in area, and is above water at high tide only by some 0.7 metres.[194] The ICJ found that only QS 32 constituted an island within the definition in Article 121(1) of the UNCLOS, and that the other 53 features identified at Quitasueño were low-tide elevations.[195] Here the Court noted that

> [i]t has not been suggested by either Party that QS 32 is anything other than a rock which is incapable of sustaining human habitation or economic life of its own under

[185] The *Black Sea* case, Memorial Submitted by Romania, vol I, 19 August 2005, 141–94, [10.1]–[10.132]; Reply Submitted by Romania, 22 December 2006, 127–87, [5.1]–[5.184]; Presentation by Mr Aurescu, Verbatim Record, CR 2008/19, 52–71, [1]–[55]; presentation by Lowe, n 64, 39–53, [1]–[75]; and Presentation by Lowe, n 97, 10–18, [1]–[34]. See also Van Dyke, n 161, 43–60.

[186] The *Black Sea* case [2009] ICJ Rep 70, [16].

[187] Memorial Submitted by Romania, n 183, 154, [10.28] et seq.

[188] ibid, 163, [10.50] et seq.

[189] ibid, 173, [10.80] et seq. See also presentation by Lowe, Verbatim Record, n 64, 16 September 2008, 14–15, [21]–[23].

[190] Counter-Memorial of Ukraine, 19 May 2006, 25, [3.47].

[191] The *Black Sea* case, n 186, [2009] ICJ Rep 109–10, [149].

[192] ibid, 123, [188].

[193] The Philippines, in the *South China Sea* arbitration, referred to the *Nicaragua v Colombia* case as an example of the interpretation of Art 121(3) by the ICJ. The Memorial of the Philippines, vol I, 122–23, [5.27].

[194] *Nicaragua v Colombia*, n 10, [2012] ICJ Rep 640–41, [24]; 645, [37]; and 699, [202].

[195] ibid, 692, [181].

Article 121, paragraph 3, of UNCLOS, so this feature generates no entitlement to a continental shelf or exclusive economic zone.[196]

The Court concluded that 'Quitasueño is *a rock* incapable of sustaining human habitation or an economic life of its own and thus falls within the rule stated in Article 121, paragraph 3, of UNCLOS'.[197] As a consequence, the Court established a 12-nautical mile envelope of arcs around Quitasueño.[198] The Judgment in *Nicaragua v Colombia* is an exceptional case where the ICJ explicitly regarded a maritime feature as a rock under Article 121(3). One can draw similarities between the ICJ's decision on Quitasueño and the Tribunal's decision on Scarborough Shoal, Johnson Reef, Cuarteron Reef, Fiery Cross Reef, Gaven Reef (North) and McKennan Reef.[199] However, it must be noted that in the *Nicaragua v Colombia* case, the ICJ decided the legal status of Quitasueño on the basis of the statements of the Parties.[200]

Sixth, in *Costa Rica v Nicaragua* (2018), the Parties were divided with regard to the placement of base points on the Corn Islands. The Corn Islands are located approximately 26 nautical miles off the coast of Nicaragua in the Caribbean Sea. Great Corn Island has an area of 9.6 square kilometres and Little Corn Island has an area of 3 square kilometres. The total population of the Corn Islands is approximately 7,400 inhabitants. According to Nicaragua, they also sustain a vibrant economic life. While fishing became the economic mainstay during the 1960s and 1970s, more recently tourism has grown considerably.[201] The ICJ considered that the Corn Islands have a significant number of inhabitants and sustain economic life. Therefore it held that they 'amply satisfy the requirements set forth in Article 121 of UNCLOS for an island to be entitled to generate an exclusive economic zone and the continental shelf'.[202] In any case the Court, in *Costa Rica v Nicaragua*, did not undertake a thorough investigation of natural conditions of the Corn Islands.

Some mention must also be made of the *Eritrea/Yemen* Arbitration. There, Yemen employed both the small single island of al-Tayr and the group of islands called al-Zubayr as controlling base points. Nonetheless, the Arbitral Tribunal decided that both the single island of al-Tayr and the island group of al-Zubayr should have no effect upon the median line international boundary,

[196] ibid, 693, [183].

[197] ibid, [238] (emphasis added).

[198] ibid.

[199] The Philippines drew such similarities in the *South China Sea* Arbitration. See presentation by Mr Martin, Merits Hearing (Day 2), 25 November 2015, 91–92. See also the *South China Sea* Arbitration Award (Merits), n 1, [423].

[200] Y Tanaka, 'Reflections on the Territorial and Maritime Dispute between Nicaragua and Colombia before the International Court of Justice' (2013) 26 *LJIL* 909, 911.

[201] Counter-Memorial of Nicaragua, 60, [3.7] and 122, [3.104]; *Maritime Delimitation in the Caribbean Sea and the Pacific Ocean (Costa Rica v Nicaragua)*, Judgment, [2018] ICJ Rep (not yet reported), [49].

[202] ibid, [140]. However, only half effect was given to the Corn Islands when constructing a maritime boundary: ibid, [154].

partly because of their barren and inhospitable nature.[203] While the Tribunal used the term 'island' in relation to al-Tayer and al-Zubayr, it did not examine the legal status of these maritime features for the purpose of Article 121(3) of the UNCLOS. Since no effect was given to the maritime features of al-Tayer and al-Zubayr, because of their barren and inhospitable nature, it seems questionable whether the Arbitral Tribunal actually treated al-Tayer and al-Zubayr as fully entitled islands.

All in all, normally international courts have been wary about determining the legal status of maritime features for the purposes of Article 121(3). In light of the paucity of the jurisprudence on this subject, it is difficult to identify any uniform interpretation of Article 121(3) in the jurisprudence.

C. Legal Reasoning Supporting the Tribunal's Interpretation

The survey in the preceding sections suggests that no uniform interpretation or application of Article 121(3) can be drawn from state practice or the jurisprudence. Accordingly, it may have to be admitted that the Tribunal's interpretation of Article 121(3) is not anchored in state practice and the jurisprudence. If this is the case, the validity of the Tribunal's interpretation relies on the legal reasoning. In this regard, two elements merit highlighting.

The first element concerns the *raison d'être* of the EEZ. Here the Tribunal stressed the inter-linkage between the EEZ and 'the benefit of the local population':

> [T]he purpose of the exclusive economic zone that emerges from the history of the Convention … was to extend the jurisdiction of States over the waters adjacent to their coasts and to preserve the resources of those waters for the benefit of the population of the coastal State.[204]

In the view of the Tribunal, 'the human habitation with which the drafters of Article 121(3) were concerned was the habitation by a portion of the population for whose benefit the exclusive economic zone was being introduced'.[205] Therefore, 'without human habitation (or an economic life), the link between a maritime feature and the people of the coastal State becomes increasingly slight'.[206] It is of particular interest to note that the Tribunal focused on the benefit of the population, not on the interest of individual states, as the *raison d'être* of the EEZ. This is not an original view of the Tribunal. For instance, Judge Vukas, in the *Volga* case, stated that 'the protection of the economic interests of the coastal States, and in particular of *their population in the coastal*

[203] The *Eritrea/Yemen* Arbitration, n 32, 368, [147]–[148].
[204] The *South China Sea* Arbitration Award (Merits), n 1, [513]. See also ibid, [515].
[205] ibid, [520].
[206] ibid, [517].

areas, has been the essential factor in establishing this new regime at sea'.[207] Similarly, Guilfoyle argued that '[t]he historical conclusion presented here is straightforward: the *purpose* of the EEZ was primarily to benefit developing states, by giving their populations greater control over the marine resources in adjacent waters'.[208] In summary, according to the Tribunal, Article 121(3) of the UNCLOS performs a preventive function to 'disable tiny features from unfairly and inequitably generating enormous entitlements to maritime space that would serve not to benefit the local population, but to award a windfall to the (potentially distant) State to have maintained a claim to such a feature'.[209]

The second element pertains to the safeguarding of the common heritage of mankind. In this regard, the Tribunal referred to the statement of Ambassador Koh of Singapore, the President of the Third UN Conference on the Law of the Sea:

> The rationale for the proposal that coastal States should have the right to establish an economic zone was essentially based upon the interests of the people and the desire to marshal the resources of ocean space for their development … However, it would be unjust, and the common heritage of mankind would be further diminished, if every island, irrespective of its characteristics, was automatically entitled to claim a uniform economic zone. Such an approach would give inequitable benefits to coastal States with small or uninhabited islands scattered over a wide expanse of the ocean.[210]

In the view of the Tribunal, Article 121(3) functions as a safeguard of the common heritage of mankind.[211] The Tribunal's view echoed that of Kwiatkowska and Soons: '[T]here is no doubt that the exception established by Article 121, paragraph 3, whatever its exact scope, has been incorporated into the Convention with a view to preventing a further substantial limitation of the area of the Common Heritage of Mankind.'[212] Notably, China has also stressed the importance of the safeguarding of the common heritage of mankind when implementing Article 121(3), stating that:

> How to implement this provision [Article 121(3)] relates to the interpretation and application of important principles of the Convention, and the overall interests of the international community, and is a key issue for the proper consideration of relevant

[207] Declaration of Vice-President Vukas in the *Volga* case, n 156, 43–44, [5] (emphasis added).

[208] D Guilfoyle, 'The South China Sea Award: How Should We Read the UN Convention on the Law of the Sea?' (2018) 8 *Asian Journal of International Law* 51, 61–62 (original emphasis). See also Gjetnes, n 62, 194; and Van Dyke and Brooks, n 103, 286.

[209] The *South China Sea* Arbitration Award (Merits), n 1, [516].

[210] 'Summary Records of Meetings of the Second Committee, 39th Meeting', UN Doc A/CONF.62/C.2/SR.39, 285, para 72 (14 August 1974) (Statement of the Representative of Singapore), *Official Records of the Third United Nations Conference on the Law of the Sea, Volume II (Summary Records of Meetings of the First, Second and Third Committees, Second Session).*

[211] The *South China Sea* Arbitration Award (Merits), n 1, [535].

[212] Kwiatkowska and Soons, n 63, 144.

> submission concerning the outer limits of the continental shelf, and the safeguarding of the common heritage of mankind.[213]

Furthermore, referring to the general obligation of good faith in Article 300 of the UNCLOS, China emphasised the 'overall interests of the international community':

> [C]oastal States should comply fully with the Convention, taking into account *the overall interests of the international community*, and should not interpret the Convention in a biased way, nor put their own interests above the overall interests of the international community, nor encroach upon the Area as *the common heritage of mankind*.[214]

In summary, the Tribunal's interpretation of Article 121(3) relies on two key concepts: the benefit of the local population in the EEZ and the safeguarding of the common heritage of mankind.[215] Given that the latter aims to protect the benefit of mankind as a whole,[216] it can be said that the Tribunal's interpretation of Article 121(3) focuses on the benefit of people and mankind at the same time.[217]

The validity of the Tribunal's interpretation of Article 121(3) needs to be considered within the broad context of the development of the law of the sea since World War II. This period can be characterised as reflecting a tension between unilateralism and universalism in the law. On the one hand, the unilateral extension of coastal state jurisdiction towards the high seas to control natural resources has been a driving force of development of the law of the sea.[218] This movement was promoted by unilateralism focused on the interests of individual states. On the other hand, like international law in general, protection of the common interests of the international community as a whole

[213] People's Republic of China Note Verbale to the Secretary-General of the United Nations, 21 May 2009, in United Nations Convention on the Law of the Sea, Meeting of States Parties, *Proposal for the Inclusion of a Supplementary Item in the Agenda of the Nineteenth Meeting of States Parties*, UN Doc. SPLOS/196, 22 May 2009, [4] (emphasis added), available at http://undocs.org/SPLOS/196. The statement was cited in the *South China Sea* Arbitration Award (Merits), n 1, [455].

[214] Note Verbale from the People's Republic of China to the Secretary-General of the United Nations, n 213, [2] (emphasis added). The statement was cited in the *South China Sea* Arbitration Award (Merits), n 1, [453].

[215] See also Van Dyke and Brooks, n 103, 288.

[216] UNCLOS, Art 140.

[217] The Tribunal's interpretation seems to be connected with a 'new *jus gentium* of the twenty-first century, an International Law for humankind' claimed by Judge Cançando Trindade. AA Cançando Trindade, 'International Law for Humankind: Towards a New *Jus Gentium* (2005) 316 *RCADI* 9, 42. Judge Cançando Trindade, in his General Course, presented the basis outlook of international law as 'a *corpus juris* increasingly oriented to the fulfilment of the needs and aspirations of human beings, of peoples and of humankind as a whole': ibid, 33.

[218] The Truman Proclamations of 1945 can be regarded as the first demonstration of unilateralism of coastal states after World War II. R-J Dupuy, 'Droit de la mer et communauté internationale' in R-J Dupuy, *Dialectiques du droit international: souveraineté des Etats, communauté internationale et droits de l'humanité* (Pedone, 1999) 173, 175.

is increasingly important in the law of the sea. The protection of the common interests of the international community is linked to universalism in the oceans. It can be said that the law of the sea after World War II has vacillated between unilateralism and universalism.

The Tribunal's view can be thought to be the antithesis of the unilateralism demonstrated by China's claim in the South China Sea. In this sense, the Tribunal's interpretation of Article 121(3) appears to reflect the universalism in the law of the sea that seeks to safeguard community interests at sea. Indeed, the Tribunal's interpretation of Article 121(3) aims to contribute to the achievement of a goal of the UNCLOS, that is 'the realisation of a just and equitable international economic order which takes into account the interests and needs of mankind as a whole and, in particular, the special interests and needs of developing countries, whether coastal or land-locked'.[219] It can be said that the Tribunal's interpretation is in line with international law in the twenty-first century that seeks to protect community interests. In accordance with the Tribunal's interpretation, however, it is foreseeable that many maritime features would fall within the scope of Article 121(3). There are many coastal states that have put in place an EEZ and a continental shelf respecting a maritime feature that may, according to the Tribunal's view of Article 121(3), not be entitled to such ocean jurisdiction.[220] Accordingly, it is debatable whether the Tribunal's interpretation of Article 121(3) will be accepted by other states. However, the value of the Tribunal's interpretation should not be decided by the reaction of states alone. It is important to note that the issue of the interpretation of Article 121(3) relates to a more essential question of whether the law of the sea in the twenty-first century should encourage unilateralism to safeguard the interests of individual states or, conversely, universalism to promote community interests at sea. Notably, the Tribunal, in the *South China Sea* Arbitration Award (Merits), did seem to favour development of the law of the sea towards universalism focusing on the interests of the mankind as a whole or community interests.

V. CONCLUSIONS

This chapter has examined three principal questions: (i) the determination of the legal status of maritime features above/below high tide; (ii) the appropriation of low-tide elevations in international law; and (iii) the interpretation of Article 121(3) of the UNCLOS. These considerations may be summarised in three points.

[219] Preamble to the UNCLOS. The Tribunal explicitly referred to the goal. The *South China Sea* Arbitration Award (Merits), n 1, [515].

[220] See Nordquist and Phalen, n 111, 66 et seq.

First, according to the Tribunal, whether a particular feature is or is not above water at high tide must be decided on the basis of investigation that combines methods, including potentially direct, in-person observation covering an extended period of time across a range of weather and tidal conditions. However, this approach is hard to apply where maritime features have been significantly modified by human activities. In this case, it becomes necessary to investigate the 'best available evidence of the *previous* status of the feature'. In this regard, the Tribunal attributed much weight to historical records when deciding the legal status of maritime features as above/below high tide. However, care should be taken, noting that historical records may not always be clear and consistent. Accordingly, the relevance of historical records must be examined carefully on a case-by-case basis.

Second, the Tribunal, in its Award on the Merits, considered that low-tide elevations do not form part of the land territory and, thus, they cannot be appropriated. The Tribunal's view is in line with the jurisprudence of the ICJ. It follows that low-tide elevations fall within the legal regimes for the territorial sea or continental shelf, and that these elevations cannot be a subject of appropriation by a third state.[221]

Third, the Tribunal, for the first time, provided a detailed review of the interpretation and application of Article 121(3) of the UNCLOS. In this regard, it specified the qualitative and temporal requirements. The Tribunal's interpretation of Article 121(3) relies on two key elements: the benefit of the local population in the EEZ and the safeguarding of the common heritage of mankind. It is noteworthy that the Tribunal's interpretation focuses on the benefit of people, not on the interests of an individual state. According to the Tribunal, Article 121(3) has a preventive function of disabling tiny features from unfairly and inequitably generating large entitlements to maritime space that would not serve to benefit the local population.

It remains to be seen whether and to what extent the Tribunal's interpretation will affect state and juridical practice. As McDorman stated, however, 'it is difficult to conclude other than the Tribunal was providing a framework or direction for States and future tribunals to determine whether features are rocks or island'.[222] Furthermore, as Gullett observed, 'it can be expected that the South China Sea Arbitral Award will at minimum be referenced by the next court or tribunal to examine Article 121(3) and it can be anticipated to be influential'.[223] It would be erroneous to underestimate the influence of the Tribunal's interpretation, since other courts or tribunals will be required to provide

[221] See also T Davenport, 'Island-Building in the South China Sea: Legality and Limtis' (2018) 8 *Asian Journal of International Law* 76, 89.

[222] TL McDorman, 'The South China Sea *Tribunal Awards: A Dispute Resolution Perspective*' (2018) 3 *Asia-Pacific Journal of Ocean Law and Policy* 134, 143.

[223] Gullett, n 109, 37.

more persuasive reasons if they wish to adopt an interpretation different from that of the Tribunal.[224] In any event, as typically shown in the law of maritime delimitation, an accumulation of case law will be needed to elaborate the interpretation of norms of international law, and the same applies to Article 121. It would be fair to say that the Tribunal's interpretation may be a first and important step in the clarification of this provision, regardless of some criticism of certain aspects of its interpretation.[225]

FURTHER READING

Anderson, DH, 'British Accession to the UN Convention on the Law of the Sea' (1997) 46 *ICLQ* 761.

——, 'Some Aspects of the Regime of Islands in the Law of the Sea' (2017) 32 *IJMCL* 316.

Benzing, M, 'Evidentiary Issues' in A Zimmermann et al (eds), *The Statute of the International Court of Justice: A Commentary*, 2nd edn (Oxford University Press, 2012) 1234–75.

Borton, J (ed), *Islands and Rocks in the South China Sea: Post-Hague Ruling* (Xlibris, 20017).

Bowett, DW, *The Legal Regime of Islands in International Law* (Oceana, 1979).

Caflisch, L, 'Les espaces marins attachés à des îles ou roches' in M Forteau and J-M Thouvenin (eds), *Traité de droit international de la mer* (Pedone, 2017) 477–89.

Charney, JI, 'Rocks That Cannot Sustain Human Habitation' (1999) 93 *AJIL* 863.

Choo-Ho Park, 'The Changeable Legal Status of Islands and "Non-Islands" in the Law of the Sea: Some Instances in the Asia-Pacific Region' in DD Caron and HN Scheiber (eds), *Bringing New Law to Ocean Waters* (Brill/Nijhoff, 2004) 483–91.

Churchill, R, 'Maritime Delimitation in the Jan Mayen Area' (1985) 9 *Marine Policy* 16.

——, 'Norway: Supreme Court Judgment on Law of the Sea Issues' (1996) 11 *IJMCL* 576.

——, 'United Kingdom's Decision to Defer Accession to the UN Convention on the Law of the Sea: A Convincing Move?'(1997) 12 *IJMCL* 110.

Davenport, T, 'Island-Building in the South China Sea: Legality and Limtis' (2018) 8 *Asian Journal of International Law* 76.

Dundas, CW, 'Middle American and Caribbean Maritime Boundaries' in DA Colson and RW Smith (eds), *International Maritime Boundaries*, vol V (Brill/Nijhoff, 2005) 3405–23.

Fitzmaurice, G, *The Law and Procedure of the International Court of Justice*, vol I (Cambridge University Press, 1993).

[224] Lee-Iwamoto, n 43, 47; E Franckx, 'The Arbitral Tribunal's Interpretation of Paragraph 3 in Article 121: A First but Important Step Forward' in Jayakumar et al (eds), n 13, 154, 175.

[225] Franckx considered the Tribunal's interpretation as 'a most timely and necessary first step': Franckx, n 224, 175. Gullet also stated that the Tribunal's interpretation of Art 121(3) and the standard it set 'should be welcomed by those who seek clarify in international law, especially due to the apparent abuse of the provision by many States': Gullett, n 109, 27–28.

Franckx, E, 'The Regime of Islands and Rocks' in DJ Attard, M Fitzmaurice and NA Martínex Gutiérrez (eds), *The IMLI Manual on International Maritime Law*, vol I: *The Law of the Sea* (Oxford University Press, 2014) 99–124.

——, 'The Arbitral Tribunal's Interpretation of Paragraph 3 in Article 121: A First but Important Step Forward' in S Jayakumar et al (eds), *The South China Sea Arbitration: The Legal Dimension* (Edward Elgar, 2018) 154–75.

Gidel, G, *Le droit international public de la mer, Le temps de paix*, Tome III (reprint) (Duchemin, 1981).

Gjetnes, M, 'The Spratlys: Are They Rocks or Islands?'(2001) 32 *ODIL* 191.

Guilfoyle, D, 'The South China Sea Award: How Should We Read the UN Convention on the Law of the Sea?' (2018) 8 *Asian Journal of International Law* 51.

Guillaume, G, 'Les haute-fonds de´couvrants en droit international' in *La mer et son droit, Mélanges offerts à Laurent Lucchini et Jean-Pierre Que´neudec* (Pedone, 2003) 287–302.

Gullett, W, 'The South China Sea Arbitration's Contribution to the Concept of Juridical Islands' (2018) 47 *Questions of International Law Zoom-in* 5.

Gullett, W and Schofield, C, 'Pushing the Limits of the Law of the Sea Convention: Australian and French Cooperative Surveillance and Enforcement in the Southern Ocean' (2007) 22 *IJMCL* 545.

Hafetz, JL, 'Fostering Protection of the Marine Environment and Economic Development: Article 121(3) of the Third Law of the Sea Convention' (2000) 15 *American University International Law Review* 583.

Karagiannis, S, 'Les rochers qui ne se prêtent pas à l'habitation humaine ou à une vie économique Propre et le droit de la mer' (1996) *Revue belge de droit international* 559.

Klein, N, 'Islands and Rocks after the South China Sea Arbitration' (2016) 34 *Australian Year Book of International Law* 21.

Kolb, R., 'L'interprétation de l'article 121, paragraph 3, de la Convention de Montego Bay sur le droit de la mer: les "roches qui ne se prêtent pas à l'habitation humaine ou à une vie économique propre …"' (1994) 40 *Annuaire Français de Droit International* 876.

Kwiatkowska, B and Soons, AHA, 'Entitlement to Maritime Areas of Rocks Which Cannot Sustain Human Habitation or Economic Life of Their Own' (1990) 21 *The Netherlands Yearbook of International Law* 139.

Lyons, Y, Luu Quang Hung and Tkalich, P, 'Determining High-tide Features (or Islands) in the South China Sea under Article 121(1): a Legal and Oceanography Perspective' in S Jayakumar et al (eds), *The South China Sea Arbitration: The Legal Dimension* (Edward Elgar, 2018) 128–53.

McDorman, TL, 'An International Law Perspective on Insular Features (Islands) and Low-tide Elevations in the South China Sea' (2017) 32 *IJMCL* 298.

Murphy, SD, 'International Law Relating to Islands' (2017) 386 *RCADI* 21.

Nordquist, MH, 'Textual Interpretation of Article 121 in the UN Convention on the Law of the Sea' in HP Hestermeyer et al (eds), *Coexistence, Cooperation and Solidarity: Liber Amicorum Rüdiger Wolfrum*, vol I (Njihoff, 2012) 991–1036.

——, 'UNCLOS Article 121 and Itu Aba in the South China Sea Final Award: A Correct Interpretation?' in S Jayakumar et al (eds), *The South China Sea Arbitration: The Legal Dimension* (Edward Elgar, 2018) 176–204.

Nordquist, MH and Phalen, WG, 'Interpretation of UNCLOS Article 121 and Itu Aba (Taiping) in the South China Sea Arbitration Award' in MH Nordquist, JN Moore and R Long (eds), *International Marine Economy: Law and Policy* (Brill/Nijhoff, 2017) 30–78.

Oral, N, 'The South China Sea Arbitral Award: Casting Light on Article 121 of UNCLOS' (2017) 16 *The Law and Practice of International Courts and Tribunals* 354.

Oude Elferink, AG, 'The Islands in the South China Sea: How Does Their Presence Limit the Extent of the High Seas and the Area and the maritime Zones of the Mainland Coasts?' (2011) 32 *ODIL*169.

——, 'The South China Sea Arbitration's Interpretation of Article 121(3) of the UNCLOS: A Disquieting First' *The JCLOS Blog*, 7 September 2016, available at http://site.uit.no/jclos/2016/09/07/the-south-china-sea-arbitrations-interpretation-of-article-1213-of-the-losc-a-disquieting-first/.

Oxman, BH, 'Complementary Agreements and Compulsory Jurisdiction' (2001) 95 *AJIL* 277.

Papanicolopulu, I, 'The Land Dominates the Sea (Dominates the Land Dominates the Sea)' (2018) 47 *Questions of International Law Zoom-in* 39.

Prescott, V and Schofield, C, *The Maritime Political Boundaries of the World*, 2nd edn (Brill/Njihoff, 2005).

Pereira, ES, 'Islands and Rocks Recent Developments by South China Sea Arbitral Award' in TM Ndyiaye and RF More (eds), *Prospects of Evolution of the Law of the Sea, Environmental Law and the practice of ITLOS: New Challenges and Emerging Regimes* (SaG Serv, 2018) 213–32.

Riddell, A and Plant, B, *Evidence before the International Court of Justice* (British Institute of International and Comparative Law, 2009).

Roach, JA, 'Offshore Archipelagos Enclosed by Straight Baselines: An Excessive Claim?' (2018) 49 *ODIL*176.

——, 'Rocks versus Islands: Implications for Protection of the Marine Environment' in S Jayakumar et al (eds), *The South China Sea Arbitration: The Legal Dimension* (Edward Elgar, 2018) 247–75.

Roach, JA and Smith, RW, *Excessive Maritime Claims*, 3rd edn (Brill/Nijhoff, 2012).

Rosenne, S (ed), *League of Nations: Conference for the Codification of International Law 1930*, vol II (New York, Oceana, 1975).

Sakamoto, S, 'Legal Status of Island: Focusing on the Interpretation of Article 121 (3) of UNCLOS by the South China Sea Arbitration Award' (in Japanese) (2018) 69 *The Doshisha Law Review* 2029.

Saunders, I, 'The *South China Sea Award*, Artificial Islands and Territory' (2016) 34 *Australian Yearbook of International Law* 31.

Schofield, C, 'The Trouble with Islands: The Definition and Role of Islands and Rocks in Maritime Boundary Delimitation' in Seoung-Yong Hong and JM Van Dyke (eds), *Maritime Boundary Disputes, Settlement Processes, and the Law of the Sea* (Brill/Nijhoff, 2009) 19–37.

Sheng-ti Gau, M, 'The Interpretation of Article 121(3) of UNCLOS by the Tribunal for the South China Sea Arbitration: A Critique' (2019) *ODIL* at https://doi.org/10.1080/00908320.2018.1511083.

Symmons, C, *The Maritime Zones of Islands in International Law* (Nijhoff, 1979).

——, 'Some Problems Relating to the Definition of 'Insular Formations' in International Law: Islands and Low-Tide Elevations' *Maritime Briefing* 1 No 5 (International Boundaries Research Unit, 1995).

Tanaka, Y, 'Low-Tide Elevations in International Law of the Sea: Selected Issues' (2006) 20 *Ocean Yearbook* 189.

——, 'Passing of Sovereignty: the *Malaysia/Singapore* Territorial Dispute before the ICJ' (2008) 3 *Hague Justice Journal* 5.

——, 'Reflections on the Territorial and Maritime Dispute between Nicaragua and Colombia before the International Court of Justice' (2013) 26 *LJIL* 909.

——, 'Reflections on the Interpretation and Application of Article 121(3) in the *South China Sea* Arbitration (Merits)' (2017) 48 *ODIL* 365.

——, 'Reflections on the *South China Sea* Arbitration Award (Merits): Historic Rights and the Interpretation of Article 121(3)' (in Japanese) (2018) 117(2) *The Journal of International Law and Diplomacy* 1.

Tiff Yu-Ting Bowes-Lin, 'Certain Historical Evidence (and Their Implications) Overlooked by the Arbitral Tribunal of the South China Sea Arbitration: Application of Article 121(3) on Spratly Islands' (2018) 10 *Asian Politics and Policy* 341.

Ulfstein, G, 'Jan Mayen' in R Wolfrum (ed), *Max Planck Encyclopedia of Public International Law* (online, Oxford University Press, 2009).

United Nations, Office for Ocean Affairs and the Law of the Sea, *The Law of the Sea: Régime of Islands, Legislative History of Part VIII (Article 121) of the United Nations Convention on the Law of the Sea* (United Nations, 1988).

Van Dyke, JM, 'The Romania-Ukraine Decision and Its Effect on East Asian Maritime Delimitation' in Seoung-Yong Hong and JM Van Dyke (eds), *Governing Ocean Resources: New Challenges and Emerging Regimes, A Tribute to Judge Choon-Ho Park* (Brill/Nijhoff, 2013) 43–60.

Van Dyke, JM and Brooks, RA, 'Uninhabited Islands: Their Impact on the Ownership of the Oceans' Resources' (1983) 12 *ODIL* 265.

Van Dyke, JM and Bennett, DL, 'Islands and the Delimitation of Ocean Space in the South China Sea' (1993) 10 *Ocean Yearbook* 54.

Van Dyke, JM, Morgan, JR and Gurish, J, 'The Exclusive Economic Zone of the Northwestern Hawaiian Islands: When Do Uninhabited islands Generate an EEZ?' (1988) 25 *San Diego Law Review* 425.

van Overbeek, W, 'Article 121(3) UNCLOS in Mexican State Practice in the Pacific' (1989) 4 *IJMCL* 252.

Yann-huei Song, 'Okinotorishima: A "Rock" or an "Island"? Recent Maritime Boundary Controversy between Japan and Taiwan/China' in Seoung-Yong Hong and JM Van Dyke (eds), *Maritime Boundary Disputes, Settlement Process, and the Law of the Sea* (Brill/Nijhoff, 2009) 145–75.

——, 'The Application of Article 121 of the Law of the Sea Convention to the Selected Geographical Features Situated in the Pacific Ocean' (2010) 9 *CJIL* 663.

——, 'Article 121(3) of the Law of the Sea Convention and the Disputed Offshore Islands in East Asia: A Tribute to Judge Choon-Ho Park' in Seoung-Yong Hong and JM Van Dyke (eds), *Governing Ocean Resources: New Challenges and Emerging Regimes, A Tribute to Judge Choon-Ho Park* (Brill/Nijhoff, 2013) 61–98.

——, 'The South China Sea Arbitration Case Filed by the Philippines against China: Arguments Concerning Submerged Features, Low Tide Elevations and Islands' in Wu Shicun and Keyuan Zou (eds), *Arbitration Concerning the South China Sea: Philippines versus China* (Routledge, 2016) 157–83.

——, 'The July 2016 Arbitral Award, Interpretation of Article 121(3) of the UNCLOS, and Selecting Examples of Inconsistent State Practices' (2018) 49 *ODIL* 247.

5

Lawfulness of Chinese Activities in the South China Sea

I. INTRODUCTION

After the examination of the legal status of maritime features, the Tribunal moved on to consider the lawfulness of Chinese activities in the South China Sea. In this connection, the Tribunal wrestled with a wide array of issues in international law. Among other things, the following issues deserve serious consideration:

(a) Can diplomatic statements and communications themselves be regarded as a breach of the UNCLOS?
(b) What is the obligation to have 'due regard to the rights and duties' under Article 58(3) of the Convention?
(c) What are the rules applicable to the traditional fishing rights under the UNCLOS?
(d) What is the 'general obligation' under Article 192 of the Convention, and what are the requirements for fulfilling the obligation of due diligence in the context of environmental protection?
(e) How is it possible to determine the breach of the obligation to conduct an environmental impact assessment?
(f) Is it legally possible to conduct construction activities on low-tide elevations in a third state's EEZ or continental shelf?
(g) What is the relationship between Article 94 of the UNCLOS and the Convention on the International Regulations for Preventing Collisions at Sea (COLREGS)?
(h) What are the criteria for deciding the breach of the obligation of non-aggravation in international law?

Beyond the scope of the settlement of the dispute between the Philippines and China, the Tribunal's view on these matters sheds some light on the interpretation or application of rules and obligations of international law. Thus this chapter addresses the above issues in light of the *South China Sea* Arbitration

Award (Merits).[1] Following this Introduction, section II examines: alleged interference with the Philippines' sovereign rights in its EEZ and continental shelf, alleged failure to prevent Chinese nationals from exploiting the Philippines' living resources, China's actions in respect of traditional fishing at Scarborough Shoal, the protection and preservation of the marine environment, occupation and construction activities on Mischief Reef, and the operation of law enforcement vessels in a dangerous manner. Section III addresses the obligation of non-aggravation and future conduct of the parties, and the chapter ends by offering conclusions in section IV.

II. LAWFULNESS OF CHINA'S ACTIONS IN THE SOUTH CHINA SEA

A. Alleged Interference with the Philippines' Sovereign Rights in its EEZ and Continental Shelf

i. Jurisdiction of the Tribunal

The first issue relates to China's interference with the Philippines' sovereign rights in its EEZ and continental shelf. In its Submission No 8, the Philippines requested the Tribunal to declare:

> (8) China has unlawfully interfered with the enjoyment and exercise of the sovereign rights of the Philippines with respect to the living and non-living resources of its exclusive economic zone and continental shelf.[2]

In this connection, the Philippines claimed that China interfered with the Philippines' sovereign rights and jurisdiction over the living resources by the following conduct:

- (a) China's prevention of fishing by Philippine vessels at Mischief Reef since 1995,
- (b) The 2012 moratorium on fishing in the South China Sea north of 12° N latitude,
- (c) China's revision of the Hainan Regulation,[3] and
- (d) China's prevention of fishing by Philippine vessels at Second Thomas Shoal since 1995.[4]

China did not directly respond to the Philippines' allegations. Referring to various statements made by China, however, the Tribunal held that apparently China considered that it had sovereignty and sovereign rights in the areas where

[1] PCA Case No 2013–19. The *South China Sea Arbitration Award* (Merits) ('the *South China Sea* Arbitration Award (Merits)'), 12 July 2016.

[2] ibid, [649]. See also ibid, [685]; the Philippines' Memorial, vol I, 165, [6.17]–[6.19]; presentation by Sands, Merits Hearing Tr (Day 2), 140–42.

[3] People's Republic of China, Hainan Province, *Hainan Provincial Regulation on the Control of Coastal Border Security*, 31 December 2012. This document was reproduced in Annex 123 to the Philippines' Memorial, vol V.

[4] The *South China Sea* Arbitration Award (Merits), n 1, [686].

the Philippines launched a petrol exploration, and that it had sovereign rights with respect to fisheries in the areas in question.[5]

In the Award on Jurisdiction, the Tribunal reserved a decision on its jurisdiction with respect to the Philippines' Submission No 8 for consideration in conjunction with the merits of the Philippines' claims.[6] At the same time, it held that this was not a dispute concerning sovereignty or maritime boundary delimitation, nor was it barred from the Tribunal's consideration by any requirement of Section 1 of Part XV of the Convention.[7] This point was confirmed by the Tribunal in its Award on the Merits.[8]

In the Award on the Merits, the Tribunal found that there was no legal basis for any Chinese historic rights in the South China Sea encompassed by the 'nine-dash line';[9] and that none of the high-tide feature in the Spratly Islands was a fully entitled island for the purposes of Article 121 of the UNCLOS.[10] Accordingly, there was no maritime feature in the Spratly Islands capable of generating an entitlement to an EEZ or continental shelf in the areas of Mischief Reef or Second Thomas Shoal, or in the areas of the GSEC101 bloc, Area 3, Area 4, or the SC58 block. It followed that there was no situation of overlapping entitlement that would call for maritime delimitations in accordance with Articles 15, 74 and 83 of the UNCLOS.[11] Since the areas of the South China Sea at issue in Submission No 8 could only constitute the EEZ of the Philippines, the Philippines possessed sovereign rights with respect to resources in these areas by virtue of Articles 77 and 56 of the Convention.[12]

Article 297(3)(a) and the law enforcement exception in Article 298(1)(b) of the Convention serve to limit compulsory dispute settlement where a claim is brought against a state's exercise of its sovereign rights in respect of living resources in its *own* EEZ. In the view of the Tribunal, however, these provisions do not apply where a state is alleged to have violated the Convention in respect of the EEZ of another state. As the areas of the South China Sea at issue in the Philippines' Submission No 8 constituted the EEZ of the Philippines,

[5] ibid, [68]–[689]. In this regard, the Tribunal referred to the following instruments: Note Verbale from the Embassy of the People's Republic of China in Manila to the Department of Foreign Affairs, Republic of the Philippines, No (10) PG-047 (22 February 2010); Memorandum from Rafael E Seguis, the Undersecretary for Special and Ocean Concerns, Department of Foreign Affairs, Republic of the Philippines, to the Secretary of Foreign Affairs of the Republic of the Philippines (30 July 2010); Note Verbale from the Embassy of the People's Republic of China in Manila to the Department of Foreign Affairs, Republic of the Philippines, No (11) PG-202 (6 July 2011); and 'Fishing ban starts in South China Sea', *Xinhua* (17 May 2012).

[6] PCA Case No 2013–19. The *South China Sea* Arbitration (Jurisdiction and Admissibility) (hereinafter 'the *South China Sea* Arbitration Award (Jurisdiction and Admissibility)'), 29 October 2015, [405].

[7] ibid.

[8] The *South China Sea* Arbitration Award (Merits), n 1, [690].

[9] ibid, [1203]B(2). See also [277]–[278].

[10] ibid, [626].

[11] ibid, [692]–[694].

[12] ibid, [697]–[700].

these provisions posed no obstacle to the jurisdiction of the Tribunal. The Tribunal thus concluded that it had jurisdiction with regard to the Philippines' Submission No 8.[13]

ii. Lawfulness of China's Actions

The Tribunal then turned to examine the legal consequences of China's interference with the Philippines' sovereign rights in its EEZ and continental shelf. In this regard, three types of conduct can be identified:

(a) diplomatic communications;[14]
(b) physical actions;[15] and
(c) a statement that may have a deterring effect.[16]

It is beyond serious argument that provisions of the UNCLOS can be breached by physical actions of a state. In fact, the Tribunal held that China's actions that induced the MV *Veritas Voyager* to cease operations and to depart from an area that constituted part of the continental shelf of the Philippines amounted to a breach of Article 77 of the UNCLOS, which accords sovereign rights to the Philippines with regard to its continental shelf in the area of Reed Bank.[17] In contrast, the Tribunal held that there was no distinct evidence concerning China's prevention of fishing by Philippines vessels at Mischief Reef and Second Thomas Shoal; and that the provisions of the Convention concerning fisheries were not implicated.[18] However, the legal effect of diplomatic communications and a statement needs further consideration. In this regard, two issues arise.

The first issue is whether diplomatic statements and communications themselves can be regarded as a breach of the UNCLOS. In this regard, the Tribunal took the view that '[i]t is an altogether normal occurrence that States will have different understandings of their respective rights'.[19] For the Tribunal, 'If the expression of such differences were itself sufficient to place the State whose understanding of the law ultimately proved incorrect in breach of the underlying

[13] ibid, [695].

[14] In this regard, the Philippines referred to two types of Chinese statements: (i) diplomatic statements, ie China's objections to the Philippines Government regarding the conversion of the GSEC101 contract, the SC58 contract, and the tender for Area 3 and Area 4; and (ii) a statement by a Chinese official to a representative of Nido Petroleum Ltd: ibid, [702].

[15] Specifically the Philippines objected to actions by Chinese Marine Surveillance (CMS) vessels to order the MV *Veritas Voyager* to halt operations and leave the area of Reed Bank, and to China's prevention of fishing by Philippines vessels at Mischief Reef and Second Thomas Shoal: ibid, [702] and [709].

[16] In this connection, the Philippines objected to China's extension of its jurisdiction over fisheries in the South China Sea through the 2012 moratorium on fishing in the area north of 12° N latitude and through the Hainan Regulation: ibid, [709].

[17] ibid, [708], [716].

[18] ibid, [714]–[715].

[19] ibid, [705].

obligation, it would cast an unacceptable chill on the ordinary conduct of diplomacy.'[20]

The Tribunal did not exclude the possibility that 'it could reach a different conclusion in the case of diplomatic statements claiming rights in bad faith, or in the case of attempts by one State to induce another to relinquish its rights through repeated statements, veiled threats, or diplomatic coercion'.[21] However, this was not the case on the record before the Tribunal. It thus concluded that China's diplomatic statements to the Philippines regarding their respective rights did not constitute breaches of the UNCLOS, even though incorrect with respect to the law.[22] Likewise it found that China's action in merely informing a private party of its claims in the South China Sea did not constitute breaches of the Convention.[23] Yet the reasoning of the Tribunal seems to lack consistency. As discussed in chapter 3, the Tribunal held that China's *claims* to historic rights, or other sovereign rights or jurisdiction, with respect to the maritime areas of the South China Sea encompassed by the relevant part of the 'nine-dash line' were contrary to the Convention. In so doing, the Tribunal judged the illegality of China's *claims*, not China's physical conduct to implement its alleged historic rights in marine spaces encompassed by the 'nine-dash line'. If China claimed its rights in good faith,[24] this did not automatically preclude the wrongfulness of those claims that were at variance with the Convention. Indeed, the Tribunal, in its Award on the Merits, clearly stated that China's understanding of its rights concerning non-living resources in the South China Sea was 'incorrect with respect to the law'.[25]

The second issue pertains to the legal effect of a statement that may have a deterring effect. The question of interest here was whether China's 2012 promulgation of the fishing moratorium[26] and the Hainan Regulation[27] infringed on the right of the Philippines and constituted a breach of the Convention, irrespective of whether the moratorium was directly enforced.[28] As regards China's moratorium, the Tribunal considered that it was intended to apply to areas of the Philippines' EEZ north of 12° N latitude and was not limited to Chinese flagged vessels. In contrast to mere statements, the fishing moratorium established a 'realistic prospect' that Filipino fishermen could be exposed to the punitive measures spelled out in the moratorium, including the possible confiscation of

[20] ibid.
[21] ibid.
[22] ibid.
[23] ibid, [706].
[24] ibid, [704].
[25] ibid, [705].
[26] People's Republic of China, Ministry of Agriculture, South China Sea Fishery Bureau, *Announcement on the 2012 Summer Ban on Marine Fishing in the South China Sea Maritime Space* (10 May 2012). This document was reproduced in Annex 118 to the Philippines' Memorial, vol V.
[27] Hainan Provincial Regulation, n 3.
[28] The *South China Sea* Arbitration Award (Merits), n 1, [711].

the fishing vessels in question. The Tribunal considered that such developments might have a deterring effect on Filipino fishermen and their activities.[29] It thus ruled that such an assertion of jurisdiction amounted to a breach of Article 56 of the Convention, which accords sovereign rights to the Philippines with respect to the living resources of its EEZ.[30] In contrast, the Tribunal found no provision in the Hainan Regulation that would restrict the rights of the Philippines over the resources of its EEZ. Furthermore, the Regulation applies only within 12 nautical miles of Hainan. Accordingly, the Tribunal ruled that the Hainan Regulation did not infringe on the rights of the Philippines or amount to a breach of the provisions of the UNCLOS concerning the EEZ.[31]

According to the Tribunal's approach, where a statement may have a deterring effect, that statement violates relevant provisions of the UNCLOS. Hence the existence of a deterring effect becomes the key element. An issue that arises in this regard is how it is possible to determine the existence of a deterring effect. Here the Tribunal applied a 'realistic prospect' test. According to this test, the existence of a deterring effect is to be decided on the basis of the existence of a 'realistic prospect' that punitive measures arising from a statement could be brought to bear in the *future*. Thus if a statement presents a realistic prospect that the exercise of the sovereign rights of a coastal state would be deterred in its EEZ in the *future*, that statement has a deterring effect.

While the deterring effect is a matter for the future, the existence or non-existence of a 'realistic prospect' is a matter for the present. In this sense, the 'realistic prospect' test can be thought to be a temporal concept. Yet the concept of a 'realistic prospect' is not wholly unambiguous. An question that arises in this regard is how it is possible to assess the existence of a 'realistic prospect'. Since the 'prospect' relies on the subjective perception of states, it may be less easy for an international court or tribunal to objectively determine the content of such 'prospect'. Furthermore, the adjective 'realistic' seems to be a matter of degree. Yet the Tribunal offered scant explanation to answer the question to what extent the prospect of the future events must exist. Moreover, unlike the China's 2012 promulgation of the fishing moratorium, the Tribunal did not apply the 'realistic prospect' test to China's diplomatic statements regarding the conversion of the GSEC101 contract, the SC58 contract, and the tender for Area 3 and Area 4. This is a double standard. With regard to SC58 contract, however, the Chinese Government stated, in its Memorandum of 30 July 2010, that it considered this as a 'very serious matter', and that it reserved the 'right to unilaterally act on this matter to protect [its] interests'.[32] Accordingly, there appears to

[29] ibid, [712].
[30] ibid; see also ibid, [716].
[31] ibid, [713].
[32] Memorandum from the Undersecretary for Special and Ocean Concerns, Department of Foreign Affairs, Republic of the Philippines, to the Secretary of Foreign Affairs of the Republic of the Philippines, 30 July 2010, quoted ibid, [663].

be some scope to reconsider the question regarding whether the Memorandum would create a deterring effect.

B. Alleged Failure to Prevent Chinese Nationals from Exploiting the Philippines' Living Resources

i. Jurisdiction of the Tribunal

The next issue concerns the alleged failure of China to prevent Chinese nationals from exploiting the Philippines' living resources. In this regard, the Philippines, in its Submission No 9, requested the Tribunal to declare:

> (9) China has unlawfully failed to prevent its nationals and vessels from exploiting the living resources in the exclusive economic zone of the Philippines.[33]

The above submission related to developments at Mischief Reef and Second Thomas Shoal, both of which are low-tide elevations lying within 200 nautical miles of the Philippines' baselines.[34] In this connection, the Philippines argued that China had violated its obligations under Article 56 of the UNCLOS concerning the sovereign rights and jurisdiction of the Philippines.[35] According to the Philippines, China prevented fishing by Philippine vessels in the South China Sea, while tolerating fishing by Chinese nationals and vessels, including in areas that comprise the Philippines' EEZ.[36] The Philippines thus claimed that whereas China was not responsible per se for the actions of its fishermen, it was responsible for its own failure to control their illegal and damaging activities.[37] China has never directly addressed the above-mentioned allegation. In light of China's contemporaneous statements, however, the Tribunal observed that China did not consider the Philippines to have rights in the area of Second Thomas Shoal and Mischief Reef. In fact, China repeatedly demanded that the Philippines withdraw its personnel from Second Thomas Shoal.[38]

[33] ibid, [717].

[34] ibid, [718].

[35] ibid, [723].

[36] ibid, [724]. See also Memorial, [6.36].

[37] The *South China Sea* Arbitration Award (Merits), n 1, [728]; presentation by Professor Sands, Merits Hearing Tr Day 4, 88.

[38] The *South China Sea* Arbitration Award (Merits), n 1, [730]–[731]. In this regard, the Tribunal relied on numerous statements of China, such as: Note Verbale from the Ministry of Foreign Affairs, People's Republic of China to the Embassy of the Republic of the Philippines in Beijing, No (2015) Bu Bian Zi No 5 (20 January 2015); Note Verbale from the Embassy of the People's Republic of China in Manila to the Department of Foreign Affairs, Republic of the Philippines, No 14 (PG)-195 (30 June 2014) (Annex 675); Note Verbale from the Embassy of the People's Republic of China in Manila to the Department of Foreign Affairs, Republic of the Philippines, No 14 (PG)-197 (4 July 2014); Note Verbale from the Embassy of the People's Republic of China in Manila to the Department of Foreign Affairs, Republic of the Philippines, No 14 (PG)-264 (2 September 2014).

In its Award on Jurisdiction, the Tribunal reserved a decision on its jurisdiction with respect to the Philippines' Submission No 9 for consideration in conjunction with the merits of the Philippines claims.[39] As had been seen, the Tribunal, in its Award on the Merits, determined that Mischief Reef and Second Thomas Shoal are both low-tide elevations and that no high-tide feature in the Spratly Islands is capable of generating an entitlement to an EEZ. It follows that there existed no legal basis for any entitlement by China to maritime zones in the area of Mischief Reef and Second Thomas Shoal. Nor was there any situation of overlapping entitlement that would call for maritime delimitations in accordance with Articles 15, 74 and 83 of the Convention. Furthermore, since the areas of the South China Sea at issue in Submission No 9 were able to constitute the EEZ of the Philippines only, Article 297(3)(a) and the law enforcement exception in Article 298(1)(b) of the UNCLOS posed no obstacle to the Tribunal's jurisdiction. The Tribunal thus held that it had jurisdiction with regard to the Philippines' Submission No 9.[40]

ii. Lawfulness of China's Actions

As the relevant areas could only constitute the EEZ of the Philippines, the Philippines had sovereign rights with regard to resources in those areas.[41] Under Articles 61 and 62 of the UNCLOS, it is clear that the Philippines could control the process of granting and regulating access to the fisheries of its EEZ under the Convention.

When considering the lawfulness of China's actions, the Tribunal highlighted the difference between Article 62(4) and Article 58(3) of the UNCLOS. According to the Tribunal, Article 62(4) imposes an obligation directly on *private* parties engaged in fishing. Under this provision, Chinese nationals are required to comply with the licensing and other access procedures of the Philippines within the EEZ of the Philippines.[42] In contrast, Article 58(3) provides for obligations of *states*. Under this provision, states must have 'due regard to the rights and duties of the coastal State' in exercising their rights and performing their duties under the Convention in the EEZ. In its Advisory Opinion of 2015, ITLOS interpreted the obligation of due regard as requiring the obliged states to 'take the necessary measures to ensure that their nationals and vessels flying their flag are not engaged in illegal, unreported and unregulated (IUU) fishing activities', by reading it in conjunction with the obligation directly imposed upon nationals by Article 62(4).[43] According to ITLOS, '[t]he flag State is under the

[39] The *South China Sea* Arbitration Award (Jurisdiction and Admissibility), n 6, [406].

[40] The *South China Sea* Arbitration Award (Merits), n 1, [734].

[41] ibid, [735].

[42] ibid, [740].

[43] *Request for an Advisory Opinion Submitted by the Sub-Regional Fisheries Commission (SRFC)*, Advisory Opinion, ITLOS Case No 21, [2015] ITLOS Rep 4, 38, [124].

"due diligence obligation" to take all necessary measures to ensure compliance and to prevent IUU fishing by fishing vessels flying its flag'.[44] This is an obligation of conduct.[45]

The interpretation of Article 58(3) was further amplified by Judge Paik, stating that:

> Although 'States' are direct [addressees] of the obligation to comply with the laws and regulations of the coastal State, private actors, be they natural or juridical persons, are the ultimate regulatory targets under this provision, as they are the main actors engaging in various activities in the foreign EEZ. Thus in order to perform its duties under article 58, paragraph 3, of the Convention, the State must ensure that those subject to its jurisdiction comply with the laws and regulations adopted by the coastal State in accordance with the provisions of the Convention. Through article 94, paragraph 1, of the Convention, those subject to jurisdiction of the State should include a ship flying its flag.[46]

According to the learned judge, '[t]aking article 94 and article 58, paragraph 3, of the Convention together, it can be stated that the flag State has an obligation to ensure that fishing vessels flying its flag comply with the laws and regulations adopted by the coastal State when fishing in its EEZ'.[47]

In this connection, ITLOS specified certain measures to be taken. In the words of ITLOS:

> While the nature of the laws, regulations and measures that are to be adopted by the flag State is left to be determined by each flag State in accordance with its legal system, the flag State nevertheless has the obligation to include in them enforcement mechanisms to monitor and secure compliance with these laws and regulations. Sanctions applicable to involvement in IUU fishing activities must be sufficient to deter violations and to deprive offenders of the benefits accruing from their IUU fishing activities.[48]

The dictum of ITLOS was echoed by the Tribunal in the Award on the Merits. For the Tribunal:

> [A]nything less than due diligence by a State in preventing its nationals from unlawfully fishing in the exclusive economic zone of another would fall short of the regard due pursuant to Article 58(3) of the Convention.[49]

As the Tribunal admitted, evidence with regard to China's activities at Mischief Reef and Second Thomas Shoal was rather limited. Despite this, the Tribunal accepted that Chinese fishing vessels, accompanied by the ships of the CMS,

[44] ibid, [129].
[45] ibid.
[46] Separate Opinion of Judge Paik [2015] ITLOS Rep 102, 107–08, [14].
[47] ibid, 108, [16].
[48] [2015] ITLOS Rep 42, [138]. Further, see A Prölss, 'Article 58' in A Proelss (ed), *United Nations Convention on the Law of the Sea: A Commentary* (Beck/Hart Publishing/Nomos, 2017) 456.
[49] The *South China Sea* Arbitration Award (Merits), n 1, [744].

were engaged in fishing at both Mischief Reef and Second Thomas Shoal in May 2013 for two reasons. First, China asserted sovereign rights and jurisdiction in the South China Sea and issued a 'Nansha Certification of Fishing Permit', which extended to the area of Mischief Reef and Second Thomas Shoal. Second, the pattern of Chinese fishing activity at Mischief Reef and Second Shoal was consistent with that exhibited at other reef formations for which the Tribunal had information.[50]

In conclusion, the Tribunal, in its Award on the Merits, established that Chinese vessels had been engaged in fishing at Mischief Reef and Second Thomas Shoal in May 2013. It further observed that in all reported instances, Chinese fishing vessels had been closely escorted by government CMS vessels, and that the officers aboard the Chinese Government vessels in question were fully aware of the actions being taken by Chinese fishermen. Nonetheless, the Chinese Government vessels did not put a stop to them. Obviously the actions of the Chinese Government ships constituted official acts of China and were all attributable to China as such.[51] The Tribunal thus ruled that China failed to exhibit due regard for the Philippines' sovereign rights with respect to fisheries in its EEZ, by tolerating and failing to exercise due diligence to prevent fishing by Chinese -flagged vessels at Mischief Reef and Second Thomas Shoal in May 2013, and that China breached its obligations under Article 58(3) of the Convention.[52]

As noted, the obligation to have 'due regard to the rights and duties' constitutes the key element in Article 58(3) of the UNCLOS. It appears that the Tribunal, in its Award on the Merits, virtually equated the obligation of due regard with the obligation of due diligence. Due diligence is an elusive concept, and the degree of due diligence may vary depending on the nature of the specific activities, the technical and economic capabilities of states, and the effectiveness of territorial control, etc.[53] The standard of due diligence may also change over time. In this connection, the view of the ITLOS Seabed Disputes Chamber deserves to be quoted:

> Among the factors that make such a description difficult is the fact that 'due diligence' is a variable concept. It may change over time as measures considered sufficiently diligent at a certain moment may become not diligent enough in light, for instance, of new scientific or technological knowledge.[54]

In light of the variable nature of due diligence, it may not be easy for an international court or a tribunal to determine the breach of the obligation.[55]

[50] ibid, [745]–[748].

[51] ibid, [755].

[52] ibid, [757]; see also ibid, [753].

[53] Y Tanaka, 'Principles of International Marine Environmental Law' in R Rayfuse (ed), *Research Handbook on International Marine Environmental Law* (Edward Elgar, 2015) 31, 38.

[54] *Responsibilities and Obligations of States Sponsoring Persons and Entities with Respect to Activities in the Area*, Advisory Opinion, ITLOS Case No 17, [2011] ITLOS Rep 10, 36, [117].

[55] Tanaka, n 53, 38.

The difficulty associated with the obligation of due diligence was also recognised by the Tribunal in its Award on the Merits. In the words of the Tribunal:

> In many cases, the precise scope and application of the obligation on a flag State to exercise due diligence in respect of fishing by vessels flying its flag in the exclusive economic zone of another State may be difficult to determine.[56]

According to the Tribunal, however, that is not the case in the *South China Sea* arbitration. In the present case, there was evidence before the Tribunal to prove the existence of the fishing activity of Chinese vessels at Mischief Reef and Second Thomas Shoal in May 2013, and the escorting of the fishing vessels by Chinese Government vessels. The Tribunal thus considered:

> The obligation to have due regard to the rights of the Philippines is unequivocally breached when vessels under Chinese Government control act to escort and protect Chinese fishing vessels engaged in fishing unlawfully in the Philippines' exclusive economic zone.[57]

On the basis of the dictum of the Tribunal, with caution and prudence, it can be argued that a state breaches the obligation of due regard when that state was aware of illegal fishing activities conducted by its nationals in an EEZ of another state and, nonetheless, failed to prevent them.

C. China's Actions in Respect of Traditional Fishing at Scarborough Shoal

i. Jurisdiction of the Tribunal

Another fishery-related issue in the Award on the Merits concerns China's actions with respect to the traditional fishing activities of Philippine nationals at Scarborough Shoal. This issue relates to the Philippines' Submission No 10:

> (10) China has unlawfully prevented Philippine fishermen from pursuing their livelihoods by interfering with traditional fishing activities at Scarborough Shoal.[58]

In this connection, the Philippines referred to a series of incidents that occurred between Philippine and Chinese vessels at Scarborough Shoal that heightened tensions between the Parties on 10 and 28 April 2012 and 26 May 2012. According to the Philippines, efforts to negotiate a mutual withdrawal of government vessels were not successful and, as tensions intensified, fishermen active in the vicinity of Scarborough Shoal were affected by the

[56] The *South China Sea* Arbitration Award (Merits), n 1, [754].
[57] ibid, [756].
[58] ibid, [758].

Parties' dispute.[59] The Philippines thus argued that China violated its obligations under Articles 2(3), 51(1) and 62(3) of the UNCLOS;[60] and that China breached its obligations under Article 2(3) of the UN Charter and Article 279 of the UNCLOS to resolve disputes through peaceful means.[61] On the other hand, China asserted that waters surrounding Scarborough Shoal constitute a traditional fishing ground for Chinese fishermen and set out its own account of the events that took place on 10 April 2012.[62] China also responded to the Philippines' allegations that China's conduct fell short of its obligation to resolve the Parties' dispute peacefully.[63]

In the view of the Tribunal, the Philippines' Submission No 10 did not relate to a dispute concerning sovereignty or maritime boundary delimitation. In its Award on the Jurisdiction, the Tribunal noted that traditional fishing rights may exist even within the territorial waters of another state. According to the Tribunal, its jurisdiction to address this dispute was not dependent on a prior determination of sovereignty over Scarborough Shoal. As Articles 297 and 298 of the Convention have no application in the territorial sea, these provisions imposed no limitation on the Tribunal's jurisdiction. Accordingly, to the extent that the claimed rights and alleged interference occurred within the territorial sea of Scarborough Shoal, the Tribunal concluded that it had jurisdiction to address the matters raised in the Philippines' Submission No 10.[64] This view was confirmed by the Tribunal in the Award on the Merits.[65]

ii. Lawfulness of China's Actions

Traditional fishing rights constituted the key concept in the Philippines' Submission No 10.[66] Indeed, both the Philippines and China consider Scarborough Shoal to be a traditional fishing ground for their nationals.[67] In this connection, two issues arise: the nature of traditional fishing rights; and the law applicable to such rights.

[59] ibid, [767]–[770]; the Philippines' Memorial, vol I, 171–74, [6.40]–[6.46].

[60] The *South China Sea* Arbitration Award (Merits), n 1, [771].

[61] ibid, [780].

[62] ibid, [787]–[788]. See also Embassy of the People's Republic of China in the Republic of the Philippines, *Ten Questions Regarding Huangyan Island* (15 June 2012), reproduced in the Philippines' Memorial, vol V, Annex 120.

[63] The *South China Sea* Arbitration Award (Merits), n 1, [790]. See also Memorandum from the Embassy of the Republic of the Philippines in Beijing to the Secretary of Foreign Affairs of the Republic of the Philippines, No ZPE-080-2012-S (24 May 2012), reproduced in the Philippines' Memorial, vol IV, Annex 81.

[64] The *South China Sea* Arbitration Award (Jurisdiction and Admissibility), n 6, [407].

[65] The *South China Sea* Arbitration Award (Merits), n 1, [759].

[66] On this issue, see also J Mossop, 'Can the South China Sea Tribunal's Conclusions on Traditional Fishing Rights Lead to Cooperative Fishing Arrangements in the Region?' (2018) 3 *Asia-Pacific Journal of Ocean Law and Policy* 210.

[67] The *South China Sea* Arbitration Award (Merits), n 1, [792].

First, with regard to the nature of the traditional fishing rights, the Tribunal stated that:

> [T]raditional fishing rights in international law [stem] from the recognition that traditional livelihoods and cultural patterns are fragile in the face of development and modern ideas of interstate relations and warrant particular protection.[68]

According to the Tribunal, traditional fishing rights are not the historic rights of states but private rights.[69] In approaching this issue, the Tribunal seemed to assimilate traditional fishing to artisanal fishing, referencing the *Eritrea/Yemen* arbitration:

> 'Artisanal fishing' is used in contrast to 'industrial fishing'. It does not exclude improvements in powering the small boats, in the techniques of navigation, communication or in the techniques of fishing; but the traditional regime of fishing does not extend to large-scale commercial or industrial fishing nor to fishing by nationals of third States …, whether small-scale or industrial.[70]

The specific practice of artisanal fishing will vary from region to region. In contrast with industrial fishing, however, artisanal fishing will be carried out on 'a small scale, using fishing methods that largely approximate those that have historically been used in the region'.[71] According to the Tribunal, 'Scarborough Shoal has been a traditional fishing ground for fishermen of many nationalities, including the Philippines, China (including from Taiwan), and Viet Nam'.[72] In this connection, the Tribunal observed that at least some of the fishing carried out at Scarborough Shoal was of a traditional and artisanal nature.[73] Nonetheless, the Tribunal offered little evidence in this matter. Nor did the Tribunal specify precise threshold for those fishing methods that would qualify as artisanal fishing.[74] Related to this, attention must be paid to the evolutionary nature of traditional fishing. As the Tribunal admitted,[75] traditional fishing may gradually change over time owing to the development of technology. In this sense, the concept of traditional fishing contains a temporal element. This view was echoed by the arbitral tribunal in the *Eritrea/Yemen* arbitration, which stated

[68] ibid, [794].

[69] ibid, [798]. In this regard, the Philippines stressed that it did not 'make a claim to "historic rights" that were … superseded by UNCLOS'. The Philippines' Memorial, vol I, 171, [640].

[70] The *Eritrea/Yemen* Arbitration (Second Phase: Maritime Delimitation), Award of 17 December 1999, (2001) 22 *RIAA* 335, 360, [106]. See also The *South China Sea* Arbitration Award (Merits), n 1, [796]. According to the Food and Agriculture Organization of the UN (FAO), 'artisanal fishing' refers to '[t]raditional fisheries involving fishing households (as opposed to commercial companies), using [a] relatively small amount of capital and energy, relatively small fishing vessels (if any), making short fishing trips, close to shore, mainly for local consumption'. FAO Term Portal, available at http://www.fao.org/faoterm/en/?defaultCollId=21. See also Mossop, n 66, 224.

[71] The *South China Sea* Arbitration Award (Merits), n 1, [797].

[72] ibid, [805].

[73] ibid.

[74] ibid, [806].

[75] ibid, [806]–[807].

that '[t]he term "artisanal" is not to be understood as applying in the future only to a certain type of fishing exactly as it is practised today.'[76] Given that the level of artisanal skills may change over time, there is a need to explore a standard to determine whether certain fishing activities would fall within the scope of artisanal fishing.

Second, the law applicable to traditional fishing must be considered. This differs according to jurisdictional zones. The Tribunal identified the law applicable to traditional fishing in the three distinct jurisdictional zones: archipelagic waters, EEZ and the territorial sea. In archipelagic waters,[77] traditional fishing rights are expressly protected by Article 51(1) of the UNCLOS, which provides:

> Without prejudice to article 49, an archipelagic State shall respect existing agreements with other States and shall recognize traditional fishing rights and other legitimate activities of the immediately adjacent neighbouring States in certain areas falling within archipelagic waters …

In contrast, traditional fishing rights are extinguished in the EEZ. Article 62(3) of the UNCLOS requires the coastal state to take into account 'the need to minimize economic dislocation in States whose nationals have habitually fished in the zone' in giving access to any surplus in the allowable catch. In the view of the Tribunal, the inclusion of this provision confirms that the drafters of the Convention did not intend to preserve such rights.[78] The Tribunal's view was echoed by McDorman, stating that '[t]he promise of the EEZ for coastal state fishing interests effectively precluded any significant arguments that might have been made to respect or even take into account any traditional or historic fishing that arguably existed in the merging 200 n. mile national exclusive zone.'[79]

As for the law applicable to the traditional fishing rights in the territorial sea, the Tribunal held:

> The Tribunal sees nothing that would suggest that the adoption of the Convention was intended to alter acquired rights in the territorial sea and concludes that within that zone – in contrast to the exclusive economic zone – established traditional fishing rights remain protected by international law. The Tribunal also notes that the vast majority of traditional fishing takes place in close proximity to the coast.[80]

According to the Tribunal, the rule of international law on the treatment of the vested rights of foreign nationals falls squarely within the 'other rules of

[76] The *Eritrea/Yemen* Arbitration (Second Phase: Maritime Delimitation), n 70, 360, [106].

[77] The *South China Sea* Arbitration Award (Merits), n 1, [804](a).

[78] ibid, [804](b). As the Tribunal noted, 'States may continue to recognise traditional fishing rights in the exclusive economic zone in their legislation, in bilateral fisheries access agreements, or through regional fisheries management organisations.'

[79] TL McDorman, 'The Law of the Sea Convention and the U-Shaped Line: Some Comments' in Shicun Wu and Keyuan Zou (eds), *Arbitration Concerning the South China Sea: Philippines versus China* (Routledge, 2017) 147, 153.

[80] The *South China Sea* Arbitration Award (Merits), n 1, [804](c).

international law' applicable to the territorial sea.[81] At the same time, the Tribunal went to add that 'traditional fishing rights are not absolute or impervious to regulation', and 'the careful regulation of traditional fishing may be necessary for conservation and to restrict environmentally harmful practices.'[82]

Since May 2012, Chinese Government vessels have acted to prevent entirely fishing by Filipino fishermen at Scarborough Shoal for significant, but not continuous, periods of time, while permitting China's own nationals to continue fishing there.[83] As the actions of Chinese Government vessels constitute official acts of China, these actions are attributable to China.[84] In the view of the Tribunal, 'the complete prevention by China of fishing by Filipinos at Scarborough Shoal over significant periods of time after May 2012 is not compatible with the respect due under international law to the traditional fishing rights of Filipino fishermen.'[85] It thus concluded that China unlawfully prevented Filipino fishermen from engaging in traditional fishing at Scarborough Shoal.[86] On the other hand, it did not find it sufficient to support the Philippines' claim with regard to the breach of Article 2(3) of the UN Charter and Article 279 of the UNCLOS by China.[87]

However, the legal basis for protecting the traditional fishing rights in the territorial sea needs further consideration. On this issue, the Tribunal took the view:

> The legal basis for protecting artisanal fishing stems from the notion of vested rights and the understanding that, having pursued a livelihood through artisanal fishing over an extended period, generations of fishermen have acquired a right, akin to property, in the ability to continue to fish in the manner of their forebears.[88]

Accordingly, 'traditional fishing rights extend to artisanal fishing that is carried out largely in keeping with the longstanding practice of the community'.[89] As shown in the terms 'an extended period' and 'longstanding practice of community', the temporal element can be thought to be the key element of traditional fishing. This view was echoed by Sir Gerald Fitzmaurice, who stated:

> [I]f the fishing vessels of a given country have been accustomed from *time immemorial*, or *over a long period*, to fish in a certain area, on the basis of the area being high seas and common to all, it may be said that their country has through them … acquired a vested interest that the fisheries of that area should remain available to its fishing

[81] ibid, [808].
[82] ibid, [809].
[83] ibid, [810] and [812].
[84] ibid, [810].
[85] ibid, [812].
[86] ibid, [814].
[87] ibid, [813].
[88] ibid, [798].
[89] ibid.

> vessels (of course on a non-exclusive basis) – so that if another country asserts a claim to that area as territorial waters, which is found to be valid or comes to be recognized, this can only be subject to the acquired rights of the fishery in question, which must continue to be respected.[90]

However, there is no objective standard to determine the length of time necessary to establish traditional fishing. Accordingly, it is difficult to determine the existence of traditional fishing rights in certain marine spaces. The Tribunal, in its Award on the Merits, offered scant explanation of its understanding of the question as to how long traditional fishing by Filipino has continued.

In reality, it may be less easy to establish traditional fishing rights in the territorial sea. In this connection, O'Connell's view deserves to be quoted:

> There is no precedent for a successful claim to continued fishing rights in waters newly converted into territorial waters, so that the claim made in the case of adjacent fishery zones had the appearance of a novel legal institution – in the absence of treaty rights – which could be rationalised only on the basis of practice. However, the practice has favoured phasing-out rather than maintenance of rights, and phasing out presupposes a concession rather than a recognition of a right ... most traditional fishing rights are opposable to State extending their fishery limits ... only when derived from treaty.[91]

D. Alleged Failure to Protect and Preserve the Marine Environment

i. Jurisdiction of the Tribunal

As pointed out earlier, the South China Sea is rich in biological diversity.[92] Thus environmental protection of the South China Sea is of critical importance. In this connection, the Philippines, in its Submission No 11 as amended[93] and Submission No 12, claimed that:

> (11) China has violated its obligations under the Convention to protect and preserve the marine environment at Scarborough Shoal, Second Thomas Shoal, Cuarteron Reef, Fiery Cross Reef, Gaven Reef, Johnson Reef, Hughes Reef and Subi Reef;

[90] G Fitzmaurice, 'The Law and Procedure of the International Court of Justice, 1951–54: General Principles' (1953) 30 *British Yearbook of International Law* 1, 51.

[91] DP O'Connell, *The International Law of the Sea*, vol I, ed IA Shearer (Clarendon Press, 1982) 538.

[92] See ch 1, section I of this book.

[93] The Philippines' Submission No 11 in its original form was limited to China's failure to protect and preserve the marine environment at Scarborough Shoal and Second Thomas Shoal. Subsequently the Tribunal allowed the Philippines to amend Submission No 11 to encompass the marine environment at Cuarteron Reef, Fiery Cross Reef, Johnson Reef, Hughes Reef, Gaven Reef (North) and Subi Reef. In this regard, the Tribunal considered that the amendments were incidental to the original Submissions and did not involve the introduction of a new dispute between the Parties. The *South China Sea* Arbitration Award (Merits), n 1, [933].

(12) China's occupation of and construction activities on Mischief Reef

(a) …

(b) violate China's duties to protect and preserve the marine environment under the Convention.[94]

The Philippines Submission No 11 as amended relates to the protection and preservation of the marine environment under Articles 192 and 194 of the UNCLOS. In this regard, the Philippines argued that China had allowed its fishermen to harvest coral, giant clams, turtles, sharks and other threatened or endangered species that inhabit the reefs, and that it had allowed them to use dynamite to kill fish and destroy coral, and to use cyanide to harvest live fish.[95] According to the Philippines, extracting giant clams is especially problematic, because they are important elements of the coral reef structure and also because the method of harvesting them entails crushing surrounding corals.[96] Furthermore, the Philippines' Submission No 12(b) reflects a dispute concerning China's activities on Mischief Reef and their effects on the marine environment. In summary, the Philippines alleged that China had breached Articles 123, 192, 194, 197, 205 and 206 of the UNCLOS.[97] China did not directly clarify its position concerning the above issues. Even so, the Tribunal considered that China's position could be discerned from contemporaneous official statements.[98]

In its Award on Jurisdiction, the Tribunal was satisfied that the incidents alleged by the Philippines could involve violations of obligations under Articles 192 and 194 of the UNCLOS to take measures to prevent, reduce and control pollution of the marine environment. It also acknowledged that the factual allegations made by the Philippines could potentially give rise to a dispute under both the UNCLOS and the Convention on Biological Diversity (CBD).[99] According to the Tribunal, this did not necessarily exclude its jurisdiction to consider Submissions No 11 and 12(b). The Tribunal thus concluded that it had jurisdiction over Submission No 11, as involving a dispute over the interpretation and application of Articles 192 and 194 of the Convention.[100]

On the other hand, the Tribunal's jurisdiction to address the Philippines' Submission No 12 was dependent on the status of Mischief Reef as an 'island', 'rock' or 'low-tide elevation'. If the Tribunal were to find that Mischief Reef was an 'island' or 'rock' and thus constituted land territory, the Tribunal would lack

[94] ibid, [112].

[95] Presentation by Professor Boyle, Merits Hearing Tr (Day 3), 12.

[96] Memorial of the Philippines, vol I, 30 March 2014, [6.57]; the *South China Sea* Arbitration Award (Merits), n 1, [897].

[97] ibid, [906].

[98] ibid, [912] et seq.

[99] Convention on Biological Diversity (adopted 22 May 1992, entered into force 29 December 1993) 1760 *UNTS* 79.

[100] The *South China Sea* Arbitration Award (Jurisdiction and Admissibility), n 6, [175]–[178] and [408].

jurisdiction to consider the lawfulness of China's construction activities or the appropriation of the feature. Since the status of Mischief Reef was a matter for the merits, the Tribunal reserved a decision on its jurisdiction with respect to the Philippines' Submission No 12 for consideration in conjunction with the merits of the Philippines' claims.[101]

As discussed earlier,[102] the Tribunal, in its Award on the Merits, ruled that Mischief Reef was a low-tide elevation and that it formed part of the EEZ and continental shelf of the Philippines.[103] It followed that China had no entitlement over Mischief Reef. Furthermore, the Tribunal, in its Award on the Merits, ascertained whether its jurisdiction over the Philippine's Submissions No 11 and 12(b) was constrained by the military activities exception in Article 298(1)(b) of the UNCLOS. In this regard, the Tribunal took note of China's repeated statements that its installations and island-building activities were intended to fulfil civilian purposes.[104] It followed that China's conduct fell outside the scope of Article 298(1)(b). The Tribunal thus concluded that it had jurisdiction to consider the Philippine's Submission Nos 11 and 12(b).[105]

ii. Lawfulness of China's Actions

In considering the Philippines' Submissions Nos 11 and 12(b), the Tribunal examined three obligations: the obligation of due diligence; the obligation to conduct an environmental impact assessment; and the obligation to cooperate.[106]

a. Obligation of Due Diligence

The first issue that needs discussion concerns the obligation of due diligence. Article 192 of the UNCLOS provides a general obligation to protect the marine environment as follows:

> States have the obligation to protect and preserve the marine environment.

When interpreting this provision, two points must be noted. The first noteworthy point concerns a time element incorporated in Article 192. According to the

[101] ibid, [409].
[102] See ch 4, section III.D of this book.
[103] The *South China Sea* Arbitration Award (Merits), n 1, [647].
[104] ibid, [934]–[935].
[105] ibid, [938].
[106] The present writer briefly examined the three obligations in Y Tanaka, 'The *South China Sea* Arbitration: Environmental Obligations under the Law of the Sea Convention' (2018) 27 *RECIEL* 90, 91–94. See also C Kojima, 'South China Sea Arbitration and the Protection of the Marine Environment: Evolution of UNCLOS Part XII Through Interpretation and the Duty to Cooperate' (2017) 27 *Asian Yearbook of International Law* 166; Z Scanlon and R Beckman, 'Assessing Environmental Impact and the Duty to Cooperate: Environmental Aspects of the Philippines v China Award' (2018) 3 *Asia-Pacific Journal of Ocean Law and Policy* 5.

Tribunal, the 'general obligation' under Article 192 extends both to 'protection' of the marine environment from *future* damage and 'preservation' in the sense of maintaining or improving its *present* condition. Article 192 thus entails a positive obligation to take active measures to protect and preserve the marine environment, and a negative obligation not to degrade the marine environment at the same time.[107] The marine environment, including marine ecosystems, is dynamic by nature, and ecological conditions in the oceans may change over time. Environmental knowledge and technology are also developing rapidly. Hence it is important to take account of time elements in the interpretation of environmental norms in order to adopt them flexibly to new situations. It is significant that the Tribunal incorporated an inter-temporal element, namely the obligation to protect the marine environment from *future* damage, into Article 192.

The second noteworthy point pertains to the systemic interpretation. At present, complex webs of treaties are developing in multiple branches of international law. The coexistence of treaties necessitates a systemic outlook.[108] Notably, the Tribunal read Article 192 in light of 'the corpus of international law relating to the environment' and 'other applicable international law'.[109] In this connection, the Tribunal made an explicit *renvoi* to the 1973 Convention on the International Trade in Endangered Species of Wild Fauna and Flora (CITES).[110] As CITES is the subject of nearly universal adherence, including by the Philippines and China, it forms part of the general corpus of international law that informs the content of Articles 192 and 194(5) of the UNCLOS. Accordingly, the Tribunal considered that the general obligation to 'protect and preserve the marine environment' in Article 192 included a 'due diligence obligation to prevent the harvesting of species that are recognised internationally as being at risk of extinction and requiring international protection'.[111] The Tribunal's interpretation provides an interesting example of the systemic interpretation of environmental treaties.[112]

[107] The *South China Sea* Arbitration Award (Merits), n 1, [941]; Tanaka, n 106, 91.

[108] Related to this, the ICJ stated that 'an international instrument has to be interpreted and applied within the framework of the entire legal system prevailing at the time of the interpretation': *Legal Consequences for States of the Continued Presence of South Africa in Namibia (South West Africa) notwithstanding Security Council Resolution 276 (1970)*, [1971] ICJ Rep 16, 31, [53]. See Separate Opinion of Judge Cançado Trindade in *Whaling in the Antarctic (Australia v Japan, New Zealand intervening)*, [2014] ICJ Rep 348, 357–58, [25]–[26].

[109] The *South China Sea* Arbitration Award (Merits), n 1, [941] and [959]. See also MM Mbengue, 'The South China Sea Arbitration: Innovations in Marine Environmental Fact-Finding and Due Diligence Obligations' (2016) 110 *AJIL Unbound* 285, 286.

[110] Convention on the International Trade in Endangered Species of Wild Fauna and Flora (adopted 3 March 1973, entered into force 1 July 1975) 993 *UNTS* 243.

[111] The *South China Sea* Arbitration Award (Merits), n 1, [956]. See also ibid, [959].

[112] See also N Oral, 'The South China Sea Arbitral Award, Part XII of UNCLOS, and the Protection and Preservation of the Marine Environment' in S Jayakumar et al (eds), *The South China Sea Arbitration: The Legal Dimension* (Edward Elgar, 2018) 223, 237.

An issue that needs further consideration is the legal basis for systemic interpretation. In this regard, Article 31(3)(c) of the Vienna Convention on the Law of Treaties merits particular attention.[113] This provision stipulates that:

> There shall be taken into account, together with the context:
>
> …
>
> (c) any relevant rules of international law applicable in the relations between the parties.

The Tribunal, in its Award on the Merits, did not refer to this provision when considering the Philippines' Submissions Nos 11 and 12(b). In its Award on Jurisdiction, however, the Tribunal made a clear reference to Article 31(3), stating:

> The Tribunal is satisfied that Article 293(1) of the Convention, together with Article 31(3) of the Vienna Convention on the Law of Treaties, enables it in principle to consider the relevant provisions of the CBD for the purposes of interpreting the content and standard of Articles 192 and 194 of the Convention.[114]

It would seem to follow that Article 31(3) of the Vienna Convention provides a basis for the Tribunal's systemic interpretation regarding Articles 192 and 194(5) of the UNCLOS. In this regard, it might have been useful if the Tribunal had been able to further explore the role of Article 31(3)(c) of the Vienna Convention in systemic interpretation of environmental norms.

According to the Tribunal, there was no doubt that the harvesting of corals and giant clams from the waters surrounding Scarborough Shoal and features in the Spratly Islands had a harmful impact on the fragile marine environment. It follows that a failure to take measures to prevent these practices would constitute a breach of Articles 192 and 194(5) of the UNCLOS.[115] In this connection, the Tribunal specified two components of the obligation of due diligence. The first concerned an obligation to *adopt* rules and measures to prevent harmful acts; and the second element related to an obligation to *maintain* a level of vigilance in enforcing those rules and measures.[116] Given that the obligation to maintain is a continuous one, it can be considered that that obligation contains a temporal

[113] Vienna Convention on the Law of Treaties (adopted 22 May 1969, entered into force 27 January 1980) 1155 *UNTS* 331. For a monograph on this subject, see H van Asselt, *The Fragmentation of Global Climate Governance: Consequences and Management of Regime Interactions* (Edward Elgar Publishing 2014); R Wolfrum and N Matz, *Conflicts in International Environmental Law* (Springer 2003); P Merkouris, *Article 31(3)(c) VCLT and the Principle of Systemic Integration: Normative Shadows in Plato's Cave* (Brill/Nijhoff, 2015). See also G Distefano and PC Mavroidis, 'L'interprétation systémique: le liant de l'ordre international' in O Guillod and C Müller (eds), *Pour un droit équitable, engagé et chaleureux, Mélanges en l'honneur de Pierre Wessner* (Helbing Lichtenhan, 2011) 743.

[114] The *South China Sea* Arbitration Award (Jurisdiction and Admissibility), n 6, [176].

[115] The *South China Sea* Arbitration Award (Merits), n 1, [960].

[116] ibid, [961].

element. An issue thus arises with regard to the impact of the passage of time on the level of vigilance. In this regard, the Seabed Disputes Chamber of ITLOS, in its Advisory Opinion of 2011, took the view that 'The standard of due diligence may vary over time and depends on the level of risk and on the activities involved.'[117] However, the Tribunal, in the *South China Sea* Arbitration Award (Merits), did not refer to the variability of the standard of due diligence over time.[118] In any event, an inquiry was made whether China had breached the obligation of due diligence. When considering this issue, the Tribunal noted two points.

First, according to the Tribunal, the harvesting of sea turtles and species threatened with extinction constitutes a harm to the marine environment as such. There is no doubt that the harvesting of corals and giant clams from the waters surrounding Scarborough Shoal and features in the Spratly Islands would have a harmful impact on the fragile marine environment. Accordingly, a failure to take measures to prevent these practices would constitute a breach of Articles 192 and 194(5) of the Convention.[119]

Second, even though China enacted a Law of the Protection of Wildlife in 1989, '[t]here is no evidence in the record that would indicate that China has taken any steps to enforce those rules and measures against fishermen engaged in poaching of endangered species'.[120] Instead, China provided armed government vessels to protect the fishing boats. Therefore the Tribunal held that:

> China has, through its toleration and protection of, and failure to prevent Chinese fishing vessels engaging in harmful harvesting activities of endangered species at Scarborough Shoal, Second Thomas Shoal and other features in the Spratly Islands, breached Articles 192 and 194(5) of the Convention.[121]

A particular issue that needs further consideration concerns China's responsibility for environmental degradation caused by propeller chopping for giant clams across the Spratly Islands. According to the Tribunal, '[g]iant clams (*Tridacnidae*) and many of the corals found in the Spratly Islands are listed in Appendix II to CITES and are unequivocally threatened'.[122] In this regard, the Ferse Report noted that:

> More recently, fishermen in the South China Sea are reported to utilise the propellers of their boats to excavate shells from reef flats in the Spratly Islands on an industrial scale, leading to near complete destruction of the affected reef areas.[123]

[117] [2011] ITLOS Rep 74, [242](3).

[118] Furthermore, Mbengue argued that the Tribunal defined 'a very high standard of due diligence in Part XII of the UNCLOS'. See Mbengue, n 109, 286.

[119] The *South China Sea* Arbitration Award (Merits), n 1, [960].

[120] ibid, [964].

[121] ibid, [992].

[122] ibid, [957].

[123] *Ferse Report: Assessment of the Potential Environmental Consequences of Construction Activities on Seven Reefs in the Spratly Islands in the South China Sea*, 26 April 2016, 11 (footnote omitted).

In addition to the Ferse Report, the Tribunal referred to other reports that testified to significant damage to coral reefs and the marine environment.[124]

The Tribunal considered that the small propeller vessels involved in harvesting the giant clams were within China's jurisdiction and control, and that China was fully aware of the practice and had actively tolerated it as a means to exploit the living resources of the reefs. It thus found that China breached its obligation to protect and preserve the marine environment in respect of its toleration and protection of the harvesting of giant clams by the propeller-chopping method.[125]

On the other hand, the Tribunal noted that in 2000, China updated its Fisheries Law and prohibited in Article 30 the 'use of explosives, poisons, electricity and any other means in fishing that impairs the fishery resources'.[126] Furthermore, according to the Tribunal:

> In contrast to the situations of harvesting of endangered species and harmful construction activities, there is scant evidence in the case record about the use of explosives and cyanide over the last decade or Philippine complaints about its use. This suggests China may have taken measures to prevent such practices in the Spratly Islands. In any event, the Tribunal is not prepared to make a finding on the evidence available, under Submission No 11 with respect to cyanide and explosives.[127]

Therefore the Tribunal did not accept the Philippines' Submission No 11 with respect to cyanide and explosives.[128] According to the logic of the Tribunal's argument, the lack of evidence would lead to the presumption that a state – in this case, China – took preventive measures. It would seem to follow that hard evidence is needed to prove the breach of environmental obligations by a state. It may be said that the Tribunal treated evidence carefully.[129]

The further issue relates to the lawfulness of China's construction activities on seven reefs in the Spratly Islands: (i) Cuarteron Reef, (ii) Fiery Cross Reef, (iii) Gaven Reef (North), (iv) Johnson Reef, (v) Hughes Reef, (vi) Subi Reef, and (vii) Mischief Reef. While Chinese construction activities reportedly commenced at Cuarteron Reef in 1992, more substantial land reclamation began in the spring of 2014. Chinese land reclamation intensified throughout 2015, and it is estimated that as at November 2015, China's construction work had resulted in the creation of at least 231,000 square metres of new land on Cuarteron Reef.[130] Likewise, land reclamation at Fiery Cross Reef was intensified throughout 2015, and by November 2015 approximately 2,740,000 square metres of land had

[124] These reports include: report by VR Lee, McManus Report, First, Second, and Third Carpenter Reports; The *South China Sea* Arbitration Award (Merits), n 1, [848]–[851]. See also Memorial of the Philippines, vol I, 177–79, [6.52]–[6.54]; 187–88, [6.73]–[6.74].

[125] The *South China Sea* Arbitration Award (Merits), n 1, [965]–[966].

[126] ibid, [974].

[127] ibid, [972], [975]. See also question by Judge Wolfrum, Merits Hearing Tr (Day 3), 46.

[128] The *South China Sea* Arbitration Award (Merits), n 1, [975].

[129] Mbengue, n 109, 289.

[130] The *South China Sea* Arbitration Award (Merits), n 1, [864]–[866].

been created at Fiery Cross Reef.[131] At Gaven Reef (North), intense reclamation work began in the spring of 2014, and within the span of a year, China transformed Gaven Reef (North) from a coral reef to an artificial island measuring approximately 300 by 250 metres, created from 136,000 square metres of materials dredged from the seabed.[132] Furthermore, in the spring of 2014, China began extensive reclamation activities at Johnson Reef, which is classified as a rock for the purpose of Article 121(3) of the UNCLOS. By November 2015, China transformed Johnson Reef to an artificial island measuring approximately 109,000 square metres, nearly 1,000 times larger than the previous structure.[133] Likewise, by November 2015, China had created an artificial island on Hughes Reef measuring around 75,000 square metres.[134] Lastly, Subi Reef is classified as a low-tide elevation.[135] Nonetheless, the massive scale of China's work on Subi Reef transformed nearly the entire atoll into an artificial island.[136]

The artificial island-building programme is clearly part of an official Chinese policy and programme implemented by organs of the Chinese state.[137] A pivotal issue in this regard concerns the impact of the construction activities on the marine environment. In considering this issue, scientific evidence becomes a key element. Hence, the Tribunal referred to various expert reports, such as the Ferse Report. The Ferse Report clearly stated that '[t]he construction activities have impacted reefs on a scale unprecedented in the region'.[138] According to the Report:

> China's recent construction activities have [caused] and will cause environmental harm to coral reefs at Cuarteron Reef, Fiery Cross Reef, Gaven Reef, Johnson Reef, Hughes Reef, Mischief Reef, and Subi Reef; beyond the pre-existing damage to reefs that resulted from destructive fishing and the collection of corals and clams, storm damage, Crown-of-Thorns starfish, and the human presence on small garrisons on the reefs. The scale of these previous impacts generally cannot be compared with the environmental harm caused by the construction activities, both in terms of spatial extent and duration.[139]

On the basis of the observation, the Tribunal found that through its construction activities, China had breached its obligations under Articles 192 and 194(1) and (5) of the UNCLOS.[140] It is notable that the expert reports significantly affected the decision of the Tribunal in the *South China Sea* arbitration.

[131] ibid, [869].
[132] ibid, [873].
[133] ibid, [877].
[134] ibid, [881].
[135] ibid, [368].
[136] ibid, [886].
[137] ibid, [976].
[138] *Ferse Report*, n 123, 3.
[139] ibid, 59; The *South China Sea* Arbitration Award (Merits), n 1, [979].
[140] The *South China Sea* Arbitration Award (Merits), n 1, [983].

This highlights the role of experts in the settlement of international environmental disputes.[141]

b. Environmental Impact Assessment and Monitoring

The next issue pertains to the obligation to conduct an environmental impact assessment and monitoring.[142] Development of a project, such as land reclamation, may entail the risk of damaging the environment. Environmental impact assessment is a device to detect potential environmental risks arising from a proposed project before authorising or funding it.[143] Environmental harms themselves belong to the future, but the risks of environmental harms belong to the present since the risks must be detected in the present. From them, the future can to some extent be predicted. In this sense, an environmental impact assessment can be considered a legal device to address inter-temporality in environmental protection. By identifying potential risks, an effective environmental impact assessment can assist decision makers in determining whether precautionary action must be taken, and indeed whether the project should go ahead or not.[144]

The obligation to carry out an environmental impact assessment under general international law was affirmed by the International Court of Justice (ICJ) in the *Pulp Mills* case, stating:

> [I]t may now be considered a requirement under general international law to undertake an environmental impact assessment where there is a risk that the proposed industrial activity may have a significant adverse impact in a transboundary context, in particular, on a shared resource.[145]

The dictum of the ICJ was echoed by the ITLOS Seabed Disputes Chamber in its Advisory Opinion of 2011. According to the Chamber, 'It should be stressed that the obligation to conduct an environmental impact assessment is a direct obligation under the Convention and a general obligation under customary international law.'[146]

In the UNCLOS, obligations to conduct an environmental impact assessment and monitoring are provided in Articles 204, 205 and 206. Under Article 204(1),

[141] This issue will be discussed in ch 6, section III.D.ii of this book. See also Oral, n 112, 233–34.

[142] On this issue, see Oral, n 112, 237–41; Tanaka, n 106, 92–94.

[143] The 1991 Convention on Environmental Impact Assessment in a Transboundary Context (the Espoo Convention) defines 'environmental impact assessment' as 'a national procedure for evaluating the likely impact of a proposed activity on the environment' (Art 1(vi)). Text in (1991) 30 *ILM* 802. Entered into force 10 September 1997.

[144] Environmental impact assessment and the precautionary approach are arguably integrally interlinked, in the sense that it is difficult to detect potential risks that may trigger the application of the precautionary approach unless an effective environmental impact assessment is carried out before a proposed project has begun.

[145] *Pulp Mills on the River Uruguay (Argentina v Uruguay)* [2010] ICJ Rep 14, 83, [204].

[146] *Responsibilities and Obligations of States*, n 54, [2011] ITLOS Rep 50, [145].

states are under the obligation to endeavour, as far as practicable, to observe, measure, evaluate and analyse the risks or effects of pollution of the marine environment. Article 205 requires states to publish reports of the results obtained pursuant to Article 204 to the competent international organisations, which should make them available to all states. Furthermore, Article 206 seeks to ensure that planned activities with potentially damaging effects may be effectively controlled and that other states are kept informed of their potential risks.[147] This provision deserves to be quoted in full:

> When States have reasonable grounds for believing that planned activities under their jurisdiction or control may cause substantial pollution of or significant and harmful changes to the marine environment, they shall, as far as practicable, assess the potential effects of such activities on the marine environment and shall communicate reports of the results of such assessments in the manner provided in article 205.

Arguably, a state whose activities cause serious environmental damage would not be able to deny breach of the obligation of due diligence on grounds of non-foreseeability if it had not conducted an environmental impact assessment.[148] This view seems to be echoed by the 2010 *Pulp Mills* judgment, which stated:

> [D]ue diligence, and the duty of vigilance and prevention which it implies, would not be considered to have been exercised, if a party planning works liable to affect the régime of the river or the quality of its waters did not undertake an environmental impact assessment on the potential effects of such works.[149]

An issue in point in the *South China Sea* arbitration was whether China had fulfilled obligations to conduct an environmental impact assessment under the Convention. China repeatedly asserted that it had undertaken thorough environmental studies. According to the Tribunal, however,

> neither the Tribunal, the Tribunal-appointed experts, the Philippines, nor the Philippines' experts have been able to identify any report that would resemble an environmental impact assessment that meets the requirements of Article 206 of the Convention, or indeed under China's own Environmental Impact Assessment Law of 2002.[150]

Therefore the Tribunal had to admit that it could not make a definitive finding that China had prepared an environmental impact assessment, but neither could it definitely find that China had failed to do so.[151]

Nonetheless, such a finding is not necessary in order to establish a breach of Article 206. In the view of the Tribunal, what is more important is the obligation

[147] The *South China Sea* Arbitration Award (Merits), n 1, [948].
[148] AE Boyle, 'Land-based Sources of Marine Pollution: Current Legal Regime' (1992) 16 *Marine Policy* 20, 23; P-M Dupuy, 'Soft Law and the International Law of the Environment' (1991) 12 *Michigan Journal of International Law* 420, 434.
[149] *Pulp Mills on the River Uruguay*, n 145, [2010] ICJ Rep 83, [204].
[150] The *South China Sea* Arbitration Award (Merits), n 1, [989].
[151] ibid, [991].

to communicate. As noted, Article 206 obliges states to communicate reports of the results of assessments on the potential effects of planned activities on the marine environment, when states have 'reasonable grounds for believing that planned activities under their jurisdiction or control may cause … significant and harmful changes to the marine environment'. According to the Tribunal, 'the obligation to communicate reports of the results of the assessment is absolute.'[152] Furthermore, the Tribunal considered that 'China could not reasonably have held any belief other than that the construction "may cause significant and harmful changes to the marine environment."'[153] Thus China was under an obligation to communicate the result of the assessment.[154] Under Article 205 of the UNCLOS, states are obliged to publish reports of the results of monitoring of the risk or effects of pollution or provide such reports to the 'competent international organizations'. Although the Tribunal directly asked China for a copy of any environmental impact assessment it had prepared, China did not provide one. Nor did it deliver an assessment in writing to that forum or to any other international body as far as the Tribunal was aware. The Tribunal accordingly concluded that China had not fulfilled its duties under Article 206 of the Convention.[155]

Three points can be made with regard to the interpretation and application of this provision.[156] The first point relates to the interlinkage between an environmental impact assessment and the obligation to communicate. As explained earlier, the Tribunal found that China had not fulfilled its duties under Article 206 of the Convention with regard to environmental impact assessment because of the absence of communication.[157] Given that it may be less easy to determine whether a state properly carried out an environmental impact assessment, the Tribunal's approach focusing on the non-fulfilment of a procedural requirement, that is communication, is noteworthy.[158] Concerning the manner of communication, however, the Tribunal generally stated that China 'has delivered no assessment in writing to that forum or any other international body as far as the Tribunal is aware'.[159] In so stating, the Tribunal did not examine the question to which organisation the environmental impact assessment report should have been provided, nor the question as to whether

[152] ibid, [948].
[153] ibid, [988].
[154] ibid.
[155] ibid, [991].
[156] Tanaka, n 106, 93–94.
[157] The *South China Sea* Arbitration Award (Merits), n 1, [991].
[158] The ICJ, in *Costa Rica v Nicaragua/Nicaragua v Costa Rica*, also linked the obligation to notify with the obligation to conduct an environmental impact assessment. *Certain Activities carried out by Nicaragua in the Border Area (Costa Rica v Nicaragua); Construction of a Road in Costa Rica along the San Juan River (Nicaragua v Costa Rica)* ('*Costa Rica v Nicaragua/Nicaragua v Costa Rica*'), Judgment, [2015] ICJ Rep 665, 707, [104]. See also Tanaka, n 106, 93–94.
[159] The *South China Sea* Arbitration Award (Merits), n 1, [991].

a relevant organisation exists in the South China Sea region.[160] It might have been useful if the Tribunal could have provided its view regarding the manner of communication.

Second, the quality of environmental impact assessments is at issue. The Tribunal, in its Award on the Merits, reviewed the China's own legislative standards and ruled that the alleged Chinese environmental impact assessments were 'far less comprehensive' than environmental impact assessments reviewed by other international courts and tribunals.[161] In so stating, the Tribunal stressed 'comprehensiveness' as an important characteristic of an environmental impact assessment.[162] Yet it offered scant explanation about the meaning of 'comprehensiveness' of an environmental impact assessment.[163] It might have been helpful if the Tribunal had been able to clarify the specific contents of an environmental impact assessment in more detail, since Article 206 of the UNCLOS contains no guidance on this matter.[164]

The third point pertains to a condition for triggering an environmental impact assessment. Under Article 206, the obligation to conduct an environmental impact assessment is limited to the situation where 'States have reasonable grounds for believing that planned activities under their jurisdiction or control may cause substantial pollution of or significant and harmful changes to the marine environment'. However, this provision provides no further precision with regard to the standard of 'reasonable grounds'. Related to this, it is relevant to note that the ICJ, in the *Costa Rica v Nicaragua* case, specified a dual assessment: first, the state is obliged to ascertain whether there is a risk of significant transboundary harm that would trigger the duty to conduct an environmental impact assessment (preliminary assessment); second, only if such a risk exists is the state further required to carry out an environmental impact assessment.[165] In this regard, the ICJ ruled that a preliminary assessment must be carried out 'on the basis of an objective evaluation of all the relevant circumstances'.[166] Yet the evidential standard for determining 'significant' transboundary harm remains less clear and is a matter of subjective appreciation. As a consequence, there is

[160] Scanlon and Beckman, n 106, 15. In this regard, Scanlon and Beckman argued that 'where there is no such organisation, there is an obligation to "publish" the report instead': ibid, 16.

[161] The *South China Sea* Arbitration Award (Merits), n 1, [990].

[162] Mbengue, n 109, 287.

[163] ibid.

[164] In practice, a dispute may arise with regard to the quality of an environmental impact assessment and monitoring. In this regard, see Tanaka, n 106, 94; P Birnie, A Boyle and C Redgwell, *International Law and the Environment* (Oxford University Press, 2009) 170. For a thorough analysis of interstate disputes concerning environmental impact assessment, see N Craik, *The International Law of Environmental Impact Assessment: Process, Substance and Integration* (Cambridge University Press, 2008) 111–20.

[165] *Costa Rica v Nicaragua/Nicaragua v Costa Rica* case, n 158, [2015] ICJ Rep 720, [153].

[166] ibid.

the risk that the obligation to conduct an environmental impact assessment may not be appropriately triggered by the state causing the risk.[167]

c. International Cooperation

The obligation of international cooperation is key in environmental protection.[168] Its importance in marine environmental protection was stressed by ITLOS in the *MOX Plant* case: '[T]he duty to cooperate is a fundamental principle in the prevention of pollution of the marine environment under Part XII of the Convention and general international law.'[169] More generally, the ICJ, in the *Pulp Mills on the River Uruguay* case, has emphasised that 'it is by cooperating that the States concerned can jointly manage the risks of damage to the environment that might be created by the plans initiated by one or other of them, so as to prevent the damage in question'.[170]

Under the UNCLOS, Article 197 places a general obligation upon states to cooperate on a global or regional basis,

> directly or through competent international organizations, in formulating and elaborating international rules, standards and recommended practices and procedures consistent with this Convention, for the protection and preservation of the marine environment, taking into account characteristic regional features.

Furthermore, Article 123 provides an obligation to cooperate between states bordering enclosed or semi-enclosed seas, including the obligation to 'coordinate the implementation of their rights and duties with respect to the protection and preservation of the marine environment'. As the South China Sea is regarded as a semi-enclosed sea, the application of this provision is important in the environmental protection of the South China Sea. According to the Tribunal, however, there was no convincing evidence of China's attempting to cooperate or coordinate with the other states bordering the South China Sea with regard to China's island-building programme. This lack of coordination is not unrelated to China's lack of communication.[171] Indeed, China had delivered no report of the results of environmental impact assessments. For these reasons, the Tribunal ruled that China had breached Articles 123 and 197 of the Convention.[172] Yet the Tribunal's reasoning on this matter needs further consideration.

[167] Tanaka, n 106, 94.

[168] For an analysis of the obligation of international cooperation, see Tanaka, n 53, 52–55; Tanaka, n 106, 95.

[169] *MOX Plant* case *(Ireland v United Kingdom)*, ITLOS Case No 10, [2011] ITLOS Rep 110, [82]. See also *Case concerning Land Reclamation by Singapore in and around the Straits of Johor (Malaysia v Singapore)*, Provisional Measures, ITLOS Case No 12, [2003] ITLOS Rep 10, 25, [92].

[170] *Pulp Mills on the River Uruguay* [2010] ICJ Rep 49, [77].

[171] The *South China Sea* Arbitration Award (Merits), n 1, [986].

[172] ibid, [993].

First, Article 197 provides an obligation to cooperate 'in formulating and elaborating international rules, standards and recommended practices and procedures consistent with this Convention, for the protection and preservation of the marine environment, taking into account characteristic regional features'. Environmental damage from China's land-building activities and the formulation and elaboration of relevant rules are two different matters. In this regard, the Tribunal seemingly failed to specify how China's land-building activities breached the obligation set out in Article 197.[173]

Second, Article 123 sets out an obligation of states to endeavour to 'coordinate the implementation of their rights and duties with respect to the protection and preservation of the marine environment'. Even though China's land-building activities might certainly cause environmental damage, this does not directly lead to the breach of the obligation to coordinate under Article 123.[174]

Overall the Tribunal seemed to assimilate the obligations under Articles 123 with a duty to notify or communicate.[175] This point can be deduced from the statement of the Tribunal: 'This lack of coordination is not unrelated to China's lack of communication ….'[176] Yet there appears to be scope to consider the question whether this is a correct interpretation of Articles 123 and 197 of the Convention.[177] In any event, the Tribunal concluded that China had breached Articles 192, 194(1), 194(5), 197, 123 and 206 of the UNCLOS.[178]

E. Occupation and Construction Activities on Mischief Reef

i. Jurisdiction of the Tribunal

The next issue pertains to the lawfulness of occupation and construction activities on Mischief Reef by China. In this regard, the Philippines, in its Submission No 12(a) and (c), requested the Tribunal to declare that:

> (12) China's occupation of and construction activities on Mischief Reef
>
> (a) violate the provisions of the Convention concerning artificial islands, installations and structures;
>
> …
>
> (c) constitute unlawful acts of attempted appropriation in violation of the Convention.[179]

[173] Scanlon and Beckman, n 106, 21.
[174] ibid, 23.
[175] ibid, 24.
[176] The *South China Sea* Arbitration Award (Merits), n 1, [986].
[177] As an alternative approach, Scanlon and Beckman argued that the Tribunal could have applied a legal duty to notify and consult relying directly on a general principle of international law or on Part XII of the UNCLOS read in light of customary international law. Scanlon and Beckman, n 106, 28.
[178] The *South China Sea* Arbitration Award (Merits), n 1, [1203]B(12) and (13).
[179] ibid, [994].

At least, Chinese construction activities on Mischief Reef reportedly date back to January 1995.[180] According to data presented by the Philippines, China's construction work had resulted in the creation of 5,580,000 square metres of new land on Mischief Reef as of November 2015.[181]

In its Award on Jurisdiction, the Tribunal held that its jurisdiction to address these questions would rely on the status of Mischief Reef as an 'island', 'rock' or 'low-tide elevation'. If the Tribunal were to find that Mischief Reef was an 'island' or 'rock', and thus constituted land territory, the Tribunal would lack jurisdiction to consider the lawfulness of China's construction activities or the appropriation of the feature. Furthermore, Article 298(1)(b) of the UNCLOS excludes disputes concerning military activities from the Tribunal's jurisdiction. In the view of the Tribunal, the specifics of China's activities on Mischief Reef and whether such activities were military in nature, were matters best assessed in conjunction with the merits. Given that the possible jurisdictional objections with respect to the dispute underlying Submission No 12 therefore did not possess an exclusively preliminary character, the Tribunal reserved a decision on its jurisdiction with respect to the Philippines' Submission No 12 for consideration in conjunction with the merits of the Philippines' claims.[182]

In its Award on the Merits, the Tribunal found that Mischief Reef was a low-tide elevation and, as such, generated no entitlement to maritime zones of its own.[183] As noted, none of the high-tide features in the Spratly Islands is a fully entitled island for the purposes of Article 121 of the UNCLOS. Consequently, there was no situation of overlapping entitlements that would require maritime delimitation by applying Articles 15, 74 and 83 of the Convention.[184] Moreover, China repeatedly stated that its installations and island construction were intended to fulfil civilian purposes.[185] In this regard, the Tribunal took note of the public statement of China's President Xi Jinping, that 'Relevant construction activities that China are undertaking in the island of South – [sic] Nansha Islands do not target or impact any country, and China does not intend to pursue militarization.'[186] As civilian activity, the Tribunal considered that China's

[180] ibid, [996]; Memorial of the Philippines, 193–94, [6.92].

[181] The *South China Sea* Arbitration Award (Merits), n 1, [1008]; Supplemental Documents of the Philippines, vol IV, Annex 782, 19 November 2015.

[182] The *South China Sea* Arbitration Award (Jurisdiction and Admissibility), n 6, [409].

[183] The *South China Sea* Arbitration Award (Merits), n 1, [1025].

[184] ibid, [1025].

[185] ibid, [1027].

[186] US, The White House, Office of the Press Secretary, 'Press Release: Remarks by President Obama and President Xi of the People's Republic of China in Joint Press Conference' (25 September 2015), Annex 664, Supplemental Documents of the Philippines, vol I, Annexes, 19 November 2015; the *South China Sea* Arbitration Award (Merits), n 1, [1027].

conduct fell outside the scope of Article 298(1)(b). It thus concluded that it had jurisdiction to consider the Philippines' Submission.[187]

ii. Lawfulness of China's Actions

Two issues arise with regard to China's occupation and construction activities on Mischief Reef. The first issue pertains to their lawfulness. In approaching this issue, it must be noted that Mischief Reef is a low-tide elevation, and that it can only constitute part of the EEZ and continental shelf of the Philippines; and that it does not lie within any entitlement that could be generated by any feature claimed by China.[188] In accordance with Article 60 of the UNCLOS, it is clear that only the Philippines could construct or authorise artificial islands, installations and structures.[189] Nonetheless, China's activities at Mischief Reef had evolved into the creation of an artificial island. Given that China's conduct took place in the face of the Philippines' protests, it is equally clear that China proceeded without receiving the permission of the Philippines.[190] Accordingly, China's violation of its obligations was manifest.[191] In conclusion, the Tribunal ruled that China breached Articles 60 and 80 of the UNCLOS with respect to the Philippines' sovereign rights in its EEZ and continental shelf.[192]

The second issue concerns the lawfulness of China's appropriation of Mischief Reef. Since low-tide elevations form part of the submerged landmass of a state, low-tide elevations, as distinct from land territory, cannot be appropriated.[193] Since Mischief Reef as a low-tide elevation falls within the legal regime for the continental shelf, it is incapable of appropriation by occupation or otherwise.[194] Related to this, the Tribunal already held that China's actions at Mischief Reef unlawfully interfered with the Philippines' enjoyment of its sovereign rights. Hence the Tribunal ruled that there was no need to address Submission No 12(c).[195]

The findings of the Tribunal require two comments. First, it must be stressed that the legal status of maritime features cannot be changed by land reclamation. In fact, the Tribunal made it clear that if what was originally a reef platform that submerged at high tide was elevated into an island that was permanently

[187] The *South China Sea* Arbitration Award (Merits), n 1, [1028].

[188] ibid, [1025], [1030]. See also Memorial of the Philippines, vol I, 198, [6.103].

[189] The *South China Sea* Arbitration Award (Merits), n 1, [1036].

[190] ibid, [1037].

[191] ibid, [1038].

[192] ibid, [1043]. In this regard, it is relevant to recall that the Tribunal found that through its construction activities, China also breached its obligations under Arts 192, 194(1) and (5) of the UNCLOS with regard to environmental protection: ibid, [983].

[193] See ch 4, section II of this book.

[194] The *South China Sea* Arbitration Award (Merits), n 1, [1040].

[195] ibid, [1042].

exposed by land reclamation, 'such an island is undoubtedly "artificial" for the purpose of Article 60.'[196] This view echoed what the Tribunal had stated earlier, that 'a low-tide elevation or area of seabed cannot be legally transformed into an island through human efforts'.[197]

Second, attention must be paid to the interrelationship between destruction of evidence and the obligation of non-aggravation of disputes. China, through its construction activities on Mischief Reef, permanently destroyed evidence of the natural status of the maritime feature. As will be discussed in section III of this chapter, it can be argued that the China's action might also lead to the breach of the obligation of non-aggravation of disputes.

F. Operation of Law Enforcement Vessels in a Dangerous Manner

i. Jurisdiction of the Tribunal

Lastly, the lawfulness of operation of Chinese law enforcement vessels must be examined. In its Submission No 13, the Philippines requested a declaration:

> (13) China has breached its obligations under the Convention by operating its law enforcement vessels in a dangerous manner causing serious risk of collision to Philippine vessels navigating in the vicinity of Scarborough Shoal.[198]

This Submission concerned interactions between Chinese law enforcement vessels and Philippine coast guard and surveillance ships on 28 April 2012 and on 26 May 2012.[199] In this connection, the Philippines alleged that China breached its obligations relating to safe navigation under Articles 94 and 21 of the UNCLOS and related provisions in the 1972 Convention on the International Regulations for Preventing of Collisions at Sea (COLREGS), by operating its law enforcement vessels in a dangerous manner.[200]

In the Award on Jurisdiction, the Tribunal found that this was not a dispute concerning sovereignty or maritime boundary delimitation, nor was it barred from the Tribunal's consideration by any requirement of Section 1 of Part XV of the UNCLOS. It also found that Article 298(1)(b) had no application in the territorial sea and that the Tribunal's jurisdiction was not dependent on a prior determination of sovereignty over Scarborough Shoal. Accordingly, to the extent that the claimed rights and alleged interference occurred within the territorial sea of Scarborough Shoal, the Tribunal concluded that it had jurisdiction to

[196] ibid, [1037].
[197] ibid, [508].
[198] ibid, [1044].
[199] ibid, [1046].
[200] ibid, [1059].

address the matters raised in the Philippines' Submission No 13.[201] The conclusion was confirmed by the Tribunal in the Award on the Merits.[202]

ii. Lawfulness of China's Actions

Both China and the Philippines ratified the COLREGS.[203] Even though the Philippines did not become a party to the 1972 Convention until 2013, the Tribunal considered that the COLREGS was binding upon the two states relating to the conduct of their respective vessels by virtue of Article 94 of the UNCLOS.

Article 94(1) of the Convention places a general obligation upon every state to 'effectively exercise its jurisdiction and control in administrative, technical and social matters over ships flying its flag'. This obligation is further amplified by Article 94(5):

> In taking the measures called for in paragraphs 3 and 4 each State is required to conform to generally accepted international regulations, procedures and practices and to take any steps which may be necessary to secure their observance.

The Tribunal took the view that Article 94 incorporates the COLREGS into the UNCLOS, since the COLREGS constitutes a 'generally accepted international regulation'.[204] It follows that a violation of the COLREGS constitutes a violation of the Convention itself.[205]

The Tribunal's view rests on 'rules of reference'. The UNCLOS often incorporates a 'no less effective' standard or an 'at least have the same effect obligation' into its relevant provisions.[206] For instance, Article 208(3) requires coastal states to adopt seabed operations laws that 'shall be no less effective than international rules, standards and recommended practices and procedures'. Such international rules include the 1990 International Convention on Oil Pollution Preparedness, Response and Cooperation[207] and the 2000 Protocol to the Convention. Article 210(6) obliges states to adopt dumping regulations that 'shall be no less effective in preventing, reducing and controlling such pollution than the

[201] The *South China Sea* Arbitration Award (Jurisdiction and Admissibility), n 6, [410].

[202] The *South China Sea* Arbitration Award (Merits), n 1, [1045].

[203] Convention on the International Regulations for Preventing Collisions at Sea (adopted 20 October 1972, entered into force on 15 July 1977) 1050 *UNTS* 1976. China and the Philippines ratified the Convention in 1980 and in 2013, respectively.

[204] The *South China Sea* Arbitration Award (Merits), n 1, [1083]. This view was supported by the IMO: IMO, *Implications of the United Nations Convention on the Law of the Sea for the International Maritime Organization*, LEG/MISC.8, 30 January 2014, 15 and 113. See also Memorial of the Philippines, vol I, 208, [6.130].

[205] The *South China Sea* Arbitration Award (Merits), n 1, [1083].

[206] The list of legal instruments corresponding to 'generally accepted international rules and standards' is available in IMO, *Circular Letter No 2456, Implication of UNCLOS for the Organization*, 17 February 2003, Annex II.

[207] (1991) 30 *ILM* 735. Entered into force 13 May 1995.

global rules and standards'. It is generally considered that such global rules and standards are set out by the 1972 London Dumping Convention and its 1996 Protocol.[208] Similarly, Article 211(2) stipulates that flag-state regulation of vessel pollution must 'at least have the same effect as that of generally accepted international rules and standards established through the competent international organization or general diplomatic conference'. Such international rules are embodied in MARPOL.[209] The reference to internationally agreed rules and standards was also made in relation to atmospheric and land-based pollution under Articles 207(1) and 212(1), though only in a weaker manner.

The legal technique of 'rules of reference' seeks to maintain uniformity of national and international regulation with regard to marine environmental protection. By updating 'generally accepted international rules and standards', it also becomes possible to adapt relevant rules of the UNCLOS to a new situation. Accordingly, 'rules of reference' can be considered a useful tool to take the new demands of the international community into account in the interpretation and application of existing rules and standards.[210]

In considering the Philippines Submission, the facts are of central importance. What is of particular interest in this regard is the role of experts. To assess the Philippines' claims, the Tribunal appointed an independent expert, Captain Gurpreet S Singhota, in accordance with Article 24 of the Rules of Procedure.[211] Captain Singhota submitted his report on 15 April 2016.[212] In the report, Captain Singhota concluded that China had breached its obligations under Rules 2, 6, 8, 15 and 16 of the COLREGS.[213]

As the Tribunal observed, all Chinese-flagged vessels involved in the abovementioned incidents belonged to one of two Chinese agencies: the CMS or the Fisheries Law Enforcement Command of China (FLEC). It followed that the alleged incidents were caused by vessels falling directly under the command and control of the Chinese Government. Hence the conduct of the Chinese vessels was automatically attributable to China.[214] The Tribunal then applied

[208] LA De La Fayette, 'The London Convention 1972: Preparing for the Future' (1998) 13 *IJMCL* 515, 516.

[209] International Convention for the Prevention of Pollution from Ships and Its Protocol (adopted 2 November 1973 (Convention), 1978 (Protocol), the combined instrument entered into force on 2 October 1983) 1340 *UNTS* 61.

[210] Y Tanaka, *The International Law of the Sea*, 3rd edn (Cambridge University Press, 2019) 333–35.

[211] The *South China Sea* Arbitration Award (Merits), n 1, [1084]. According to the Tribunal, Captain Singhota's experience includes 26 years of service with the IMO's Maritime Safety Division, Sub-committee on Safety of Navigation, and other departments, as well as 14 years of seagoing experience: ibid.

[212] Captain Gurpreet S Singhota, *Report of the International Navigational Safety Expert appointed by the Permanent Court of Arbitration, The Hague, The Netherlands* (15 April 2016) ('Singhota Report').

[213] The *South China Sea* Arbitration Award (Merits), n 1, [1085].

[214] ibid, [1091].

the relevant Rules of the COLREGS presented by the Singhota Report to the alleged incidents. Basically the Tribunal confirmed the conclusions of the Singhota Report.[215] It thus concluded that China had violated Rules 2, 6, 7, 8, 15 and 16 of the COLREGS and, as a consequence, was in breach of Article 94 of the Convention.[216] At the same time, the Tribunal added that its determination in Submission No 13 did not involve any finding of sovereignty over Scarborough Shoal and its waters.[217] In assessing the manner of law enforcement operation by Chinese vessels, the Tribunal relied heavily on the Singhota Report. In light of the technicality of the rules of COLREGS, it would be less easy for judges to determine breaches of that Convention. Thus, as the *South China Sea* arbitration demonstrated, the appointment of independent experts by the judicial body is an option well worth considering. Given that an international court or tribunal rarely addresses breaches of COLREGS in the jurisprudence, the *South China Sea* Arbitration Award on the Merits provides an important precedent that undertook a detailed review of this matter.

III. AGGRAVATION OR EXTENSION OF THE DISPUTE BETWEEN THE PARTIES

A. Aggravation of the Dispute between the Parties

i. Jurisdiction of the Tribunal

Given that international disputes may escalate over time, it is necessary to prevent their aggravation. Hence the obligation not to aggravate a dispute is of critical importance.[218] This obligation can be regarded as a corollary of the obligation of peaceful settlement of international disputes. It is no coincidence that the 1970 Friendly Relations Declaration refers to the two obligations at the same time. In fact, the Declaration first states that 'Every State shall settle its international disputes with other States by peaceful means in such a manner that international peace and security and justice are not endangered.'[219] It then continues:

> States parties to an international dispute, as well as other States shall refrain from any action which may aggravate the situation so as to endanger the maintenance of

[215] ibid, [1090]–[1105].

[216] ibid, [1109].

[217] ibid, [1108].

[218] The obligation not to aggravate a dispute is also called the 'obligation of restraint'. The Tribunal, in its Award of 2016, used the term 'obligation not to engage in acts that might aggravate a dispute': ibid, [1135].

[219] UN General Assembly, *Declaration on Principles of International Law Concerning Friendly Relations and Co-operation among States in accordance with the Charter of the United Nations*, UN Doc A/RES/25/2625 (24 October 1970), Principle 2, [1].

> international peace and security, and shall act in accordance with the purposes and principles of the United Nations.[220]

The 1982 Manila Declaration also confirmed the two obligations at the same time.[221]

In the particular context of the *South China Sea* dispute, the 1992 ASEAN Declaration on the South China Sea emphasised 'the necessity to resolve all sovereignty and jurisdictional issues pertaining to the South China Sea by peaceful means, without resort to force'; and it urged 'all parties concerned to exercise restraint with the view to creating a positive climate for the eventual resolution of all disputes'.[222] The 2002 Declaration on the Conduct of Parties in the South China Sea, adopted by ASEAN and China, also stressed that:

> The Parties undertake to exercise self-restraint in the conduct of activities that would complicate or escalate disputes and affect peace and stability including, among others, refraining from action of inhabiting on the presently uninhabited islands, reefs, shoals, cays, and other features and to handle their differences in a constructive manner.[223]

An issue that needs to be considered in this context was whether the conduct of the Chinese Government in the South China Sea was at variance with the obligation of restraint. In this regard, the Philippines, in its Submission No 14 as amended, requested the Tribunal to declare:

> (14) Since the commencement of this arbitration in January 2013, China has unlawfully aggravated and extended the dispute by, among other things:
> (a) interfering with the Philippines' rights of navigation in the waters at, and adjacent to, Second Thomas Shoal;
> (b) preventing the rotation and resupply of Philippine personnel stationed at Second Thomas Shoal;
> (c) endangering the health and well-being of Philippine personnel stationed at Second Thomas Shoal; and
> (d) conducting dredging, artificial island-building and construction activities at Mischief Reef, Cuarteron Reef, Fiery Cross Reef, Gaven Reef, Johnson Reef, Hughes Reef and Subi Reef.[224]

[220] ibid, [4].

[221] UN General Assembly Resolution 37/10, Manila Declaration on Peaceful Settlement of Disputes between States, para I(8). See also *Electricity Company of Sofia and Bulgaria (Belgium v Bulgaria)*, Order of 5 December 1939 Request for the Indication of Interim Measures of Protection, Series A/B 79, [1939] PCIJ Rep 194,199.

[222] ASEAN Declaration on the South China Sea adopted 22 July 1992, available at https://cil.nus.edu.sg/wp-content/uploads/2017/07/1992-ASEAN-Declaration-on-the-South-China-Sea.pdf.

[223] Para 5. The text of the Declaration is available at http://asean.org/?static_post=declaration-on-the-conduct-of-parties-in-the-south-china-sea-2.

[224] The *South China Sea* Arbitration Award (Merits), n 1, [1110].

Paragraph (d) was newly added to the amended Submission No 14, while paragraphs (a) to (c) were included in the initial formulation of this Submission.[225] In addition, the Philippines' Submission No 14 related to China's activities after the commencement of the *South China Sea* arbitration.

In considering Submission No 14, the Tribunal first needed to ascertain whether it had jurisdiction to deal with the submission. In the Award of Jurisdiction, the Tribunal ruled that 'this is not a dispute concerning sovereignty or maritime boundary delimitation, nor is it barred from the Tribunal's consideration by any requirement of Section 1 of Part XV [of the Convention]'.[226] At the same time, the Tribunal held that its jurisdiction to address these questions might depend on the status of Second Thomas Shoal as an 'island', 'rock' or 'low-tide elevation'. Furthermore, the question of whether China's activities in and around Second Thomas Shoal were military in nature under Article 298 of the Convention must be assessed in conjunction with the merits. Since the possible jurisdictional objections with respect to the dispute underlying Submission No 14 did not possess an exclusively preliminary character, the Tribunal reserved a decision on its jurisdiction with respect to the Philippines' Submission No 14 for consideration in conjunction with the merits of the Philippines' claims.[227]

As had been seen, the Tribunal found that Second Thomas Shoal was a low-tide elevation. Nor were there any high-tide features within 12 nautical miles of Second Thomas Shoal. Since there was no legal basis for any entitlement by China to marine zones in the area of Second Thomas Shoal, no maritime delimitation issues arose. Furthermore, as Second Thomas Shoal was located within the EEZ of the Philippines, there was no need for the Tribunal to address sovereignty over Second Thomas Shoal.[228] However, the application of the military activities exception set out in Article 298(1)(b) needs further consideration. In this regard, two issues arise.

The first issue concerns the question of whether the optional exception under Article 298(1) must be specifically invoked by the respondent state. While China activated this exception through its Declaration of August 2006,[229] the Philippines took the position that '[t]he decision to rely on those options is a matter of choice',[230] and that if China did not specifically invoke Article 298(1)(b) in the course of these proceedings, there was no need for the Tribunal to examine the application of this provision.[231] However, the Tribunal was not

[225] ibid, [1111].
[226] The *South China Sea* Arbitration Award (Jurisdiction and Admissibility), n 6, [411].
[227] ibid.
[228] The *South China Sea* Arbitration Award (Merits), n 1, [1153].
[229] ibid, [1154].
[230] Presentation by Professor Oxman, Jurisdiction Hearing Tr (Day 2), 74.
[231] The *South China Sea* Arbitration Award (Merits), n 1, [1156].

persuaded by the Philippines' argument. In the view of the Tribunal, there was nothing to suggest that a provision of Article 298(1) must be specifically invoked. The Tribunal thus held that '[o]nce made, a declaration under Article 298(1) excludes the consent of the declaring State to compulsory settlement with respect to the specified categories of disputes' and '[s]uch a declaration stands until modified or withdrawn'.[232] In so stating, the Tribunal can be said to have clarified the automatic application of Article 298(1)(b).

The second issue pertains to the application of optional exceptions to aggravation of disputes subsequent to the commencement of proceedings. This issue concerns the time frame of the application of Article 298(1)(b). In this regard, the Philippines argued that 'Articles 297 and 298 do not apply to aggravation and extension of the dispute'.[233] The Philippines' argument seemed to suggest that insofar as any obligation not to aggravate the dispute concerns events subsequent to the commencement of proceedings, it is not separately subject to the limitations on dispute resolution set out in the Convention.[234] In this regard, the Tribunal took the view:

> Where a State Party has initiated compulsory dispute settlement under the Convention in respect of a dispute that does not concern military activities, Article 298(1)(b) would not come into play if the other Party were later to begin employing its military in relation to the dispute in the course of proceedings. Nor does the Tribunal see that Article 298(1)(b) would limit its ancillary jurisdiction to prescribe provisional measures in respect of military activities taking place in relation to a dispute that does not, itself, concern military activities.[235]

For the Tribunal, it was necessary to consider 'whether the claim of aggravation remains dependent on an underlying dispute, or whether it constitutes itself a distinct dispute to which the military activities exception would be applicable'.[236] In this connection, the Tribunal considered that 'China's actions in and around Second Thomas Shoal and its interaction with the Philippine military forces stationed there constitute a distinct matter, irrespective of their effect in potentially aggravating other disputes before the Tribunal.'[237] Accordingly, there was a need for the Tribunal to consider the question whether this dispute concerned military activities for the purposes of Article 298(1)(b).[238] The essential facts at Second Thomas Shoal concerned the opposition between the Philippines' armed forces and China's Navy and Coast Guard and other government agencies. According to the Tribunal, these facts represented a

[232] ibid.
[233] Presentation by Professor Oxman, Merits Hearing Tr (Day 3), 84.
[234] The *South China Sea* Arbitration Award (Merits), n 1, [1157].
[235] ibid, [1158].
[236] ibid, [1159].
[237] ibid, [1160].
[238] ibid.

quintessentially military situation and fell within the exception for the purposes of Article 298(1)(b).[239] The Tribunal thus concluded that it lacked jurisdiction to consider the Philippines' Submission No 14(a), (b) and (c).[240]

In this regard, the Tribunal applied another ancillary test.[241] Where the military action aggravating the dispute is ancillary to non-military action that triggered compulsory dispute settlement under the Convention by a state party, Article 298(1)(b) would not limit the jurisdiction of an international court or tribunal. Thus continuity between the original action creating an international dispute and the action ancillary to the original action constitutes the key element in deciding the applicability of Article 298(1)(b). If such a continuity exists, the applicability of Article 298(1)(b) rests on the nature of the original action creating the dispute in question. If no continuity exists, the applicability of the provision relies on the nature of the action aggravating the dispute that is distinct from the original action.

On the other hand, China's dredging and construction activities were not military in nature since China itself consistently resisted such classification. As civilian activity, China's conduct fell outside the scope of Article 298(1)(b).[242] The Tribunal thus concluded that it had jurisdiction with regard to the matter raised in the Philippines' Submission No 14(d).[243] The Tribunal thus turned to the examination of the Philippines' Submission No 14(d).

ii. Lawfulness of China's Actions

a. The Obligation of Non-aggravation

The pivotal issue before the Tribunal was whether, as the Philippines alleged, China aggravated and extended the disputes between the Parties through its dredging, artificial island-building and construction activities.[244] After the examination of four materials, namely, (i) the jurisprudence of the PCIJ and ICJ concerning provisional measures, (ii) multilateral treaties and UN instruments, (iii) provisions of the UNCLOS, and (iv) general international law, the Tribunal ruled that the obligation not to aggravate a dispute constituted a 'principle of international law that is applicable to States engaged in dispute settlement as such'.[245] Accordingly, the principle was applicable to the *South China Sea*

[239] ibid, [1161].
[240] ibid, [1162].
[241] The ancillary test was at issue when deciding the jurisdiction of an international court or tribunal with regard to the mixed disputes involving land and maritime issues at the same time. See ch 2, section IV.C of this book.
[242] The *South China Sea* Arbitration Award (Merits), n 1, [1164].
[243] ibid, [1165].
[244] ibid, [1166].
[245] ibid, [1173].

case as one of the 'other rules of international law not incompatible with this Convention' pursuant to Article 293 of the UNCLOS.[246]

It is significant that the Tribunal regarded the obligation not to aggravate a dispute as a 'principle of international law'.[247] In this connection, by referring to the jurisprudence of the PCIJ[248] and the ICJ,[249] the Tribunal accepted the existence of a 'duty on parties engaged in a dispute settlement procedure to refrain from aggravating or extending the dispute or disputes at issue during the pendency of the settlement process'.[250] For the Tribunal:

> This duty exists *independently* of any order from a court or tribunal to refrain from aggravating or extending the dispute and stems from the purpose of dispute settlement and the status of the States in question as parties in such a proceeding. Indeed, when a court or tribunal issues provisional measures directing a party to refrain from actions that would aggravate or extend the dispute, it is not imposing a new obligation on the parties, but rather recalling to the parties an obligation that already exists by virtue of their involvement in the proceedings.[251]

Beyond the scope of the *South China Sea* arbitration, the dictum may affect the ICJ's power to indicate provisional measures. It is common practice that the Court indicates provisional measures to ensure that the parties in dispute take no action that might aggravate or extend the dispute before the Court. These can be called 'non-aggravation measures'. However, opinions of commentators are divided whether the Court has the power *proprio motu* to indicate non-aggravation measures.

According to a narrow view, the Court does not have the power *proprio motu* to indicate non-aggravation measures unless such measures are linked with the protection of the rights of the parties. For instance, Merrills argued that 'the powers of the Court under Article 41 have the specific purpose of preserving the rights in issue in litigation and so it is only in that context that the Court is entitled to act to prevent extension or aggravation of the dispute'.[252] This view was echoed by Palchetti, stating that 'the Court's practice reveals that the element of aggravation must in any case be linked with the protection of the rights of the parties which are at issue in a case'.[253]

[246] ibid.

[247] ibid, [1173].

[248] *Electricity Company of Sofia and Bulgaria (Belgium v Bulgaria)* [1939] PCIJ Rep 199. By referring to this case, the Philippines asserted that '[a]lthough the PCIJ's views were stated in connection with its decision on provisional measures, there is no reason to presume that the principle is not of universal application'. Memorial of the Philippines, vol I, 174, [646].

[249] *LaGrand (Germany v United States of America)*, Judgment, [2001] ICJ Rep 466, 503, [102]–[103].

[250] The *South China Sea* Arbitration Award (Merits), n 1, [1169].

[251] ibid, [1169] (emphasis added).

[252] J Merrills, 'Interim Measures of Protection in the Recent Jurisprudence of the International Court of Justice' (1995) 44 *ICLQ* 90, 123.

[253] P Palchetti, 'The Power of the International Court of Justice to Indicate Provisional Measures to Prevent the Aggravation of a Dispute' (2008) 21 *LJIL* 623, 634.

According to a less restrictive view, however, the Court may indicate non-aggravation measures in the absence of linkage between the measures and the alleged rights in the principal request. For instance, Thirlway took the view that 'the existence of a bar to the indication of preservative measures does not necessarily signify that the Court cannot indicate non-aggravation measure'.[254] To some extent, this position seems to be supported by the practice of the Court. By way of illustration, the ICJ, in the *Cameroon v Nigeria* case, held:

> Considering that, independently of the requests for the indication of provisional measures submitted by the Parties to *preserve specific rights*, the Court possesses by virtue of Article 41 of the Statute the power to indicate provisional measures with a view to preventing the aggravation or extension of the dispute whenever it considers that circumstances so require.[255]

This passage seems to suggest that the Court has the power to indicate non-aggravation measures independently of any preservative measures.[256] This interpretation was supported by Judge Greenwood in the *Costa Rica v Nicaragua* case. According to the learned judge:

> It is, however, open to the Court to indicate measures different from those requested, or even to act *proprio motu* without a request having been made (see Article 75 of the Rules of Court) but, if it does so, it is still bound to satisfy itself that the measures which it proposes to order meet the requirements set out above, since those requirements follow from the provisions of Article 41 of the Statute. The only exception – and that only a partial one – is the indication of measures requiring the parties to refrain from action which might aggravate or extend the dispute. Such measures are not limited to the protection of rights which might be adjudged to belong to either party but serve a wider purpose.[257]

If, as the Tribunal ruled in its Award of 2016, the non-aggravation measures are not 'imposing a new obligation on the parties, but rather recalling to the parties an obligation that already exists by virtue of their involvement in the proceedings', this interpretation will contribute to strengthening the ICJ's power *proprio motu* to indicate non-aggravation measures.[258]

[254] H Thirlway, *The Law and Procedure of the International Court of Justice: Fifty Years of Jurisprudence*, vol I (Oxford University Press, 2013) 951.

[255] *Land and Maritime Boundary between Cameroon and Nigeria (Cameroon v Nigeria: Equatorial Guinea intervening)*, Provisional Measures, [1996] ICJ Rep 13, 22–23, [41] (emphasis added).

[256] Thirlway, n 254, 949. According to Thirlway, the Chamber of the Court, in para 18 of the Order of 1986 in *Frontier Dispute (Burkina Faso v Mali)*, also implied that it could indicate non-aggravation measures independently of any finding that preservative measures were appropriate: ibid, 949; [1986] ICJ Rep 9, [18]. See also Separate Opinion of Judge Ajibola in *Cameroon v Nigeria* [1996] ICJ Rep 53.

[257] Declaration of Judge Greenwood in *Certain Activities carried out by Nicaragua in the Border Area (Costa Rica v Nicaragua)*, Provisional Measures, [2011] ICJ Rep 46, 48, [8]. See also ibid, 46–47, [2]. However, it appears that the subsequent case law of the Court does not support this dictum. See *Application of the International Convention on the Elimination of All Forms of Racial Discrimination (Qatar v. United Arab Emirates)*, Order, [2019] ICJ Rep (not yet reported), [28].

[258] However, it must be noted that in the jurisprudence of the ICJ, non-aggravation measures were ordered only as an adjunct to preservative provisional measures. *Case Concerning Pulp Mills on the*

However, the independent existence of the obligation not to aggravate a dispute does not mean that the obligation is separated from other obligations in international law. In this regard, particular attention must be paid to the interlinkage between the obligation not to aggravate a dispute, the obligation of peaceful settlement of international disputes and the principle of good faith. In the view of the Tribunal, '[t]he very purpose of dispute settlement procedures would be frustrated by actions by any party that had the effect of aggravating or extending the dispute, thereby rendering it less amenable to settlement'.[259] It follows that the obligation not to aggravate a dispute and the obligation of peaceful settlement of international disputes are closely intertwined. Furthermore, the Tribunal linked the obligation of peaceful settlement of international disputes to the principle of good faith. Indeed, by referring to Article 279 of the UNCLOS concerning the obligation of peaceful settlement of international disputes, the Tribunal held that:

> In carrying out the dispute settlement procedures of the Convention, the Parties are also under an obligation, pursuant to Article 300, to 'fulfil in good faith the obligations assumed under this Convention and … exercise the rights, jurisdiction and freedoms recognized in this Convention in a manner which would not constitute an abuse of right.'[260]

The Tribunal further considered that the obligation not to aggravate a dispute is 'inherent in the central role of good faith in the international legal relations between States' and that 'actions by either Party to aggravate or extend the dispute would be incompatible with the recognition and performance in good faith of these obligations'.[261] Accordingly, the obligation of peaceful settlement of international disputes, the obligation not to aggravate a dispute and the principle of good faith are integrally interlinked. It is important that the Tribunal clarified the interlinking of the three elements. It would seem to follow that the breach of the obligation not to aggravate a dispute also leads to the breach of the obligation of peaceful settlement of international disputes and the principle of good faith at the same time.

b. Criteria for Deciding Breaches of the Obligation Not to Aggravate a Dispute

There is little doubt that parties are under the obligation not to aggravate a dispute in international law. However, the question is what the criteria are for

River Uruguay (Argentina v Uruguay), Provisional Measures, [2007] ICJ Rep 3, 16, [49]. See also Palchetti, n 253, 635; Y Tanaka, 'A New Phase of the Temple of Preah Vihear Dispute before the International Court of Justice: Reflections on the Indication of Provisional Measures of 18 July 2011' (2012) 11 *CJIL* 191, 212–16.

[259] The *South China Sea* Arbitration Award (Merits), n 1, [1171].

[260] ibid, [1172].

[261] ibid, [1171]–[1172].

deciding breaches of the obligation. In this regard, the Tribunal specified three actions that are contrary to the obligation:

(a) actions that are alleged to violate the rights of the other party during the pendency of the proceedings, in such a way as to render the alleged violation more serious;
(b) actions that would frustrate the effectiveness of a potential decision, or render its implementation by the parties significantly more difficult; and
(c) actions that would undermine the integrity of the dispute resolution proceedings themselves.[262]

The three categories of actions provide the criteria for determining breaches of the obligation not to aggravate a dispute. By applying the criteria, the Tribunal determined breaches of the obligation by the Chinese Government. The Court's findings may be summarised in three points.

First, the Tribunal held that China effectively created a *fait accompli* at Mischief Reef by constructing a large artificial island on a low-tide elevation located within the Philippines' EEZ. As Mischief Reef cannot be returned to its original state, the China's construction work made the implementation of the Tribunal's decision difficult.[263]

Second, according to the Tribunal, China's action aggravated the dispute between the Parties concerning the marine environment at Mischief Reef and extended that dispute to encompass additional features that became the sites of large-scale construction work while this arbitration was ongoing. In this connection, the Tribunal noted that '[i]n practical terms, neither this decision nor any action that either Party may take in response can undo the permanent damage that has been done to the coral reef habitats of the South China Sea'.[264] It is notable that the breach of the obligation not to aggravate a dispute led to breaches of the substantive obligation not to cause harm to the environment at the same time.

Third, China permanently destroyed evidence of the natural status of maritime features in the Spratly Islands. The assessment of the legal status of maritime features as above/below water at high tide was rendered significantly more difficult by the China's action. Accordingly, the Tribunal ruled that China undermined the integrity of the arbitral proceedings and rendered the task before the Tribunal more difficult.[265] In this connection, Tribunal referred to non-appearance of China and stressed that:

> The decision of how best to represent China's position is a matter for China, not the Tribunal. China is not free, however, to act to undermine the integrity of these proceedings or to frustrate the effectiveness of the Tribunal's decisions.[266]

[262] ibid, [1176].
[263] ibid, [1177].
[264] ibid, [1178].
[265] ibid, [1179]. See also ibid, [1203]B(16).
[266] ibid, [1180].

All in all, the Tribunal found that during the time at which these dispute resolution proceedings were ongoing, China:

(a) had aggravated the Parties' dispute concerning their respective rights and entitlements in the area of Mischief Reef;
(b) had aggravated the Parties' dispute concerning the protection and preservation of the marine environment at Mischief Reef;
(c) had extended the scope of the Parties' dispute concerning the protection and preservation of the marine environment to Cuarteron Reef, Fiery Cross Reef, Gaven Reef (North), Johnson Reef, Hughes Reef and Subi Reef;
(d) had aggravated the Parties' dispute concerning the status of maritime features in the Spratly Islands and their capacity to generate entitlements to maritime zones.[267]

In conclusion, the Tribunal declared:

> China has breached its obligations pursuant to Articles 279, 296, and 300 of the Convention, as well as pursuant to general international law, to abstain from any measure capable of exercising a prejudicial effect in regard to the execution of the decisions to be given and in general, not to allow any step of any kind to be taken which might aggravate or extend the dispute during such time as dispute resolution proceedings were ongoing.[268]

It is noteworthy that the Tribunal, in its Award of 2016, specified three criteria for deciding breaches of the obligation not to aggravate a dispute in the judicial proceedings. In general, it could well be said that destruction of evidence and a *fait accompli* constitute the breach of the second criterion and/or third criterion. Even so, it may have to be admitted that the application of the three criteria is context-specific and that breaches of the obligations of non-aggravation must be decided on a case-by-case basis, taking account of particularities of each case.

B. The Future Conduct of the Parties

The final claim made by the Philippines pertained to the future conduct of the Parties. In its Submission No 15, the Philippines requested the Tribunal to declare:

> (15) China shall respect the rights and freedoms of the Philippines under the Convention, shall comply with its duties under the Convention, including those relevant to the protection and preservation of the marine environment in the South China Sea, and shall exercise its rights and freedoms in the South China Sea with due regard to those of the Philippines under the Convention.[269]

[267] ibid, [1181].
[268] ibid, [1203]B(16).
[269] ibid, [1182].

In its Award on Jurisdiction, the Tribunal considered that it was unable to determine whether there existed a dispute between the Parties concerning the interpretation or application of the Convention, or to assess the scope of the Tribunal's jurisdiction in this respect. It thus directed the Philippines to clarify the content and narrow the scope of its Submission No 15, and reserved the question of its jurisdiction in relation to Submission No 15 for consideration in conjunction with the merits of the Philippines' claims.[270]

Subsequently the Philippines reframed its Submission. In the view of the Tribunal, the Philippines' Submission No 15 as amended contained three components:

(a) asking the Tribunal to declare that China 'shall respect the rights and freedoms of the Philippines under the Convention';
(b) asking the Tribunal to declare that China 'shall comply with its duties under the Convention, including those relevant to the marine environmental protection in the South China Sea'; and
(c) asking the Tribunal to declare that China 'shall exercise its rights and freedoms in the South China Sea with due regard to those of the Philippines under the Convention'.[271]

According to the Philippines, the focus of Submission No 15 was prospective.[272] In the view of the Tribunal, however, it was beyond dispute that both Parties were obliged to comply with the Convention and to respect the rights and freedoms of other states under the UNCLOS. Indeed, neither Party contended this point.[273] In this connection, the Tribunal stressed that it is a fundamental principle of international law that 'bad faith is not presumed'.[274] The Tribunal thus ruled that it was not necessary nor appropriate for it to make any further declaration.[275]

IV. CONCLUSIONS

The Tribunal, in its Award on the Merits, examined a wide array of issues with regard to the lawfulness of Chinese activities in the South China Sea. The Tribunal's views on these issues shed some light on the interpretation and application of relevant rules and obligations of international law. The principal points discussed in this chapter may be summarised as follows.

[270] The *South China Sea* Arbitration Award (Jurisdiction and Admissibility), n 6, [412].
[271] The *South China Sea* Arbitration Award (Merits), n 1, [1192]–[1194].
[272] Presentation by Professor Oxman, Merits Hearing Tr (Day 3), 90.
[273] The *South China Sea* Arbitration Award (Merits), n 1, [1201].
[274] ibid, [200].
[275] ibid, [1201].

First, according to the Tribunal, a statement itself violates relevant provisions of the UNCLOS where there is a 'realistic prospect' that the statement may create a deterring effect. The Tribunal's approach may be called the 'realistic prospect' test. It is argued that the 'realistic prospect' test is regarded as an inter-temporal concept, in the sense that it seeks to envisage future events. In this regard, further consideration must be given to the questions of how it is possible to assess the existence of a 'realistic prospect' and to what extent the prospect of the future events must exist.

Second, the key element in Article 58(3) of the UNCLOS is the obligation to have 'due regard to the rights and duties'. Referring to the ITLOS Advisory Opinion of 2015, the Tribunal equated 'the obligation of due regard' with 'the obligation of due diligence'. The *South China Sea* Arbitration Award (Merits) suggests that a state breaches the obligation of due diligence when that state was aware of illegal fishing activities conducted by its nationals in an EEZ of another state and it failed to prevent them.

Third, traditional fishing rights are not the historic rights of states but private rights. By referring to the *Eritrea/Yemen* Arbitration Award (Second Phase), the Tribunal regarded traditional fishing as artisanal fishing. Yet it did not go into further detail with regard to the criteria for deciding whether certain fishing activities would fall within the scope of artisanal fishing. The law applicable to traditional fishing rights differs according to jurisdictional zones. According to the Tribunal, established traditional fishing rights in the territorial sea remain protected by international law.

Fourth, the 'general obligation' under Article 192 with regard to marine environmental protection extends both to 'protection' of the marine environment from *future* damage and 'preservation' in the sense of maintaining or improving its *present* condition. In this sense, this provision contains a temporal element. Furthermore, Article 192 must be read against the background of other applicable international law, such as CITES. The Tribunal's systemic approach to treaty interpretation merits particular notice. In this connection, it is noteworthy that the Tribunal recognised application of the obligation of due diligence to the protection of rare or fragile ecosystems and the habitat of endangered species. In this regard, the Tribunal specified two requirements of the obligation of due diligence:

(a) a duty to adopt rules and measures to prevent harmful acts; and
(b) a duty to maintain a level of vigilance in enforcing those rules and measures.

According to the Tribunal, to fulfil the obligation of due diligence, legislation of municipal law alone is inadequate; there is also a need to take steps to enforce it.

Fifth, Article 206 of the UNCLOS includes the obligation to communicate. In the view of the Tribunal, this obligation is absolute. Given that it may be less easy to determine whether a state properly carried out an environmental impact assessment, the Tribunal's approach focusing on the non-fulfilment of a procedural requirement, that is communication, is noteworthy. While there are some issues remaining regarding the obligation under Article 206, the Tribunal's finding may contribute to cementing the normative position of environmental impact assessment in international law.[276]

Sixth, according to the Tribunal, only the Philippines could construct or authorise artificial islands, installations and structures in accordance with Article 60 of the UNCLOS, since Mischief Reef was a low-tide elevation and it could only constitute part of the EEZ and continental shelf of the Philippines. It would seem to follow that construction activities on low-tide elevations in a third state's EEZ or continental shelf are contrary to the UNCLOS, unless there is a valid circumstance precluding wrongfulness.[277] As a low-tide elevation, as distinct from land territory, cannot be appropriated, Mischief Reef was incapable of appropriation by occupation.

Seventh, the COLREGS, as a 'generally accepted international regulation', is thought to be incorporated into Article 94 of the UNCLOS. It follows that a violation of the COLREGS constitutes a violation of Article 94 of the UNCLOS. When examining the manner of law enforcement operations by Chinese vessels, the Tribunal relied on the report of an independent expert, namely, the Singhota Report. In light of the highly technical nature of the rules under the COLREGS, the assessment of an independent expert was particularly useful.

Eighth, the Tribunal considered that the obligation not to aggravate a dispute may be regarded as a 'principle of international law that is applicable to States engaged in dispute settlement as such'. In this connection, the Tribunal specified three actions that are contrary to the obligation. On the basis of the three actions, it may be possible to formulate three criteria for determining breach of the obligation:

(a) Whether an action violates the rights of the other party during the pendency of the proceedings, in such a way as to render the alleged violation more serious.
(b) Whether an action would frustrate the effectiveness of a potential decision, or render its implementation by the parties significantly more difficult.
(c) Whether an action would undermine the integrity of the dispute resolution proceedings themselves.

The criteria may offer an insight into the obligation on non-aggravation of a dispute.

[276] Scanlon and Beckman, n 106, 29–30.

[277] See also T Davenport, 'Island-building in the South China Sea: Legality and Limits' (2018) 8 *Asian Journal of International Law* 76, 89.

FURTHER READING

Birnie, P, Boyle, A and Redgwell, C, *International Law and the Environment* (Oxford University Press, 2009).

Craik, N, *The International Law of Environmental Impact Assessment: Process, Substance and Integration* (Cambridge University Press, 2008).

Davenport, T, 'Island-building in the South China Sea: Legality and Limits' (2018) 8 *Asian Journal of International Law* 76.

Harrison, J, 'Significant International Environmental Law Cases: 2015–16', (2016) 28 *Journal of Environmental Law* 533.

——, *Saving the Oceans through Law: the International Legal Framework for the Protection of the Marine Environment* (Oxford University Press, 2017).

Keyuan Zou, 'Navigation in the South China Sea: Why Still an Issue?' (2017) 32 *IJMCL* 243.

Kojima, C, 'South China Sea Arbitration and the Protection of the Marine Environment: Evolution of UNCLOS Part XII Through Interpretation and the Duty to Cooperate' (2017) 27 *Asian Yearbook of International Law* 166.

Kopela, S, 'Historic Titles and Historic Rights in the Law of the Sea in the Light of the South China Sea Arbitration' (2017) 48 *ODIL* 181.

Letts, D, McLaughlin, R and Nasu, H, 'Maritime Law Enforcement and the Aggravation of the South China Sea Dispute: Implications for Australia' (2016) 34 *Australian Yearbook of International Law* 53.

Lyons, Y et al, 'Managing Giant Clams in the South China Sea' (2018) 33 *IJMCL* 467.

Martin-Bidou, P, 'Le principe de précaution en droit international de l'environnement' (1999) 103 *RGDIP* 631.

Mbengue, MM, 'The South China Sea Arbitration: Innovations in Marine Environmental Fact-Finding and Due Diligence Obligations' (2016) 110 *American Journal of International Law Unbound* 285.

McDorman, TL, 'The Law of the Sea Convention and the U-Shaped Line: Some Comments' in Shicun Wu and Keyuan Zou (eds), *Arbitration Concerning the South China Sea: Philippines versus China* (Routledge, 2017) 147–55.

McManus, JW, 'Offshore Oral Reef Damage, Overfishing, and Paths to Peace in the South China Sea' (2017) 32 *IJMCL* 199.

Merkouris, P, *Article 31(3)(c) VCLT and the Principle of Systemic Integration: Normative Shadows in Plato's Cave* (Brill/Nijhoff, 2015).

Moore, C, 'The Arbitral Award in the Matter of the South China Sea between the Philippines and China: What are the Implications for Freedom of Navigation and the Use of Force?' (2017) 2 *Asia-Pacific Journal of Ocean Law and Policy* 117.

Mossop, J, 'Can the South China Sea Tribunal's Conclusions on Traditional Fishing Rights Lead to Cooperative Fishing Arrangements in the Region?' (2018) 3 *Asia-Pacific Journal of Ocean Law and Policy* 210.

Oral, N, 'The South China Sea Arbitral Award, Part XII of UNCLOS, and the Protection and Preservation of the Marine Environment' in S Jayakumar et al (eds), *The South China Sea Arbitration: The Legal Dimension* (Edward Elgar, 2018) 223–46.

Oude Elferink, AG, 'Arguing International Law in the South China Sea Disputes: The *Haiyang Shiyou 981* and *USS Lassen* Incidents and the *Philippines* v *China* Arbitration' (2016) 31 *IJMCL* 205.

Palchetti, P, 'The Power of the International Court of Justice to Indicate Provisional Measures to Prevent the Aggravation of a Dispute' (2008) 21 *Leiden Journal of International Law* 623.

Prölss (ed), A, *United Nations Convention on the Law of the Sea: A Commentary* (Beck/Hart Publishing/ Nomos, 2017).

Scanlon, Z and Beckman, R, 'Assessing Environmental Impact and the Duty to Cooperate: Environmental Aspects of the Philippines v China Award' (2018) 3 *Asia-Pacific Journal of Ocean Law and Policy* 5.

Stephens, T, 'The Collateral Damage from China's "Great Wall of Sand": The Environmental Dimensions of the *South China Sea* Case' (2016) 34 *Australian Yearbook of International Law* 41.

Stubbs, M and Stephens, D, 'Dredge Your Way to China? The Legal Significance of Chinese Reclamation and Construction in the South China Sea' (2017) 2 *Asia-Pacific Journal of Ocean Law and Policy* 25.

Tanaka, Y, 'Principles of International Marine Environmental Law' in R Rayfuse (ed), *Research Handbook on International Marine Environmental Law* (Edward Elgar, 2015) 31–56.

——, 'A New Phase of the Temple of Preah Vihear Dispute before the International Court of Justice: Reflections on the Indication of Provisional Measures of 18 July 2011' (2012) 11 *CJIL* 191.

——, 'Reflections on Time Elements in the International Law of the Environment' (2013) 73 *ZaöRV* 139.

——, 'A Note on the M/V "Louisa" Case' (2014) 45 *ODIL* 205.

——, 'Costa Rica v Nicaragua and Nicaragua v Costa Rica (ICJ 2015): Some Reflections on the Obligation to Conduct an Environmental Impact Assessment' (2017) 27 *Review of European, Comparative and International Environmental Law* 91.

——, 'The *South China Sea* Arbitration (Merits, 12 July 2016): Environmental Obligations under the UN Convention on the Law of the Sea' (2018) 28 *Review of European, Comparative and International Environmental Law* 90.

Yen Hoang Tran, 'The South China Sea Arbitral Award: Legal Implications for Fisheries Management and Cooperation in the South China Sea' (2017) 6 *Cambridge International Law Journal* 87.

6

Legal Implications of the South China Sea *Arbitration Awards*

I. INTRODUCTION

On the basis of considerations in the previous chapters, this chapter addresses the implications of the *South China Sea* arbitration. Even though the Tribunal, in its Award on the Merits, stressed the obligation of both Parties 'to resolve their disputes peacefully and to comply with the Convention and this Award in good faith',[1] it is widely known that China refused to accept the *South China Sea* arbitration awards. On 12 July 2016, the Ministry of Foreign Affairs of the People's Republic of China explicitly stated that 'the award [on the Merits] is null and void and has no binding force. China neither accepts nor recognises it'.[2] In 'China Adheres to the Position of Settling Through Negotiation the Relevant Disputes between China and the Philippines in the South China Sea' of 13 July 2016, the Chinese Government also stressed that 'China does not accept or recognize those awards. China opposes and will never accept any claim or action based on those awards'.[3] However, it is clear

[1] PCA Case No 2013–19. The *South China Sea Arbitration Award* (Merits) (hereinafter 'the *South China Sea* Arbitration Award (Merits)'), 12 July 2016, [1200].

[2] Statement of the Ministry of Foreign Affairs of the People's Republic of China on the Award of 12 July 2016 of the Arbitral Tribunal in the South China Sea Arbitration Established at the Request of the Republic of the Philippines, available at http://www.fmprc.gov.cn/nanhai/eng/snhwtlcwj_1/t1379492.htm. Reproduced in Chinese Society of International Law (CSIL), *The South China Sea Arbitration: A Critical Study* (Foreign Languages Press, 2018) 561. This position was confirmed by the Chinese Foreign Minister Wang Yi, stating that 'The award is clearly out of the Arbitral Tribunal's acts of self-expansion of power and ultra vires, and has no legal effect.' Remarks by Chinese Foreign Minister Wang Yi on the Award of the So-called Arbitral Tribunal in the South China Sea Arbitration, 12 July 2016, available at http://www.fmprc.gov.cn/mfa_eng/zxxx_662805/t1380003.shtml. For other China's statements, see http://www.fmprc.gov.cn/nanhai/eng/. CSIL took the same position, stating that '[t]he Tribunal manifestly had no jurisdiction over the Philippines' submissions, and its awards are groundless both in fact and in law, thus null and void': CSIL, n 2, 517, [978] et seq.

[3] China Adheres to the Position of Settling through Negotiation the Relevant Disputes between China and the Philippines in the South China Sea, 13 July 2016, [120], available at http://www.fmprc.gov.cn/nanhai/eng/snhwtlcwj_1/t1380615.htm. Reproduced in CSIL, n 2, 567.

that under Article 296(1) and Article 11 of Annex VII of the UNCLOS, the Award is final and binding upon the Parties.[4]

Even though China continues to deny the binding nature of the *South China Sea* arbitration awards, this does not directly mean that the awards have no value. As McDorman aptly stated, '[t]he effectiveness (or impact) of international judicial decision is not always to be assessed by the immediate reactions of the disputing or relevant States'.[5] The value of the *South China Sea* arbitration must be examined from the multiple viewpoints. This chapter considers the role and legal implications of the South China Sea arbitration awards, focusing on the following questions:

(a) What is the role of the *South China Sea* arbitration in the peaceful settlement of the dispute between the Philippines and China?
(b) What are the implications of the *South China Sea* arbitration awards for the development of international law?
(c) What are the implications of the *South China Sea* arbitration awards for the protection of community interests at sea?
(d) What is the impact of the considerations of time elements on the interpretation or application of relevant rules of international law?

Following this introduction, this chapter discusses the role of the *South China Sea* arbitration in the peaceful settlement of the *Philippines/China* dispute (section II). Next, it addresses the contribution of the *South China Sea* arbitration to the development of international law, in particular the law of the sea (section III). Furthermore, it examines whether and to what extent the *South China Sea* arbitration affects the protection of community interests at sea (section IV). Lastly, it addresses the considerations of time elements in that arbitration (section V), before offering conclusions in section VI.

II. THE ROLE OF THE *SOUTH CHINA SEA* ARBITRATION IN DISPUTE SETTLEMENT

A. Dual Role of the *South China Sea* Arbitration Award (Merits)

The first issue that needs consideration is the role of the *South China Sea* arbitration in the settlement of the dispute between the Philippines and China.

[4] The *South China Sea* Arbitration Award (Merits), n 1, [1180]. See also TL McDorman, 'The South China Sea Arbitration: Selected Legal Notes' (2017) 21 *Asian Yearbook of International Law* 1, 6; AC Robles, Jr, *The South China Sea Arbitration: Understanding the Awards and Debating with China* (Sussex Academic Press, 2019) 247 et seq. Non-compliance with the arbitration award will also be contrary to the principle of good faith, since judicial decisions must be executed in good faith by the parties to the proceedings. R Kolb, *Good Faith in International Law* (Hart Publishing, 2017) 240. See also Art 2(2) of the UN Charter.

[5] TL McDorman, 'The South China Sea Tribunal Awards: A Dispute Resolution Perspective' (2018) 3 *Asia-Pacific Journal of Ocean Law and Policy* 134, 143. See also ibid, 145.

According to the Tribunal, the root of the disputes in the *South China Sea* arbitration lay in fundamentally different understandings of the Parties' respective rights under the Convention in the waters of the South China Sea. 'In such circumstances', the Tribunal stated, 'the purpose of dispute resolution proceedings is to clarify the Parties' respective rights and obligations and thereby to facilitate their future relations in accordance with the general obligations of good faith that both governments unequivocally recognize.'[6] The question of interest here is whether and to what extent the Tribunal could contribute to the settlement of the *Philippines/China* dispute and beyond. In considering this question, two points merit discussion: to narrow the issues; and to furnish a basis for international cooperation in the region.

i. Narrowing the Issues

The first noteworthy point pertains to narrowing the issues. Since the Tribunal could not deal with territorial and maritime delimitation disputes, its arbitration awards only dealt with some legal aspects of the *South China Sea* dispute. In this sense, the scope of the awards was limited.[7] However, the narrow scope of the *South China Sea* arbitration was part of the legal strategy of the Philippines. According to the Philippines, 'the award would perform one of the most important functions of law and legal process in facilitating cooperation: narrowing the issues'.[8] Thus the Philippines adopted a phased approach to facilitate the settlement of the dispute.

In some cases, wisdom may require that the settlement of an international dispute be divided into multiple phases, and an international court or tribunal comes into play in one of the phases of the dispute settlement process only. An illustrative example is the 1969 *North Sea Continental Shelf* cases.[9] There, Denmark and the Netherlands requested the Court to decide the principles of international law applicable to the delimitation of the continental shelf between the two kingdoms and the Federal Republic of Germany. The Court, in its judgment, held that 'delimitation is to be effected by agreement in accordance with equitable principles, and taking account of all relevant circumstances'.[10] It then specified multiple factors to be taken into account in the course of the negotiations.[11] After the judgment, the parties resumed negotiation and two bilateral agreements delimitating the continental shelves were initialled on

[6] The *South China Sea* Arbitration Award (Merits), n 1, [1198].

[7] D Tamada, 'In the Matter of an Arbitration before an Arbitral Tribunal Constituted under Annex VII to the 1982 United Nations Convention on the Law of the Sea between the Republic of Philippines and the People's Republic of China, Award on Jurisdiction and Admissibility (29 October 2015)' (in Japanese) (2016) 66 *Kobe Law Journal* 125, 155.

[8] Hearing on Jurisdiction and Admissibility, Day 2, Presentation by Oxman, 49.

[9] *North Sea Continental Shelf (Federal Republic of Germany/Netherlands) (Federal Republic of Germany/Denmark)* (hereinafter 'the *North Sea Continental Shelf* cases'), Judgment, [1969] ICJ Rep 3.

[10] ibid, 53, [101](C).

[11] ibid, 54, [101](D).

October 1970. The continental shelf dispute between the three states was finally settled by the ratification of the two agreements on 7 December 1972.[12] The judicially directed negotiation provides an insight into the interaction between international adjudication and negotiation.[13]

As discussed in chapter 3, the Tribunal ruled that 'China's claims to historic rights … with respect to the maritime areas of the South China Sea encompassed by the relevant part of the "nine-dash line" are contrary to the Convention.'[14] It also held that none of the high-tide features in the Spratly Islands generated entitlements to an EEZ or continental shelf since they were rocks for the purposes of Article 121(3) of the UNCLOS.[15] Accordingly, a great portion of the areas previously claimed as disputed constituted either the high seas or the Philippines' EEZ. In addition, the Tribunal also decided that Mischief Reef and Second Thomas Shoal were within the EEZ and continental shelf of the Philippines. As a consequence, principal issues in the *China/Philippines* dispute would be limited to territorial sovereignty over some high-tide features and territorial seas surrounding those features.[16] By neutralising many of the contentious maritime disputes in the region, the *South China Sea* arbitration could be thought to contribute to narrowing down the scope of the dispute between the Philippines and China.[17] Accordingly, there are good reasons to agree with Judge Paik's statement that 'it is hoped that the Awards, by reducing legal uncertainties surrounding their long-standing, acrimonious dispute, could help the Parties to find a constructive solution in the long run'.[18]

ii. Basis for International Cooperation

The role of decisions of an international court or tribunal is not limited to the declaration of breaches of international obligations. On the basis of the

[12] For a detailed analysis of the negotiation process following the 1969 *North Sea Continental Shelf judgment*, see AG Oude Elferink, *The Delimitation of the Continental Shelf between Denmark, Germany and the Netherlands: Arguing Law, Practicing Politics?* (Cambridge University Press, 2013) 342 et seq.

[13] Further, see Y Tanaka, *The Peaceful Settlement of International Dispute* (Cambridge University Press, 2018) 35–36.

[14] The *South China Sea* Arbitration Award (Merits), n 1, [1203]B(2). See also [277]–[278].

[15] ibid, [1203]B(7).

[16] Yen Hoang Tran, 'The South China Sea Arbitral Award: Legal Implications for Fisheries Management and Cooperation in the South China Sea' (2017) 6 *Cambridge International Law Journal* 87, 90; ASP Baviera, 'Arbitration Over, Time for China to Lead Responsibility', available at http://appfi.ph/publications/commentaries/865-arbitration-over-time-for-china-to-lead-responsibly. This paper was reproduced in (2017) 9 *Asian Politics and Policy* 136.

[17] MPT Sison III, 'Universalizing the Law of the Sea in the South China Sea Dispute' (2018) 49 *ODIL* 157, 167; Hao Duy Phan and Lan Ngoc Nguyen, 'The South China Sea Arbitration: Bindingness, Finality, and Compliance with UNCLOS Dispute Settlement Decisions' (2018) 8 *Asian Journal of International Law* 36, 50; D Rothwell, 'Cause for Optimism in the South China Sea', East Asia Forum, 25 July 2016, available at http://www.eastasiaforum.org/2016/07/25/assessing-the-damage-the-south-china-sea-arbitration/.

[18] Jin-Hyun Paik, 'South China Sea Arbitral Awards: Main Findings and Assessment' (2016) 20 *Max Planck Yearbook of United Nations Law* 367, 407.

decisions, the parties in dispute – and, in appropriate cases, other states that may have an interest in the decisions – are also required to explore relevant means to effectively implement the obligations identified by a court or tribunal. In this regard, there appears to be some scope to consider that the *South China Sea* Arbitration Award (Merits) may lay the ground work for international cooperation with regard to, inter alia, fisheries and marine environmental protection.

As discussed earlier, the Tribunal acknowledged that 'Scarborough Shoal has been a traditional fishing ground for fishermen of many nationalities, including the Philippines, China (including from Taiwan), and Viet Nam.'[19] To coordinate fishing by multiple nationals, international cooperation will be needed. In this regard, as commentators suggested, the recognition of the Tribunal may furnish a basis for the establishment of an international arrangement on traditional fishing in the territorial sea surrounding the Scarborough Shoal.[20] The creation of a joint fishing zone in which nationals of all parties may engage in fishing may be an option under such an arrangement.[21] Given that fisheries in the South China Sea are currently unsustainable,[22] arguably the establishment of an international arrangement on traditional fishing is relevant. To establish such an arrangement, there will be a need to address a wide array of issues, such as:

- The geographical scope of marine spaces where traditional fishing is permitted.
- The definition of traditional fishing.
- The range of nationals that are allowed to conduct traditional fishing.
- Sustainable use of marine living resources.
- Mechanisms for securing compliance.
- Separation of traditional fishing from territorial disputes.[23]

In reality, it would be highly difficult to reach an agreement on these points, unless the political climate were to become more favourable.[24]

As for marine environmental protection, the Tribunal highlighted the obligation to cooperate set out, inter alia, in Article 123 of the UNCLOS concerning

[19] The *South China Sea* Arbitration Award (Merits), n 1, [805].

[20] S Jayakumar et al, 'Conclusion' in S Jayakumar et al (eds), *The South China Sea Arbitration: The Legal Dimension* (Edward Elgar, 2018) 277, 285.

[21] ibid.

[22] J Mossop, 'Can the South China Sea Tribunal's Conclusions on Traditional Fishing Rights Lead to Cooperative Fishing Arrangements in the Region?' (2018) 3 *Asia-Pacific Journal of Ocean Law and Policy* 210, 213 et seq.

[23] Similarly, Mossop listed the following elements: 'To which features the rights apply; What amounts to traditional fishing as opposed to industrial fishing; How each state would limit the fishing effort in order to ensure sustainability What would happen in internal waters and beyond 12 nautical miles; How enforcement would be dealt with; That nothing in the agreement affected the claims to sovereignty': ibid, 229.

[24] ibid.

cooperation in enclosed or semi-enclosed seas and Article 206 relating to environmental impact assessment. Article 123 specifies an obligation to cooperate between states bordering enclosed or semi-enclosed seas, including the obligation to 'coordinate the implementation of their rights and duties with respect to the protection and preservation of the marine environment'. To implement the obligation, there is a need to explore mechanisms to secure international cooperation between states surrounding the South China Sea. To fulfil the obligation to conduct environmental impact assessment, it will be useful to create an institutional arrangement to ensure communication on environmental impact assessment between relevant states. In this connection, it is also relevant to set out cooperative mechanisms for the joint gathering and sharing of information, and standardisation of the procedure of environmental impact assessment.[25] Like traditional fishing, however, progress on environmental cooperation rests on the will of relevant states.

B. Non-compliance with Arbitration Awards

i. Two Options

Next, some consideration must be given to the issue of non-compliance with arbitration awards. In reality, it is not infrequent that one of the parties in dispute challenges the validity of the arbitration award and refuses to implement it. In that case, two options exist: submission of the dispute regarding non-compliance with the arbitration award to the International Court of Justice (ICJ); and settlement by negotiation, where appropriate, along with the good offices or mediation of a third party.[26]

a. Referral to the ICJ

The first option is to submit a dispute concerning non-compliance with an arbitration award to the ICJ. In this regard, two instances merit mention.

The first instance is the *King of Spain* case between Honduras and Nicaragua. On 7 October 1894, Honduras and Nicaragua concluded the Gámez-Bonilla Treaty in order to demarcate the boundary line between the two republics.[27] Although the Mixed Boundary Commission established by Article I of the Treaty succeeded in determining the boundary from the Pacific Coast to the *Portillo de Teotecacinte*, it was unable to agree on the boundary from that point

[25] Jayakumar et al, 'Conclusion', n 20, 287.

[26] Tanaka, n 13, 120–21.

[27] *Case concerning the Arbitral Award made by the King of Spain on 23 December 1906 (Honduras v Nicaragua)* (hereinafter 'the *King of Spain* case'), Judgment, [1960] ICJ Rep 192.

to the Atlantic Coast.[28] With regard to the latter section of the boundary, the King of Spain, Alphonse XIII, handed down an Arbitral Award on 23 December 1906.[29] In a Note dated 19 March 1912, however, Nicaragua challenged the validity and binding character of the award. As a consequence, a dispute arose with regard to it. Honduras and Nicaragua attempted to settle the dispute by direct negotiation or through the good offices or mediation of other states, but to no avail. On 21 July 1957, the two parties reached an agreement to submit the dispute to the ICJ.[30] Against that background, on 1 July 1958, Honduras instituted proceedings against Nicaragua before the ICJ with regard to a dispute concerning the arbitral award made by the King of Spain.[31] By this application, Honduras requested the Court to declare, inter alia, that Nicaragua was under an obligation to give effect to the award. By contrast, Nicaragua solicited the Court to adjudge and declare that the decision given by the King of Spain on 23 December 1906 did not possess the character of a binding arbitral award, and that the arbitral decision was incapable of being executed by reason of its omissions, contradictions and obscurities.[32] The Court dismissed all of the allegations made by Nicaragua and found, by 14:1, that the award made by the King of Spain on 23 December 1906 was valid and binding, and that Nicaragua was under an obligation to give effect to it.[33]

The second instance is the *Arbitral Award* case between Guinea-Bissau and Senegal.[34] By Article 3 of an arbitration agreement of 12 March 1985, Guinea-Bissau and Senegal requested the arbitral tribunal to determine whether an Agreement of 1960 between France and Portugal with respect to the maritime boundary had the force of law in relations between Guinea-Bissau and Senegal.[35] In the event of a negative response to that question, the arbitral tribunal was to proceed to draw maritime delimitation lines between Guinea-Bissau and Senegal *de novo*. On 31 July 1989, the arbitral tribunal ruled, 2:1, that the 1960 Agreement was binding on the parties so far as concerned the maritime zones – namely, the territorial sea, the contiguous zone and the continental shelf – but that it did not establish a boundary in relation to areas that at that time were not known to exist – namely, the EEZ or the fisheries zone.

[28] ibid, 202.

[29] ibid. See also *The Boundary Case between Honduras and Nicaragua*, 23 December 1906, (1961) 11 *RIAA* 101.

[30] The *King of Spain* case, n 27, [1960] ICJ Rep 203. See also C Schulte, *Compliance with Decisions of the International Court of Justice* (Oxford University Press, 2004) 127.

[31] The *King of Spain* case, n 27, [1960] ICJ Rep 194–95.

[32] ibid, 204–05.

[33] ibid, 217. Further, see Y Tanaka, 'Case concerning the Arbitral Award made by the King of Spain on 23 December 1906 (Honduras v Nicaragua), 1960' in J-M Sorel and P Wojcikiewicz Almeida (eds), *Latin America and the International Court of Justice: Contributions to International Law* (Routledge, 2016) 262.

[34] *Arbitral Award of 31 July 1989 (Guinea-Bissau v Senegal)*, Judgment, [1991] ICJ Rep 53.

[35] At that time, Senegal was a French dependent territory and Guinea-Bissau was a Portuguese colony.

In light of this 'positive' response to the first question, the tribunal did not proceed to draw a new maritime boundary for the EEZ. Neither did it indicate that the latter must follow the established line of the continental shelf.[36] The President of the Arbitral Tribunal, Mr Barberis, who had voted with the majority, appended a declaration, whilst Mr Bedjaoui appended a dissenting opinion.[37] Guinea-Bissau disputed the validity of the award of 31 July 1989 and asked the ICJ to declare that the award was null and void.[38] However, the ICJ, in its judgment of 1991, rejected the submission of the Guinea-Bissau that the arbitral award of 31 July 1989 was absolutely null and void.[39]

b. Settlement by Negotiation

The second option is settlement by negotiation. An example of this is provided by the *Chamizal* case between the United States (US) and Mexico. The *Chamizal* dispute arose over the title to the land deriving from adjustments of the original river boundary. The dispute was referred to arbitration by the International Boundary Commission. The Commission issued its arbitration award in 1911.[40] Yet the US rejected the award as ultra vires. The dispute was eventually settled in 1963, when Mexico and the US agreed to give effect to the 1911 arbitration award and concluded the Convention for the Solution of the Problem of the Chamizal.[41]

Another example in this matter is the 1978 *Beagle Channel* dispute between Argentina and Chile.[42] This dispute involved sovereignty over three islands – Picton, Nueva, and Lennox – and the maritime boundary along the Beagle Channel between Argentina and Chile at the southernmost tip of South America. There was disagreement between Argentina and Chile with regard to their entire boundary along the southern extent of South America, and sovereignty over Patagonia and the groups of islands and straits at the very south of

[36] 31 July 1989, (1994) 20 *RIAA* 153, [88]. The members of the arbitral tribunal were: Julio A Barberis (President), André Gros, and Mohammed Bedjaoui. Judge Bedjaoui voted against the award.

[37] Judge Bedjaoui, in his dissenting opinion annexed to the award of 31 July 1989, questioned the existence of a majority considering the declaration of the President of the arbitral tribunal: ibid, 212–13, [161].

[38] *Arbitral Award of 31 July 1989*, n 31, [1991] ICJ Rep 56, [10].

[39] ibid, 75, [69](2).

[40] *The Chamizal case (Mexico v United States)*, 15 June 1911, (1961) 11 *RIAA* 309.

[41] Further, see PC Jessup, 'EL Chamizal' (1973) 67 *AJIL* 423; L Caflisch, 'Règles générales du droit des cours d'eau internationaux' (1989) 219 *RCADI* 9, 81–82; G Handl, 'American-Mexican Boundary Disputes and Cooperation' in R Wolfrum (ed), *Max Planck Encyclopaedia of Public International Law* (online edition), [4].

[42] *Case concerning a Dispute between Argentina and Chile concerning the Beagle Channel* 18 February 1977, (1997) 21 *RIAA* 53. For a commentary on the *Beagle Channel* disputes, see in particular T Princen, 'International Mediation: The View from the Vatican: Lessons from Mediating the Beagle Channel Dispute' (1987) 3 *Negotiation Journal* 347; LA de La Fayette, 'Beagle Channel Dispute' in Wolfrum (ed), n 41.

the continent. Negotiations in the 1870s resulted in the 1881 Boundary Treaty between the two countries. Nonetheless, its interpretation was subsequently disputed by Argentina several times. In the 1960s, negotiations failed and the dispute was submitted to arbitration by the British Crown in 1971. In February 1977, an arbitral tribunal rendered an award, giving all three disputed islands to Chile and tracing a maritime boundary by a median line through the Beagle Channel. Yet the arbitration award of 1977 was rejected on 25 January 1978 by the Argentina Government, which claimed it was a nullity. While Chile suggested taking the matter to the ICJ, Argentina refused to do so. Both sides sent troops to the border.[43] Faced with the tense situation, on 22 December 1978, Pope John Paul II offered mediation through his special envoy Cardinal Antonio Samoré and both states accepted the offer. On 12 December 1980, the Pope proposed a settlement.[44] This was not accepted by Argentina however. After the Falklands/Malvinas war with the United Kingdom (UK), the political situation in Argentina changed dramatically and democratically elected President Raúl Alfonsin took office on 10 December 1983. The relationship between Chile and Argentina quickly improved, and, on 23 January 1984, the Joint Declaration of Peace and Friendship between Argentina and Chile was signed.[45] Subsequently, Vatican Secretary of State Cardinal Agostino Casaroli resumed mediation efforts and presented a final proposal to the parties in June 1984. They agreed to the proposal and the Treaty of Peace and Friendship was signed on 29 November 1984 at the Vatican City.[46] Overall, the *Beagle Channel* dispute was eventually settled through the mediation of the Holy See.

ii. Initiatives Taken by China and the US

As between the two options discussed in the preceding section, the first (referral to the ICJ) will not be available unless China accepts the compulsory jurisdiction of the ICJ or concludes an agreement with the Philippines to submit a dispute concerning the validity of the *South China Sea* arbitration to the Court. Accordingly, at present, diplomatic means will provide the only option to resolve the problems associated with non-compliance with the *South China Sea* arbitration awards.[47]

Non-compliance does not directly mean stalemate. In this connection, it is of particular interest to note that in 2014, the US and China signed two legally

[43] ibid, [24]–[25].

[44] Papal Proposal in the Beagle Channel Dispute, Proposal of the Mediator, 12 December 1980, reproduced in JI Charney and LM Alexander (eds), *International Maritime Boundaries*, vol I (Nijhoff, 1993) 731–35.

[45] Reproduced ibid, 735–36.

[46] Entered into force 2 May 1985. For the text of the Treaty, see ibid, 736–55.

[47] T Davenport, 'Island-Building in the South China Sea: Legality and Limits' (2018) 8 *Asian Journal of International Law* 76, 90.

non-binding Memorandums of Understanding (MOUs):[48] the MOU regarding Rules of Behaviour for Safety of Air and Maritime Encounters ('the MOU regarding the Rules of Behaviour');[49] and the MOU on Notification of Major Military Activities Confidence-Building Measures Mechanism ('the MOU on Notification').[50]

Annex I to the Rules of Behaviour for Safety of Air and Maritime Encounters requires that when military vessels and military aircraft of one side exercise their rights, freedom and lawful uses of the sea and airspace under international law, they are to have due regard for the rights, freedoms and lawful uses of the sea and airspace of the other side's military vessels and aircraft under international law.[51] Furthermore, Annex II to the MOU regarding the Rules of Behaviour provides for behaviour for the safety of surface-to-surface encounters. Specifically, Section I of Annex II states that:

> Military vessels that encounter each other at sea are to abide by the *Convention on the International Regulations for Preventing Collisions at Sea, 1972* and the *Collision Regulations* (COLREGs) contained therein and implement in good faith the *Code for Unplanned Encounters at Sea* (CUES) developed and adopted by the Western pacific Naval Symposium.[52]

Related to this, the MOU regarding the Rules of Behaviour states that:

> The primary method to assure peaceful intent in the air and maritime domain for the military vessels of both Sides is adherence to the existing safety rules and standards reflected in the *United Nations Law of the Sea Convention* and the COLREGS combined with positive and timely communication to clarify actions.[53]

It is notable that both China and the US recognise the application of the UNCLOS and COLREGS to their military vessels. In 2015, China and the US also agreed a Supplement to the MOU regarding the Rules of Behaviour.[54]

[48] For a detailed analysis of the MOUs between the US and China, see J Kraska, 'Maritime Confidence-building Measures for Navigation in the South China Sea' (2017) 32 *IJMCL* 268.

[49] The full title is Memorandum of Understanding Between the Department of Defence of the United States of America and the Ministry of National Defense of the People's Republic of China regarding the Rules of Behaviour for Safety of Air and Maritime Encounters. The text is available at: https://archive.defense.gov/pubs/141112_MemorandumOfUnderstandingRegardingRules.pdf.

[50] The full title is Memorandum of Understanding between the United States of America Department of Defense and the People's Republic of China Ministry of National Defense on Notification of Major Military Activities Confidence-building Measures Mechanism. The text is available at https://dod.defense.gov/Portals/1/Documents/pubs/141112_MemorandumOfUnderstandingOnNotification.pdf.

[51] Annex I, Section II(vi).

[52] Annex II, Section I (original emphasis, footnote omitted).

[53] Annex II, Section VI(i).3 (original emphasis).

[54] The full title is Supplement to the Memorandum of Understanding on the Rules of Behaviour for Safety of Air and Maritime Encounters between the Department of Defense of the United States of America and the Ministry of National Defense of the People's Republic of China. The text is available at http://china.usc.edu/sites/default/files/article/attachments/US-CHINA_AIR_ENCOUNTERS_ANNEX_SEP_2015.pdf.

According to the MOU on Notification, 'both sides seek to foster greater comprehension of each other's security policy, strategy, and intent through regular exchanges of information related to major official publications and statements'.[55] Furthermore, '[b]oth sides intend to exchange information voluntarily about their respective country's security polity, strategy, and legal information, … by providing briefings and information about speeches, [and] major government publications'.[56]

Whilst the bilateral MOUs are not restricted to interactions in the South China Sea, these instruments are particularly relevant to this region, since most of the dangerous incidents between the military forces of the two states have occurred there.[57] It remains to be seen whether and to what extent the MOUs can really contribute to promoting confidence-building for navigation in the South China Sea.[58] In any event, it is noteworthy that some initiatives have been taken by China and the US to address various issues in the South China Sea.

III. THE IMPLICATIONS OF THE *SOUTH CHINA SEA* ARBITRATION FOR THE DEVELOPMENT OF INTERNATIONAL LAW

A. Four Functions of the Jurisprudence in the Development of International Law

In general, international courts and tribunals perform a dual function: the peaceful settlement of international disputes and development of international law.[59] Obviously the primary task of international courts and tribunals is to peacefully resolve international disputes by applying the existing rules of international law. At the same time, an international court or tribunal can be thought to make an important contribution to the development of international law. Specifically, it contributes to developing the law at least in four ways.[60]

The first is the clarification of rules of international law. As there is no higher authority above individual states, rules of international law, customary or conventional, are interpreted and applied by states on their own. This is called auto-interpretation/auto-application. Normally states interpret rules of

[55] Annex I, Section I.

[56] Annex I, Section II.

[57] Kraska, n 48, 269–70.

[58] Kraska indicates that to promote its maritime claims, China employs a fleet of fishing vessels and other civil craft and coast guard ships, which are outside scope of the US-China bilateral MOUs. Kraska thus considers that the MOUs are unlikely to enhance navigational safety or security. ibid, 294–95.

[59] Paik, n 18, 406.

[60] Y Tanaka, 'The Impacts of the ITLOS Jurisprudence on the Development of International Law' in International Tribunal for the Law of the Sea, *The Contribution of the International Tribunal for the Law of the Sea to the Rule of Law: 1996–2016* (Brill/Nijhoff, 2017) 161.

international law in such a way as to justify their policy. Consequently, they may be interpreted in a different manner by different states. Yet the different interpretations and application of these rules are likely to create international disputes.[61] In the process of resolving these disputes, international courts and tribunals contribute to clarifying the meaning and scope of relevant rules of international law in its jurisprudence.

The second way concerns the consolidation of rules of international law. By confirming dicta and/or precedents of other judicial organs with regard to the interpretation and application of rules of international law, international courts and tribunals contribute to further consolidating the normative status of these rules.

The third way pertains to the elaboration of procedural law. In general, the procedural law of international courts and tribunals is to be elaborated through their jurisprudence over time,[62] and the same applies to a court or tribunal under Part XV, section II of the UNCLOS. Elaboration of procedural rules and procedures of international courts and tribunals can be regarded as part of the development of international law.

Lastly, the formation of rules of international law through jurisprudence must be noted. As typically shown in the law of maritime delimitation, judicial decisions may have a formative effect on the development of international law.

As these functions are interlinked, distinguishing the four ways is not clear-cut. For instance, it may be less easy to distinguish clarification of the meaning of rules of international law from judicial creativity, particularly when applying evolutionary treaty interpretation. In any event, in the *South China Sea* arbitration, it appears that the first three functions merit particular discussion.

B. Clarification of Rules of International Law

As for the clarification of rules of international law, including the law of the sea, four specific points merit attention. The first noteworthy point concerns the clarification of the concept of historic rights and title. As discussed in chapter 3, section II.B, the Tribunal, in its Arbitration Award on the Merits, made a clear distinction between the concept of historic title that refers to historic sovereignty to land or maritime areas, and that of historic rights that include more limited rights falling well short of a claim of sovereignty. Given that the UNCLOS contains no definition of historic title or historic rights, it would be fair to say that the Tribunal made a significant contribution to clarifying the

[61] Tanaka, n 13, 4.

[62] In this regard, Thirlway stated that '[o]ne specialized field in which it appears that the decision of an international tribunal can be regarded as creative of law is in the domain of the tribunal's own procedure': H Thirlway, *The Sources of International Law* (Oxford University Press, 2014) 122.

two concepts.[63] As noted, the exception to jurisdiction in Article 298(1)(a)(i) is limited to disputes involving historic titles. Accordingly, the distinction also influences the scope of the compulsory procedures under the UNCLOS.

The second noteworthy point pertains to the interpretation and application of Article 121(3) of the UNCLOS. As discussed in chapter 4,[64] the *South China Sea* Arbitration Award on the Merits made a detailed review of the interpretation of that provision. That Award can be said to be the first international decision to have delved into its interpretation. In particular, it is significant that the Tribunal clarified the qualitative and temporal requirements under Article 121(3) of the UNCLOS. Related to this, it is of particular interest to note that the Tribunal's interpretation of Article 121(3) focuses on the benefit to people, not the interests of an individual state, and the safeguarding of the common heritage of mankind. When applying this provision, the Tribunal applied the two-stage approach. Under this approach, at the first stage, the natural conditions of a maritime feature are to be examined. Where the physical characteristics of the features do not definitively indicate the capacity of the features, at the second stage the legal status of the features is to be determined on the basis of 'historical human habitation' and 'historical economic life of their own'.

The third noteworthy point concerns the interpretation and application of environmental obligations under the UNCLOS. As has been seen in chapter 5, by applying the systemic treaty interpretation, the Tribunal ruled that the general obligation to 'protect and preserve the marine environment' in Article 192 included a due diligence obligation to prevent the harvesting of species recognised internationally as being at risk of extinction and as requiring international protection. This interpretation is of particular importance in the protection of marine biological diversity. It is also notable that the Tribunal regarded the obligation to communicate the results of the assessment under Article 206 as an absolute obligation. It seems that the Tribunal's interpretation of the environmental obligations under the Convention may have positive impacts on the protection of the marine environment.[65]

The fourth point pertains to the concept of traditional fishing rights. As discussed in chapter 5, the Tribunal made it clear that traditional fishing rights are not the historic rights of states but private rights. It then assimilated the traditional fishing rights to artisanal fishing. Furthermore, the Tribunal clarified that established traditional fishing rights remain protected by international law in the territorial sea, while the rights are extinguished in the EEZ.[66]

[63] See ch 3, section II.B of this book.

[64] See ch 4, section III of this book.

[65] See ch 5, section II.D of this book. See also Z Scanlon and R Beckman, 'Assessing Environmental Impact and the Duty to Cooperate: Environmental Aspects of the Philippines v China Award' (2018) 3 *Asia-Pacific Journal of Ocean Law and Policy* 5, 30.

[66] See ch 5, section II.C of this book.

Last but not least, the Tribunal specified three actions that are contrary to the obligation not to aggravate a dispute in the judicial proceedings.[67]

As discussed earlier, the Tribunal's interpretation on these matters is not free from controversy in some respects. Even so, it would be fair to say at least that the *South China Sea* Arbitration Award (Merits) provided a precedent well worth considering in the interpretation of relevant provisions of the UNCLOS.

C. Consolidation of the Existing Rules of International Law

The next issue concerns the role of the *South China Sea* arbitration awards in the consolidation of the existing rules of international law. The interpretation of the territoriality of low-tide elevations is a case in point. Referring to the 2012 *Nicaragua v Colombia* case, the Tribunal, in its Award on the Merits, ruled that low-tide elevations do not form part of the land territory of a state in the legal sense, but are part of the submerged landmass of the state and fall within the legal regimes for the territorial sea or continental shelf.[68] As discussed in chapter 4, the Tribunal's view is in line with the jurisprudence of the ICJ. The leading case in this regard is *Qatar v Bahrain* (Merits) (2001).[69] By endorsing the views of the ICJ in this matter, the Tribunal can be said to be contributing to consolidating the legal status of low-tide elevations as part of the seabed.

Another example is the obligation not to aggravate a dispute. The Tribunal, in its Award on the Merits, found the legal basis for the obligation of non-aggravation in the jurisprudence of the PCIJ and ICJ concerning provisional measures and treaty practice. It then declared that that obligation constitutes a 'principle of international law that is applicable to States engaged in dispute settlement as such'.[70] The dictum of the Tribunal seems to contribute towards cementing the obligation as a principle of international law.

Consolidation of rules of international law through the jurisprudence raises some issues concerning the making of customary international law. Orthodox legal theory sees rules of customary law as resulting from the combination of two elements: an objective element of 'extensive and virtually uniform' state practice, and the subjective or psychological element known as the *opinio juris*, that is a belief that the practice is rendered obligatory by the existence of a rule

[67] See ch 5, section III.A of this book.

[68] The *South China Sea* Arbitration Award (Merits), n 1, [309].

[69] See ch 4, section II.B of this book.

[70] The *South China Sea* Arbitration Award (Merits), n 1, [1173]. See also ch 5, section III.A of this book.

of law requiring it.[71] A clear statement of the two-element theory can be seen in the *Libya/Malta* judgment, which stated that '[i]t is of course axiomatic that the material of customary international law is to be looked for primarily in the actual practice and *opinio juris* of States'.[72] Nonetheless, the judicial practice suggests that an international court or tribunal does not mechanically apply the two-element test to the identification of a rule of customary law. Instead, there is a trend that an international court or tribunal identifies a rule of international law, by merely referring to the dictum of another court or tribunal or the International Law Commission (ILC), without examining state practice and *opinio juris*. This is called 'institutional circularity'. As noted, the Tribunal, in the *South China Sea* Arbitration Award (Merits), relied only on the precedents of the ICJ, when it declared that low-tide elevations form part of the submerged landmass in international law. The methodology of the Tribunal in the *South China Sea* Arbitration Award is not unique and the same methodology is also used by other international courts or tribunals. One may take 'state of necessity' as an example.[73]

In the *Gabčíkovo-Nagymaros Project* case, 'state of necessity' was invoked by Hungary as a legal ground to suspend and abandon works that it had been committed to perform under the 1977 Treaty on the Construction and Operation of the Gabčíkovo-Nagymaros Barrage System and related instruments. In this regard, the ICJ held that 'the state of necessity is a ground recognized by customary international law for precluding the wrongfulness of an act not in conformity with an international obligation'.[74] It also approved the customary law character of conditions that must be cumulatively satisfied to invoke 'necessity' as a plea for precluding wrongfulness, set forth in Article 33 of the ILC Draft Articles on State Responsibility.[75] However, the Court offered scant explanation of the reasons why state of necessity and its conditions can be regarded as part of customary international law.

Subsequently, by referring to cases and incidents on this subject, including the *Gabčíkovo-Nagymaros Project* Judgment, the ILC concluded that 'On balance, State practice and judicial decisions support the view that necessity may constitute a circumstance precluding wrongfulness under certain very limited conditions, and this view is embodied in article 25.'[76] The dictum in the

[71] *North Sea Continental Shelf* cases, n 9, [1969] ICJ Rep 42–44, [73]–[77]. For an analysis of the two-element theory, see R Kolb, 'Selected Problems in the Theory of Customary International Law' (2003) 50 *NILR* 119, 120–30.

[72] *Continental Shelf (Libyan Arab Jamahiriya v Malta)* [1985] ICJ Rep 13, 29, [27]. The two-element theory was also echoed by the ILC. See ILC, 'Draft Conclusions on Identification of Customary International Law' (2018), Conclusion 2.

[73] Tanaka, n 60, 162–64.

[74] *Gabčíkovo-Nagymaros Project (Hungary/Slovakia)*, Judgment, [1997] ICJ Rep 40, [51].

[75] ibid, 41, [52].

[76] J Crawford, *The International Law Commission's Articles on State Responsibility: Introduction, Text and Commentaries* (Cambridge University Press, 2002) 183.

Gabčíkovo-Nagymaros Project Judgment was also confirmed by the ICJ in the *Wall* case, where it stated:

> As the Court observed in the case concerning *Gabčíkovo-Nagymaros Project (Hungary/Slovakia)*, 'the state of necessity is a ground recognized by customary international law' that 'can only be accepted on an exceptional basis'; it 'can only be invoked under certain strictly defined conditions which must be cumulatively satisfied; and the State concerned is not the sole judge of whether those conditions have been met'.[77]

The Court then applied one of the conditions stated in Article 25 of the ILC Draft Articles on State Responsibility.[78] Here one may find an 'institutional circularity'.[79]

The application of the defence of 'state of necessity' was also at issue in the *M/V 'SAIGA' (No 2)* case before the Tribunal.[80] In this case, the Tribunal considered whether the otherwise wrongful application by Guinea of its customs laws to the EEZ could be justified under general international law by Guinea's appeal to 'state of necessity'. Here the Tribunal relied on the ICJ's view in the *Gabčíkovo-Nagymaros Project* Judgment.[81] By applying the conditions set out in Article 33(1) of the ILC Draft Articles on State Responsibility, the Tribunal ruled that application of Guinea's customs laws to a customs radius was contrary to the Convention; and that the arrest and detention of the *SAIGA*, the prosecution and conviction of its Master, the confiscation of the cargo and the seizure of the ship were contrary to the Convention.[82] Overall, ITLOS seemed to approve the rule of the state of necessity as formulated by the ILC Draft Articles on State Responsibility.[83] It did not clarify its view with regard to the customary law nature of the state of necessity by examining state practice and *opinio juris*.

Before the *Gabčíkovo-Nagymaros Project* Judgment, it was less clear whether state of necessity enjoyed universal acceptance in international law.[84] In fact, the arbitral tribunal in the *Rainbow Warrior* arbitration considered state of necessity to be a 'controversial doctrine' and concluded that there was no

[77] *Legal Consequences of the Construction of a Wall in the Occupied Palestinian Territory*, Advisory Opinion, [2004] ICJ Rep 136, 195, [140].

[78] ibid.

[79] RD Sloane, 'On the Use and Abuse of Necessity in the Law of State Responsibility' (2012) 106 *AJIL* 447, 453.

[80] *M/V SAIGA (No 2) (Saint Vincent and the Grenadines v Guinea)*, Judgment, ITLOS Case No 2, [1999] ITLOS Rep 10, 56, [133]–[134].

[81] ibid, 56, [133].

[82] ibid, 56, [136].

[83] S Heathcote, 'Est-ce que l'état de nécessité est un principe de droit international coutumier?' (2007) 1 *Revue belge de droit international* 53, 59.

[84] D Bodansky and JR Crook, 'Symposium: The ILC's State Responsibility Articles' (2002) 96 *AJIL* 773, 788.

general principle allowing the defence of necessity.[85] However, the ICJ, in the *Gabčíkovo-Nagymaros Project* Judgment, admitted the customary law character of state of necessity, without examining state practice and *opinio juris*. The Court's view affected the work of the ILC when drafting a rule concerning state of necessity in its Draft Articles on State Responsibility. The dictum of the ICJ in the *Gabčíkovo-Nagymaros Project* Judgment and the ILC Draft Articles on State Responsibility were also applied by the Tribunal in the *MV 'SAIGA' (No 2)* case. Thus one can argue that the state of necessity was consolidated as customary international law through the ICJ, ILC and ITLOS. As Bodansky and Crook observed, it may be said that the 'legal development of state of necessity had a circular quality'.[86] The identification of a rule of customary international law through institutional circularity can contribute to preventing the fragmentation of international law. At the same time, however, care should be taken in noting that the practice of institutional circularity may entail the risk of detaching the rule from actual state practice.[87]

D. Elaboration of Procedural Rules

The *South China Sea* arbitration awards shed some light on the issues of jurisdiction and the procedure of international dispute settlement. In this regard, two issues in particular merit discussion: separation of territorial and maritime issues; and the use of experts.

i. Separation of Territorial and Maritime Issues

As discussed in chapter 2, the most contentious issue in the *South China Sea* Arbitration Award on Jurisdiction and Admissibility was whether the Annex VII Arbitral Tribunal can exercise its jurisdiction over the mixed dispute involving territorial and maritime issues. In this regard, the relationship between three categories of dispute is at issue:

- Category I: Territorial disputes,
- Category II: Maritime delimitation disputes, and
- Category III: Other maritime disputes, such as dispute concerning maritime entitlement and environmental protection.[88]

[85] *Case concerning the difference between New Zealand and France concerning the interpretation or application of two agreements, concluded on 9 July 1986 between the two States and which related to the problems arising from the Rainbow Warrior Affair*, 30 April 1990, (1960) 10 *RIAA* 254.

[86] Bodansky and Crook, n 84, 788. Yet they did not refer to the *M/V 'SAIGA' (No 2)* case.

[87] Tanaka, n 60, 167. Heathcote called the requirements for a state of necessity developed by the ICJ and ILC 'plantes de serre, [ou] perles de culture': Heathcote, n 83, 63.

[88] Tamada, n 7, 149 et seq.

In the *South China Sea* arbitration, the Tribunal took an approach that separated the third category from the first and second categories of disputes. Related to this, the Tribunal repeatedly affirmed that the Philippines' Submissions did not reflect disputes concerning sovereignty or maritime boundary delimitation.[89] The Tribunal's approach can be called the separation approach. Two issues arise here.

The first issue is whether the third category of disputes, that is maritime entitlement disputes, can exist independently of the first category of disputes, that is territorial disputes. Entitlement to maritime features is governed by Article 121 of the UNCLOS, while the international law of acquisition of territory is applicable to territorial disputes. The application of Article 121 and that of the law of acquisition of territory are two distinct issues. The application of Article 121 does not rely on the question of territorial sovereignty over maritime features. Accordingly, in theory, maritime entitlement disputes arguably can be distinct from territorial disputes. It seems that the same logic applies to marine environmental disputes. The general obligation to protect the marine environment, including biological diversity, is laid down in Article 192 of the UNCLOS. This obligation is applicable to states irrespective of where the alleged harmful activities took place.[90] The application of the environmental obligation does not depend on the question of sovereignty over particular maritime features. Therefore, it can be argued that disputes concerning maritime environmental protection are distinct from the territorial disputes. As shown in these examples, as a matter of theory, it may be possible to separate the third category of disputes from the first category of disputes.

The second issue is whether the third category of disputes can be separated from the second category of disputes, that is maritime delimitation disputes. Whilst disputes concerning entitlement to maritime features fall within the scope of Article 121 of the UNCLOS, maritime delimitation is governed by Articles 15, 74 and 83 of the Convention. Thus rules applicable to maritime delimitation differ from those applicable to entitlement to maritime features. The application of Article 121 does not rely on the application of the rules concerning maritime delimitation. Attention must also be paid to the difference in the nature of the two categories of dispute. Maritime delimitation dispute arises only where title to marine spaces of coastal states overlaps. Accordingly, maritime delimitation is effectuated primarily by agreement between relevant states. In contrast, as shown in the example of Oki-no-Tori-Shima, maritime entitlement disputes can arise even if there is no overlap of title to marine spaces. The entitlement to maritime features is a matter of objective determination and does not rely

[89] PCA Case No 2013–19. The *South China Sea* arbitration (Jurisdiction and Admissibility) (hereinafter 'the *South China Sea* Arbitration Award (Jurisdiction and Admissibility)'), 29 October 2015, [394]–[412].

[90] The *South China Sea* Arbitration Award (Merits), n 1, [927]. See also the *South China Sea* Arbitration Award (Jurisdiction and Admissibility), n 89, [408].

on agreement between states.[91] One can thus argue that maritime entitlement disputes exist independently of maritime delimitation disputes.[92]

In summary, the *South China Sea* Arbitration Award (Merits) demonstrated the possibility that the third category of maritime disputes can be separated from the first and second categories of disputes. This approach provides an alternative well worth considering when examining the jurisdiction of a court or tribunal as set out under the UNCLOS with regard to mixed disputes.[93]

ii. The Use of Experts

A remarkable feature of the *South China Sea* arbitration was that the Tribunal appointed experts to furnish an independent opinion with regard to environmental damage arising from China's activities and navigational safety in the South China Sea.[94] The power of the Tribunal to appoint experts is provided in Article 24 of the Rules of Procedure.[95] Under Article 24(1):

> After seeking the views of the Parties, the Arbitral Tribunal may appoint one or more independent experts. That expert may be called upon to report on specific issues and in the manner to be determined by the Arbitral Tribunal. A copy of the expert's terms of reference, established by the Arbitral Tribunal, shall be communicated to the Parties.

In this connection, it is of particular interest to note that Article 24 provides a procedure to secure the independence and impartiality of expert appointed by the Tribunal. In fact, Article 24(2) requires any expert to 'submit to the Arbitral Tribunal and to the Parties a description of his or her qualifications and a statement of his or her impartiality and independence'. Under the same provision, the Parties are to inform the Arbitral Tribunal whether they have any objections as to the expert's qualifications, impartiality or independence, and the Arbitral Tribunal is to decide promptly whether to accept any such objections. After the appointment has been made, a Party may object to the expert's qualifications, impartiality or independence only if the objection is for reasons of which the Party becomes aware. In this case, the Arbitral Tribunal is to decide promptly what, if any, action to take.

[91] See section IV.A of this chapter; ch 2, section IV.A of this book.

[92] Tamada, n 7, 154–55.

[93] As for another approach to mixed disputes, it may be relevant to recall that the Annex VII Arbitral Tribunal, in the *Chagos Marine Protected Area* arbitration, adopted the ancillary test. See ch 2, section IV.B of this book.

[94] Generally on this issue, see Y Tanaka, 'The *South China Sea* Arbitration: Environmental Obligations under the Law of the Sea Convention' (2018) 27 *RECIEL* 90, 95–96; T Davenport, 'Procedural Issues Arising from China's Non-participation in the South China Sea Arbitration' in Jayakumar et al (eds), n 20, 65, 86–95.

[95] Art 24 was inspired by Art 29 of the 2013 UNCITAL Arbitration Rules. MM Mbengue, 'The South China Sea Arbitration: Innovations in Marine Environmental Fact-Finding and Due Diligence Obligations' (2016) 110 *American Journal of International Law Unbound* 285, 287.

Furthermore, Article 24(3) of the Rules of Procedure places an obligation upon the Parties to 'give the expert any relevant information or produce for his or her inspection any relevant documents or goods that he or she may require of them'. Under the same provision, the Parties are also obliged to 'afford the expert all reasonable facilities in the event that the expert's terms of reference contemplate a visit to the localities to which the case relates'. Under Article 24(4) of the Rules of Procedure, if called upon to prepare an expert's report, the Arbitral Tribunal must communicate a copy of the report to the Parties; and the Parties must be given the opportunity to express, in writing, their respective opinions on the report. A Party can also examine any document on which the expert relied in his or her report. Comparatively detailed rules embodied in Article 24 go well beyond a simple rule provided in Article 50 of the Statute of the ICJ, which contains no procedure to secure the impartiality and independence of experts.[96]

The Tribunal, in the arbitral proceedings, appointed five independent experts:

- Mr Grant Boyes (expert hydrographer),
- Dr Sebastian CA Ferse (a coral reef ecologist),
- Dr Peter J Mumby (coral reef ecology),
- Dr Selina Ward (coral biologist),
- Captain Gurpreet S Singhota (expert on navigational safety).[97]

The experts submitted the following reports to the Tribunal:

- *Ferse Report: Assessment of the Potential Environmental Consequences of Construction Activities on Seven Reefs in the Spratly Islands in the South China Sea* (26 April 2016).
- *Singhota Report: Report of the International Navigational Safety Expert appointed by the Permanent Court of Arbitration, The Hague, The Netherlands* (15 April 2016).[98]

The Philippines also submitted several expert reports to the Tribunal.[99]

[96] ibid. Art 50 of the ICJ Statute stipulates that 'The Court may, at any time, entrust any individual, body, bureau, commission, or other organization that it may select, with the task of carrying out an enquiry or giving an expert opinion.'

[97] The *South China Sea* Arbitration Award (Merits), n 1, [58], [85], and [90]. The Philippines approved the appointment of the experts: ibid, [58], [86] and [90]. China made no comments on this matter: ibid, [58], [87] and [90].

[98] The two Reports are available on the website of the Permanent Court of Arbitration, at https://pca-cpa.org/en/cases/7/.

[99] The expert reports include: Dr Ryan T Bailey, *Groundwater Resources Analysis of Itu Aba* (9 March 2016) (First Bailey Report); Dr Ryan T Bailey, *Supplemental Report on Groundwater Resources Analysis of Itu Aba* (20 April 2016) (Second Bailey Report); KE Carpenter, *Eastern South China Sea Environmental Disturbances and Irresponsible Fishing Practices and their Effects on Coral Reefs and Fisheries* (22 March 2014) (First Carpenter Report); KE Carpenter & LM Chou, *Environmental Consequences of Land Reclamation Activities on Various Reefs in*

The Tribunal gave weight to the expert reports, particularly in the context of the protection of the marine environment.[100] In examining the adverse effects of harvesting giant clams, for instance, the independent experts' report provided important evidence for the Tribunal.[101] The Tribunal also referred to the independent experts' report when examining the impact of China's construction activities on the coral reefs.[102] Furthermore, the assessment of law enforcement operations by vessels in conformity with COLREGS requires expert knowledge and experience. Therefore, the Tribunal-appointed independent expert performed a crucial role in the assessment of the lawfulness of law enforcement operations by Chinese vessels.[103]

The active use of experts in the *South China Sea* arbitration contrasted with the practice of ITLOS and the ICJ.[104] Under the UNCLOS, the use of experts is provided for in Article 289:

> In any dispute involving scientific or technical matters, a court or tribunal exercising jurisdiction under this section may, at the request of a party or *proprio motu*, select in consultation with the parties no fewer than two scientific or technical experts chosen preferably from the relevant list prepared in accordance with Annex VIII, article 2, to sit with the court or tribunal but without the right to vote.

This provision is applicable to cases before all dispute settlement bodies as set out under the UNCLOS, namely, the ICJ, ITLOS, Annex VII arbitral tribunals and the special arbitral tribunals in accordance with Annex VIII.[105] While Article 15 of the Rules of Tribunal provides detailed rules concerning the appointment of experts in accordance with Article 289, ITLOS has not appointed experts. In the *Southern Bluefin Tuna* cases, for instance, the Parties differed as

the South China Sea (14 November 2015) (Second Carpenter Report); Declaration of Professor KE Carpenter (24 April 2016)(Third Carpenter Report) [5]; PP Motavalli, Expert Report on Soil Resources and Potential Self-Sustaining Agricultural Production on Itu Aba (Expert Report, 9 March 2016) (First Motavalli Report); Dr Peter P Motavalli, *Second Supplemental Expert Report on Soil Resources and Potential Self-Sustaining Agricultural Production on Itu Aba* (2 June 2016) (Second Motavalli Report); JW McManus, *Offshore Coral Reef Damage, Overfishing and Paths to Peace in the South China Sea* (rev edn, 21 April 2016) (McManus Report) 10–11; C Mora, IR Caldwell, C Birkeland and JW McManus, 'Dredging in the Spratly Islands: Gaining Land but Losing Reefs' (2016) 14(3) *PLoS Biology* 1 (31 March 2016), DOI:10.1371/journal.pbio.1002422 (Mora Report); Professor Clive Schofield, Professor JRV Prescott and Mr Robert van de Poll, *An Appraisal of the Geographical Characteristics and Status of Certain Insular Features in the South China Sea* (March 2015) (Schofield Report).

[100] In this regard, Mbenge argued that '[m]ost important, the Tribunal gives scientific expertise a new function by making it a central tool for the sound administration of international justice and for ensuring equality between the parties to a dispute': Mbengue, n 95, 288. See also Davenport, n 94, 93–94; ch 5, section II.D of this book.

[101] The *South China Sea* Arbitration Award (Merits), n 1, [957]–[958].

[102] ibid, [978]–[983].

[103] See ch 5, section II.F of this book.

[104] See also Davenport, n 94, 86–90.

[105] T Treves, 'Law and Science in the Interpretation of the Law of the Sea Convention' (2012) 3 *Journal of International Dispute Settlement* 483, 485.

to whether the scientific data available showed an upward trend from the current level and whether Japan's experimental fishing programme would have a negative impact upon the southern bluefin tuna stock.[106] Accordingly, a scientific expert was presented as a witness by New Zealand and Australia.[107] Yet ITLOS did not appoint an independent expert to investigate scientific evidence.

The *Bangladesh/Myanmar* case raised the question of whether the parties had the entitlement to a continental shelf beyond 200 nautical miles.[108] In this regard, Bangladesh presented geological and geomorphological evidence to demonstrate that the continental shelf beyond 200 nautical miles in the Bay of Bengal was the natural prolongation of Bangladesh, but was not the natural prolongation of Myanmar.[109] However, Myanmar countered that Myanmar's continental margin satisfied the appurtenance test of Article 76(4) of the UNCLOS, that is the edge of Myanmar's continental margin established in accordance with the Convention was situated beyond 200 nautical miles measured from its baseline.[110] In light of the opposition of the Parties, ITLOS had to determine whether there were entitlements to the continental shelf beyond 200 nautical miles and whether they overlapped. In this regard, the Tribunal held that '[t]he scientific data and analyses presented in this case, which have not been contested, do not establish that Myanmar's continental shelf is limited to 200 nm under article 76 of the Convention, and instead indicate the opposite'.[111] It thus concluded that '[t]he submissions of Bangladesh and Myanmar to the Commission clearly indicate that their entitlements overlap in the area in dispute in this case'.[112] In so ruling, the Tribunal did not review the scientific evidence on its own.[113] Nor did it appoint independent experts to tender an independent opinion in this matter. As for a reason regarding the reluctance of ITLOS to appoint independent experts, Treves explained that:

> In my view, the reason lies in that the scientific or technical experts as envisaged in Article 289 are too close to being judges or arbitrators: they sit with the tribunal and

[106] Request for Provisional Measures by Australia, 75, [11]; Request for Provisional Measures by New Zealand, 11, [11], available at https://www.itlos.org/en/cases/list-of-cases/case-no-3-4/. Further, see Y Tanaka, 'Toward Sustainable Management of Marine Natural Resources' in M Kotzur et al (eds), *Sustainable Ocean Resource Governance: Deep Sea Mining, Marine Energy and Submarine Cables* (Brill/Nijhoff, 2018) 110, 122–24.

[107] The *Southern Bluefin Tuna* cases, ITLOS Case Nos 3 and 4, [1999] ITLOS Rep 284, [25]; Treves, n 105, 486.

[108] *Dispute concerning delimitation of the maritime boundary between Bangladesh and Myanmar in the Bay of Bengal (Bangladesh/Myanmar)*, Judgment, ITLOS Case No 16, [2012] ITLOS Rep 4 ('the *Bay of Bengal* case').

[109] Bangladesh's Memorial, vol I, 18–28.

[110] Myanmar's Counter-Memorial, vol I, 190, [A.28] et seq.

[111] The *Bay of Bengal* case, n 108, [2012] ITLOS Rep 116, [448].

[112] ibid, 116, [449].

[113] The approach of ITLOS was criticised by a commentator. See Xuexia Liao, 'Evaluation of Scientific Evidence by International Courts and Tribunals in the Continental Shelf Delimitation Cases' (2017) 48 *ODIL* 136, 145–46.

are to be drawn from the lists set out in Annex VIII for selecting specialised arbitrators, who should have not only technical but also legal expertise.[114]

Treves also expressed his misgivings that the selection of the experts in consultation with the parties may cast doubts on their effective independence.[115]

While the ICJ is empowered to request an expert opinion by virtue of Article 50 of the Court's Statute, it has been rather rare for it to use this power.[116] One may take the *Whaling in the Antarctic* case as an example. The central issue in this case concerned the validity of Japan's scientific whaling programme. In this connection, both Japan and Australia called experts at the hearings. However, the ICJ examined the contents of the scientific programme which are in essence a matter of science on its own, without appointing its own expert.[117]

In the *Costa Rica v Nicaragua /Nicaragua v Costa Rica* cases, the Court, by itself, examined competing scientific evidence without appointing a scientific expert. Similarly, the ICJ, in the *Pulp Mills* case, did not appoint any experts under Article 50 of the Court's Statute. In this case, the Court declared:

> it is the responsibility of the Court, after having given careful consideration to all the evidence placed before it by the Parties, to determine which facts must be considered relevant, to assess their probative value, and to draw conclusions from them as appropriate.[118]

However, Judges Al-Khasawneh and Simma expressed their misgivings that '[t]he Court on its own is not in a position adequately to assess and weigh complex scientific evidence of the type presented by the Parties'.[119] According to the learned judges:

> The adjudication of disputes in which the assessment of scientific questions by experts is indispensable, as is the case here, requires an interweaving of legal process with knowledge and expertise that can only be drawn from experts properly trained to evaluate the increasingly complex nature of the facts put before the Court.[120]

[114] Treves, n 105, 485.

[115] ibid.

[116] In the *Corfu Channel* case, the Court appointed experts since it was necessary to obtain an expert opinion with regard to certain points contested between the parties. *Corfu Channel (United Kingdom of Great Britain and Northern Ireland v. Albania)*, Order, [1948] ICJ Rep 124. In the *Gulf of Maine* case, the ICJ, upon a joint request of the parties, appointed an expert using its powers under Art 50 of the Statute. *Delimitation of the Maritime Boundary in the Gulf of Maine Area (Canada/United States of America)*, Appointment of Expert, [1984] ICJ Rep165. For categories of experts of the ICJ, see Tanaka, n 13, 183–84.

[117] Some argue that as one option, the ICJ should have appointed experts under Art 50 of the ICJ Statute to advise whether Japan's Research Whaling in the Atlantic (JARPA) II can be regarded as a programme conducted for 'the purposes of scientific research'. D Peat, 'The Use of Court-Appointed Experts by the International Court of Justice' (2014) 84 *British Year Book of International Law* 271, 287. See also M Fitzmaurice, *Whaling and International Law* (Cambridge University Press, 2015) 103.

[118] *Pulp Mills on the River Uruguay (Argentina v Uruguay)*, Judgment, [2010] ICJ Rep 14, 72, [168].

[119] Joint Dissenting Opinion of Judges Al-Khasawneh and Simma, ibid, 110, [4].

[120] ibid, [3]. See also AM Weisburd, *Failings of the International Court of Justice* (Oxford University Press, 2016) 232.

Related to this, Judges Al-Khasawneh and Simma indicated the existence of internal 'experts fantômes' or 'invisible experts'. When using 'invisible experts', however, the parties before the Court have no chance to comment upon the experts' opinions. Hence the use of such experts, particularly in the fact-intensive cases, would create problems associated with the absence of transparency, openness and procedural fairness.[121]

Recently, the ICJ appointed experts in the 2018 *Costa Rica v Nicaragua* case in accordance with Articles 48 and 50 of its Statute. Their task was to inform the Court as to the state of the coast and the starting-point of the maritime boundary in the Caribbean Sea.[122] Two experts appointed by the Court conducted two site visits in December 2016 and March 2017.[123] In this case, the role of experts was of critical importance in two respects.

First, the experts observed that there was no longer any water channel connecting the San Juan River with Harbor Head Lagoon. As there was no channel, there could not be a boundary running along it. The Court thus determined that Costa Rica had sovereignty over the whole of Isla Portillos up to where the river reached the Caribbean Sea.[124]

Second, a special circumstance affecting maritime delimitation in the territorial sea consisted of the high instability and narrowness of the sandspit near the mouth of the San Juan River. The ICJ considered that it was more appropriate that the fixed point at sea on the median line be connected by a mobile line to the point on solid land on Costa Rica's coast. The Court selected the point Pv, which had been identified by the Court-appointed experts. Accordingly, the territorial sea boundary extended from the fixed point at sea landwards to the point on the low-water mark of the coast of the Caribbean Sea that was closest to point Pv.[125] The experts' opinion significantly affected the Court's decisions with regard to the settlement of the territorial disputes and the establishment of the territorial sea boundary.

It remains to be seen whether or not the 2018 *Costa Rica v Nicaragua* case will be a turning point towards the active use of experts by the ICJ. In any event, it could well be said that scientific evidence is a key element in the settlement of international environmental disputes. Given that an international court or tribunal as a judicial organ is not well placed to tackle complex scientific issues, the appointment of independent experts by the judicial body may be an alternative well worth considering.[126] The *South China Sea* Arbitration Award (Merits)

[121] Joint Dissenting Opinion of Judges Al-Khasawneh and Simma, [2010] ICJ Rep 108, 114, [14]. See also B Simma, 'The International Court of Justice and Scientific Expertise' (2012) 106 *Proceedings of the Annual Meeting of American Society of International Law* 230, 231.

[122] *Maritime Delimitation in the Caribbean Sea and the Pacific Ocean* (*Costa Rica v Nicaragua*) [2018] ICJ Rep (not yet reported), [14].

[123] ibid, [21] and [31].

[124] ibid, [71].

[125] ibid, [104].

[126] Mbengue, n 95, 287–89; Tanaka, n 94, 95–96.

seems to provide an interesting precedent with regard to the use of independent expert in international adjudication.[127]

IV. THE IMPLICATIONS OF THE *SOUTH CHINA SEA* ARBITRATION FOR THE PROTECTION OF COMMUNITY INTERESTS

As explained in chapter 1,[128] protection of community interests that encompass fundamental values shared by groups of states or the international community as a whole is becoming a crucial issue in international law, and the same applies to the international law of the sea. In the context of the *South China Sea* arbitration, two issues merit discussion: the *erga omnes* effect of the Tribunal's decisions on the maritime entitlements; and the standing of not directly injured states in response to a breach of obligations *erga omnes partes*.

A. *Erga Omnes* Effect of the Tribunal's Decisions Concerning the Maritime Entitlements

First, it is necessary to examine legal effect of the Tribunal's decisions concerning maritime entitlements. In this regard, the Philippines stressed that the question of maritime entitlements in the South China Sea is 'a matter that is most important not only to the Philippines, but also to all coastal states that border the South China Sea, and even to all the states parties to UNCLOS. It is a dispute that goes to the very heart of UNCLOS itself'.[129] The Philippines also emphasised that issues of entitlement engage the overall interests of the international community.[130]

As discussed in chapter 2, the Annex VII Arbitral Tribunal, in its Award on the Merits, held that (i) Hughes Reef, (ii) Gaven Reef (South), (iii) Subi Reef, (iv) Mischief Reef, and (v) Second Thomas Shoal were regarded as low-tide elevations and that they did not generate entitlements to a territorial sea, EEZ or continental shelf.[131] It also ruled that all of the high-tide features in the Spratly Islands were therefore legally rocks for the purposes of Article 121(3) of the UNCLOS and did not generate entitlements to an EEZ or continental shelf.[132] In this regard, three points may be made.

[127] Davenport, n 94, 95.
[128] See ch 1, section III.B of this book.
[129] Hearing on Jurisdiction and Admissibility, Day 1, 7 July 2015, presentation by Del Rosario, 13.
[130] Presentation by Oxman, Jurisdictional Hearing Tr (Day 2), 42. See also R Wolfrum, 'Identifying Community Interests in International Law: Common Spaces and Beyond' in E Benvenisti and G Nolte (eds), *Common Interests Across International Law* (Oxford University Press, 2018), 33.
[131] The *South China Sea* Arbitration Award (Merits), n 1, [383] and [1203]B(3), (4), (5).
[132] ibid, [646]; [1203]B(6) and (7).

First, entitlement to maritime features is a matter of objective determination. According to the Philippines, objective determination means that 'the same feature could not be a "rock" if it pertains to one State but an island capable of generating entitlement to an EEZ and continental shelf if it pertains to another'.[133] Indeed, the entitlement to maritime features cannot be changed by an agreement between the parties in dispute. The objective nature of the maritime entitlements can also be confirmed by the fact that disputes over claimed entitlements may exist even without overlap of legal titles claimed by the parties in dispute.[134] It would be difficult for a third state to argue for a different interpretation with regard to the entitlement to the same maritime feature.[135] Hence it may be said that the Tribunal's decision on the legal status of maritime features has effect *erga omnes*.

Second, as has been seen, none of the high-tide features in the Spratly Islands generated entitlements to an EEZ or continental shelf. The Tribunal, in its Award on the Merits, also held that China's claim to historic rights to the maritime areas of the South China Sea encompassed by the so-called 'nine-dash line' was contrary to the Convention.[136] As a consequence, the central part of the South China Sea that lay beyond the EEZ of the coastal states remained the high seas. Given that all states enjoy the freedoms in the high seas, including the freedom of navigation and overflight, one could argue that the Tribunal's decision affects community interests concerning navigational rights and freedoms in the high seas.[137]

Third, the Tribunal's decisions on maritime entitlements to the South China Sea affect the spatial scope of the Area, which is the common heritage of mankind. Given that activities in the Area are to be carried out for the benefit of mankind as a whole, one could argued that the determination of the spatial scope of the Area directly affects common interests of mankind.[138] In this regard, care must be taken in noting that the scope of the Area relies on the submissions by the coastal states on the continental shelf beyond 200 nautical miles and the recommendation by the Commission on the Limits of the Continental Shelf (CLCS).[139] In fact, on 6 May 2009, Malaysia and Viet Nam jointly submitted

[133] Supplemental Written Submission of the Philippines, [26.15].

[134] The *South China Sea* Arbitration Award (Jurisdiction and Admissibility), n 89, [156].

[135] NB O'Sullivan, 'The Case Law's Handling of Issues Concerning Third States' in AG Oude Elferink, T Henriksen and SV Busch (eds), *Maritime Boundary Delimitation: The Case Law Is It Consistent and Predictable?* (Cambridge University Press, 2018) 273.

[136] The *South China Sea* Arbitration Award (Merits), n 1, [1203]B(2).

[137] See also Jayakumar et al, 'Conclusion' in S Jayakumar et al (eds), n 20, 277, 284; Tamada, n 7, 155.

[138] UNCLOS, Art 140(1).

[139] Yen Hoang Tran, 'The South China Sea Arbitral Award: Legal Implications for Fisheries Management and Cooperation in the South China Sea' (2017) 6 *Cambridge International Law Journal* 87, 90. See also Supplemental Written Submission of the Philippines, Figure S8.4.

information on the limits of the continental shelf beyond 200 nautical miles in respect of the southern part of the South China Sea to the CLCS.[140] On 7 May 2009, Viet Nam submitted information on the limits of the continental shelf beyond 200 nautical miles in respect of the North Area (VNM-N) to the Commission.[141] In addition, the Philippines is in the process of preparing an additional submission covering areas of the South China Sea/West Philippine Sea.[142] Thus the spatial scope of the Area in the South China Sea is not yet definitely determined.

B. The *Locus Standi* of Not Directly Injured States in Response to a Breach of Environmental Norms

i. Erga Omnes Partes *Character of the Environmental Protection of the High Seas and the Area*

Given that a healthy marine environment is the foundation for all life, it could well be said that the protection of the marine environment, including marine biological diversity, relates to a common interest of the international community.[143] A particular issue that arises in this context is whether any state other than an injured state, that is a not directly injured state,[144] can bring a claim to an international court or tribunal in response to a breach of environmental obligations under the UNCLOS by another state, in vindication of a community interest, even though no damage occurred to the applicant state. This issue concerns locus standi in relation to a dispute concerning compliance with obligations *erga omnes partes*.

In accordance with Article 1 of the 2005 Resolution of the Institut de droit international, an obligation *erga omnes* is defined as:

(a) an obligation under general international law that a state owes in any given case to the international community, in view of its common values and

[140] See at http://www.un.org/Depts/los/clcs_new/submissions_files/submission_mysvnm_33_2009.htm. In response, China submitted Note Verbale CML/17/2009, along with the map of the 'nine-dash line', on 7 May 2009. See also TL McDorman, 'The South China Sea after 2009: Clarity of Claims and Enhanced Prospects for Regional Cooperation?' (2010) 24 *Ocean Yearbook* 507, 508–09.

[141] See at http://www.un.org/Depts/los/clcs_new/submissions_files/submission_mysvnm_33_2009.htm. In response, China submitted Note Verbale CML/18/2009, along with the map of the 'nine-dash line', on 7 May 2009.

[142] Supplemental Written Submission of the Philippines, [8.4].

[143] Furthermore, arguably the protection of the environment as a whole can be regarded as a community interest. In this regard, Wolfrum observed that '[d]evelopments following the 1972 Stockholm Conference continued to move towards the protection of community interests': R Wolfrum, 'Enforcing Community Interests Through International Dispute Settlement; Reality or Utopia?' in U Fastenrath et al (eds), *From Bilateralism to Community Interest, Essays in Honour of Judge Bruno Simma* (Oxford University Press, 2011) 1132, 1135.

[144] The term 'not directly injured States' is used in K Kawasaki, 'The "Injured State" in the International Law of State Responsibility' (2000) 28 *Hitotsubashi Journal of Law and Politics* 17, 22.

its concern for compliance, so that a breach of that obligation enables all states to take action; or

(b) an obligation under a multilateral treaty that a state party to the treaty owes in any given case to all the other states parties to the same treaty, in view of their common values and concern for compliance, so that a breach of that obligation enables all these states to take action.[145]

Article 1(a) defines the obligation *erga omnes* and Article 1(b) refers to the obligation *erga omnes partes*. This section focuses particularly on the obligation *erga omnes partes*, while, to a certain extent, arguments on obligations *erga omnes partes* and *erga omnes* may overlap. The question of interest here is whether any state other than an injured state, that is a not directly injured state, can invoke the responsibility of another state for breaches of obligations *erga omnes partes* enshrined in a treaty before an international court or tribunal, even though the treaty contains no express clause recognising standing. Claims to defend community interests before an international court or tribunal can be called 'community interest litigation'.[146] As will be discussed below, the *South China Sea* Arbitration Award provides an interesting example in this matter.[147]

The Philippines, in its Submission No 11 as amended, claimed that:

> (11) China has violated its obligations under the Convention to protect and preserve the marine environment at Scarborough Shoal, Second Thomas Shoal, Cuarteron Reef, Fiery Cross Reef, Gaven Reef, Johnson Reef, Hughes Reef and Subi Reef …

Among the maritime features mentioned in Submission No 11, Cuarteron Reef,[148] Fiery Cross Reef,[149] Gaven Reef[150] and Subi Reef[151] are located in the

[145] Institut de droit international, Resolution: Obligation *Erga Omnes* in International Law, Krakow Session 2005, available at www.idi-iil.org/idiE/resolutionsE/2005_kra_01_en.pdf.

[146] Tams used the term 'public interest litigation'. CJ Tams, 'Individual States as Guardians of Community Interests' in Fastenrach et al (eds), n 143, 379, 383.

[147] On this issue, see also Y Tanaka, 'Reflections on *Locus Standi* in Response to a Breach of Obligations *Erga Omnes Partes*: A Comparative Analysis of the *Whaling in the Antarctic* and *South China Sea* Cases' (2018) 17 *The Law and Practice of International Courts and Tribunals* 527, 545 et seq.

[148] Cuarteron Reef is 245.3 nautical miles from the archipelagic baseline of the Philippine island of Palawan and 585.3 nautical miles from China's baseline point 39 (Dongzhou (2)) adjacent to the island of Hainan. The *South China Sea* Arbitration Award (Merits), n 1, [285].

[149] Fiery Cross Reef is 254.2 nautical miles from the archipelagic baseline of the Philippine island of Palawan and 547.7 nautical miles from the China's baseline point 39 (Dongzhou (2)) adjacent to the island of Hainan: ibid, [286].

[150] Gaven Reef (North) is located at 203.0 nautical miles from the archipelagic baseline of the Philippine island of Palawan and 544.1 nautical miles from China's baseline point 39 (Dongzhou (2)) adjacent to Hainan; Gaven Reef (South) is located at 200.5 nautical miles from the archipelagic baseline of the Philippine island of Palawan and 547.4 nautical miles from China's baseline point 39 (Dongzhou (2)) adjacent to Hainan: ibid, [288]. In addition, Gaven Reef (South) lies within 12 nautical miles of the high-tide features at Gaven Reef (North) and Namyit Island: ibid, [384].

[151] Subi Reef is 231.9 nautical miles from the archipelagic baseline of the Philippine island of Palawan and 502.2 nautical miles from China's baseline point 39 (Dongzhou (2)) adjacent to Hainan: ibid., [289]. At the same time, Subi Reef lies within 12 nautical miles of the high-tide feature of Sandy Cay: ibid, [384].

area beyond 200 nautical miles from the coasts of the Philippines. It must also be noted that the territorial sovereignty over these maritime features remains undetermined. Hence it may be said that the Philippines suffered no material damage from Chinese activities in its jurisdictional zones. In this connection, the Tribunal made an important statement:

> [B]ecause the environmental obligations in Part XII apply to States *irrespective of where the alleged harmful activities took place, [the Tribunal's] jurisdiction is not dependent on the question of sovereignty over any particular feature*, on a prior determination of the status of any maritime feature, on the existence of an entitlement by China or the Philippines to an exclusive economic zone in the area, or on the prior delimitation of any overlapping entitlements.[152]

In the view of the Tribunal, 'Article 297(1)(c) [of the UNCLOS] expressly reaffirms the availability of compulsory dispute settlement for disputes concerning "alleged violations of international rules and standards for the protection and preservation of the marine environment"'.[153] The Tribunal accordingly concluded that it had jurisdiction to consider the Philippines' Submission No 11. It would seem to follow that the Tribunal accepted the locus standi of the Philippines, even though no material damage occurred to the Philippines. In fact, as Harrison pointedly observed, the Tribunal did not require the Philippines to demonstrate that it had suffered any environmental harm.[154]

As discussed in chapter 5, the Tribunal determined breaches of environmental obligations by China with regard to its island-building works at seven reefs, including four reefs located in the areas beyond 200 nautical miles from the coasts of the Philippines. Related to this, it also held that China had not fulfilled its duties under Article 206 of the UNCLOS with regard to environmental impact assessment and monitoring.[155] Arguably, the *South China Sea* Arbitration Award (Merits) provides a precedent with regard to the protection of community interests concerning marine environmental protection through international adjudication.

However, the Annex VII Arbitral Tribunal offered scant explanation of its understanding of the legal nature of the environmental obligations provided in the UNCLOS. In this regard, the ITLOS Seabed Disputes Chamber, in its Advisory Opinion of 2011, stated that 'Each State Party may also be entitled to claim compensation in light of the *erga omnes* character of the obligations relating to preservation of the environment of the high seas and in the Area.'[156]

[152] ibid, [927] (emphasis added). See also the *South China Sea* Arbitration Award (Jurisdiction and Admissibility), n 89, [408].

[153] The *South China Sea* Arbitration Award (Merits), n 1, [928].

[154] J Harrison, *Saving the Oceans Through Law: The International Leal Framework for the Protection of the Marine Environment* (Oxford University Press, 2017) 25.

[155] See ch 5, section II.D of this book.

[156] *Responsibilities and Obligations of States Sponsoring Persons and Entities with Respect to Activities in the Area*, Advisory Opinion, ITLOS Case No 17, [2011] ITLOS Rep 10, 59, [180].

The Seabed Disputes Chamber did not take pains to clarify the meaning of *erga omnes*. In light of the term '[e]ach State Party', however, there appears to be some scope to consider that the obligation relating to preservation of the environment of the high seas can be considered as *erga omnes partes* under the Convention. If this is the case, the dictum of the Chamber can be interpreted in a way to suggest that any states parties to the Convention may invoke responsibility for the breach of obligations in this matter.[157] In support of this view, Chandrasekhara Rao and Gautier took the view that 'any State Party to the Convention is entitled to institute proceedings with respect to a violation of a provision of the Convention relating to the preservation of the marine environment, committed outside marine areas under its jurisdiction'.[158] Related to this, they noted that the obligation under Article 192 to 'protect and preserve the marine environment' covers the ocean as a whole, without distinguishing marine spaces under and beyond national jurisdiction; and that Article 286 of the UNCLOS is drafted in general terms and envisages the possibility to take judicial action vis-à-vis 'any dispute concerning the interpretation or application of [the] Convention', without requiring that the applicant should demonstrate a special interest.[159] Hence there may be basis for arguing that the obligation to protect the marine environment under the UNCLOS can be considered as an obligation *erga omnes partes* and that any contracting parties to the Convention should have standing to protect against breaches of the obligation before an international court or tribunal.[160]

ii. Locus Standi *in Response to a Breach of Obligation* Erga Omnes Partes *in Theory and Practice*

a. The Early Jurisprudence of the ICJ

Locus standi in response to a breach of obligation *erga omnes parties* must be considered from the perspective of the development of international judiciary. Here it is necessary to briefly review the principal cases of the ICJ relating to this subject.[161] It is common knowledge that the ICJ, in the 1966

[157] RL Johnstone, *Offshore Oil and Gas Development in the Arctic under International Law: Risk and Responsibility* (Brill/Nijhoff, 2015) 223. Furthermore, Harrison argued that Art 192 of the UNCLOS concerning marine environmental protection is 'arguably *erga omnes* in character': Harrison, n 154, 24–25.

[158] P Chandrasekhara Rao and P Gautier, *The International Tribunal for the Law of the Sea: Law, Practice and Procedure* (Edward Elgar, 2018) 327.

[159] ibid.

[160] Tanaka, n 147, 551–52.

[161] Due to space restrictions, the practice of the PCIJ falls outside scope of this chapter. For an analysis of the jurisprudence on this subject, including the practice of the PCIJ, see Mariko Kawano, 'Standing of a State in the Contentious Proceedings of the International Court of Justice – Judicial

South West Africa case,[162] rejected the locus standi of Ethiopia and Liberia in vindication of a 'public interest', since the applicant states had not suffered direct injury due to South Africa's practice of apartheid in South West Africa. In this connection, the Court denied an *actio popularis* in international law. In the words of the Court:

> Looked at in another way moreover, the argument amounts to a plea that the Court should allow the equivalent of an 'actio popularis', or right resident in any member of a community to take legal action in vindication of a public interest. But although a right of this kind may be known to certain municipal systems of law, it is not known to international law as it stands at present: nor is the Court able to regard it as imported by the 'general principles of law' referred to in Article 38, paragraph 1(c), of its Statute.[163]

However, the Court went to add:

> [T]he provisions of certain treaties and other international instruments of a humanitarian character, and the terms of various arbitral and judicial decisions, are cited as indicating that, for instance, States may be entitled to uphold some general principle even though the particular contravention of it alleged has not affected their own material interests … The Court simply holds that such rights or interests, in order to exist, must be clearly vested in those who claim them, by some text or instrument, or rule of law.[164]

The last sentence could be read in a way to suggest that even though no material damage exists, states may be entitled to invoke the responsibility of a wrongdoing state, if such rights are clearly vested by treaty or customary international law.[165] If so, whether there would be no room to admit the institution of *actio popularis* in international law needs further consideration.[166]

Procedures on the Basis of the Consent of the Parties and the Development of International Legal Rules to Protect the Common Interests of the International Community as a Whole or as Established by Treaty' (in English) (2012) 55 *Japanese Yearbook of International Law* 208, 220–29; C Ishizuka, 'Expansion of Standing before the International Court of Justice: Possibility of *actio popularis* in terms of the Basis of the Court's Jurisdiction' (in Japanese) (2016) 35 *Yearbook of World Law* 64, 65–73. See also Tanaka, n 147, 530–33.

[162] *South West Africa (Liberia v South Africa) (Ethiopia v South Africa)*, Second Phase, Judgment, [1966] ICJ Rep 6.

[163] ibid, 47, [88]. However, there appears to be some scope to consider the question whether the dictum of the Court would lead to the conclusion that there would be no room to admit the institution of *actio polularis* in international law. See Kawasaki, n 144, 27; F Voeffray, *L'*actio popularis *ou la défense de l'intérêt collectif devant les juridictions internationales* (PUF, 2004) 70–71.

[164] *South West Africa*, n 162, 32, [44].

[165] See Voeffray, n 163, 70-71.

[166] Kawasaki, n 144, 27. Indeed, some members of the ICJ accepted the locus standi of Ethiopia and Liberia in the *South West Africa* case. See, for instance, Dissenting Opinion of Judge Mbanefo, [1966] ICJ Rep 492–93 and 505; Dissenting Opinion of Judge Nervo, ibid, 463 and 473; Dissenting Opinion of Judge Foster, ibid, 479–80; Dissenting Opinion of Judge Jessup, ibid, 382; Dissenting Opinion of Judge Tanaka, ibid, 259.

Four years later, the ICJ, in the 1970 *Barcelona Traction* case, explicitly referred to the concept of obligations *erga omnes*. The time-honoured dictum deserves to be quoted in full:

> [A]n essential distinction should be drawn between the obligations of a State towards the international community as a whole, and those arising vis-à-vis another State in the field of diplomatic protection. By their very nature the former are the concern of all States. In view of the importance of the rights involved, all States can be held to have a legal interest in their protection; they are obligations *erga omnes*.[167]

In the view of the Court, 'Such obligations derive, for example, in contemporary international law, from the outlawing of acts of aggression, and of genocide, as also from the principles and rules concerning the basic rights of the human person, including protection from slavery and racial discrimination.'[168] In this case, the Court provided no further precision with regard to standing in response to breaches of obligations *erga omnes*. However, the context suggests that the dictum of the Court was expressed in relation to standing before the Court.[169] In this regard, the Court held that in order to bring a claim in respect of the breach of obligations arising vis-a-vis 'another State in the field of diplomatic protection', a state must establish that its rights were violated.[170] It would seem to follow that with regard to obligations *erga omnes*, states are not required to establish the violation of their rights when bringing a claim with regard to the breach of this type of obligation; and that all states would have the locus standi to respond to breaches of obligations *erga omnes* by instituting proceedings before the ICJ.[171] This point could be supported by the fact that the dictum of the Court concerning obligations *erga omnes* was intended to move away from the 1966 *South West Africa* judgment.[172] In the words of Judge Schwebel, the holding of the ICJ on the inadmissibility of *actio popularis* in the *South West Africa* case (Second Phase) was 'rapidly and decisively displaced by the Court's Judgment in *Barcelona Traction*'.[173]

[167] *Barcelona Traction, Light and Power Company, Limited (Belgium v Spain) (New Application: 1962)*, the Second Phase, Judgment, [1970] ICJ Rep 3, 32, [33].

[168] ibid, [34].

[169] CJ Tams, *Enforcing Obligations* Erga Omnes *in International Law* (Cambridge University Press, 2005) 163.

[170] *Barcelona Traction, Light and Power Company, Limited* [1970] ICJ Rep 33–34, [35].

[171] Tams considered that the Court, in the *Barcelona Traction* case, accepted the standing of states to respond to *erga omnes* breaches by instituting proceedings of the ICJ: Tams, n 169, 164–165. This view was echoed by Villalpando: S Villalpando, *L'émergence de la communauté internationale dans la responsabilité des Etats* (PUF, 2005) 285–86. Furthermore, Orakhelashvili argued that '*Barcelona Traction* fits perfectly into the normative and jurisprudential framework admitting *actio popularis* wherever substantive obligations admit it': A Orakhelashivili, *Peremptory Norms in International Law* (Oxford University Press, 2006) 524.

[172] Tams, n 169, 163. See also H Thirlway, *The Law and Procedure of the International Court of Justice: Fifty Years of Jurisprudence*, vol I (Oxford University Press, 2013) 82.

[173] Dissenting Opinion of Judge Schwebel in *Military and Paramilitary Activities in and against Nicaragua (Nicaragua v United States of America)*, Provisional Measures, [1984] ICJ Rep 190, 197.

In the 1974 *Nuclear Test* cases, Australia claimed that obligations imposed on France in international law included the general one of abstaining from any kind of atmospheric nuclear tests. Related to this, it maintained:

> The feature common to all the specific expressions and confirmations of the rule as indicated above is that they are couched in terms of an *erga omnes* obligation and not in terms of an obligation owed to particular States. The duty to refrain from atmospheric nuclear testing is stated in absolute terms, rather than in terms relative to the incidence of the effect of nuclear testing upon particular States. The duty is thus owed to the international community; it is a duty of every State towards every other State.[174]

Likewise New Zealand maintained that nuclear testing undertaken by the French Government in the South Pacific region had violated 'the rights of all members of the international community, including New Zealand, that no nuclear tests that give rise to radioactive fallout be conducted'.[175] However, it cannot pass unnoticed that Australia and New Zealand also stressed the special impact of nuclear testing on their territory.[176] Thus the applicant states claimed the right to response to breaches of obligations *erga omnes* and the right to protect their special interests at the same time.[177] In any case the ICJ, the *Nuclear Test* cases, avoided examining this issue, focusing on the binding nature of the unilateral statements of the French authorities.[178] Overall it can be observed that the early jurisprudence of the ICJ remained in flux with regard to the standing of not directly injured states.

b. Doctrine

The opinions of commentators are not uniform with regard to locus standi in response to the breach of obligations *erga omnes (partes)*. In this regard, two

[174] Memorial on Jurisdiction and Admissibility Submitted by the Government of Australia, 334–35, [448]. See also ibid, 331, [431].

[175] *Application Instituting Proceedings by New Zealand*, ICJ Pleadings vol II, 8, [28], available at http://www.icj-cij.org/files/case-related/59/9447.pdf.

[176] ibid, 5–7, [12]–[22]; *Application Instituting Proceedings by Australia*, 26–28, [46]–[49], available at http://www.icj-cij.org/files/case-related/58/13187.pdf. On this point, see also comments by the following writers: M Ragazzi, *The Concept of International Obligations* Erga Omnes (Oxford University Press, 1997) 213–14; M Fitzmaurice, 'The International Court of Justice and International Environmental Law' in CJ Tams and J Sloan (eds), *The Development of International Law by the International Court of Justice* (Oxford University Press, 2013) 353, 358–59; CJ Tams, 'Roads Not Taken, Opportunities Missed: Procedural and Jurisdictional Questions Sidestepped in the Whaling Judgment' in M Fitzmaurice and D Tamada (eds), *Whaling in the Antarctic: Significance and Implications of the ICJ Judgment* (Brill/Nijhoff, 2016) 193, 204–05.

[177] Tams, n 176, 204. Related to this, Judges Onyeama, Dillard, Jiménez de Aréchaga and Waldock, in the Joint Dissenting Opinion, recognised '[t]hat States have individual as well as *common rights* with respect to the freedoms of the high seas is implicit in the very concept of such freedoms which involve rights of user possessed by every State' (emphasis added). Joint Dissenting Opinion of Judges Onyeama, Dillard, Jiménez de Aréchaga and Sir Humphrey Waldock, *Nuclear Tests (Australia v France)* [1974] ICJ Rep 312, 370, [118]. Thus they considered that 'the Applicant had a right under the Statute and the Rules to have the case adjudicated': ibid, 371, [120].

[178] *Nuclear Tests (Australia v France)*, Judgment, [1974] ICJ Rep 253, 268, [47].

contrasting views may be identified.[179] According to the negative view, the locus standi of not directly injured states was not well established in international law. For instance, Verhoeven considers that while all states parties to a treaty have a common interest to comply with the treaty, whether this would be sufficient to provide all states with the right to ask judges to determine the violation of the treaty without proper damage is a different question. Hence Verhoeven hesitates to admit that each state can institute proceedings before the ICJ in the absence of any special interest of that state.[180] Likewise Ragazzi argued that 'the concept of obligations *erga omnes* does not necessarily imply the existence of a sort of *actio popularis*. In other words, the concept of obligations *erga omnes* and *actio popularis* ... are distinct and independent of one another.'[181] Dominicé took the view that even though some treaties allow not directly injured states to institute proceedings against a state responsible for a violation of an obligation *erga omnes* before the ICJ or another tribunal, the situation in general international law remained less clear.[182] In the discussion at the Institut de droit international, Lady Fox stated that 'the question whether the recognition of an obligation *erga omnes* should not of itself give rise, in the event of its violation, of a right to take countermeasures or to require the violating State to submit to compulsory adjudication of the violation, has to date received a resounding negative'.[183]

According to the positive view, the locus standi of not directly injured states is recognised in international law. For example, Tams argued that '[w]here jurisdiction is established, all States can institute proceedings against States principally responsible for violation of obligations *erga omnes*'.[184] While Tams's view relates to obligations *erga omnes*, the same line of argument could apply to the breach of obligations *erga omnes partes*. In this connection, Tams expressed the view that 'even in the absence of an express clause recognizing standing, all States can institute proceedings if they seek to defend a small range of obligations protecting fundamental community values'.[185] Likewise Crawford stated that 'It is now generally accepted that in certain circumstances any State has standing to protect against breaches of fundamental norms, and if necessary to institute proceedings to vindicate its interest as a member of the international community.'[186] Furthermore, Zemanek, in the discussion at the Institut, expressed the view that 'if a State other than the injured State is entitled to

[179] Tanaka, n 147, 533–34.

[180] J Verhoeven, 'Belgique contre Sénégal ou quel intérêt pour se plaindre d'autrui ? (CIJ, 20 juillet 2012, Questions concernant l'obligation de pursuivre ou d'extrader)' (2013) 59 *Annuaire français de droit international* 15.

[181] Ragazzi, n 176, 212.

[182] C Dominicé, 'À la recherché des droits "*erga omnes*"' in *Droit de pouvoir, Pouvoir du droit, Mélanges offerts à Jean SALMON* (Bruylant, 2007) 357, 366–67.

[183] (2005) 71-I *Annuaire de l'Institut de Droit International*, 158.

[184] Tams, n 169, 197.

[185] Tams, n 146, 386.

[186] J Crawford, *Chance, Order, Change: The Course of International Law* (Brill/Nijhoff, 2014) 270.

invoke responsibility under certain circumstances, it would be absurd to deny it the right to submit an eventually ensuing legal dispute to a procedure for peaceful settlement if the necessary jurisdictional link exists'.[187] Likewise Gaja, in his Second Report on *Obligations and Rights Erga Omnes in International Law*, expressed the view that 'While consent to jurisdiction is required, the absence of a specific interest on the part of the claimant State does not generally debar it from bringing a dispute concerning compliance with an obligation *erga omnes*.'[188]

In this connection, the 2005 Resolution of the Institut de droit international broke new ground, stating in Article 3:

> In the event of there being a jurisdictional link between a State alleged to have committed a breach of an obligation *erga omnes* and a State to which the obligation is owed, the latter State has standing to bring a claim to the International Court of Justice or other international judicial institution in relation to a dispute concerning compliance with that obligation.[189]

This statement seems to be in line with Article 48(1) of the ILC's Articles on Responsibility of States for Internationally Wrongful Acts ('the ILC's Articles on State Responsibility'):

> Any State other than an injured State is entitled to invoke the responsibility of another State ... if:
>
> (a) the obligation breached is owed to a group of States including that State, and is established for the protection of a collective interest of the group; or
> (b) the obligation breached is owed to the international community as a whole.[190]

c. Recent Development of the ICJ Jurisprudence

In the recent jurisprudence of the ICJ, we can witness a new trend toward the locus standi of not directly injured states in response to the breach of obligations *erga omnes partes*. A leading decision on this subject is the 2012 *Belgium v Senegal* case.[191] On 19 February 2009, Belgium instituted proceedings against Senegal with regard to Senegal's compliance with its obligation to prosecute Mr Hissène Habré, former President of the Republic of Chad, or to extradite him to Belgium for the purposes of criminal proceedings. In its application, Belgium invoked, as the basis for the jurisdiction of the Court, Article 30(1)

[187] (2005) 71-I *Annuaire de l'Institut de Droit International* 168.
[188] ibid, 196.
[189] Institut de droit international, n 145. See also Thirlway, n 62, 149.
[190] *Yearbook of the International Law Commission*, 2001, vol II (Part Two). Reproduced in Crawford, n 76, 61 et seq.
[191] *Questions relating to the Obligation to Prosecute or Extradite (Belgium v Senegal)* [2012] ICJ Rep 422 ('the *Belgium v Senegal* case').

of the 1984 United Nations Convention against Torture[192] and the declaration made under Article 36(2) of the Statute of the ICJ.[193]

In this case, Belgium claimed, inter alia, that Senegal had breached its obligations under Articles 6(2) and 7(1) of the Convention against Torture. It thus requested the Court to declare that Senegal must cease these internationally wrongful acts by submitting without delay the Hissène Habré case to its competent authorities for prosecution of or, failing that, by extraditing Hissène Habré to Belgium without further ado.[194]

As Senegal claimed, none of the alleged victims of the acts said to be attributable to Mr Habré was of Belgian nationality at the time when the acts were committed,[195] and Belgium did not dispute this point.[196] Nonetheless, the ICJ accepted the locus standi of Belgium. In the words of the Court:

> The common interest in compliance with the relevant obligations under the Convention against Torture implies the entitlement of each State party to the Convention to make a claim concerning the cessation of an alleged breach by another State party. If a special interest were required for that purpose, in many cases no State would be in the position to make such a claim. It follows that any State party to the Convention may invoke the responsibility of another State party with a view to ascertaining the alleged failure to comply with its obligations *erga omnes partes*, such as those under Article 6, paragraph 2, and Article 7, paragraph 1, of the Convention, and to bring that failure to an end.[197]

It thus concluded that Belgium, as a state party to the Convention against Torture, had standing to invoke the responsibility of Senegal for the alleged breaches of its obligations under Articles 6(2) and 7(1) on the basis of Article 30(1) of the Convention[198] The Court did not consider whether its jurisdiction also existed with regard to the same dispute on the basis of the declarations made by the Parties under Article 36(2) of its Statute.[199] Therefore, it may be said that the ICJ, in the *Belgium v Senegal* judgment, accepted

[192] Convention against Torture and Other Cruel, Inhuman or Degrading Treatment or Punishment (adopted 10 December 1984, entered into force 26 June 1987) 1465 *UNTS* 85. Art 30(1) provides: 'Any dispute between two or more States Parties concerning the interpretation or application of this Convention which cannot be settled through negotiation shall, at the request of one of them, be submitted to arbitration. If within six months from the date of the request for arbitration the Parties are unable to agree on the organization of the arbitration, any one of those Parties may refer the dispute to the International Court of Justice by request in conformity with the Statute of the Court.'

[193] The *Belgium v Senegal* case, n 191, [2012] ICJ Rep 427, [1].

[194] ibid, 429–30, [14]; Verbatim record 2012/6, 19 March 2012, 59–60.

[195] The *Belgium v Senegal* case, n 191, [2012] ICJ Rep 448, [64].

[196] ibid, [65].

[197] ibid, 450, [69]. The dictum of the Court was echoed by the International Criminal Tribunal for the Former Yugoslavia. *Prosecutor v Anto Furundžija*, (IT-95-17/1), Judgment, 10 December 1998, 58, [151]. At the same time, it must be noted that the ICJ recognised the *erga omnes partes* character of Arts 6(2) and 7(1) of the Convention only, not the Convention as a whole. Ishizuka, n 161, 73.

[198] The *Belgium v Senegal* case, n 191, [2012] ICJ Rep 448, [63] and 450, [70]. See also Separate Opinion of Judge Cançado Trindade, [2012] ICJ Rep 527–29, [104]–[108].

[199] Judgment, ibid, 448, [63].

the standing of a not directly injured state in response to a breach of obligation *erga omnes partes*.[200] In conclusion, the Court held that Senegal had breached its obligations under Article 6(2) and 7(1) of the Convention against Torture, and that Senegal must, without further delay, submit the case of Mr Hissène Habré to its competent authorities for the purpose of prosecution, if it did not extradite him.[201]

The *Belgium v Senegal* judgment was seemingly followed by the 2014 *Whaling in the Antarctic* judgment.[202] On 31 May 2010, Australia instituted proceedings before the ICJ against Japan in respect of a dispute concerning the illegality of Japan's continued pursuit of a large-scale programme of whaling under the JARPA II, on the basis of Article 36(2) of the Statute of the ICJ.[203] A pivotal issue in this case was whether the Japan's scientific whaling programme, JARPA II, was contrary to Article VIII of the International Convention for the Regulation of Whaling (ICRW),[204] which provides for whaling for the purposes of scientific research. In this case, however, no rights of Australia in its maritime zones were breached by JARPA II.[205] Nor did Australia suffer any material damage from JARPA II.[206] In this connection, Judge Bhandari asked the following question of Australia:

> What injury, if any, has Australia suffered as a result of Japan's alleged breach of the ICRW through JARPA II?[207]

Counsel for Australia answered that:

> Australia does not claim to be an injured State because of the fact that some of the JARPA II take is from waters over which Australia claims sovereign rights and jurisdiction … Every party has the same interest in ensuring compliance by every other party with its obligations under the 1946 Convention. Australia is seeking to uphold its collective interest, an interest it shares with all other parties.[208]

[200] This view was supported by commentators, including: Crawford, n 186, 273; Johnstone, n 157, 217; Kawano, n 161, 230; D Tamada, 'Objective Litigation in the International Court of Justice' (in Japanese) (2017) 116 *The Journal of International Law and Diplomacy* 1, 21; Hiroyuki Banzai, *Study on State Responsibility for Internationally Wrongful Act: Basic Problems of the Theory on State Responsibility* (in Japanese) (Seibundo, 2015), 297.

[201] The *Belgium v Senegal* case, n 191, [2012] ICJ Rep 462–63, [122].

[202] *Whaling in the Antarctic (Australia v Japan: New Zealand intervening)*, Judgment, [2014] ICJ Rep 226. See also Tanaka, n 147, 535 et seq.

[203] The Statute of the International Court of Justice. Entered into force on 24 October 1945. The text is available at http://www.icj-cij.org/en/statute. Australia and Japan accepted the jurisdiction of the ICJ in 2002 and 2007, respectively.

[204] The electronic text of the ICRW is available at https://iwc.int/convention.

[205] Australia did not contend that JARPA II is unlawful because the whaling activities envisaged in the programme take place in the maritime zones over which Australia asserts sovereign rights or in adjacent areas: *Whaling in the Antarctic*, n 202, [2014] ICJ Rep 246, [40]; 244, [35].

[206] H Sakai, 'After the Whaling in the Antarctic Judgment: Its Lessons and Prospects from a Japanese Perspective' in Fitzmaurice and Tamada (eds), n 176, 308, 314.

[207] Verbatim Record, 3 July 2013, CR 2013/13, 73, [35].

[208] Presentation by H Burmester, Verbatim Record, CR 2013/18, 9 July 2013, 28, [19].

Likewise another Counsel for Australia replied to Judge Bhandari's question, 'Australia, like all the other States parties to the 1946 Convention, has a common interest in maintaining the integrity of the régime deriving from the Convention'[209] and that 'all States parties to that Convention have a common interest in each State complying with its obligations under the Convention and the régime deriving from it'.[210]

The remedies sought by Australia did not include any reparation in the sole interest of the applicant.[211] The remedies requested by Australia seemed to coincide with the remedies available under Article 48(2) of the ILC's Articles on State Responsibility.[212] In the words of Judge Crawford, Australia invoked 'Japan's obligations *erga omnes partes* under the Whaling Convention'.[213] In light of the above considerations, there may be basis for arguing that the *Whaling in the Antarctic* case is regarded as an instance of the application of Article 48 of the ILC's Articles on State Responsibility.[214]

The ICJ, in its judgment of 2014, accepted the locus standi of Australia.[215] It would seem to follow that the Court, in the *Whaling in the Antarctic* case, accepted the locus standi of a not directly injured state in response to the breach of obligations *erga omnes partes*.[216] It is of particular interest to note that in this case, the Court based its jurisdiction on Article 36(2) of the Statute of the ICJ, not a compromissory clause. The *Whaling in the Antarctic* judgment seems to suggest that if a treaty contains no compromissory clause, the standing of a not directly injured state in response to the breach of obligations *erga omnes partes* may be accepted on the basis of the optional clause.[217]

On the other hand, *Obligations Concerning Negotiations Relating to Cessation of the Nuclear Arms Race and to Nuclear Disarmament* between the Marshall Islands and the UK needs careful consideration.[218] On 24 April 2014, the

[209] Presentation by L Boisson de Chazournes, CR 2013/18, 9 July 2013, 23, [18] (translation).

[210] ibid, [19] (translation). See also ibid, [20].

[211] Australia requested that the Court declare that Japan shall: '*(a)* refrain from authorizing or implementing any special permit whaling which is not for purposes of scientific research within the meaning of Article VIII; *(b)* cease with immediate effect the implementation of JARPA II; and *(c)* revoke any authorization, permit or licence that allows the implementation of JARPA II.' *Whaling in the Antarctic*, n 202, [2014] ICJ Rep 239, [25].

[212] J Crawford, *State Responsibility: The General Part* (Cambridge University Press, 2013) 373.

[213] J Crawford, 'Responsibility for Breaches of Communitarian Norms: An Appraisal of Article 48 of the ILC Articles on Responsibility of States for Internationally Wrongful Acts' in Fastenrath et al (eds), n 143, 224, 236.

[214] Crawford, n 186, 273; Tamada, n 200, 22.

[215] *Whaling in the Antarctic*, n 202, [2014] ICJ Rep 246, [41]. One reason was that Japan did not dispute the locus standi of Australia in the present case. It is obscure why Japan did not challenge the jurisdiction of the Court as a preliminary objection. In this regard, Sakai indicated that 'Japan's plan to settle the case without submitting any preliminary objections to the Court probably represented its aim to resolve the matter as definitely and quickly as possible': Sakai, n 206, 313.

[216] Fitzmaurice, n 117, 110.

[217] Ishizuka, n 161, 75.

[218] *Obligations Concerning Negotiations Relating to Cessation of the Nuclear Arms Race and to Nuclear Disarmament (Marshall Islands v United Kingdom)*, Preliminary Objections, Judgment, [2016] ICJ Rep 833 ('the *Marshall Islands v United Kingdom* case').

Marshall Islands instituted proceedings against the UK with regard to breaches of treaty and customary obligations concerning nuclear disarmament.[219] In this case, the Marshall Islands requested that the Court declare breaches of nuclear disarmament obligations under the 1968 Treaty on the Non-Proliferation of Nuclear Weapons (NPT)[220] and under customary international law, and that the Court order the UK to take all steps necessary to comply with its obligations under Article VI of the NPT and under customary international law.[221] In this regard, the Marshall Islands made clear that '[t]his case involves obligations of an *erga omnes* character, engaging RMI [the Republic of the Marshall Islands] as a member of the international community'.[222] By referring to Article 42 and Article 48 of the ILC's Articles on State Responsibility,[223] it claimed that 'Given the immeasurable destructive consequences of even a limited nuclear war and given the *erga omnes* character of the obligations at stake in this case the Applicant has *locus standi* and the Application is admissible.'[224]

As Judge Xue observed, the Marshall Islands did not institute the proceedings merely for the protection of its own interest. Rather, the case served more the interest of the international community.[225] Hence there may be scope for arguing that the *Marshall Islands v United Kingdom* case can be regarded as community interest litigation.[226]

The Court, in its judgment of 2016, dismissed a case on the ground that no dispute existed between the applicant and the respondent prior to the filing of the application instituting proceedings, after 8:8, by the President's casting vote.[227] By rigidly interpreting the existence of disputes, the Court, in the

[219] ibid, 837, [1]. The Marshall Island filed separate applications against the nine states that possess, or are believed to possess, nuclear weapons: China, France, India, Israel, North Korea, Pakistan, Russia, the UK and the US. In the cases against India, Pakistan and the UK, the Marshall Islands relied on the optional clause as the basis for the Court's jurisdiction. The cases against other six states were not entered on the Court's General List because of the absence of a jurisdictional basis. MA Becker, 'The Dispute that Wasn't There: Judgments in the Nuclear Disarmament Cases at the International Court of Justice' (2017) 6 *Cambridge International Law Journal* 4, 5–6.

[220] Treaty on the Non-Proliferation of Nuclear Weapons (adopted 12 June 1968, entered into force 5 March 1970) 729 *UNTS* 161.

[221] The *Marshall Islands v United Kingdom* case, n 218, [2016] ICJ Rep 839, [11].

[222] *Memorial of the Marshall Islands*, 16 March 2015, 19, [26].

[223] ibid, 49, [110].

[224] ibid, 98, [231].

[225] Declaration of Judge Xue in the *Marshall Islands v United Kingdom* case, n 218, [2016] ICJ Rep 1029, 1031, [8].

[226] In fact, Judge Crawford considered that this was a case of the application of Art 48 of the ILC's Articles on State Responsibility. Dissenting Opinion of Judge Crawford in the *Marshall Islands v United Kingdom* case, n 218, [2016] ICJ Rep 1093, 1102, [22]. See also I Venzke, 'Public Interests in the International Court of Justice: A Comparison between Nuclear Arms Race (2016) and South West Africa (1966)' (2017) 111 *AJIL Unbound* 68 et seq; Tamada, n 200, 25.

[227] The *Marshall Islands v United Kingdom* case, n 218, [2016] ICJ Rep 856, [59]. For the same reason, the ICJ also dismissed the cases between Marshall Islands on the one hand and India and Pakistan on the other hand: *Obligations concerning Negotiations relating to Cessation of the Nuclear Arms Race and to Nuclear Disarmament (Marshall Islands v Pakistan)*, Judgment of 5 October 2016, Jurisdiction of the Court and Admissibility of the Application, [2016] ICJ Rep 552;

Marshall Islands v United Kingdom judgment, seemed to restrict the possibility of community interest litigation.[228] However, it is not suggested that the locus standi in response to a breach of obligation *erga omnes partes* was denied by the Court in the *Marshall Islands v United Kingdom* case. In fact, the Court dismissed the application because of the non-existence of a dispute between the parties, and it did not address the question of the standing of the Marshall Islands. Furthermore, as some members of the Court observed, in theory it might have been possible for the Marshall Islands to immediately file a new case to the same effect, since the dispute had been crystallised through the application.[229]

iii. Discussion

a. The Role of International Courts and Tribunals in the Protection of Community Interests

Whilst further development of case law is needed to draw more general conclusions, the *Belgium/Senegal* and *Whaling in the Antarctic* cases seemed to hint that, in appropriate cases, the ICJ would accept locus standi in relation to a dispute concerning compliance with obligations *erga omnes partes*, if it could establish its jurisdiction.[230] If this is so, as a matter of theory, it appears that

Obligations concerning Negotiations relating to Cessation of the Nuclear Arms Race and to Nuclear Disarmament (Marshall Islands v India), Judgment of 5 October 2016, Jurisdiction of the Court and Admissibility of the Application, [2016] ICJ Rep 255. The rejection of the existence of a dispute by the majority opinion, in particular the 'awareness' requirement, has been the subject of extensive debate. For a recent study on this subject, see Becker, n 219; L Marotti, '"Establishing the Existence of a Dispute before the International Court of Justice": Glimpses of Flexibility within Formalism?' (2017) 45 *Questions of International Law: Zoom-out* 77; E Stoppioni, 'Decentring the ICJ: A Critical Analysis of the Marshall Islands Judgments' (2017) 45 *Questions of International Law: Zoom-out* 65; A Miron, '"Establishing the existence of a dispute before the International Court of Justice": Between Formalism and Verbalism' (2017) 45 *Questions of International Law: Zoom-out* 43; BI Bonafé, 'Establishing the existence of a dispute before the International Court of Justice: Drawbacks and Implications' (2017) 45 *Questions of International Law: Zoom-out* 3; H Thirlway, 'Establishing the Existence of a Dispute before the International Court of Justice: A Response to Professor Bonafé's Criticisms of the ICJ' (2017) 45 *Questions of International Law: Zoom-out* 53; O Pomson, 'The *Obligations concerning Negotiations* Cases and the "Dispute" Requirement in International Court of Justice' (2017) 16 *The Law and Practice of International Courts and Tribunals* 373; J McIntyre, 'Put on Notice: the Role of the Dispute Requirement in Assessing Jurisdiction and Admissibility before the International Court' (2018) 19 *Melbourne Journal of International Law* 1; *Symposium on the Marshall Islands Case* (2017) 111 *AJIL Unbound* 62 et seq.

[228] Venzke, n 226, 70.

[229] Declaration of Judge Xue in the *Marshall Islands v United Kingdom* case, n 218, [2016] ICJ Rep 1030, [4]; Dissenting Opinion of Vice-President Yusuf, ibid, [24]–[26]; Dissenting Opinion of Judge Bennouna, ibid, 901; Declaration of Judge Gaja, [2016] ICJ Rep 1038; Separate Opinion of Judge Bhandari, [2016] ICJ Rep 1057, 1059–60, [13]; Dissenting Opinion of Judge Robinson, [2016] ICJ Rep 1084, [55]; Dissenting Opinion of Judge ad hoc Bedjaoui, [2016] ICJ Rep 1121, [48]. See also Bonafé, n 227, 21; Thirlway, n 227, 54.

[230] In the *Marshall Islands v United Kingdom* case, Judge Crawford clearly stated that: 'It is now established – contrary to the inferences commonly drawn from the merits phase of *South West Africa* – that States can be parties to disputes about obligations in the performance of which they have no specific material interests.' Dissenting Opinion of Judge Crawford, [2016] ICJ Rep 1093, 1102, [22]. See also Tams, n 176, 210–11.

the international judiciary may open a path for *actio popularis* in response to a breach of obligations *erga omnes partes*.[231] The *South China Sea* Arbitration Award (Merits) seems to be in line with the development of the jurisprudence of the ICJ.

The locus standi of not directly injured states raises a more fundamental issue regarding the relationship between the procedural law and substantive law. The procedural law and substantive law are not completely separate but are dynamically interlinked.[232] As Main pointedly observed, '[p]rocedure is an instrument of power that can, in a very practical sense, generate or undermine substantive rights'.[233] Hence the availability of procedure is key in effectuating the substantive law. If the substantive law were to lack procedure to effectuate it, its effectiveness would be compromised. This would be particularly true of rules concerning community interests. In this regard, Nollkaemper stated as follows:

> [T]he fact that the recognition of community interests has not resulted in a right to protection, which any state could invoke in the general interest, casts doubt on the status and meaning of the substantive rules themselves, if only because conduct contravening the public good is validated.[234]

Accordingly, it could well be said that procedure affects the normative strength of substantive rules concerning community interests. Furthermore, procedure also relates to the process for identifying the *erga omnes* nature of obligations protecting community interests.[235] If a court accepts the locus standi of not directly injured states in response to a breach of an international obligation, it can be reasonably considered that that obligation has an *erga omnes* nature. In this sense, procedure may influence the legal nature of the substantive rules and obligations.[236] Overall, it may be said that international courts and tribunals can perform an active role in the protection of community interests.[237]

b. Limitations with Community Interest Litigation

Community interest litigation may provide a way to effectuate obligations *erga omnes partes* regarding marine environmental protection. At the same time,

[231] cf GRB Galindo, 'On Form, Substance, and equality between States' (2017) 111 *AJIL Unbound* 75, 78. However, care should be taken in noting that obligations *erga omnes partes* do not mean that not directly injured states are *obliged* to take action in response to breach of such obligations, only that not directly injured states *may* take such action. According to Thirlway, what is at issue is 'an obligation *omnium*, an obligation shared by all': Thirlway, n 62, 152.

[232] A Nollkaemper, 'International Adjudication of Global Public Goods: The Intersection of Substance and Procedure' (2012) 23 *EJIL* 769, 773 et seq.

[233] TO Main, 'The Procedural Foundation of Substantive Law' (2010) 87 *Washington University Law Review*, 801, 802.

[234] Nollkaemper, n 232, 784 (footnote omitted).

[235] ibid, 781.

[236] Tanaka, n 147, 537–38.

[237] Nollkaemper, n 232, 786–87.

however, it contains some limitations. Unlike in the *Whaling in the Antarctic* case, the Tribunal's findings in its Award on the Merits are limited to the declaration of China's breach of environmental obligations under the UNCLOS. In this regard, some doubts can be expressed whether the *ex post facto* declaration of unlawfulness of China's activities alone would be adequate to protect the environment of the South China Sea. This point relates to the scope of the rights of not directly injured states that may be invoked against the responsible state. In this connection, four observations may be made.[238]

First, it can be argued that not directly injured states are entitled to seek, when necessary, the cessation and the assurance of non-repetition of the wrongful act from the state responsible for the internationally wrongful act.[239] This is supported by Article 48(2)(a) of the ILC's Articles on State Responsibility.[240] Furthermore, the ILC's Articles on State Responsibility make it clear in Article 30 that the state responsible for the internationally wrongful act is under an obligation to cease that act if it is continuing, and to offer appropriate assurances and guarantees of non-repetition, if circumstances so require. As the ILC stated, 'the responsible State's obligation of cessation thus protects both the interests of the injured State or States and the interests of the international community as a whole in the preservation of and reliance on, the rule of law'.[241]

Second, not directly injured States may be entitled to invoke restitution in kind where damage was caused on the high seas by the responsible state,[242] although a demand for restitution in kind is excluded if restitution itself has become impossible.[243] Unfortunately this is true in the South China Sea. In fact, the Ferse Report stated that 'the harm caused by direct burial of reef habitat during the construction of artificial islands is near-permanent' and that 'there is little prospect for recovery on ecological time scales'.[244] As the ICJ stated in the *Gabčíkovo-Nagymarous Project* case, environmental damage is often irreversible.[245] Thus it may have to be admitted that invocation of state responsibility in community interest litigation after irreversible environmental damage has occurred contains an essential limitation.

[238] Tanaka, n 147, 552–53.

[239] Kawasaki, n 144, 26; J Crawford, 'State Responsibility' in Wolfrum, n 41, [49]. See also G Gaja, 'The Protection of General Interests in the International Community: General Course on Public International Law' (2012) 364 *RCADI* 9, 107.

[240] See also Art 2 of the Resolution of the Institut, n 145.

[241] Crawford, n 76,197.

[242] K Kawasaki, 'Subsystems of State Responsibility in International Law (2)' (in Japanese) (1996) 19 *Shudo Law Review* 105; G Gaja, 'Obligations and Rights *Erga Omnes* in International Law: The First Report' (2005) 71 *Annuaire de l'Institut de droit international: Part I* 81, 137.

[243] Crawford, n 76, 280.

[244] *Ferse Report: Assessment of the Potential Environmental Consequences of Construction Activities on Seven Reefs in the Spratly Islands in the South China Sea*, n 98, 59–60.

[245] *Gabčíkovo-Nagymaros Project* (Hungary/Slovakia), Judgment, [1997] ICJ Rep 7, 78, [140]. The ILC also stressed the importance of prevention. Draft Articles on Prevention of Transboundary Harm from Hazardous Activities, ILC *Yearbook* 2001/II (2), General Commentary, 148, [2].

Third, not directly injured states may not be entitled to obtain satisfaction from the wrongful state since these states do not personally suffer any damage, material or moral, and satisfaction must be made to the true victims.

Fourth, as noted, the ITLOS Seabed Disputes Chamber took the view that each state party may be entitled to claim compensation.[246] If not directly injured states obtain some compensation without any damage having been caused to them, however, that would amount to a sort of undue profit.[247] Thus it seems reasonable to consider that not directly injured states may be entitled to claim compensation not in their own interest, but *only in the interest of the directly injured state or the true victims*.[248] If, for instance, a fund were established to protect the environment of the high seas, not directly injured states might be entitled to require the responsible state to pay compensation to the fund. To date, however, no fund exists with regard to environmental protection of the high seas. Accordingly, it will be difficult for not directly injured states to claim compensation for environmental damage to the high seas. Furthermore, compensation is not free from difficulty, since it is hard to translate environmental damage into a monetary amount.[249] In this regard, it is significant that in *Certain Activities Carried Out by Nicaragua in the Border Area*, the ICJ decided amounts for the compensation due from Nicaragua to Costa Rica for environmental damage caused by Nicaragua's unlawful activities on Costa Rican territory.[250] In this case, the ICJ was to assess the value to be assigned to the restoration of the damaged environment, as well as for the impairment or loss of environmental goods and services prior to recovery.[251] To this end, the Court adopted an overall assessment of impairment or loss of goods and services. Specifically, it took into account the four categories of environmental goods and services: trees, other raw materials, gas regulation and air quality services, and biodiversity.[252] This case seems to demonstrate that amounts for environmental damage can be determined by a judicial organ, here the ICJ. Yet it remains to be seen whether the overall assessment approach adopted by the Court could also apply to other instances, such as environmental damage to the high seas.

More generally, community interest litigation contains limitations at least in three respects.[253] The first limitation pertains to the consensual basis for jurisdiction of an international court or tribunal. The ICJ continues to apply a

[246] *Responsibilities and Obligations of States*, n 156, [2011] ITLOS Rep 59, [180].

[247] Kawasaki, n 144, 27.

[248] ibid, 27. See also Gaja, n 242, 137; Nguyen Quoc Dinh et al, *Droit international public*, 8th edn (LGDJ, 2009) 900; T Scovazzi, 'Some Remarks on International Responsibility in the Field of Environmental Protection' in M Ragazzi (ed), *International Responsibility Today: Essays in Memory of Oscar Schachter* (Brill/Nijhoff, 2005) 209, 219.

[249] Johnstone, n 157, 229. See also Scovazzi, n 248, 221.

[250] *Certain Activities Carried out by Nicaragua in the Border Area (Costa Rica v Nicaragua)*, Compensation owed by the Republic of Nicaragua to the Republic of Costa Rica, Judgment, [2018] ICJ Rep (not yet reported).

[251] ibid, [53].

[252] ibid, [75] and [83].

[253] Tanaka, n 147, 542–45.

rigid approach to this matter.[254] For example, the Court, in the *East Timor* case, stressed:

> However, the Court considers that the *erga omnes* character of a norm and the rule of consent to jurisdiction are two different things. Whatever the nature of the obligations invoked, the Court could not rule on the lawfulness of the conduct of a State when its judgment would imply an evaluation of the lawfulness of the conduct of another State which is not a party to the case. Where this is so, the Court cannot act, even if the right in question is a right *erga omnes*.[255]

In this case, the ICJ held that it could not in the present case exercise its jurisdiction because, according to the Court, the rights and interests of Indonesia would constitute the 'very subject-matter' of the Court's decision.[256] The *East Timor* judgment seems to suggest that the *Monetary Gold* rule applies to obligations *erga omnes*.[257] However, it must be noted that the circumstances surrounding the *East Timor* case were rather peculiar, in the sense that proceedings were not instituted against the state principally responsible for the breach of the obligation *erga omnes*, that is Indonesia. The East Timor judgment clarified that litigation must be directed against principally responsible states.[258] However, the judgment did not prejudice the question of locus standi in response to the breach of obligations *erga omnes partes*.[259] In any event, it can be considered that the Court, in the *East Timor* case, confirmed the consensual basis of its jurisdiction. This point was also echoed by the Court in the *Armed Activities* case, stating that 'the mere fact that rights and obligations *erga omnes* may be at issue in a dispute would not give the Court jurisdiction to entertain that dispute'.[260] Furthermore, the ICJ, in the *Application of the Convention on the Prevention and Punishment of the Crime of Genocide* case, stressed that the jurisdiction of the Court in this case was based solely on Article IX of the Genocide Convention:

> It has no power to rule on alleged breaches of other obligations under international law, not amounting to genocide, particularly those protecting human rights in armed conflict. That is so even if the alleged breaches are of obligations under peremptory norms, or of obligations which protect essential humanitarian values, and which may be owed *erga omnes*.[261]

[254] M Kawano, 'The Role of Judicial Procedures in the Process of the Pacific Settlement of International Disputes' (2009) 346 *RCADI* 9, 419–21; 424. See also Gaja, n 242, 110 et seq.

[255] *East Timor (Portugal v Australia)*, Judgment, [1995] ICJ Rep 90, 102, [29].

[256] ibid, 102–06, [23]–[38].

[257] For the *Monetary Gold* rule, see T Thienel, 'Third States and the Jurisdiction of the International Court of Justice: The Monetary Gold Principle' (2014) 57 *GYIL* 321; Tanaka, n 13, 202–04. See also ch 4, section III.D of this book.

[258] Tams, n 169,183–84.

[259] See also ibid, 185; Kawasaki, n 144, 30.

[260] *Armed Activities on the Territory of the Congo (New Application: 2002) (Democratic Republic of the Congo v. Rwanda)*, Jurisdiction of the Court and Admissibility of the Application, Judgment, [2006] ICJ Rep 6, 32, [64].

[261] *Application of the Convention on the Prevention and Punishment of the Crime of Genocide (Bosnia and Herzegovina v Serbia and Montenegro)* [2007] ICJ Rep 43, 104, [147].

Given that the jurisdiction of the ICJ or any other international courts relies on the consent of the parties, the Court must deal with its cases with caution so as not to lose the confidence of the parties.[262] Hence it is hardly surprising that the Court applied the rigid approach to the consensual basis of its jurisdiction.

Second, if international litigation on the basis of obligations *erga omnes partes* increases, there is the risk that states may withdraw from, or make reservations to, the optional clause of the ICJ Statute.[263] In reality, after the *Whaling in the Antarctic* judgment, Japan made a new reservation to preclude 'any dispute arising out of, concerning, or relating to research on, or conservation, management or exploitation of, living resources of the sea' from the jurisdiction of the ICJ.[264] Furthermore, after the *Marshall Islands/United Kingdom* judgment, the UK precluded 'any claim or dispute in respect of which the claim or dispute in question has not been notified to the United Kingdom by the State or States … at least six months in advance of the submission of the claim or dispute to the Court' and 'any claim or dispute that arises from or is connected with or related to nuclear disarmament and/or nuclear weapons' from the jurisdiction of the Court.[265] Ironically, the increase of community interest litigation might entail the risk of undermining the acceptance of the jurisdiction of the ICJ.

Third, a more fundamental issue arises with regard to a dilemma between the bilateral nature of international adjudication and need for collective action in protection of community interests. As international adjudication is bilateral by nature,[266] a dispute concerning community interests must be formulated as a bilateral dispute in order to bring a claim before an international court or tribunal. However, normally these interests can be protected only through the international cooperation of multiple states. Here a sharp tension arises between the bilateral structure of international adjudication and the collective nature of community interests.[267] In reality, some doubts might be expressed regarding the question to what extent the settlement of a bilateral dispute by an international court or tribunal can contribute to safeguarding community interests. Marine environmental protection is an example. Since marine pollution may easily spread beyond man-made delimitation lines, the protection of the marine environment from pollution can hardly be achieved by a single state. Accordingly, as ITLOS stated in the *MOX Plant* case, 'the duty to cooperate is a fundamental principle in the prevention of pollution of the marine environment

[262] OJ Lissitzyn, *The International Court of Justice: Its Role in the Maintenance of International Peace and Security* (Carnegie Endowment for International Peace, 1951) 17.

[263] Nollkaemper, n 232, 783.

[264] Declaration of 6 October 2015, available at http://www.icj-cij.org/en/declarations.

[265] Declaration of 22 February 2017, available at http://www.icj-cij.org/en/declarations.

[266] M Benzing, 'Community Interests in the Procedure of International Courts and Tribunals' (2006) 5 *The Law and Practice of International Courts and Tribunals* 369, 374 et seq.

[267] Nollkaemper, n 232, 785. See also B Simma, 'From Bilateralism to Community Interest in International Law' (1994-IV) 250 *RCADI* 217, 249.

under Part XII of the Convention and general international law'.[268] Similarly, collective action is needed in the conservation of marine living resources and biological diversity, since it cannot be achieved by a single state. To this day, however, there is no regional legal framework for securing international cooperation, thereby protecting the environment of the South China Sea. To protect the environment of the South China Sea, there will be a need to establish such a framework in the future.

V. CONSIDERATIONS OF TIME ELEMENTS IN THE *SOUTH CHINA SEA* ARBITRATION AWARDS

As noted earlier, in broad terms, the impact of time elements in international law can be divided into two categories: the impact on the interpretation or application of rules; and the impact on space.[269] Likewise, the influence of time elements in the *South China Sea* arbitration can also be divided into two categories.

A. Time Elements in the Interpretation of Provisions of the UNCLOS

One of the remarkable features of the *South China Sea* arbitration awards is that the Tribunal incorporated time elements into the interpretation or application of relevant rules of the UNCLOS. In this regard, four points may be made.

First, as discussed in chapter 5, the Tribunal incorporated a time element into the interpretation of Article 192. According to the Tribunal, the 'general obligation' under Article 192 covers 'preservation' in the sense of maintaining or improving the *present* condition of the marine environment and its 'protection' from *future* damage at the same time. As the marine environment is dynamic by nature, the ecological and physical conditions of the oceans may change with the passage of time. Environmental knowledge and technology concerning the oceans are also developing rapidly. Accordingly, there is a need to take account of time elements in the interpretation and application of rules of international law concerning marine environmental protection.[270] Hence the Tribunal's interpretation of Article 192 is relevant. In light of the irreversible nature of environmental damage, *ex post facto* responsibility has only a modest role to play in the protection of the marine environment. Thus the focus should be on

[268] The *MOX Plant* case, Request for provisional measures, ITLOS Case No 10, [2001] ITLOS Rep 95, 110, [82].

[269] See ch 1, section III.C of this book.

[270] Y Tanaka, 'Reflections on Time Elements in the International Law of the Environment' (2013) 73 *ZaöRV/Heidelberg Journal of International Law* 139, 141; Y Tanaka, *The International Law of the Sea*, 3rd edn (Cambridge University Press, 2019) 324.

the prevention of environmental damage,[271] and the precautionary approach is of particular importance in the protection of the environment. The Tribunal's interpretation seems to have an affinity to the precautionary approach,[272] even though it did not refer to that approach in its Award on the Merits.

Second, a time element is incorporated into the 'realistic prospect' test. The Tribunal applied this test to the China's moratorium on fishing in the South China Sea with regard to living resources, and declared that China breached Article 56 of the Convention with respect to the Philippines' sovereign rights over the living resources of its EEZ. According to the 'realistic prospect' test, the lawfulness of a statement is to be determined on the basis of the existence of a realistic prospect that punitive measures arising from the breach of the statement could be imposed in the future. Where a statement may deter the exercise of the sovereign rights of a coastal state in its EEZ in the future, the statement constitutes unlawful assertion of jurisdiction that amounts to a breach of Article 56 of the UNCLOS. While 'prospect' concerns the possibility of future events, decisions on the existence or non-existence of a 'realistic prospect' belong to the present. Thus the 'realistic prospect' test can be thought of as an intertemporal concept. As discussed in chapter 5,[273] however, the manner of assessment of the existence of a 'realistic prospect' and the degree of the prospect need further clarification.

Third, time elements are incorporated into the concept of traditional fishing rights in two respects. First, 'longstanding practice' is needed to establish traditional fishing rights. In this sense, the passage of time is a prerequisite to establish such rights. Yet the Tribunal, in its Award on the Merits, remained mute on this question. Second, the concept of 'tradition' is not static but evolutionary, in the sense that the mode of traditional fishing may evolve over time owing to the development of technology. While the Tribunal equated traditional fishing with artisanal fishing, the borderline between artisanal and modern fishing is not always clear-cut. The scope of 'traditional' or 'artisanal' fishing must be examined, taking account of evolutionary elements such as technological development.

Fourth, it is crucial to note that international disputes may escalate with the passage of time. Thus states are under an obligation not to aggravate these disputes. As the settlement of international disputes is a continuous process, it must be envisaged within a certain time frame. In this sense, the obligation not to aggravate international disputes can be thought to contain an intertemporal element. The obligation is essentially a future-orientated one, in the sense that it

[271] See Y Tanaka, 'Land-based Marine Pollution' in A Nollkaemper and I Plakokefalos (eds), *The Practice of Shared Responsibility* (Cambridge University Press, 2017) 294, 309.

[272] In his oral presentation before the Tribunal, Boyle argued that Arts 192 and 194 of the UNCLOS require the application of the precautionary approach. Presentation by Professor Boyle, Merits Hearing Tr (Day 3), 23 and 29–30.

[273] Ch 5, section II.A of this book.

aims to prevent further aggravation of a dispute in the future. As has been seen, a particular issue that may arise in this context concerns the applicability of the military activity exception provided for in Article 298(1)(b).[274] When deciding the applicability of this provision, a key element is continuity between the original action creating the international dispute and the action ancillary to the original action. If the original action concerns military activities and the action aggravating the dispute is ancillary to the original action, the military activity exception under Article 298(1)(b) applies. If the action aggravating a dispute is detached from the original action, the applicability of the military activity exception relies on the nature of the action aggravating the dispute. Accordingly, the nature of the action aggravating a dispute needs to be examined in connection with the original action, when considering the application of the military activity exception.

B. Impact of Time Elements on an International Spatial Order

Next, some consideration should be given to the impact of time elements on an international spatial order. The primary function of international law involves the spatial distribution of jurisdiction of states. The establishment of a spatial order in the international community is a crucial function of international law. As noted earlier, time elements may affect an international spatial order in three possible ways: (i) the acquisition of sovereignty over territory; (ii) the establishment of boundaries; and (iii) the entitlement to marine spaces.[275] The consideration of time elements in the *South China Sea* Arbitration Award (Merits) relates to the entitlement to marine spaces. Before examining this issue, however, for the sake of comparative analysis, it is necessary to briefly discuss the first two ways.

i. Impact of Time Elements in the Acquisition of Sovereignty over Territory

Above all, time elements may influence the acquisition of sovereignty over territory. As territory is an essential component of a spatial order in international law, the impact of time elements in the acquisition of sovereignty over territory should be a crucial issue.[276] An essential point in this regard relates to the reconciliation between change and stability in the international law governing the acquisition of territory. While stability of territory based on title requires

[274] See ch 5, section III.A of this book.

[275] See ch 1, section III.C of this book.

[276] Generally on this issue, see G Distefano, 'Time Factor and Territorial Disputes' in MG Kohen and M Hébité (eds), *Research Handbook on Territorial Disputes in International Law* (Edward Elgar Publishing, 2018) 397.

the maintenance of the status quo, *effectivités* stress the reality of governance of territory by taking account of changing situations in international relations. Since the tension between stability and change derives from the passage of time, the consideration of time elements becomes key.

In the jurisprudence of the ICJ concerning territorial disputes, the dictum expounded in the *Frontier Dispute* case provides a key legal framework in this field. The dictum of the Court may be called the *Burkina Faso/Mali* paradigm.[277] According to the paradigm:

> Where the act corresponds exactly to law, where effective administration is additional to the *uti possidetis juris*, the only role of *effectivité* is to confirm the exercise of the right derived from a legal title. Where the act does not correspond to the law, where the territory which is the subject of the dispute is effectively administered by a State other than the one possessing the legal title, preference should be given to the holder of the title. In the event that the *effectivité* does not co-exist with any legal title, it must invariably be taken into consideration. Finally, there are cases where the legal title is not capable of showing exactly the territorial expanse to which it relates. The *effectivités* can then play an essential role in showing how the title is interpreted in practice.[278]

Under the *Burkina Faso/Mali* paradigm, where title of one party is established, the title prevails over *effectivités*. Thus, time is fixed at the moment when title was established and *effectivités* which are contrary to the title, that is *effectivités contra legem*, do not affect the rights of the holder of the title. By the same token, in principle, acts of the party after establishing its title to territory do not affect the existence of its rights. To this extent, the *Burkina Faso/Mali* paradigm is also thought to be static. In the *Cameroon v Nigeria* case, for instance, it was submitted that the number of Nigerian nationals living in the Bakassi Peninsula had grown considerably.[279] Under the *Burkina Faso/Mali* paradigm, however, 'these facts of themselves do not establish Nigerian title over Bakassi territory; nor can they serve as an element in a claim for historical consolidation'.[280] Here a tension between law and fact may arise.[281] While the tension may make it difficult to implement the judgment of the Court,[282] the *Burkina Faso/Mali* paradigm does not adequately address the question how it is possible to address the tension between law and fact in the international law of acquisition of territory.

[277] MG Kohen, 'La relation titre/effectivités dans le contentieux territorial à la lumière de la jurisprudence récente' (2004) 108 *RGDIP* 561, 563.

[278] *Frontier Dispute (Burkina Faso/Republic of Mali)* [1986] ICJ Rep 554, 586–87, [63].

[279] *Land and Maritime Boundary between Cameroon and Nigeria (Cameroon v Nigeria: Equatorial Guinea intervening)*, Judgment, [2002] ICJ Rep 303, 414, [221]. According to Brownlie, the permanent population of Nigeria living in the Bakassi territory was 156,000. CR 2002/9 (Brownlie), 65, [226].

[280] The *Cameroon v Nigeria* case, n 279, [2002] ICJ Rep 414, [221].

[281] G Oduntan, *International Law and Boundary Disputes in Africa* (Routledge, 2015) 238–39.

[282] Limitations of space preclude examining the implementation process of the *Cameroon v Nigeria* judgment. On this issue, see ibid, 227–35.

In this connection, it is relevant to recall that in 1928, Max Huber, the sole arbitrator in the *Island of Palmas* case, presented a different paradigm with regard to acquisition of territory. The essence of this paradigm can be seen in the following statement:

> As regards the question which of different legal systems prevailing at successive periods is to be applied in a particular case (the so-called intertemporal law), a distinction must be made between the creation of rights and the existence of rights. The same principle which subjects the act creative of a right to the law in force at the time the right arises, demands that the existence of the right, in other words its continued manifestation, shall follow the conditions required by *the evolution of law*.[283]

The formula presented by Max Huber may be called the *Island of Palmas* paradigm.[284] This paradigm is evolutionary in the sense that title to territory must be maintained through continuous and peaceful display of sovereignty.[285] At the same time, it is intertemporal by nature.

To a certain extent at least, the evolutionary approach reflected in the *Island of Palmas* paradigm seems to have been taken by the ICJ in the 2008 *Malaysia/Singapore* case.[286] The central issue in the *Malaysia/Singapore* dispute related to sovereignty over the Pedra Branca/Pulau Batu Puteh. In this regard, the Court held that in 1844 Pedra Branca was under the sovereignty of the Sultan of Johor, a predecessor of Malaysia.[287] Nonetheless, the ICJ moved on to examine the question whether Malaysia had retained sovereignty over Pedra Branca after 1844, or whether sovereignty had since passed to Singapore.[288]

In considering this issue, the ICJ gave much weight to 1953 correspondence as evidence to show that Johor understood that it did not have sovereignty over Pedra Branca.[289] It further ruled that multiple actions of Singapore could be seen as conduct *à titre de souverain*.[290] In the view of the Court, the relevant facts reflected 'a convergent evolution' of the positions of the Parties concerning title to Pedra Branca. The Court thus found that by 1980, sovereignty over Pedra Branca had passed to Singapore.[291] It is notable that when considering

[283] *Island of Palmas* case *(the Netherlands v United States)* (1928) 2 *RIAA* 829, 845 (emphasis added).

[284] This paradigm is linked to Max Huber's approach to international law. For Huber's approach, see J Dlbrück, 'Max Huber's Sociological Approach to International law Revisited' (2007) 18 *European Journal of International Law* 97; J Klabbers, 'The Sociological Jurisprudence of Max Huber: An Introduction' (1992) 43 *Austrian Journal of Public International Law* 197.

[285] *Island of Palmas* case, n 283, 839.

[286] In fact, the ICJ explicitly referred to the *Island of Palmas* case. *Sovereignty over Pedra Branca/Pulau Batu Puteh, Middle Rocks and South Ledge (Malaysia/Singapore)*, Judgment of 23 May 2008, [2008] ICJ Rep 12, 50, [121].

[287] ibid, 49, [117].

[288] ibid, 50, [118]–[119].

[289] ibid, 80, [223]; 82, [230]. See also Separate Opinion of Judge *ad hoc* Sreenivasa Rao, [2008] ICJ Rep153, 170, [35].

[290] Judgment, [2008] ICJ Rep 82–95, [231]–[272].

[291] ibid, 96, [276]–[277]; 101, [300](1).

the passing of sovereignty over Pedra Branca from Malaysia to Singapore, the Court referred to the concept of 'evolving views of the authorities',[292] 'evolving understanding shared by the Parties'[293] or a 'convergent evolution of the position of the Parties'.[294] Overall it can be observed that in the *Malaysia/Singapore* judgment, time elements significantly affected the passing of sovereignty over the Pedra Branca/Pulau Batu Puteh.

ii. Impact of Time Elements in the Establishment of Boundaries

Time elements may also influence the establishment of boundaries. As territories are separated by boundaries,[295] the establishment of the boundaries is crucial to stabilise an international spatial order. In some cases, time elements may significantly affect the establishment of boundaries between states. Changes of international watercourses as natural boundaries are a case in point.[296] When an international watercourse constitutes a boundary between states, a natural alteration of the watercourse taking place over time would affect the location of the boundary between the coriparian states.[297] Specifically, two types of alteration exist: accretion (*alluviso*) and avulsion (*avulsio*). According to the phenomenon known as accretion, material sediments flowing downstream in a particular river deposit themselves on one of the riverbanks or on the river bed. In contrast, avulsion may be caused either by a geological phenomenon or by a natural disaster, such as an extraordinary flood. In both cases, an issue arises whether and how changes in the course of a river over time affect the boundary line.[298]

Likewise, maritime boundaries may be affected by time elements. Relevant coasts are one of the key elements of maritime delimitations. The coasts may change with the passage of time. A difficulty arises when relevant coasts may be supposed to change significantly over time. By way of illustration, in particular, two cases merit mention.

The first is *Nicaragua v Honduras*.[299] A particular feature of this case concerned the very active morpho-dynamism of the relevant coasts. In light of the highly unstable coastlines, the ICJ observed that 'continued accretion

[292] ibid, 65, [162].
[293] ibid, 80, [224].
[294] ibid, 96, [276]. It appears that the three terms are used interchangeably in the *Malaysia/Singapore* judgment.
[295] Generally on this subject, see L Caflisch, 'Les frontiers, limites et délimitations internationals: Quelle importance aujourd'hui?' (2013) 368 *RCADI* 9.
[296] While international watercourses have been qualified as natural boundaries, the consent of relevant states makes them international boundaries in international law. M Querol, 'Freshwater Boundaries Revisited: Recent Developments in International River and Lake Delimitation' (2016) 1 *Brill Research Perspectives in International Water Law* 1, 2.
[297] Further, ibid, 46 et seq; Caflisch, n 295, 80 et seq.
[298] Querol, n 296, 47.
[299] *Territorial and Maritime Dispute between Nicaragua and Honduras in the Caribbean Sea (Nicaragua v Honduras)*, Judgment, [2007] ICJ Rep 659.

at the Cape might render any equidistance line so constructed today arbitrary and unreasonable in the near future'.[300] According to the Court, whatever base points would be used for the drawing of an equidistance line, the configuration and unstable nature of the relevant coasts would make these base points uncertain within a short period of time. Given the set of circumstances, the Court considered that in the current case, it was impossible to identify base points and construct a provisional equidistance line for the single maritime boundary delimiting maritime areas off the Parties' mainland coasts. Accordingly, the Court found itself within the exception provided for in Article 15 of the UNCLOS, namely, facing special circumstances in which it could not apply the equidistance principle.[301] In conclusion, the Court held that the bisector method was to be applied in the present case.[302] *Nicaragua v Honduras* demonstrated that changes of relevant coasts over time did affect the methodology of maritime delimitations.

The second instance is the *Costa Rica v Nicaragua* case. Because of the instability of the coast, the ICJ encountered a difficulty when identifying the starting-point of the maritime boundary in this case. In this regard, the Court took the view:

> [T]he great instability of the coastline in the area of the mouth of the San Juan River … prevents the identification on the sandspit of a fixed point that would be suitable as the starting-point of the maritime delimitation. It is preferable to select a fixed point at sea and connect it to the starting-point on the coast by a mobile line. Taking into account the fact that the prevailing phenomenon characterizing the coastline at the mouth of the San Juan River is recession through erosion from the sea, the Court deems it appropriate to place a fixed point at sea at a distance of 2 nautical miles from the coast on the median line.[303]

It thus connected the fixed point at sea on the median line to the point on solid land on Costa Rica's coast that was closest to the mouth of the river by a mobile line.[304] The fixed point at sea constituted the starting-point of the maritime boundary. According to the concept of a mobile boundary, a time element, that is the future change of relevant coasts over time, is to be built into the boundary itself. The mobile boundary line appears to be an interesting solution well worth considering in response to instable coastlines.

iii. Impact of Time Elements on Maritime Entitlement

As territorial disputes were precluded from the jurisdiction of the Tribunal in the *South China Sea* arbitration, the issue of the impact of time elements in the

[300] ibid, 742, [277].
[301] ibid,742–43, [277]–[281].
[302] ibid, 746, [287].
[303] *Maritime Delimitation in the Caribbean Sea and the Pacific Ocean (Costa Rica v Nicaragua)*, Judgment, [2018] ICJ Rep (not yet reported), [86].
[304] ibid, [104].

acquisition of sovereignty over territory was not raised in this case. By the same token, maritime delimitations were precluded from the scope of the jurisdiction of the Tribunal in the *South China Sea* arbitration. Accordingly, the issue regarding the impact of time elements in the establishment of boundaries did not arise. Nonetheless, the *South China Sea* Arbitration Award (Merits) did demonstrate that time elements may influence an international spatial order in a different way, that is, in the determination of entitlements to marine spaces. In this arbitration, the Tribunal took two contrasting approaches to this subject.

As discussed in chapter 3, the passage of time can be thought to be at the heart of *historic* rights. However, the Tribunal did not examine the 'long course of history' with regard to Chinese activities in the South China Sea when considering the question of whether China historically had rights to living and non-living resources beyond the limits of the territorial sea in the South China Sea.[305] Instead, the Tribunal focused on the freedom of the high seas and the exceptional nature of historic rights. Furthermore, the Tribunal ruled that upon China's accession to the Convention and its entry into force, any historic rights that China may have had to the living and non-living resources within the 'nine-dash line' were superseded by the limits of the maritime zones provided for by the Convention.[306] In the view of the Tribunal, historic rights that are at variance with the Convention cannot be defended on the basis of the long course of history. As discussed in chapter 3, it may be said that the Tribunal, in its Award on the Merits, minimised the role of the time element when determining the legality of China's claimed historic rights in the South China Sea.

In contrast, the Tribunal incorporated time elements into Article 121(3) of the UNCLOS. Specifically, the temporal elements are reflected in:

- the 'non-transient character' of the human habitation,
- the existence of factors to support a group of persons living on a maritime feature for an 'indeterminate period of time',
- the existence of 'not one-off or short-lived' support and provision,
- provision necessary to keep humans alive and healthy over 'a continuous period of time',
- 'historical evidence' of natural conditions on maritime features,
- 'historical' human habitation, and
- maritime features' 'historical' economic life of their own.

Among the above elements, the concepts of 'historical evidence' of natural conditions, 'historical human habitation' and 'historical economic life of their own' serve to freeze the legal status of maritime features at a certain period in

[305] The *South China Sea* Arbitration Award (Merits), n 1, [264].
[306] ibid, [262].

the past.[307] In this sense, the Tribunal's interpretation of Article 121(3) is essentially static. The time elements tighten the conditions provided in Article 121(3). By rigidly applying this provision, the Tribunal seemed to prevent the situation that disables tiny features unfairly and inequitably generates enormous entitlements to maritime space and, accordingly, reduces the scope of the common heritage of mankind.

Overall it may be observed that time elements significantly affected the Tribunal's decision on the maritime entitlement to marine spaces in the South China Sea. On the one hand, it minimised the impact of time or historic elements when examining the China's claim of historic rights to marine spaces encompassed by the 'nine-dash line'. On the other hand, the Tribunal incorporated time elements into the interpretation and application of Article 121(3). In so doing, the Tribunal rigidly applied Article 121(3) to maritime features in the South China Sea. Despite the differences, both approaches commonly seek to prevent unilateral expansion of the coastal state jurisdiction as regards the high seas. In any event, the entitlement to marine spaces directly affects an international spatial order in the oceans. Thus the *South China Sea* arbitration provides an interesting instance of how the time elements affect an international spatial order.

VI. CONCLUSIONS

This chapter has examined four issues in the *South China Sea* arbitration: the role of the *South China Sea* arbitration in the peaceful settlement of the *Philippines/China* dispute; the implications of the *South China Sea* arbitration for the development of international law; the role of judiciary in the protection of community interests at sea; and consideration of time elements. The matters covered in this chapter may be summarised as follows.

First, by deciding the entitlement to marine spaces in the South China Sea, it is argued that the Tribunal contributed to narrowing down the scope of the *South China Sea* dispute. By reducing legal uncertainties surrounding the dispute, the *South China Sea* arbitration can potentially contribute to clarifying the issues in future negotiations between the Parties.

Second, the *South China Sea* arbitration awards contribute to the clarification, consolidation and elaboration of relevant rules of international law. As Judge Paik observed, it would be fair to say that the *South China Sea* arbitration awards have made a significant contribution to developing international law.[308] Of course, the Tribunal's views are not free from controversy. If an international

[307] N Klein, 'Islands and Rocks after the South China Sea Arbitration' (2016) 34 *Australian Year Book of International Law* 21, 27.
[308] Paik, n 18, 407.

court or tribunal were to disagree with the interpretation pronounced in the *South China Sea* arbitration awards, however, it would have to present an alternative interpretation of the law. In this sense, the arbitration awards can be thought to provide a non-negligible precedent in the interpretation or application of the relevant rules of international law.

Third, the jurisdiction of international tribunals set out under the UNCLOS over mixed disputes remains debatable. Mixed disputes may concern three issues: (i) territorial disputes; (ii) maritime delimitation disputes; and (iii) other maritime disputes, such as maritime entitlement disputes and marine environmental disputes. According to the Tribunal's approach, the third category of disputes is distinct from the first and second categories. This approach made it possible for the Tribunal to decide maritime entitlement disputes independently of territorial and maritime delimitation disputes.[309] It seems to provide an alternative well worth considering when dealing with a mixed dispute. Under the Tribunal's approach, however, the relationship between the first and second categories of disputes remains open. In this regard, further consideration must be given to the ancillary test presented in the *Chagos Marine Protected Area* arbitration.[310]

Fourth, in the *South China Sea* arbitration, the experts' report performed a significant role in the assessment of adverse effects from the harvesting of endangered species, the impact of China's construction activities on the coral reefs and the dangerous manner of law enforcement operations carried out by Chinese vessels. While scientific data constitute a key element in international disputes concerning environmental protection, an international court or tribunal as a judicial body encounters challenges with regard to the assessment of complex scientific issues. Assessment of the manner of ship handling also requires technical and expert knowledge. To secure the objectiveness of the scientific assessment, the independence and impartiality of experts can be regarded as crucial requirements. Hence the use of independent experts by the judicial body is an option well worth considering.

Fifth, the Tribunal's decision on entitlements to the South China Sea affects the spatial scope of the high seas and the Area, which is the common heritage of mankind. Given that all states enjoy the freedom of the sea in the high seas, arguably the spatial scope of the high seas affects the common interests of the international community as a whole. The spatial scope of the Area also affects community interests, since the Area and its natural resources are the common heritage of mankind. In this sense, the decisions can be thought to concern common interests of the international community as a whole. As the entitlements to marine spaces are a matter of objective determination, the Tribunal's

[309] See section III.D of this chapter.
[310] See also ch 2, section IV.B of this book.

decisions on this matter have effect *erga omnes*. Hence the Tribunal's decisions on entitlement to maritime features have implications that go far beyond the scope of the bilateral dispute between the Philippines and China.

Sixth, the Philippines' Submission No 11 as amended, concerning breaches of environmental obligations, partly covered the marine spaces beyond 200 nautical miles from the coasts surrounding the South China Sea. Even though the Philippines suffered no material damage from Chinese fishing activities there, the Tribunal accepted the locus standi of the Philippines. It may be considered that the Tribunal, in the *South China Sea* arbitration, implicitly recognised the locus standi of a not directly injured state in response to the breach of obligations *erga omnes partes* concerning marine environmental protection. The *South China Sea* arbitration, along with the *Whaling in the Antarctic* and the *Belgium/Senegal* cases, appears to hint that an international court or tribunal would accept locus standi in relation to international disputes concerning compliance with obligations *erga omnes partes*, if that international court or tribunal could establish its jurisdiction.

Last but not least, time elements performed an important role in the interpretation and application of relevant provisions of the UNCLOS and other rules of international law. In the *South China Sea* arbitration awards, the impact of time elements can be seen, inter alia, on the following matters:

- historic rights,
- the interpretation of Article 121(3) of the UNCLOS
- the interpretation of Article 192 of the UNCLOS,
- the 'realistic prospect' test,
- traditional fishing rights, and
- the obligation of non-aggravation.

In particular, consideration of time elements became crucial with regard to entitlement to the South China Sea. In this regard, the Tribunal took a contrasting approach. On the one hand, the Tribunal, in its Award on the Merits, took an approach that minimised the role of the historical or time element when determining the legality of China's claimed historic rights in the South China Sea. Given that the rules concerning the temporal elements in formulating historic rights remain less clear, the Tribunal's approach is a useful way to avoid any controversy with regard to historical evidence. In contrast, the Tribunal incorporated time elements into the interpretation and application of Article 121(3). Overall, the *South China Sea* Arbitration Award (Merits) demonstrated that time elements may affect spatial order in the oceans. In this sense, the award provides an interesting insight into the interaction between space and time in international law.

In conclusion, it can be observed that the issues regarding key elements of an international spatial order, *space*, *time* and *community interests*, were vividly raised in the *South China Sea* arbitration awards. In this sense, the awards should act as a crucial precedent when considering a spatial order in international law.

FURTHER READING

Andenas, M and Leiss, JR, 'The Systemic relevant of "Judicial Decisions" in Article 38 of the ICJ Statute' (2017) 77 *ZaöRV* 907.

Banzai, H, 'Disputes on State Responsibility for the Restoration of a Common Interest in International Law' (in Japanese) (2018) 117 *The Journal of International Law and Diplomacy* 25.

Bateman, S, 'Building Cooperation for Managing the South China Sea Without Strategic Trust' (2017) 4 *Aisa and the Pacific Policy Studies* 251.

Becker, MA, 'The Dispute that Wasn't There: Judgments in the Nuclear Disarmament Cases at the International Court of Justice' (2017) 6 *Cambridge International Law Journal* 4.

Benzing, M, 'Community Interests in the Procedure of International Courts and Tribunals' (2006) 5 *The Law and Practice of International Courts and Tribunals* 369.

Bodansky, D and Crook, JR, 'Symposium: The ILC's State Responsibility Articles' (2002) 96 *AJIL* 773.

Chandrasekhara Rao, P and Gautier, P, *The International Tribunal for the Law of the Sea: Law, Practice and Procedure* (Edward Elgar, 2018).

Crawford, J, *The International Law Commission's Articles on State Responsibility: Introduction, Text and Commentaries* (Cambridge University Press, 2002).

——, *State Responsibility: The General Part* (Cambridge University Press, 2013).

——, *Chance, Order, Change: The Course of International Law* (Brill/Nijhoff, 2013).

——, 'Responsibility for Breaches of Communitarian Norms: An Appraisal of Article 48 of the ILC Articles on responsibility of States for Internationally Wrongful Acts' in U Fastenrath et al (eds), *From Bilateralism to Community Interest: Essays in Honour of Judge Bruno Simma* (Oxford University Press, 2011) 224–40.

——, 'State Responsibility' in R Wolfrum (ed), *Max Planck Encyclopedia of Public International Law* (online edition).

Davenport, T, 'Legal Implications of the *South China Sea Award* for Maritime Southeast Asia' (2016) 34 *Australian Yearbook of International Law* 65.

Desierto, DA, 'Enforcement Options and Paths to Compliance: Disputants and Global Stakeholders in Philippines v China' (2018) 8 *Asian Journal of International Law* 64.

Distefano, G, 'Time Factor and Territorial Disputes' in MG Kohen and M Hébité (eds), *Research Handbook on Territorial Disputes in International Law* (Edward Elgar Publishing, 2018) 397–416.

Espenilla, JJF, 'Judicial Fact-Finding Initiatives in the South China Sea Arbitration' (2019) 9 *Asian Journal of International Law* 20–30.

Fitzmaurice, M, *Whaling and International Law* (Cambridge University Press, 2015).

Fitzmaurice, M and Tamada, D (eds), *Whaling in the Antarctic: Significance and Implications of the ICJ Judgment* (Brill/Nijhoff, 2016).

Gaja, G, 'The Protection of General Interests in the International Community: General Course on Public International Law' (2012) 364 *RCADI* 9.

——, 'Obligations and Rights *Erga Omnes* in International Law: The First Report' (2005) 71 *Annuaire de l'Institut de droit international: Part I* 119; (2005) 71 *Annuaire de l'Institut de droit international: Part II* 81.

Galindo, GRB, 'On Form, Substance, and equality between States' (2017) 111 *AJIL Unbound* 75.

Hamamoto, S, 'Paradoxical Role of Experts in the *Whaling in the Antarctic* Case' (2017) 59 *Japanese Yearbook of International Law* 345.

Harrison, J, *Saving the Oceans Through Law: The International Leal Framework for the Protection of the Marine Environment* (Oxford University Press 2017).

Heathcote, S, 'Est-ce que l'état de nécessité est un principe de droit international coutumier?' (2007) 1 *Revue belge de droit international* 53.

Ishizuka, C, 'Expansion of Standing before the International Court of Justice: Possibility of *actio popularis* in terms of the Basis of the Court's Jurisdiction' (in Japanese) (2016) 35 *Yearbook of World Law* 64.

Kolb, R, *Good Faith in International Law* (Hart Publishing, 2017).

——, 'Selected Problems in the Theory of Customary International Law' (2003) 50 *NILR* 119.

Kawano, M, 'The Role of Judicial Procedures in the Process of the Pacific Settlement of International Disputes' (2009) 346 *RCADI* 9.

——, 'Standing of a State in the Contentious Proceedings of the International Court of Justice – Judicial Procedures on the Basis of the Consent of the Parties and the Development of International Legal Rules to Protect the Common Interests of the International Community as a Whole or as Established by Treaty' (2012) 55 *Japanese Yearbook of International Law* 208.

Kawasaki, K, 'The "Injured State" in the International Law of State Responsibility' (2000) 28 *Hitotsubashi Journal of Law and Politics* 17.

Kraska, J, 'Maritime Confidence-building Measures for Navigation in the South China Sea' (2017) 32 *IJMCL* 268.

Lee-Iwamoto, Y, 'Legal Implications of the Awards and Procedure in the South China Sea Arbitration' (in Japanese) (2018) 177 (2) *The Journal of International Law and Diplomacy* 30.

Mbengue, MM, 'The South China Sea Arbitration: Innovations in Marine Environmental Fact- Finding and Due Diligence Obligations' (2016) 110 *American Journal of International Law Unbound* 285.

Mbengue, MM and Das, R, 'Rules Governing the Use of Experts in International Disputes' (2018) 17 *The Law and Practice of International Courts and Tribunals* 415.

McDorman, TL, 'The South China Sea after 2009: Clarity of Claims and Enhanced Prospects for Regional Cooperation?' (2010) 24 *Ocean Yearbook* 507.

Mossop, J, 'Can the South China Sea Tribunal's Conclusions on Traditional Fishing Rights Lead to Cooperative Fishing Arrangements in the Region?' (2018) 3 *Asia-Pacific Journal of Ocean Law and Policy* 210.

Nollkaemper, A, 'International Adjudication of Global Public Goods: The Intersection of Substance and Procedure' (2012) 23 *EJIL* 769.

Nguyen Hong Thao and Amer, R, 'Coastal States in the South China Sea and Submissions on the Outer Limits of the Continental Shelf' (2011) 42 *ODIL* 245.

Orakhelashivili, A, *Peremptory Norms in International Law* (Oxford University Press, 2006).

O'Sullivan, NB, 'The Case Law's handling of Issues Concerning Third States' in AG Oude Elferink, T Henriksen and SV Busch (eds), *Maritime Boundary Delimitation: The Case Law Is It Consistent and Predictable?* (Cambridge University Press, 2018) 262–90.

Peat, D, 'The Use of Court-Appointed Experts by the International Court of Justice' (2014) 84 *BYIL* 271.

Ragazzi, M, *The Concept of International Obligations* Erga Omnes (Oxford University Press, 1997).

Schoenbaum, TJ, 'The South China Sea Arbitration Decision and a Plan for Peaceful Resolution of the Disputes' (2016) 47 *Journal of Maritime Law and Commerce* 451.

Scovazzi, T, 'Some Remarks on International Responsibility in the Field of Environmental Protection' in M Ragazzi (ed), *International Responsibility Today: Essays in Memory of Oscar Schachter* (Brill/Nijhoff, 2005) 209–22.

Simma, B, 'The International Court of Justice and Scientific Expertise' (2012) 106 *Proceedings of the Annual Meeting of American Society of International Law* 230.

Sison III, MPT, 'Universalizing the Law of the Sea in the South China Sea Dispute' (2018) 49 *ODIL* 157.

Sloane, RD, 'On the Use and Abuse of Necessity in the Law of State Responsibility' (2012) 106 *AJIL* 447.

Tamada, D, 'In the Matter of an Arbitration before an Arbitral Tribunal Constituted under Annex VII to the 1982 United Nations Convention on the Law of the Sea between the Republic of Philippines and the People's Republic of China, Award on Jurisdiction and Admissibility (29 October 2015)' (in Japanese) (2016) 66 *Kobe Law Journal* 125.

——, 'Objective Litigation in the International Court of Justice' (in Japanese) (2017) 116 *The Journal of International Law and Diplomacy* 1.

Tams, CJ, Enforcing Obligations *Erga Omnes* in International Law (Cambridge University Press, 2005).

——, 'Individual States as Guardians of Community Interests' in U Fastenrach et al (eds), *From Bilateralism to Community Interest: Essays in Honour of Judge Bruno Simma* (2011) 379–405.

——, 'Roads Not Taken, Opportunities Missed: Procedural and Jurisdictional Questions Sidestepped in the Whaling Judgment' in M Fitzmaurice and D Tamada (eds), *Whaling in the Antarctic: Significance and Implications of the ICJ Judgment* (Brill/Nijhoff, 2016) 193–217.

Tanaka, Y, *The Peaceful Settlement of International Dispute* (Cambridge University Press, 2018).

——, 'Case concerning the Arbitral Award made by the King of Spain on 23 December 1906 (Honduras v Nicaragua), 1960' in J-M Sorel and P Wojcikiewicz Almeida (eds), *Latin America and the International Court of Justice: Contributions to International Law* (Routledge, 2016) 262–72.

——, 'The Impacts of the ITLOS Jurisprudence on the Development of International Law' in International Tribunal for the Law of the Sea, *The Contribution of the International Tribunal for the Law of the Sea to the Rule of Law: 1996–2016* (Brill/Nijhoff, 2018) 161–78.

——, 'Toward Sustainable Management of Marine Natural Resources' in M Kotzur et al (eds), *Sustainable Ocean Resource Governance: Deep Sea Mining, Marine Energy and Submarine Cables* (Brill/Nijhoff, 2018) 110–33.

——, 'Bakassi Decision: International Law and the Acquisition of Sovereignty over Land Territory' in E Egede and M Igiehon (eds), *Bakassi Dispute on the International Court of Justice: Continuing Challenges* (Routledge, 2018) 100–16.

——, 'Reflections on *Locus Standi* in Response to a Breach of Obligations *Erga Omnes Partes*: A Comparative Analysis of the *Whaling in the Antarctic* and *South China Sea* Cases' (2018) 17 *The Law and Practice of International Courts and Tribunals* 527.

Thirlway, H, *The Sources of International Law* (Oxford University Press, 2014).

Treves, T, 'Law and Science in the Interpretation of the Law of the Sea Convention: Article 76 Between the Law of the Sea Tribunal and the Commission on the Limits of the Continental Shelf' (2012) 3 *Journal of International Dispute Settlement* 483.

Venzke, I, 'Public Interests in the International Court of Justice: A Comparison between Nuclear Arms Race (2016) and South West Africa (1966)' (2017) 111 *AJIL Unbound* 68.

Villalpando, S, *L'émergence de la communauté internationale dans la responsabilité des Etats* (PUF, 2005).

Voeffray, F, *L'actio popularis ou la défense de l'intérêt collectif devant les juridictions internationales* (PUF, 2004).

Wolfrum, R, 'Identifying Community Interests in International Law: Common Spaces and Beyond' in E Benvenisti and G Nolte (eds), *Common Interests Across International Law* (Oxford University Press, 2018) 19–35.

Xuexia Liao, 'Evaluation of Scientific Evidence by International Courts and Tribunals in the Continental Shelf Delimitation Cases' (2017) 48 *ODIL* 136.

Yen Hoang Tran, 'The South China Sea Arbitral Award: Legal Implications for Fisheries Management and Cooperation in the South China Sea' (2017) 6 *Cambridge International Law Journal* 87.

7

General Conclusion

OVERALL THE VALUE of the *South China Sea* arbitration needs to be considered from the perspective of the changing paradigm of the international law of the sea.[1] From a broad perspective, the history of the international law of the sea after World War II shows vacillation between two contrasting approaches: a voluntarist approach and an objectivist approach. The voluntarist approach aims to safeguard the interests of individual states by expanding national jurisdiction to the high seas. Arguably, the voluntarist approach was a driving force of the establishment of the traditional paradigm of the law of the sea, that is, the law of the divided oceans. Given that the world is divided into sovereign states, the traditional paradigm of the law of the sea will in no way lose its importance. By contrast, the objectivist approach seeks to protect community interests at sea. This approach leads to a new paradigm that aims to safeguard community interests, by providing a legal framework for ensuring international cooperation in marine affairs. In essence, the Tribunal's approach, in the *South China Sea* arbitration, seems to be in line with the development of this novel paradigm in the law of the sea.

The Tribunal's basic stance is essentially characterised by two elements. The first relates to the maintenance of the integrity of the UNCLOS. It is beyond serious argument that an international legal order of the oceans is established primarily by the UNCLOS. To secure the legal order, there is a need to maintain the integrity of the Convention. It appears that the essential line of the Tribunal's interpretations in the *South China Sea* arbitration awards was to ensure the integrity of the UNCLOS, by preventing unilateral expansion of coastal state jurisdiction that is contrary to the Convention. This point is exemplified by the Tribunal's interpretation that the Convention superseded any historic rights, or other sovereign rights or jurisdiction, in excess of the limits imposed therein.[2]

The second element concerns the prevention of unilateralism at sea and strengthening the international dispute settlement procedures in the UNCLOS. Given that unilateralism runs the serious risk of creating international disputes, securing the effectiveness of the compulsory procedures of international dispute settlement set out as an integral part of the UNCLOS is of critical importance.

[1] See ch 1, section III.B of this book.
[2] See ch 3 of this book.

It appears that the Tribunal, in the *South China Sea* arbitration, adopted an interpretation that allowed it to exercise its jurisdiction as effectively as possible. In this regard, the Tribunal's interpretation of Article 281[3] and the separation of maritime entitlement disputes from territorial and maritime delimitation disputes are noteworthy.[4] It is also notable that the Tribunal accepted the locus standi of the Philippines in response to the alleged breach of environmental obligations under the UNCLOS, even though the Philippines suffered no material damage there. This would open the way to protecting community interests concerning marine environmental protection through international adjudication.

The *South China Sea* arbitration did seem to disclose the opposition of fundamental values existing in the international community, such as between unilateral expansion of national jurisdiction (ie unilateralism) and the integrity of the UNCLOS (ie multilateralism), between the promotion of states' interests and that of community interests, and between the voluntary procedure and the compulsory procedure of international dispute settlement. In some respects at least, the *South China Sea* arbitration seems to press us to choose the value we wish to support. In this sense, that arbitration may be considered as a touchstone against which we can measure the degree of maturity of the international community and decide *an orientation* for the future development of an international legal order in the oceans.[5]

[3] See ch 2, section V of this book.

[4] See ch 2, section IV.A and ch 6, section III.D of this book.

[5] In this connection, the words of Virally deserve to be quoted in the original: 'Bien mieux, il [le droit] peut même précéder, en quelque sorte, les mouvements historiques, les orienter et les canaliser, revêtir une valeur révolutionnaire, en brisant des habitudes cristallisées, des traditions, paralysantes, en vue d'instaurer un ordre nouveau.' M Virally, *La pensée juridique* (LGDJ, 2010) 188.

Index

Note: Alphabetical arrangement is word-by-word, where a group of letters followed by a space is filed before the same group of letters followed by a letter, eg 'law of the sea' will appear before 'lawfulness'. In determining alphabetical arrangement, initial articles and prepositions are ignored.